Global Business Strategies
Text and Cases

Global Business Strategies

TEXT AND CASES

U.C. Mathur
Director MDP
Integrated Academy of Management and Technology
Ghaziabad

I.K. International Publishing House Pvt. Ltd.
NEW DELHI • BANGALORE

Published by
I.K. International Publishing House Pvt. Ltd.
S-25, Green Park Extension
Uphaar Cinema Market
New Delhi–110 016 (India)
E-mail : info@ikinternational.com

ISBN 978-93-80578-65-1

10 9 8 7 6 5 4 3 2 1

Published by Krishan Makhijani for I.K. International Publishing House Pvt. Ltd., S-25, Green Park Extension, Uphaar Cinema Market, New Delhi–110 016 and Printed by Rekha Printers Pvt. Ltd., Okhla Industrial Area, Phase II, New Delhi–110 020.

Dedicated to
Bina my best friend and wife with love

Preface

The Indian ancient philosophical thought of "Vasudhaiv Kutumbkam" meaning the analogy of the present-day world with a global village or more rightly of the world being a world family signifies the importance of cooperation among the nations, more especially in the area of trade and commerce. *Global Business Strategies* is meant for Indian and international student community taking their needs; while cutting across global boundaries it covers the subject in totality. It deals with basic principles; concepts and practices to enable managers perform effectively in today's global business environment. The theories and institutions of global trade and investment are dealt with in detail. The cultural and human aspects that make global business different from domestic business form a significant part of the book. The readers will learn to apply the concepts, principles and the practices of global business in the global environment. The following have been covered for the benefit of the student community and corporate world.

Global environment and the major differences between MNCs and non-MNCs and formulation and implementation of strategies of MNCs.

Analytical skills needed for the unique aspects of global operations are provided. Global business in the 21st century would be driven by among other things like the innovations and technological developments especially in the field of information technology. The World Wide Web, or www, has made inroads into most countries in the homes and offices of those countries. No one can remain untouched anywhere in the world with the developments around the world. Information about latest products, on different uses of the products is instantly available through the click of a mouse and if perestroika and glasnost had not happened when they did, the IT revolution would have brought about the desired changes in the erstwhile USSR.

The book is full of global examples in the case studies that help in understanding the diverse routes countries and even companies take in developing their global business.

The book has been designed by harmonizing the variety of global business opportunities, and threats to enable the students get a cohesive picture of the relevant areas required for success in the field of global business.

Global business would necessarily have some common features with the domestic business and yet it differs in several ways. Companies have a variety of reasons for planning global business and these have been dealt with in the book in some detail, with emphasis on Indian viewpoint. Topics like global buyer profile; global business contracts and controls have been dealt with in detail.

In global business a lot of emphasis is being given to the study of the social, cultural, political and demographic aspects of each country. Therefore, in order to familiarize the students with these aspects of some selected countries, brief information is given about them at the end of the chapters. It is hoped that these will be useful for the students. The information given in book as Countries of the World has been collected from various global sources, is only indicative with no guarantee of its timeliness and authenticity. Businesspersons planning global business would organize full-scale marketing research to get the correct picture on these counts.

The book contains topics being taught in the best business schools of the country and overseas taking their syllabi into account. It also includes areas of business interests from the author's interaction with the corporate brass and academia. The cases given in the book have been carefully selected and their analysis would provide students an insight into the global business world. Method of handling the case studies is given in the beginning of the book. Besides, certain topics are given as guidelines to the teaching faculty as points to ponder and discussion points. It is therefore felt that the book would be useful in learning the subtleties of Global/International Business.

My thanks are due to Ms. Punam Dayal and Mr. Pankaj Mathur. The author wishes to place on record his gratitude to the publishers for their encouragement during the period the book was being written.

U.C. MATHUR

Contents

Method for Handling Case Studies

Please find below a logical method of handling case studies.

- Read the case
- Study the figures, charts if any, look for exceptions, too high or too low figures
- Frame questions
- Use five force model to analyze the questions
- Find alternative solutions
- Focus on the best solutions
- Write the answers in rough
- Discuss with peer group and group leader
- Check recommendations
- Finalize the report with your recommendations

There is no standard method of analyzing the cases and reporting the results of the analysis. The way of presentation can differ, but usually for analyzing the cases all or some of the tools are used, which are listed below:

- Strategic intents—vision, mission, goals and objectives
- External business environment analysis
- Internal analysis of the firm using critical success factors, value chain, core process and systems, balance scorecard, qualitative, quantitative analysis, activity based cost analysis
- Firm's competitive advantage, through differentiation, cost leadership, quick response, market focus, strategies through market life cycle
- Firm's competitive advantage from its operations, including, TQM, TCM, and core process reengineering
- Corporate level competitive advantage from diversifications, mergers, acquisitions
- Competitive advantage from global strategy of the firm
- Strategy implementations and resultant competitive advantage
- Firms' organizational structure and its culture
- Firms' resources—information, capital and human and their deployment for strategic advantage
- Leadership advantage of firms—the CEO and the board of directors
- Mackenzie 7S Model

At times students try to write to many recommendations, which are vague, meandering and they do not provide the guidelines for making strategies. **The right way is to give three to four recommendations; they should be unambiguous, hard hitting and to the point so that the firm can use them to modify its strategy effectively.** If it is necessary to give several recommendations they should all be hard hitting and to the point and relevant to the problems or the improvement opportunities the firm has.

While most cases do not give the business general environmental factors, their effect on the firm can never be underestimated. In such events, if it is possible, use your own knowledge of the general environment factors or just ignore them.

Case study method is of great help in understanding the concepts of strategic management as it takes the student in the real corporate world albeit vicariously. The student is able to use hands-on the tools, techniques learnt in the strategic management course for a lasting impression, which would come handy in the corporate world in better organizational understanding, much before he comes to the position of strategic planning.

CHAPTER
1

Global Business Strategies: An Introduction

Country's culture, economic strength and geography define its role in the global business. Besides, its political structure focuses on its place in the global business community.

Most businesses start in a small way, with vendors tapping the local town's market, either by selling house to house on a cart or through a retail shop. As they grow, they extend their areas of operation to cover the state in the first place and then the entire country. The next logical step is taking the goods to cater to global markets around the world. Global business can therefore be defined as follows:

Global business covers all business transactions involving two or more countries.

If USA is considered the benchmark nation for global business, it can be seen that in 1970s USA's global trade was only 5% of the total trade. Now it far exceeds even 10%. Reasons for the growth are given below:

1. Technological innovations, including transportation which is now much quicker. Communication technology has allowed remote control of business easy and effective.
2. Trade policy liberalization in the US, as the citizens there want better access to greater variety of goods and at lower competitive price. This adds to greater domestic efficiency and gives fillip to reciprocal liberalization.
3. Development of trading institutions, both trade bodies and global banks have grown during this period. Trade and banking help in improving transportation facilities. These also assist in global credit, the LCs and global insurance.
4. Increase in global competition helps US as overseas players bring in lower prices, faster deliveries and also provide latest technological products.

The global business gets underway with the help of visible merchandise trade, the invisible trade of services besides going through the route of direct investments and portfolio investments.

Economics for Global Business

Firms start global business to expand sales territories and sales volumes, acquire resources and diversify their sources of sales and supplies. Company's increased sales depend on greater product acceptance by the customers in the selected market segment, besides the customers' ability and readiness to buy the same. Higher sales bring in larger profits in the normal course, unless the company is trying penetration pricing to gain a bigger market share. With higher sales the cost gets amortized on larger numbers bringing the cost of manufacture per unit down.

Global businesses are to a large extent, governed by the general and competitive business environment as can be seen from the following:

General business environment factors are demographic, social, cultural, legal, political, macroeconomic, technical and global.

Competitive business environment can be seen with the help of Michael Porter's 5 Force Model.

Besides the companies should look at the following competitive areas.

1. Advantage in pricing, innovation and other marketing mix factors
2. Number of competitors and their strengths and weaknesses and core competencies
3. Country's competitive strategy regarding foreign companies

The company must understand the host country's buyers value system, their attitude towards company's products and the geographic proximity with its home country.

The company has to decide the following before entering into global business:

1. Importing and exporting
2. Licensing and franchising
3. Turnkey operations
4. Management contracts
5. Direct and portfolio management
6. Tourism and transportation

Besides the company must decide about its choice of the country where it wants to do business. It needs to have an organization and control plans for the business and the plan level of integration among operations of several countries where the company may be operating and the stage of local inputs in each country.

Companies look for the following in the global markets:

1. Products and services, raw materials and components made overseas
2. Foreign capital–a direct investment
3. Technology
4. Information about the markets, new developments in the markets
5. Manufacturing technologies for cost reduction
6. Partners who can be trusted for outsourcing of their own product range or part of it.

Outsourcing is done if the purchased product matches with the home product and is lower in cost. This gives additional profits that can be used to for competition or given to the customer for increasing his purchases.

Global markets provide the cushion against sales losses incurred due to the home market for any reason. They can compete at home better with the extra sales in the global markets. The reasons for increase in global business in the twenty-first century are given below:

1. Technological innovations
2. Several countries getting into the market economy mode like India
3. Development of support organizations and infrastructures in different parts of the world
4. Worldwide increase in competition

The greatest innovation has been in the information and communication technology with cell phones and Internet. Besides transportation area has also seen rapid growth with supersonic jets moving around the world. Genetic engineering has revolutionized the farm sector bringing in vast resources of food in the markets of the world.

Several countries including India have eased cross-border movement of goods with reduced entry barriers, both tariff and non-tariff barriers. There is also greater awareness of the availability of a large variety of goods in the market that helps in consumers demanding the products from across the border at affordable prices. The spin-off of global players entry in the home country is the improvement of product and service quality of the domestic suppliers. Market forces along with bodies like WTO are trying to reduce the barriers to global movement of goods.

Influences on the Global Business

The following figure depicts the areas of influence on the global business.

External influences Political, legal, social, cultural, macroeconomic, technological, demographic, global competition	→ / ←	Operations Objectives Strategy Resources

Competitive business environment plays a decisive role in global business as given below.

External environment Competitive environment Advantage in lower costs, price, marketing, innovation Competitors and their strengths Difference in levels of competition country-wise
↑ ↓
Operations Objectives Strategy Resources

Companies have to undergo the following exercise when they plan global business.

A. Find out if the host country is similar or dissimilar to the home country businesswise. The scale can be made as given below:
Very similar
Moderately similar
Very different
B. Find out the imperative for going global as given below:
Passive thought process like responding to enquiries
Dynamic search for business opportunities
C. Find out the best way of managing global operations as given below:
External contracts framed out
The company handles on its own
D. Find out the mode of operations that shows the level of company's commitment in global operations as given below:
Limited foreign functions, exports and imports
Limited foreign production and multiple functions
Extensive production overseas with FDI and all functions
E. Find out the number of countries the company operates as follows:
One
Several
Many

Companies compete in the global markets to gain production efficiency on a global scale. For the purpose, product selection, its manufacture and location, shifting to the host country are important inputs.

Countries too compete in the global business. However, countries have their own agenda of improving the lot of its citizens and countries use their economic strength for leveraging their political clout with other nations. Countries compete for FDIs, technology updates and improving the social standards. Countries know that they have to cooperate with other countries for solving their economic problems that cannot be taken care of on their own.

Summarizing, the following needs to be considered.

1. Companies get into global business to expand sales, acquire resources, diversify the resources of sales and supplies and reduce risk of competitive action.
2. The reason for increase in global business is the advancement in technology, liberalization in various countries, policies on trade and increase in global competition.

A firm can start global business in various ways, like exports and imports of goods and services, direct and indirect portfolio investments and strategic alliance with other firms for mutual advantage, monetary, logistic or human.

Multinational firms operate in highly diversified external business environment. Profit-making in global markets becomes difficult due to different business conditions and at times confusing situations in foreign countries, rivalry between countries, cross-national treaties, bilateral and at times multilateral. There are ethical issues due to cultural differences between countries as well.

Multinational firms operate beyond national boundaries. When firms operate in different countries they become global firms, the firms, which allow a lot of autonomy to their foreign operations, are known as Multi- Domestic Firms. Even in multi-domestic firms a sense of integration and belonging is required to preserve the firm's identity.

Global Human Business Environment

Today most of the countries are involved in global business. Every country has certain physical, demographic and behaviour standards and norms, which forms the basis of their national identity. Therefore, study of these differences in country characteristics is essential for doing business in that country. However, it is important to overcome the fear of the unknown as demand and supply, money transactions remain similar all over the world.

The culture of a country is based on the attitudes, values system of its people and their beliefs, which are part of every society. Cultural variations give different levels of importance to the role of gender, family, age, work, career and self-reliance. Firms have to decide the extent to which they must adopt the home country practices to the foreign environment or get the host country people to accept something new. Each culture is unique with its special qualities. Contacts with people of other countries provide an insight into the cultures of those countries, while business dealing tends to become more formal and professional.

While doing business in other countries there is a need to have knowledge of their political and legal systems, which may vary from one country to another in a big way. Firms must develop a deep understanding of political and legal environments of the host countries, which would help them in formulating and implementing their business strategies.

Political and Legal Environment

Political and legal systems differ from one country to another; MNCs must understand these before formulating and implementing their strategies. There are two basic political systems in the world, both at two ends of spectrum, the democracies and totalitarianism. While in democracy decision-making process is a collective one, in communism the decisions are taken by one person or by a group of people, who control the power. This leads to vast differences in the way the governments deal with or interfere with business, especially with the overseas players. Political stability in the host country is another area that needs careful handling.

Political systems are designed to integrate the different parts of a society into a viable effective functional organization. The political thought and its ideology is a combination of a set of ideas, theories and objectives that form a sociopolitical programme. There are some pluralistic societies where a variety of ideologies coexist. In pure democracy citizens are directly into decision-making process. In representative democracy citizens elect representatives to make decisions in the parliament. In a totalitarian state, a single person or a group monopolizes political power.

Democracy has the following main characteristics.

1. Freedom of opinion, expression, press and freedom to organize
2. Fair and free elections to legislative bodies
3. Term limit for elected representatives
4. Independent and fair judiciary system and fair court system with high regard for individual rights and property

Democracy gives political rights as given below.

1. Fair and competitive elections
2. Elected representatives to have real power
3. Right to organize political parties and groups of individual choice
4. Safeguards on the rights of minorities

Democracy gives the following civil liberties.

1. Freedom of the press
2. Equality under the law to all citizens irrespective of their position status, caste, religion or sex
3. Personal social freedom
4. Freedom from extreme governmental interference or corruption

Totalitarian systems can be based on religious fundamentalism like in Iran or like secular in Cuba.

Countries have different norms or standards of legal, moral and ethical issues. At times law in counties is inadequate to cover these areas fully and the firms need to have a clear idea of what can be permissible and what would cross the ethical boundary in a given country.

Democracies provide great degree of freedom to their citizens in political areas with voting rights, which empower them for electing their own government. They get civil liberties allowing them to operate in any part of the country, worship any religion, and speak for or against the government without fear.

The Economic Environment

The world is divided in several economic zones. Basically there are the poor and the rich nations. Certain countries are in different stages of development. The levels of economic development, and the resultant differences in the living standards of different countries force companies to take management decisions in significantly different ways. In market economy, the CEO is authorized to take resource generation and allocation decisions, while in centrally planned economic states, the government takes such decisions. However, it can be safely assumed that most countries work in between the two extremes. Following are the key areas that affect the business decisions of companies in the overseas markets.

1. Status of privatization
2. Rate of inflation
3. Balance of payment situations between nations
4. External debts
5. Economic growth

Countries have to utilize their human and natural resources most efficiently to enable them to occupy the position of highest economic growth. However, the developing nations in general provide large market potentials. They may have strong overall growth yet; rich nations find it risky to invest in them. This is the result of some unscrupulous dealers, who have at times duped the rich nations in their desire of becoming rich quickly.

Governments play a major role in the development of tyeir country's economy as given below.

1. Protect liberty of citizens for engaging in businesses they opt for
2. Promote the welfare of citizens
3. Provide for national defence, transportation and communication systems
4. Control market flaws
5. Deal with external problems like incursions
6. Plan for check of pollution

There are several types of economies in the world, with large differences among each other. These differences make a major impact on the decision-making process in the corporate world with the MNCs as they plan to do business in other countries. The ownership of business can be public or private. Resource allocation could be market driven or totalitarian in approach. There are examples of combination of the two as well, which can be termed capitalist, socialist and mixed economies.

In market economy adequate wages are paid to the workmen. Prices of products are driven by demand and supply equation and are based on competitive forces as well. Resources allocation, wage levels are both market dependent. In socialist economies the government's spend a lot on social welfare and services. In consumer economy, there is minimal government's interference and high labour turnover. In economies that are driven administratively there is cooperation between the governments, management and the workers like in Japan.

In market based economic model most factors are privately owned and markets are highly competitive. These have strong currencies. In such economies the institutions like banks provide strong support to the economy. They have good infrastructure support like transport, warehousing, ports, communications, schools and hospitals and hotels. They provide MNCs with good investment opportunities.

In totalitarian economy the government sets the objectives, decides about the 4Ps, product to be made and sold, its price, the distribution network, who will manufacture it and who will be the buyers. Such economies have mostly become history now. In the mixed system, the role of the government depends on the revenue the government gets from the venture and the resource allocation and disbursement is as a percentage of the GDP. In fully mixed economies called the democratic socialism, not even a part of economy is owned by the government. In case of several erstwhile socialist countries, several companies are now becoming privately owned.

In market economy individuals become entrepreneurs and they allocate and control the economic resources, while in the government planned economies the government carries out this task. Most countries are placed between these two extremes. The main indicators of a country's economy are, per capita income, quality of life and the percentage GDP from the agriculture sector.

MNCs should understand the following economic issues in today's global business as given below.

East and South-East Asia is having the fastest economic growth in the recent times, in the last decade of the twentieth century and the first few years of the present century.

1. France and some countries in the Latin America have had a spate of privatization of several government companies.
2. Inflation has been on a all time high in most countries.
3. Balance of payment between countries has been suffering from imbalances.
4. External debts play an important role in global business.

Summarizing, certain main issues that have an impact on the business of MNCs are, economic growth, rate of privatization, inflation, payment imbalances between nations and external debts.

MNCs entering the global markets should have a good idea of the following:

1. The economic system of the host country
2. The industry divides between private and public sectors
3. If the industry is in the public sector does the government accept competition?
4. If the industry is in private sector is it moving towards government control and becoming public sector company?

MNCs should understand if the host government is encouraging foreign capital investment to compete with local companies. Besides it is important to understand the manner the government controls private business. Also it is essential to know the contribution of private sector in the formulation of country's economic policies.

Global Trade Theory

Global trade theory oversees the locations where companies can produce a product efficiently and competitively, depending on factors like availability of raw materials, manpower and vicinity of markets. The companies have to understand the host country's governmental policies and practices regarding foreign investments. Stability of the government and its structure are the important factors for taking investment decisions in the global trade.

Looking at the history of global trade it can be seen that trade between India, China and Middle East countries thrived much before any theories on global trade could be developed or propounded. Theories, however, help the companies in the global trade as they plan their operations. It can be presumed that when there are large differences in countries there would be greater trade potential. However, it can be seen from the past trade that most of the world trade is taking place between countries with similar levels of economic development and characteristics. It can be however presumed that free trade would be the result of most efficient utilization of world's natural and human resources. Trade theories cover the cost benefits of different countries. Actual decisions on global trade are taken at the corporate level only.

Government and Trade

Countries try to locate areas in the world, where they can influence trade for economic, social and political aims and objectives. If you go by the history the English, French and Portuguese found India as the ideal marketplace. They came as traders in the country and looking at the political opportunities took over the governance of parts of the country. Several rich countries exploit the poor countries by giving them the 'so-called doles' which in fact are a way of selling their surpluses and other obsolete products and technologies. However, even the genuine desire of the rich nations of doing business with the third world countries is designed to balance conflicting objectives and satisfying a number of varied interests. At times it could be to gain political mileage or it could be to obtain some rare material available only there. As such there is always governmental influence in global trade.

Governments of countries involved in global trade interfere because of political motives in the region, rather than economic concerns. These issues have led to conflicts within and between nations.

Rich countries use WTO and regional economic cooperation to remove trade barriers among the countries on multilateral basis. They also simplify global trade mechanism within these countries. It is the basic difference between nations that would limit the spread of trade liberalization on a global basis. On their part the government wants to ensure and expand employment opportunities for its population and for this purpose it has to interfere in the global trade. However, as both imports and exports provide job opportunities, such interference could become counterproductive as the other country may retaliate. This can be seen from the Indo-American outsourcing of jobs, which has become a political debate in the US.

Foreign Direct Investments

Foreign direct investments (FDIs) have been a source of concern to the host countries, as can be seen from pre-1991 Indian scene. However, since then FDIs have been welcomed even in India as they bring in progress to the country as well as to the firms getting the investments.

Countries seeking FDIs must understand the reasons why foreign investors would like to invest in their organizations. It could be for their own market expansion, or for acquiring foreign resources. FDIs involve the following:

1. Control by the foreign investor of the company to the extent of his investment percentage in the total investments of the company.
2. Helps the company in obtaining foreign technology easily and freely.

3. Company gets easy access to investors' personnel, raw materials, and components besides finance.
4. FDIs stimulate trade rather than inhibit them.

FDIs are one way of gaining equity participation. Besides foreign companies can transfer technology as investment in equity, or supply equipment, consultancy or manpower. Companies obtain FDI for selling in the host countries or even third countries to take advantage of some basic inherent advantage in operating in the host country. This could be low cost labour, easy availability of raw materials, proximity to global markets for the product. FDI could also be utilized to gain resources in the host country. The other advantage to the company making FDI is that it tends to be more profitable, and would have more stable sales and profits.

There are market related motivations for foreign investors coming to other country as given below.

1. Horizontal expansion of products which are not sensitive to scale economics
2. To achieve economies of scale
3. Lack of domestic market or saturation in the domestic market makes FDIs interesting
4. Actual or potential trade restrictions
5. Changing consumer tastes or requirements
6. Locals prefer local products
7. Late delivery risks from home country reduced
8. It is easy to follow customers, their needs and competitors who have expanded to the host country

There are resource related motivations for making FDI as given below.

1. To organize vertical integration especially for getting raw materials
2. To take advantage of low cost labour
3. To improve access to knowledge
4. To take advantage of the stages of PLC in which the product lies
5. At times to take advantage of incentives given by the host country's government
6. To obtain political gains by adding to the company's sphere of influence

There are purchase related motivations for FDIs as given below.

1. To avoid start up search time for raw materials and components
2. To avoid increase in home country capacity
3. To gain brand acceptance and goodwill
4. To reduce initial cost by taking over an ongoing concern, maybe a company going bankrupt

There can be a debate before making an FDI whether the investor should buy a company or start a company. The buy or build decision will depend on the factors given below.

1. Investors will have to build if there is no company available for acquisition
2. Acquisitions are loaded with problems

3. Financing is difficult for old companies whereas concessionary finance is available for new ventures

Companies plan FDIs overseas to expand markets or to acquire foreign resources. The main features of FDIs are given below.

1. It is a well-known fact that MNCs are more profitable
2. MNCs have more stable incomes
3. Most FDIs have been between rich industrial nations
4. Growth rate has been highest in the services sector FDIs

Companies that have made foreign investments are known to be more profitable having more sales and earnings than others. FDIs imply controlling authorities, permit companies to decide to maximize global performance. FDIs help in improving global efficiency. Countries can however try to restrict movements of investments by giving incentives for local companies.

FDI allows companies to make bold decisions to maximize global performance as they get better control on the host firm's activities. It helps in becoming globally more efficient although there is the inherent danger that some host countries may restrict inward or outward flow of goods and finance. Incentives like cash subsidies, tax benefits or import quotas are meant to support local companies to the detriment of companies making the FDI.

Foreign Exchange

1. Global trade requires the use of more than one currency. Making payments overseas requires special checks and other financial instruments, which are collectively known as foreign exchange. It is important to understand the term and definition of foreign exchange and how its market operates for short-term and long-term transactions. The main factor of exchanging one currency into another is convertibility. Some governments have imposed restrictions for controlling easy access to the foreign exchange, which might be in short supply in that country. Global banks provide the vital link for flow of global transactions. They provide the common link between the economies of the world.
2. Global trade has given rise to speculations about the value and availability of foreign currency and the speculators are ready to destabilize the world monetary system. Buying and selling commodities globally both have an element of risk, with enough chances of making profits. These risks give voice to the speculators. They can even push the market demand up or in the direction it wants to go. In such a case as the governments face the market realities they help in contributing to its long-term stability.

The basic difference between national and global business is the use of more than one currency. The special control points and other instruments for making payments abroad are collectively known as Foreign Exchange.

It is important for MNCs to know the terms, definitions connected with foreign exchange, how its market operates, governmental restrictions in countries regarding control of access to foreign exchange and how the global transactions take place.

Exchange Rates

Exchange rate is the number of units of one currency required for obtaining one unit of another currency. Spot rate is the rate quoted for inter-bank transactions that require delivery within two business days; this exchange is called settlement.

The inter-bank market is the foreign exchange market among commercial banks. Inter-banks transactions are transactions in the inter-bank market. The spot rate applies to Over-the-counter (OTC) transactions that involve non-bank customers and same day settlement. Forward rate is quoted for transactions for delivery after two business days. A trader can buy at the bid price and sell at the offer price; the spread becomes the difference. Direct quote is the number of units of domestic currency needed to purchase a unit of the required foreign currency, called the US terms or the American system. Indirect quote is the reciprocal of the number of foreign currency units required to purchase one unit of local currency, called European or Continental terms. The cross rate is computed from the two other exchange rates. Forward discount exists when the forward rate is less than the spot rate. Forward premium exists when the forward rate becomes more than the spot rate. Forward spread is the difference between the spot and the forward rates.

Foreign exchange brokers are the specialists who help in transactions in the inter-bank markets. Swap is a simultaneous spot and forward transaction; an outright forward contract is not connected to a spot transaction. Derivatives are the non-spot foreign exchange instruments, while future contracts are forward contracts for specific periods and amounts. Options are the rights, but not the obligations to trade at a specific rate.

Convertibility of Currency

In countries where the currency is fully convertible both residents and non-residents can purchase unlimited amounts of foreign exchange as and when they want. Hard currencies like the US dollar, yen, mark, pound are fully convertible, strong and stable. Other currencies are known as soft and weak. There can be exchange restrictions like having licensing agreements for selling only to central bank at the official conversion rates. There can be multiple exchange rates, import deposit requirements and control on quantities that can be purchased.

The main factor of exchanging one currency into others is convertibility. Some governments impose exchange restrictions to control access to foreign exchange.

Companies wanting to do global trade would do well to understand the methods in which the exchange rates are fixed, as it will help them in taking decisions about situations influenced by fluctuations in the exchange rates. Thus, they will be able to maintain a balance in a constantly changing environment.

There are three major categories of exchange rate arrangements, first, is pegged, second is limited flexibility and the third is more flexible. If the exchange rate arrangement is not reflecting the real demand and supply position, it will develop black market. The major systems for defining exchange rates are: freely fluctuating, managed fixed and automatic fixed. Country's inflation rate, interest rates differential, confidence level for doing business and technical factors influence the exchange rates.

Exchange rates are predicted by using Balance of Payment statistics, economics fundamentals and technical factors. Surprising as it may appear today, after the First World War, it was thought that a system of fixed exchange rate would help to bring stability and growth to the free world. It was later realized that this system created rigidity rather than stability, and the system was restructured to allow greater exchange rate flexibility. Largest markets of global transaction are UK, USA and Japan.

In the global transactions arbitrage is known as buying and selling of foreign currencies at a profit due to price discrepancies. (Arbitrage means simultaneous buying and selling of the same negotiable or commodity in different markets to make immediate profits.) Interest arbitrage comes from investing in debt instruments in different countries. Speculation means taking a risk with the basic objective of earning quick and substantial profits.

Summarizing, global banking is a means for facilitating the flow of global transactions. It provides the link between the economies of the world.

Some people believe that currency speculators are destabilizing the world monetary system. Speculations in buying and selling of a commodity provides for an element of risk along with chances of high profit-making. Speculators can push the market in the direction it should be moving. In such an event, they may contribute to long-term market stability to make the governments focus on the market realities.

Exchange Rate Study

MNCs must understand the manner the exchange rates are fixed and why they change so that they can make decisions about situations influenced by the changes. This will help the MNCs in keeping a balance in a constantly changing economic environment. MNCs should learn about the following aspects in this regard.

1. Exchange rate arrangements evolution
2. The current exchange rate arrangements
3. How the exchange rates are determined
4. Forecasting the exchange rate movement
5. Implications on business on exchange rate changes

Evolution of Exchange Rate Arrangements

In 1944, The Bretton Wood Agreement established a system of fixed exchange rates, variable within a narrow range of one percentage. In 1945, the IMF was set up to help build exchange rate stability and help the flow of global currencies. In 1970, Special Drawing Rights the SDRs were designed to increase global reserves. In 1971, exchange rate flexibility spread from one per cent to 2.25 per cent; 8 per cent devaluation of the dollar. In 1973, dollar devalued by 10 per cent; major currencies started unauthorized floating against one another. In 1997, Jamaica Agreement formally accepted the floating exchange rate.

IMF has made country classifications with some having pegged exchange rates and others having limited flexibility within 2.25 per cent of a single currency, while UK and Italy discarded it to allow deviations of 15 per cent. However, there are black market transactions depending on the supply and demand situation of different currencies. In some countries their central banks intervene to control the value of their currency. In India the Reserve Bank of India carries out this task. Bank of Global Settlement helps in monetary cooperation between countries.

The three main categories of IMF exchange rate are pegged, limited flexibility and more flexible. When the arrangement does not reflect the real demand supply position, black market develops.

Rates Determination

When the USA inflation increases as compared to the Japanese inflation, Japan finds US products expensive and would buy lesser quantities. Hence, the demand for dollar would reduce and the price of dollar will decline as compared to the yen resulting in devalued dollar.

The government buys and sells its currency to maintain its price parity. If it goes down it will increase the cost of imports and increase inflation rate. If the price goes up the demand for country's export would reduce and cause unemployment. Rates change when the exchange reserves are low.

The domestic money supply is based on the basis of reserve assets. When the domestic currency comes under pressure, gold reserves are sold or mortgaged to support the currency strength. As reserves go down so does the money supply, while the interest rates increase and investments decline. Moreover, in such conditions unemployment increases and prices take a beating. Next, exports start to increase and that strengthens the currency.

The exchange rate fixation is also dependent on the inflation, interest rate differentials and technical factors.

When the relative inflation changes, it can result in changes in exchange rates to maintain price parity. For example, if Japanese inflation is 2 per cent and the USA inflation is 3.5 per cent, then the value of the dollar will go down by 1.5 per cent.

The Fisher Effect

The Fisher Effect states that the nominal interest rate in a country is defined by the real interest rate and the inflation rate. If the real interest rates are same in two countries, the country with the higher rate of inflation will have higher nominal interest rate.

The Global Fisher Effect states that the interest rate differential between two countries is an unbiased forecaster of the future changes in the spot exchange rate. Higher relative interest rates will make a country's currency weak.

Technical factors that define the exchange rates are the level of confidence in the currency, release of economic statistical data and seasonality of demand for the currency.

The prime systems of finding out the exchange rates are, freely fluctuating, managed fixed and automatic fixed. Rates are affected by inflation, confidence and technical factors too.

Rate forecasting comes from the Balance of Payments statistics, balance of merchandise trade, current account balance and basic balance. While there is fundamental forecasting of exchange rates, there is also technical forecasting where people keeping statistical charts use past trends in rates to spot future trends.

The changes in exchange rate have far reaching impact on the following:

1. Marketing decisions on price modifications
2. Production decision regarding the most appropriate location
3. Financial decision on fund sources, disbursement of funds and financial reporting

The balance of payment statistics, economic basics and the technical factors are used in forecasting exchange rate movements.

Multinational Companies Impact

Multinational companies influence the countries in which they operate; their influence, however, could be conflicting with respect to the countries' commercial objectives. That makes evaluating the MNCs commercial influence on countries difficult to assess.

MNCs do affect growth and employment of the countries in which they operate. This effect does not necessarily benefit one country at the expense of the other. Balance of payment gains are a zero sum situation.

Political concerns about MNCs centre around the fear that they may be used as foreign policy instruments of home country or host country governments or that they may avoid the control of any government.

MNCs do contribute to growth and employment in the host country by utilizing the idle resources more efficiently and even improving the quality of the resources. This is done by providing training to the employees and using better production technology. Growth and employment are affected by the location in which the MNCs operate, product sophistication, competitiveness of local companies, government policies, and the degree of product differentiation.

Negotiations and Diplomacy in the Global Trade

Governments try to improve their economic positions through global trade and they plan their strategies, policies and enact laws favouring their business and economic objectives. Global companies too plan their overseas ventures to get the best out of their global competitive advantage. The business diplomacy of the concerned countries and the other global firms operating in the host country, influence MNCs operations. The business diplomacy can take the shape of declaring some countries as the Most Favoured Nation with the give and take business philosophy, like reduction in tariffs and easy import formalities.

MNCs operate in host countries on the basis of their relative need of each other. Entry in the global markets is increasingly being negotiated to define the terms under which the company would be allowed to operate in the country. For example, some government may ask the company to partly invest their yearly profits in the country. The company has to decide to enter in the country's market depending on its needs of that market.

Rich countries use the promise of giving financial assistance to the poor nations. They also use the threat of trade sanctions against the nations not falling in line with the commercial forays through their companies in the host country. Developed countries are known to have used military interventions and related economic coercion to ensure that the terms of business are agreed upon between their investing companies and the poor recipient nations as dictated by them.

However, no global business can thrive unless there are separate types of resources available between the two countries setting up the business. If the resources of one nation can be combined with the resources of the other both the countries can achieve their objectives. However, if one country or both the countries withhold the resources, business would suffer and cause conflicts.

The difficulty between countries engaged in global negotiations arise due to the following reasons.

1. Cultural differences
2. Level of education, resultant skills
3. Expectations from the global operations

Countries have to look at each other's business sentiments. It would help them in preparing convincingly arguments in favour of the global business.

Evaluation and Selection of Country

Before entering into a new nation a country needs to have proper evaluation of the possible host countries. It is almost impossible for companies to have enough resources to enter into all the countries where there is a scope of business for them. Therefore, it is better for the company to establish methodology for determining the markets they should enter and where they should locate their production base for serving that market. An integrated approach would be to identify the similarities and the differences between the nations, in terms of the economic levels, technological advances to enable the planners to ensure that these complement each other and that there is no conflict at all.

The main thrust areas to understand are the market size, cost and availability of resources. These would help the company in taking decision regarding its entry into the market. They would also be in a better position regarding allocation of resources for optimizing the results. After the company has gained the information the host country can be rated in the context of a predetermined diversification or concentration strategy; to go all out in the country or keep it as one of the areas for doing business. In the early stages of entering a country, a company responds to opportunities as they unfold before it. Later, companies realize that they cannot take advantage to all possible opportunities.

Companies have to, at some stage, choose between diversification and concentration, either to rush to several countries and then build up the business slowly, or go to one or just a few and build up fast, before going to others.

Collaborations in the Global Business

Companies use different ways of having forays in the global markets, like getting into licensing, franchising, joint venture or having a wholly owned subsidiary. Company's business strategy would depend on the following factors in this regard.

1. Company's business experience in the global business and its business acumen
2. Competitive forces as can be studied with the help of Michael Porter's 5 Force Model
3. Political and economic risks
4. The nature of assets and resources to be used

Foreign investment or involvement takes the shape of a joint venture, licensing, franchising, and managing contracts, turnkey contracts, and equity with or without controlling interests.

Companies can decide to have different strategies for different countries and even have different strategies for different products in one country. With operations in several countries of numerous products coordinating and managing global operations become complex needing a set of expertise in each of the key business areas.

Therefore, companies doing global business have a variety of foreign operations depending on their internal and external activity handling capabilities. These also depend on the proportion of resources allocated to home operations as against the global activities. While dealing with its global operations the company's form would be examined in terms of company's strategic objectives, the choice would be mostly made involving some trade-off among the objectives. It would be a good idea for the students to analyze the possible trade-offs in this regard. The company, for example, fixes the global price of the product taking only the variable cost plus a small element of fixed costs, while increase the home country price by adding the balance amount thus lost to price the product in the home market, by amortizing it on the numbers sold locally.

Control Points

Company's objectives can be achieved with having control points during the strategic planning stage, where parameters are provided to the planners. Besides, implementation of the plan, its evaluation and online correction of any aberrations are the important features of the controls.

Decisions in the global business are made depending on the relative competence of the managers handling the business and the cost of decision-making at different levels and the effect of the decisions taken on the overall corporate performance.

The difficulties arise in controlling the global business due to the following reasons.

1. Cultural diversities between countries
2. Economic differences
3. Geographic distances

4. The need to operate differently in different host countries
5. The large amount of uncontrollable in overseas business
6. Uncertainties of data availability and its rapid changes

Therefore, in global business total centralization and total decentralization may be considered as the two extremes. In real life situations companies take the middle road; they do not go for centralization or decentralization in their decision-making process.

Companies need to have formal control over its foreign subsidiary. The degree of this control required governs the degree of control imposed by the home office on the selection of overseas top managers.

Global Marketing

Like marketing in the home country, global marketing requires tailor-made approaches to analysis of the market potential. Special care is needed in selection of product, pricing, promotion, branding, and distribution plans.

Depending on the product, companies can opt the global approach to marketing by having standardized products and business terms and strategies in different countries where it plans to market its products. This approach reduces the marketing expense drastically, however, most companies make changes in their plans to fit the host country needs.

Products can be in different stages of the Product Life Cycle in different countries. If the product is in introduction or growth stage the company can influence the product pricing. Global pricing gets complicated with fluctuations in currency rates and differences in preferences of the product. Furthermore, branding, promotion and distribution areas of the marketing mix factors are sensitive to the social and cultural values systems of the host countries, consumer attitudes and the host country's laws. However, it is possible that as the world becomes one big global village, companies could plan global strategies with much less differentiated approach and more of standard global planning.

It may be argued that the principles of marketing do not differ between the home country and the host countries, global business calls for dealing with less known business environment, which may be changing rapidly too. Even with common marketing principles in the global business, the environmental differences often force the managers either to overlook important variables or to misinterpret the information.

Strategies for Imports and Exports

The 21st century is poised for growth in the global economy. Furthermore, barriers to global business are expected to reduce. As a result global exports trade is likely to increase. While planning exports strategies, companies should take the following steps.

1. Assess export potential in the target country through a reputed local market research agency
2. Select markets by taking advice from experts in the host country
3. Formulate strategy regarding product specification, packaging, aesthetics
4. Determine the export channels, direct or indirect

Besides, there are three major areas which need immediate attention relating to finance. They are export pricing, method of payment and the financing of the receivables.

From experience it can be stated that large companies probability of becoming exports is more as, with its size, the company must export if it wants to increase sales. However, the extent of exports does not directly correlate with the company's size. Several large companies have a small percentage of exports to its total sales. At times smaller companies outperform the large companies in exports as they are more focused.

Outsourcing Global Operations

Outsourcing and production bases in the global arena imply that companies need to understand the location advantage of manufacturing parts, components or even complete units globally. Companies need to decide about making manufacturing plans should global or multi-domestic. Then there is a necessity of integrating the global operations for becoming globally competitive. For example, if an Indian company wants to export to Africa it may consider setting up manufacturing base in Maldives or Seychelles. This would reduce the transportation cost to a large extent. MNCs would do well to start coordinating with the host country's suppliers at the design stage to develop products with low cost and high quality.

The production sharing method is used in one or several countries for exporting products to the final third country markets. Intermediate goods like components are increasingly being made in several countries and these are then transported to other countries for assembly and sales.

Multinational Finance Planning

Companies use their internal or external sources of funds for their foreign operations. Companies must understand global cash management and risk management.

The Eurocurrency market can be considered still as banked by outside their countries of origin, especially, dollars banked outside the USA. These could become an important source of funds for the MNCs. Other major internal fund source for MNCs are dividends, royalties, management fees, inter-company loans and the equity generated by the parent company. An important task of the company is to protect company's assets from losses on account of inflation and exchange fluctuations by using managerial techniques.

Net present value and internal rate of returns can be successfully used for evaluating investment decisions. As the companies make foreign investment decisions, they must compare the net present value and the internal rate of return of the project with that of other projects and that of others available in the host country.

Scientific developments, like the supersonic transport planes, Internet and faster telecom covering practically the entire world has made it a small place. Further, the information technology has speeded up the globalization process for business collaborations and political understanding which are so very important for business. Foreign firms are invading practically most countries in the world and unless we know how to handle the situation, we would be left behind in the race for a place in the market leave alone the market leadership in the world.

To start with it is necessary to understand the basic outline of business, which is given below.

a) Purchase of raw materials b) Conversion of the raw materials into a salable product or manufacturing c) Reaching the product to the customer or marketing.

The business starts with sourcing of raw materials and with the use of machinery and human resources these raw materials are converted/or a saleable product is manufactured for which a need exists in the marketplace. However, to reach the ultimate consumer, firms take the help of middlemen who distribute/sell the product through a channel to the consumers.

Firms starting global business enter into exports and at times imports from other countries, where according to the 18th century economist Adam Smith, the country has either absolute advantage or at least comparative advantage over other countries in the selected product.

Firms go for global business for:

1. Gaining market extensions, when they find their own country's market getting saturated when they are into exports.
2. Lower labour cost, easy availability of raw materials, technological base and lack of competition are the other major imperatives of global business for the firms.

Objectives of Global Business

The firms need to have a clear objective for going into the global business and then they can decide on the plans of achieving the same. The major objectives are given below.

- Finding profitable markets for increased production
- Using local technological advantage in the global market
- Using the firms brand equity in the global market
- Using local low cost labour as competitive advantage
- Obtaining new source of raw materials, subassemblies and even completely built units at reasonable prices for sale in own country and even in third countries
- Fighting competition from global firms on the home ground

When firms plan to increase their production to achieve economies of scale of manufacture, they build excess capacity, which cannot be sold in the local market due to the saturation levels it has reached. Matching machine's manufacturing capacity with fine-tuned demand in the local market is not easy and hence, firms plan to go overseas with their excess capacity. Once the firms get into the overseas market, they even plan manufacturing just for that market, taking care of the exact specifications of the product needed there.

Product technology can be patented and scarce. The firm having the technology can take advantage by locating markets needing the products and then they can almost dictate the price of the product in the global markets. Such skimming prices can give additional profits till competition comes in with similar product but at lower prices. However, if the firm's brand equity is high it can still sell the product on the strength of its brand.

Labour cost in most products is a sizable costing area. Developing nations like India still enjoy low cost labour and therefore can produce goods cheaply as compared to affluent nations. These nations like the USA are giving up manufacture of labour intensive products and they are ready to buy from a country, which gives them quality product and does not have political risks attached to it.

USA has been outsourcing a number of products and their firms are happy to give the following to the firms in other countries ready to take up manufacture on their behalf.

- Technology of manufacture
- Quality planning and control
- Managerial expertise
- Markets
- Financial assistance

When global firms have invaded the country, the only recourse for Indian firms is to look for markets elsewhere. This will make the firms stronger to deal with foreign firms in their own country as well.

Global business strategy has to look at alternative plans before the final decision can be taken. The correctness of assessment of global markets, which comes from Global Marketing Research, is the Critical Success Factor in the global business. Firms need to look at the following areas.

1. The country or countries most suited for the firm
2. Synergy in the operations within the country and with other countries
3. Absolute or comparative advantage of the product or any other P, like, the price or distribution network
4. The other country's financial strengths
5. The other countries balance of payment situations in respect to the home country
6. Availability of labour, distribution network, raw materials
7. Possibilities of exporting to third countries from that country
8. Entry barriers for overseas players by the government of the host countries
9. Other forms of entry barriers like non-availability of channel network as they may be already tied-up with existing players
10. Tax regulations, profit repatriation rules of the host countries

The suitability of country would depend on the product demand level, competitive strengths, product quality and its availability and the long-term product perspective on demand growth. Physical distance, transportation costs may become the major barriers, unless of course the firm wants to use either low cost labour there or if the country has immense business potential. Political climate, governmental controls are the other areas, which the firms need to examine especially from the historical point of view. Availability of market information, transparency in business dealings and business ethics are major components of decisions on countries to be selected for doing business with.

Firm's home country operations, which have been honed to perfection over a period of time, may not work elsewhere at all. The business culture of the host country becomes an important decision criterion as otherwise a lot of time would be lost in understanding what went wrong. A study of consumer behaviour patterns would give a better idea of the business culture. Host country's social milieu, which governs most of the consumer business, is yet another area of thorough investigation before business can be started. In other words, firms need an in-depth market study before taking the plunge in any unknown global market. Like people countries too behave differently with each other; what is good for one country may not be good for another.

Firms seek competitive advantage and this comes from several sources as given below.

- Effective management leadership, policies and their implementation
- Product differentiation
- Brand equity
- Cost leadership
- Market responses
- Production efficiency
- Soft numbers like employees' motivation levels

Leadership

Leadership in an organization includes justice and fair play, motivation through being a role model, settlement of disputes among workers, providing information by being a good and effective communicator. In global business leaders must have a broad perspective of the global business, its advantages and its pitfalls. The leader has to provide the firm its strategic intents like, vision, mission goals and objectives and he has to ensure that the workforce becomes committed to these intents.

Differentiation

Differentiation can be made in product, price, and placement as well as in promotion, all the 4 Ps. In India, all the scooters looked almost identical till the Kinetic Honda came on the scene, which looked distinctly different from the rest. Buyers are always looking for products, which are unique in some ways. While the differentiated products give the firm a competitive advantage, it is useful to watch for "me too" or copied products coming into the market, which can be a bit better because the competition would have learnt the negative points of the firm's products. Therefore, firms should be on constant look out for making a difference in any of the 4Ps, to keep competition a few steps behind them.

The other danger in differentiation is that the firm may increase the product cost, resulting in a selling price, which is not acceptable in the market. For example, in an electrical gadget, where copper wire would do the job, there is no need for putting gold wire, which would increase the cost with no benefit to the customer.

Brand Equity

Firms spend huge amounts of money in building their brands. A good product with a powerful brand gets the competitive advantage as customers buy the product on the reputation and the goodwill the firm and its product has generated in the market. Firms use its brand to price its products as good brand equity gets a higher price as well.

Cost Leadership

Most of the discerning customers are looking for **value for money** products. With better looks and mass production, Japan has taken a lead in car entertainment electronics and watches sales the world over. With lower production costs they are able to use the money for R& D, product innovations, and for fighting price wars if required. Cost is built up of two factors, namely:

- Fixed costs
- Variable costs

The fixed costs include the cost of money, salaries, rentals and depreciation, while variable costs include cost of raw materials, labor and consumables.

Fixed costs per unit of manufacture get reduced when the economies of production scale are achieved, and variable cost gets reduced with the effect of experience curve.

Suppose the total fixed cost of manufacturing 10,000 cars is Rs. 30,00,000. The fixed cost per car comes to Rs. 300. now if the production is increased by 20 per cent, to 12,000 cars and if the fixed cost does not change, then the fixed cost per car would come to Rs. 250 per car (worked in a straight-line method). Such ideal situation may not occur as with increase of production by thirty to forty percent would increase the total fixed cost to some extent with increase in shift managers, bigger floor space. The firm can get the benefit of larger purchase of raw materials, bigger and hence cheaper advertising campaigns, because of the bulk rates offered by the media.

Variable costs decrease due to the time experience factor. When the workers start the manufacture in the initial stages the rejection rates are high. As they become familiar with the manufacturing process the rejection rate falls, decreases the cost of raw materials and labor. A typical example is of electronic semiconductor devices. In the beginning the rejection rate used to be up to 70 percent and hence the price of Integrated circuits was between 200 to 300 rupees. Today when the rejection rate has reduced to 1 to 2 percent the prices have come down to twenty to thirty rupees only.

Firms use the low cost benefit to their advantage as follows:

- Enjoying extra profit and using it for expansion
- Innovating the product and other Ps for maintaining their market share.
- Cross Parry-fighting price wars, hitting competition at their weak links, if they start the price war and hit the firm in its vulnerable market.

Costs leadership works through the firm as follows:

- Flatter firm less costs
- Employee-oriented policies to reduce their turnover
- Training to reduce wastage and increase productivity
- Long term relationship with the vendors
- Economies of scale in production

- Experience curve to reduce variable costs
- Long term advertising budget for lowering costs
- Expert servicing for being right always

It is useful to understand the risks associated in the factors, which can collectively or individually provide the competitive advantage, the risks are given below:

- Differentiation—if it increases the manufacturing cost to such an extent that the product out-prices itself, beyond the reach of the customers in the market segment, than such a differentiation is not worthwhile at all and should be eschewed. A typical example is of TV sets. Imagine it having gold wires inside making electrical contacts, while copper is much cheaper and does the same job well.
- Cost Leadership—firms trying to bring down costs should not go overboard by compromising on quality of the product; otherwise, instead of gaining any advantage the firm would be in real danger of losing total market. It can be a clearly demarcated win or lose situation.
- Quick Response—if the firm's response to market demand is half baked, not well planned then, it could lose out to competitors who would become wiser from the firm's mistakes and counter the firms strategy with a much better one and the initial advantage gained, if any would be totally lost to the firm.

Out of the three methods firms can plan to use one, two or all the three at the same time depending on the need. The fourth method is however likely to provide sustainable competitive advantage, which is provoding unique customer service

Customer Service: Sustainable Competitive Advantage

The first three methods do provide competitive advantage to the firm, but these could be temporary, as the competition knocks off the advantage usually with a flair, by not only copying the differentiation, but doing one better than the firm, as they have seen the customers reactions on the differentiated product or the other Ps. Service is one element of the product, which is less likely to be copied. It is not possible to copy the genuine smile of the salesman, his ways of ingrating himself with the customer, his relationship building techniques, which although can be taught, yet they remain in the realm of soft factors, which cannot be easily quantified, much less copied. Service therefore is one of the ways of creating and maintaining sustainable competitive advantage.

Market Focus

Firms trying to cater to the entire market can face problems, as the variety of customers and their requirements is huge. Firms are finding it increasingly appropriate to focus their marketing efforts on a selected market segment, where the product is best accepted. For example, in India Mercedes sells only in the top market segment; trying to sell it in any other segment would be complete waste of time and money.

The danger in going in a big way for cost reduction to achieve cost leadership is that, the firm may compromise on product quality and lose the entire business in the bargain. Firms need to watch out that price reduction is never made at the cost of product quality.

Market Response

Firms who are proactive to the market needs, whether overt or covert (known or unknown) and who understand the stated and unstated requirements can be taking preemptive measures by providing the needs at the right time. This calls for continuous vigil on the market without any letup at all. The firm offering the required product first gets the initial advantage; it can flood the market, even mould it to make it receptive to the product. Of course, the first marketer has the job of concept selling, making the customers aware of the product and its benefits. Quick response to market needs can be an effective competitive advantage.

Production Efficiency

Firms have to keep their manufacturing in top gear always, with the help of total quality management and process reengineering. These lead to optimum levels of production and to high quality production, both essential for gaining competitive advantage.

Motivation and Commitment of the Employees

Employees are referred to, as **human resource** in today's management. If we accept the term only as indicative of the employees it is acceptable. However, human beings are, thinking, sensitive people and should not be considered as herd. One should not forget the impact the employees have on the total organizational picture.

Genesis of Global Business

Global business is perhaps as old as the hills. We can trace it as far back as the 9th century AD, when in Europe and Asia, the civilized people were living on land where they grew agricultural products and the rest, the barbaric lived in the Steppes where they grazed the cattle and sheep, hunted animals for food and bartered their skin in exchange of their other needs. The countries were not well defined; there were clans who lived in a particular geographic area.

In the 10th century the Chinese introduced paper money, which were introduced after having bullion reserves of gold and silver nuggets. Chinese also printed books about the same time using block-printing method.

In the 11th century King Rajendra of Chola Kingdom in the south India found his realm's business was being usurped by the Malaya who were dominating the Indian Ocean trade. He ordered a naval attack on Malaya to end the domination. Seafaring folks of coastal India were going to far off places including China, Europe, Africa with their wares for sale.

11th century saw China with a lot of paper money, mass production of iron items and its prosperity came from trade with other nations as ocean voyages had become safer by now, with the invention of mariner's compass.

In the 13th century Genghis Khan controlled north China and most of Asia. He promoted global trade and revived the Chinese silk route. About the same time, Marco Polo, the Viennese merchant went to the Chinese court and because of his business acumen, he was made the commercial agent of the court. He travelled throughout the country to gain knowledge of its trade.

In the 14th century Brugge, which is located in the North Sea near Europe became a major trading centre for England, France and other countries bordering Atlantic Ocean. The Scandinavian Vikings were seafaring people, who were proving a threat to the other ocean traders.

15th century Japan and China prohibited foreign trade to suppress piracy; the only countries allowed to trade were the tributary countries. Chinese ships reached the African shores for trading and in return they got exotic animals from their emperor. Chinese expeditions explored the Indian Ocean during this time.

On May 10th, 1498, Vasco da Gama came to India for adding to the trade efforts of Portugal. His trade efforts were not so successful due to fierce competition from Muslim traders operating in the country.

In the 18th century the Dutch, the French and the English came to India as traders, formed the Dutch East India Company, the British East India Company, and started trade from Madras and Bombay. How the English came to rule India is history.

In the 17-18th century industrial revolution was taking place in the west. Steam engine had changed the way people travelled.

In 1807, the USA banned European trade because of the Napoleonic wars.

The industrial revolution, mass production techniques resulted in imbalances in the demand and supply of several products in their own countries, forcing firms to seek global markets. The dip in the global business can be seen during the two world wars of the 20th century. Countries' culture, literature, commerce are the victims of any wars and on a serious note, no one really wins a war, which leaves behind massive destruction of human life and property.

Classical Theory of Trade

In 1776, Adam Smith propounded the theory of absolute advantage between nations. Later scholars gave the theory of comparative advantage. The theory of absolute advantage says that a country has to have absolute advantage in their product offerings, in order that they can export their wares in other countries. They should be able to manufacture the product, cheaper, better and faster than other nations. While this theory still holds good—countries have recognized the importance of theory of comparative advantage, which recognizes the advantage of one country in a particular area only, like availability of raw materials or low cost labour, which can sustain the country in the global market theory.

The **Theory of Absolute Advantage** conveys the following:

(a) If country A has absolute advantage in manufacturing a product over other countries, then it can export it to those countries.
(b) If the country B does not enjoy the absolute advantage, then it cannot export at all.

The **Theory of Comparative or relative advantage** says that the "relative advantage of a country in manufacturing a product is different or better than that of another country's ability to manufacture the same product. This advantage acts as a lever in exporting the product from the first country to the second country." Recardo propounded this theory of comparative advantage.

The above statement gives an idea of how the comparative advantage works. However, other considerations like the political situation, investments made and market trends play a vital role in the export trade today.

Global Business Methods

The usual route firm's take while embarking on global business is as follows: Exports → Licensing → Franchise → Joint venture → Wholly owned subsidary (at each step company's investments increase)

Area of operation	Control country	Area of operation	Location of operation
Exports	Home country	Goods/services	Host country
Licensing	Home country	Tech. Know-how	Host country
Franchise	Home country	Management help, technology, Brand	Host country
Joint venture	Home country	Part investment, technology, management, raw materials	Host country
Wholly owned subsidary	Host country	Total organization	Host country

The other areas of operations are given below.

- Import-export
- Tourism
- Transport
- Consultancy
- Investments
- Manpower
- Management

Advantages of Global Business

Firms look for expanding their geographic horizons in order to increase their sales volumes. The product, which has been successful in the home market, may not necessarily succeed in a different country. Therefore, firms have to conduct market surveys in different countries. The ideal situation is to arrange information through the embassies, chamber of commerce including global chamber of commerce, the WTO, and other UN agencies as secondary research. Once the firm can shortlist a few countries, primary research should be undertaken to understand the product needs, buying patterns market segments suited to the product, competition and the price, placement and promotion of competitive firms already operating in the countries. The information must be then used to decide about the country(ies) best suited. Information about the country's government's known and covert intentions and plans regarding foreign firms entering their markets is absolutely essential for the progress of the firm in the global markets.

SUMMARY

Firms realizing the importance of doing business in different parts of the world, have to start locating the markets most favourable for their products and then only they can chart their route on way to doing global business.

India has over the years especially since 1991, the watershed year in the country's economy, has gained comparative advantage over several countries of the world as follows:

- Low labour cost
- Trained manpower
- Leadership in software development
- Availability of raw materials

Globally, firms try to gain competitive advantage through the following as well:

- Economic scale of production due to large customer base globally
- Patent laws
- Quota system
- Product differentiation
- High exit costs

CHAPTER 2

Global Marketing

"Vasudhaiv Kutumbkam" the two words aptly describe the business world of the twenty-first century. It means that the entire world is one family. With faster supersonic jets, travel time has been drastically reduced. Internet, Fax, and Cell phones have made communications as fast as anybody can want. Flow of technology, finance and market information has become rapid, making it easier to plan global business. It however has opened the doors to wide range of countries creating severe global, competition in practically all areas of business. There have been global or multinational firms for a long time now, like the Lever Brothers, Shell, Exxon, Ford, Nestle. Today, a much larger contingent of firms are either already in the market or are entering it to vie for the customers globally. There is hardly a nation left which is not a player in the global arena. It depends on the **Supply-Demand** paradigm, which decides the supply point while the economic levels of the countries support the product's sales in different countries.

The importance of global marketing has never been felt in India with such intensity as today. With increasing global competition on our shores, Indian firms have to compete with them and find other markets as well. With partial **convertibility of rupee,** export earnings become a major source of foreign exchange, which helps in firm's imports of raw materials and components. Now even completely built units are allowed for imports, and many firms are using the benefits to import samples for user trials and sales. Firms have to find markets overseas to survive in the Indian market. It is also true that first the product must be proven in the Indian market before the firm ventures out for its export, unless of course, the product has been manufactured with foreign customer's specifications and requirements in mind.

Our manufacturers have been by and large handicapped in the world market, with a few exceptions, because of the following reasons:

1. Indian products have a low brand equity, foreigners consider them of low quality.
2. Our advertising in the world market is below the mark.

3. Our embassies need to do much more to promote Indian products.
4. India has been considered a country of snake-charmers and elephant ride and the land of Maharajas. This needs to be changed.
5. Our knowledge about the world market is restricted to traditional products and traditional markets. We need to widen our product range as also our geographic world coverage.
6. Till the eighties of the last century, the firms in India found that the home market was more attractive and they had no reason to go overseas.
7. Surprisingly, perhaps, it was some small firms, which had ventured into exports and built a name for them.
8. With rupee value in favour of exports, now is the time to take full advantage of the situation.
9. Besides, till now, India has low cost of labour, which can make our top quality products competitive.
10. To a new exporter, global business remains a mystery until he ventures out and finds out the benefits and methods of going overseas.

Global marketing requires fine-tuned approaches for understanding market potential, analyzing the same. Next, product has to be selected, price fixed and strategies for distribution, promotion, advertising, branding and packaging need to be finalized. Knowledge and understanding of the global markets are the sound basis for success worldwide.

The company should, therefore, arrange for the following:

1. Market demand analysis
2. Product policy
3. Pricing policy
4. Promotion plans
5. Branding policy
6. Distribution channels

Some of the indicators of market size are given below.

Relationship between sales and per capita income as compared to sales of the same product in another country and its per capita income should be studied. The comparison of per capita income would help in predicting sales in the other country. Companies should find if product demand is dependent on income and would it change with the change in income. If the change in demand with unit change in income is greater than one, then the demand can be considered elastic. If it is less than one, then it is inelastic as given below.

$$\text{Income elasticity} = \frac{\%\text{ change in demand}}{\%\text{ change in income}}$$

Elastic would mean the ratio to be > 1
Inelastic would mean the ratio to be < 1

The company can use time series analysis for projecting the future demand by understanding the past sales patterns. Market size analysis can be undertaken by the following methods as well.

1. Regression analysis by working out the relationships between demand and other economic indicators.
2. Analysis of the gap between demand and supply, usage, product line, distribution and competition gaps can be studied for the purpose.

Taking from the above guidelines, the company has to select the product to be sold in the selected global market.

In the past, companies were selecting products on the basis of production orientation. "What the company can make we will sell". In product groups where the demand exists and there is little or no competition the policy can still work. However, as is generally acknowledged, there is hardly any product with no competition, the policy would not work, because competitive companies will sell products needed by the customers and not what they make.

The next level of product selection comes from sales orientation with the hypothesis that what is sold in home country will sell in the host county as well, because the customers are having similar needs. This would not work today because different countries have different mindsets, consumer behaviour patterns and income levels.

Strategic marketing orientation would require the companies to select the product only what the customer wants and manufacture the same. This customer-centric approach is most likely to succeed as the company is just meeting an obvious or a dormant demand.

Product selection strategy would also have to take into account the host country's legal issues like safety, health hazards coverage as given below.

1. Legal factors like safety norms given by the host country government
2. Health based norms for food products, medicines
3. Cultural factors of product acceptance in the host country's markets like no perfumes, bath oils and suntan in Japan
4. Income levels or the economic factors
5. Cost of product modification as compared to its benefits

Summing up, the companies in the global market should realize that while standard market approach would mean maximum uniformity in product and other marketing strategies in countries they are selling the products, as it brings in minimizing of expenses, it will not work in today's severe competition and the companies must make product modifications as required in the host country.

Global Pricing

Companies should look at the following areas in fixing product prices in the global markets.

In some countries the government sets the formula for price fixation. They give the maximum and minimum limits for prices. In some of the countries the degree of governmental intervention in pricing varies widely. In some there are price control rules. Products have different acceptance levels, brand equity and usage and all these contribute to the final product price. Global markets have mostly longer channels of distribution, which need to be given their commission, which becomes an add-on to the price. Countries have different tariff schedules that keep changing. These factors need to be considered for finalizing the prices.

The other areas of consideration in fixing the price are given below.

1. Rate of inflation
2. Replacement cost of the product
3. Currency stability—it is preferable to quote in hard currency like the dollar or the pound
4. The level of customer bargaining applicable in the country
5. The level of global competition

While it is the duty of the company to fix the price in the host country, at times the prices may be given to the first channel member, like a distributor, who can put a mark depending on the market situation for fixing the price. In other words, the distributor and retailer can put their own price on the product.

Companies can influence pricing of the product in its growth stage. However, product may be in different stages of life cycle in different countries. Currency value changes, customer preference changes—both contribute in product price fixation.

Promotion Plans

Product sales can be promoted by using both the pull strategy of advertising and the push strategy of personal selling. In most cases, however, both the push and the pull strategies are used. In places where self-service is not prevalent it is better to have extensive use of push strategy. Besides the push strategy works well where the product is a highly priced, compared to the general per capita income of the place. It is used in places where advertising usage is restricted.

Global advertising, when standardized, brings about the following:

1. Cost benefits
2. Local level better quality
3. Fast entry in different countries

The company must take care in advertising in the global markets to ensure that the body copy of the advertising gets translated in the local language with the right nuances of the original copy. For instance, in China, old friend becomes former friend. A homely girl in England is a girl from decent respectable family, while in America it suggests an uncultured girl.

Selection of brand names for the global market must take the following into consideration.

1. The brand name should not mean something unpalatable in local language
2. It should be easy to pronounce, with a pleasant sound
3. It should not be too long
4. Brand names with high equity worldwide should be used provided the company is not going to dilute the product quality; otherwise it may affect the company's business elsewhere in the world
5. Care should be taken to avoid usage of brands that have become generic, like Dalda, Mobiloil.

Distribution Channels

Distribution is the route the product takes from manufacturing unit to the consumer. Since products and consumers are so different in different parts of the world, the selection of the right distribution channel is a difficult task. The distribution system reflects the ground realities of the market, like the way the consumers buy the product, ease of accessibility of the channel for the consumers. Legal, economic and cultural factors are embodied in the channel operations. Distributor networks are national or regional in geographic coverage and seldom global.

Companies should consider the following points while selecting a distributor for their products in the global market.

1. Suitability for handling company's products
2. Financial strength required
3. Capability for servicing the product
4. Good market standing
5. Synergy between the existing products and the company's products
6. Capacity for handling the required volumes of business
7. Adequate storage capacity
8. Keen desire to take up the distribution

The company may plan to distribute the product directly to the consumer on its own for the following reasons.

1. Volumes are high
2. Direct dealing with the customers is required
3. For gaining competitive advantage
4. Business-to-business sales is more prominent
5. After-sales service is important
6. Control over distribution is important

The distribution costs increase when the levels of distribution are several, as each channel member takes his commission for his role. Besides distribution channels can cause major sales debacle if they are not selected, motivated and controlled properly. The other reasons for inefficient distribution are given below.

1. Inefficient retail outlets with untrained salespersons
2. Inadequate stocks, insufficient display of merchandise

3. Lack of sales counters in retail outlets
4. Product stock outs, low or no inventory of the company's products

Summing up, product brands, promotion plans and distribution networks are sensitive to the social and cultural ethos of the host country. Besides, consumer behaviour, attitudes towards brands and host country laws play a significant role in deciding these. With greater degree of globalization, as the world shrinks in business paradigm, companies would be able to operate worldwide with more uniform systems.

The easy and most suitable way of doing global business is to look at the market as it is done for the local market as follows.

General Business Environment

Understand the following **General Business Environment** factors:

- Demographic: It gives a population-profile in terms of income, age, sex, ethnic differences, languages spoken, religions followed, urban, semi-urban, rural population. Besides migration of population, seasonal or permanent helps in product demand patterns
- Socio-cultural: It gives information on areas like, health awareness, educational standards, population of working women, family sizes
- Political-legal: The political system of the country, number of political parties, form of the government—monarchy, democracy—legal restrictions and aids to the business, especially foreign firms. Business law as related to the specific country
- Technology: Level of technology available in the firm's area of interest. Speed of technology upgradation. R&D efforts going on in the country.
- Macro-economics: It deals with levies and taxes, balance of payment between the countries, interest rates for borrowing
- Global: It gives information about the business globalization process going on in the country
- Governmental view: How the country's government views foreign investments and entry of foreign goods into their country. Do they have a long-range perspective on foreign firms?

Countries try to influence trade for economic, social and political objectives. They use a variety of means to satisfy different interest groups and conflicting objectives. Host country governments use different types of trade controls. Host country's government has a role in companies' entry into the country due to the following reasons.

1. Level of unemployment in the country. The unemployed persons can be powerful pressure group in favour of protecting local industry as potential employers. These restrictions can lead to retaliation, which is less likely if practised by smaller countries
2. Status of industry in the country—infancy or in early adulthood. Production can be more competitive with time as companies gain economies of scale and experience curve benefits. However, consumer may be getting a raw deal in terms of low level of technology, higher prices due to lack of competition.

3. Low level of country's industrialization. With the government's intervention country will get faster industrial growth, even faster than agricultural growth. It would help in economic diversification and export oriented growth with favourable plans for import substitution. The government can adjust balance of payment by opting for affected products as opposed to devaluation or deflation this way the countries can prevent dumping of unwanted goods.
4. Country's economic relation with other countries. It can be a part of economic trade pact.
5. Country's political agenda and objectives. Rich countries can opt for export restrictions to keep world prices high like in the oil industry. This would prevent smuggling of goods and keep domestic prices low.

Other political objectives could be keeping essential industries like defence under its control and management. This would stop export to enemy countries, while preserving national identity and help the country in keeping its sphere of influence in the comity of nations. It would help in preserving national identity.

Government interference in the global trade is influenced by political rather than economic issues. These concerns create serious conflicts within and among nations. Government could, for example, increase the prices of imported competitive goods through tariff disciplines. Or it could just use it as a source of additional tariff income. Non-tariff barriers imposed by governments are given below.

1. Subsidies for exports
2. Increased custom valuation
3. Import or export quota systems
4. Legislation to exhort buyers to buy only indigenous goods
5. Making tough standards for MNC products
6. Having strict foreign exchange control regimen
7. Having administration delay, which make foreign players lose interest in India

WTO, on the other hand, has a set of rules for negotiations between countries, and it promises to monitor them. Due to their efforts, average tariff has been going down worldwide as it oversees world trade.

There has been economic integration in some areas of the world as given below.

1. Free Trade Area (FTA): Member countries of FTA do away with internal tariffs
2. Customs Union: These have FTA plus common external tariff
3. Common markets have all of the above plus factor mobility
4. Complete integration has the above and common fiscal and monetary policies

The examples of the above are the EU, NAFTA, LAFTA, CARICOM, and ASEAN.

To add to the national efforts countries have used GATT and WTO now and regional economic integration to multilaterally reduce trade barriers and plan for simple methods for conducting global trade. In certain nations there are fundamental differences, which would inhibit trade liberalization on a global basis.

The basis of governmental interference remains, unemployment levels in the home country, lack of industrialization and political will of the government. The governments create both tariff and non-tariff type barriers to protect their own business. WTO's role, on the contrary remains that of organizing free trade. Countries have on their own making different types of economic free trade zones. Some hope these may get converted into political unions.

As the governments keep interfering in trade for the benefit of being able to secure and expand employment opportunities for its population, there is a possibility of retaliation from other nations. Imports and exports create jobs; it may not be easy to understand the effect on employment of protecting the industry. In fact, the entrepreneurs can, with creativity, organizing power and strategic planning significantly multiply opportunities for prosperity and progress in the country.

The firms should understand the competitive environment factors also, in order to plan pro-active activities to nip competition in the bud or put it in its place. Michael Porters 5 Force Model should be used to gain knowledge on competition in the country, which is given below.

	Threat of new entrants	
Bargaining power of suppliers	Rivalry amongst existing players	Bargaining power of buyers
	Threat of substitute products	

Competitive Forces

A detailed discussion on competitive forces is given below.

- Rivalry amongst existing players: This is the most important area, where the competing firms have to understand each other's, strengths and weaknesses in the basic 4 Ps, product, price, placement and promotion.
- Bargaining power of suppliers: It depends on the volume purchases and payment terms, a large volume manufacturer enjoys the lower price as he helps the supplier in reaching at their economies of scale. If there were less number of suppliers of a product and several buyers, the suppliers would hold the advantage and the bargaining power. Further, manufacturers/suppliers of customized product for a buyer hold the upper hand, as the same product is not available to the buyer elsewhere. For example, maker of car seats for a particular make of a car would have the upper hand. In order to beat this, some firms start subsidiaries for making such components like the car seats.
- Bargaining power of buyers: If the sellers of a product are only a few then they hold the bargaining power as is amply exemplified in the pre-1991 era, when there were only three or four car makers in the country and they sold their cars at prices which they fixed and took booking money for delayed deliveries. In 1960, Fiat had a booking time of nearly fifteen years. The firm would take Rs. 10,000 as booking amount and ask you to wait for several years before the car was delivered to the buyer at a price,

which was prevailing then, at the time of delivery. Today, with a plethora of car makers in the fray, the buyers have the bargaining power, which is evident from the extras being offered by the car sellers. Global players have created severe competitive conditions for the Indian firms, much to the delight of the customers.

- Threat of new entrants: It is of a high order where the entry barriers do not exist. These entry barriers are: a) high project costs, b) government regulations, c) scarcity of raw materials, d) difficulty in getting proper distribution network. After the 1991 government of India's policy of liberalization, privatization and globalization, entry barriers for most industries have disappeared.
- Threat of substitute products must be carefully analyzed, as at times the solutions could be take-over of the substitute products and at other times it could be cooperation with them. For example, a motorcycle maker if threatened by scooters, start masking the scooters as well. A paint maker can tie up with wood panel maker for bidding for a tender for interiors.

The firm wanting to do overseas business should understand the Competitor's 4Ps—Product, Price, Placement and Promotion. This is to ensure that apples are compared with apples only and not with oranges. The firm must know who are the competitors, what are their products in competition to their own products and their strengths and weaknesses.

After doing the analyses, the firm should take a look at their own strengths and weaknesses vis-à-vis; competition and then take the following decisions.

1. To go overseas or not
2. If yes, which market or markets to enter and the priority of markets selected
3. The methods of entering the market; direct sales to customers, through channels, having their own outlets, franchisee operations or even having own production overseas. Production could be from component stage, semi-knocked down product assemblies or import of completely built units
4. Having own offices and sales
5. Technology transfers to local business/industry
6. Deciding on marketing programme, including market share to be captured and marketing expense to be incurred
7. Deciding on marketing organization

Managers must be aware of global complexities in business. The following needs to be considered in this area.

- Global perspectives, is their product acceptable in the global market or does it need any modifications to ensure its acceptance?
- Options available, like keeping the same product, which has had a successful run in the domestic market and educate the customers about its benefits and proper usage
- Possible strategies could be offering a differentiated product better suited to the customer in a particular country
- Global marketing and government relations: Keeping the host country's government officials on its right side is a must for an global player. It is important that all the

laws of the land like that of taxation, environment protection or of imports are strictly adhered to.

Advantages of Global Marketing

Global marketing helps tide over problems, which may arise while doing business in one market only. It becomes an insurance against political risks as well. However, the firms should well understand the cultural diversities of different countries. Cultural differences can be converted into firm's advantage by positioning products as attractive ethnic ones.

The three strategies possible in global marketing are as given below.

1. Global
2. Multi-domestic
3. Hybrid

In global strategy, the firms adapt their global planning on the lines of their single global strategy. Mercedes remains the same all over the world. There is no change in its marketing plans as well. Lever Brothers, however, have different products, brands and other marketing features for each country. This is called multi-domestic strategy. A combination of the two is the hybrid strategy.

Firms who have a universally accepted product, like Coke, Mercedes, Toyota, keep the global marketing policy, as the product remains the same the world over.

However, firms with products where the tastes of countries differ use the multi-domestic policy. In this case, they change the product specifications, pricing policy, and advertising according to local conditions and tastes. FMCG Firms like Unilever, Proctor & Gamble follow this strategy.

The most popular strategy is the hybrid one, where the firms use the global product, but change its advertising and promotion to suit the local conditions. Even Coke changes its advertising and promotion to suit the country, while keeping the product same universally.

Levis jeans are the dress of the workers in the USA, while in France, Italy and India it is a fashion statement. Mercedes is mostly used as taxi in Germany, while it is considered a status symbol in the rest of the world.

Bar codes have made a global presence, as Levis link system helps their retailers the world over, to transfer, sale and control their inventories with the help of these codes.

If value is added in upstream activities like commercial aircraft it is global strategy. If the value is added in downstream like house or prepared food it is multi-domestic strategy.

In most countries, the foreign firms can get competitive advantage by having quality **relations with the government.**

Advantages of global or global marketing for India are as follows:

- Can leverage our low labour cost as a cost leadership advantage vis-à-vis competition
- Get foreign exchange as per partial convertibility of rupee

Disadvantages for global marketing are given below.

- Currency changes (exchange rate fluctuations)

- Country's strategies for foreign firm
- Lack of global experience

Firms take the following route to global business.

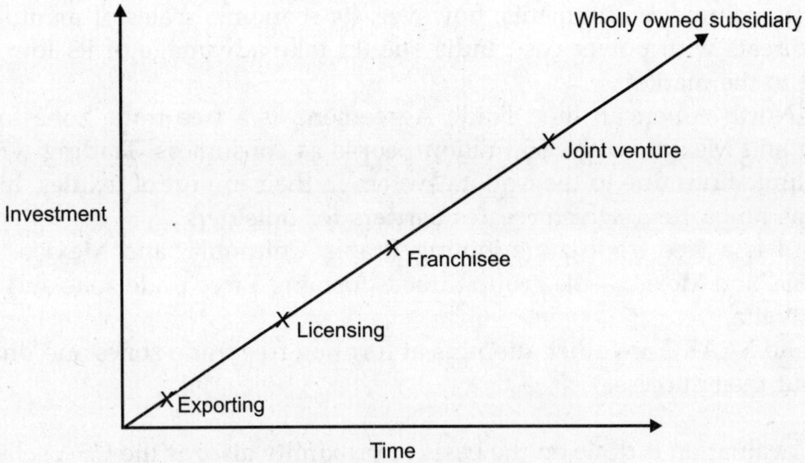

Route for Global Business

As can be seen, the firms normally start by exporting, followed by licensing the manufacture of the product for the sale. Next comes franchisee operation where the local businessman franchisee can use the brand name of the firm get managerial support. On being successful, the firm can start a joint venture manufacturing unit and finally, the firm can have it own organization to manufacture and market products in that and in other countries as well. With firms in global market, firms can enter new global market from any place depending on their own plans and the host government's rules and regulations.

The firms have to decide the markets they want to enter globally. The three markets, which cater to the major part of global business, are the European market, the USA and the Far East markets. The decision should be taken depending on the host country's policy on foreign firms, besides its economic standards. Distances become important, as freight of goods to be exported is dependent on it. India as a market looked attractive to the western nations due to its large population, which consists of nearly 200 million people belonging to the consumer group.

Seeing the importance of inter-country trade, several geographic economic blocks or zones have been formed to not only do easy and free business with one another, but also to put barriers for outsiders from doing business with them.

Free Trade Zones

Some of the free trade zones are listed below:

- European Union: They have recently introduced a common currency, the Euro, with the help of which the countries of Europe can do business with each other without any tax levies or other type of barriers. Most of the countries of Europe are members of the Union. Some like the U.K. have not fully accepted the idea yet and have kept their own currency, the Pound, as valid tender for business within and overseas. With nearly 400 million consumers in the Union, they amount to more than 20% of world trade. European Union offers a large market to other countries, including India due to its volume requirements, however; its economic scales of manufacture shall create threats with power cost. India should take advantage of its low cost labour and get to the market.

- Nafta—North American Free Trade Agreement, is a free trade zone for the USA, Canada and Mexico, with 365 million people as consumers. Trading with the USA has its limitations due to their quota system in their import of textiles. Inter-country trade has no barriers, which creates barriers for outsiders.
- Mercosul is a free trade zone joining Brazil, Columbia, and Mexico. Venezuela, Columbia, and Mexico—the group three is forming a free trade zone and these could all join Nafta.
- Asean and SAARC are other attempts at forming free trade zones and only time will tell about their success.

Market evaluation is done on the basis of proximity also, as the USA sells maximum to Canada, its immediate neighbour.

Exports

Global marketing is started as **exports** to other countries. In India in the 1960s, firms found that their local market is not expanding to the expected level and they have surplus product. It was enough to spur the firm to try and enter the export trade. However, once the Indian market came up, these firms diverted export goods in the then more lucrative local market. This inconsistency of supplies, sporadic at times did no good to the firms or countries export effort. Firms had to build export production capacities like the Bajaj Motors did and they reaped the harvest in terms of export earnings and long-range benefits. Some exporting organizations after their initial success, started exporting products of several manufacturers to different countries. The small-scale industry was the first to take up the challenge of exporting from India. Exports help in gaining economies of scale, improving quality to global levels, and Cross Parry.

Cross Parry is defined as a method of fighting competition in India from the foreign firms by hitting them in their own country.

Some took up direct exports like, Bajaj, and they could select from one of the following routes.

- Exports through local export department of the firm
- Overseas branches
- Export travelling salespersons
- Foreign distribution networks
- Overseas liaison offices
- Indian embassies

A company's experience, global competitive advantage, political and economic risks and the nature of the assets to be exploited all affect the operating forms the company would employ in its foreign operations.

Forms of foreign activities comprise exporting, licensing, franchising, management contract resulting in joint ventures, turnkey operations, fully owned subsidiaries. Companies may use different forms of the activities in different countries and even for different products. As the diversity increases, the task of coordinating and managing the foreign operations become more complex.

The company's foreign operations differ in terms of intra-activities and inter-activities, handling of actions inside and outside of the company. They also differ in the resources committed in the home and the host country. Foreign operations of the company are examined in terms of its strategic objectives, usually there are tradeoffs involved, as for gaining overseas advantage the company may have to forgo some of its local plus points.

Besides exports, the normal methods of going global are given below.

Licensing

The next level of global marketing is through licensing. In licensing the firm gets into overseas business by giving technology, trade name, brand and process of manufacturing against a fee or/and royalty to the local firm, of the country the firm wants to do business with. The firm gains entry in the foreign market without much investment. The firm taking the licence gets the technology of manufacturing a well-known brand in the world, a proven technology. India has had a number of such arrangements so far, including Maruti-Suzuki, Alcatel-Modi. Some survived the open market economy of the country; others were bought out by the licensers.

The failure can be attributed to the following:

- Low control of the licenser over the local operations
- Sale of some vital components by the licenser to the firm at high prices to make extra profits reducing margins for the firm.
- Licensing can be done without looking at the firm's synergy
- Distrust between the two partners

Franchising

It is more detailed and complete form of licensing. The franchiser provides entire product marketing concepts, branding building plans and processes. The firm pays the franchiser a fee and invests in the venture, like the McDonald franchise arrangements.

Joint Ventures

Two firms, one local and the other foreign join hands and they form a third company to exploit the strengths of the respective firms. It became expedient for entering some countries as the governments of those countries were opposed to foreign firm's equity beyond a certain level. Joint ventures suffer because of a) cultural differences between the two partners, b) level of expertise required being absent for even absorbing the technology of the foreign firm c) difference of opinion in running the firm, d) financial disagreements.

Fully Owned Foreign Subsidiary

It is usually the last step and is taken after the firm has been in the foreign market for a time and established it there. It is dependent on the local government's policy with respect to investments by foreign firms in the country. Countries like India and China have been the focus of western world as these countries are welcoming Direct Foreign Investments in their countries.

Overview of Global Marketing

Firms which do not take full advantage of the global opportunities will in time lose their home base as well as, they will suffer loses by their business being taken over by strong foreign players.

Hence, Global Marketing is the process for focusing the firm's resources and its objectives on global opportunities. Each firm has some driving and stimulating forces in this regard as also some restraining forces, like laid-back ideas, rigidity of views and fear of the unknown. The fact, however, remains that global market provides enormous potential of business. Overall it is the place of perfect competition, lots of sellers and lots of buyers too.

Products sold can be undifferentiated products like, ores and raw materials (sold on the basis of price only.) With differentiated or branded product firms charge higher prices and they sell on their brand equity the world over.

Countries differ from each other in their wealth, GNP, per capita income, education, religious beliefs, size and their ethnicity. Firms planning global marketing must understand other country's human resources, economics, politics and social situations.

Major assumptions in the global trade are given below.

1. Environment is a determinant in global marketing. Geography, distances and climatic conditions have an impact on business.
2. Scientific and industrial revolution helps the firms/business to make things happen even when the environment says no it cannot be done. Technology helps in doing more with less effort.
3. Ways in which the firms do business and produce goods are different in different parts of the world.
4. The statement that, "Firm's country is the best for business" may not remain true with global competition with better products.

We can thus conclude that, the trend in growth in the world business is a result of the interaction of specific driving and restraining forces. The driving forces must overcome the restraining forces.

Let us discuss the driving force in the world business. Mainly we can see the supply and demand situation and the gap therein. New products, newer needs of old products and worldwide communication links like television and the Internet have fuelled the world of business as follows:

- Worldwide TV network and worldwide web have driven the markets. Product information, its usage and advantages from its use are now known the world over through these media.
- Technology helps in reducing human drudgery. Products like washing machines, vacuum cleaners, and microwave ovens are ample proof in this regard.
- Costs: The cost of the product to the customer is usually of vital interest to him. Low cost manufacture with the help of economies of scale, experience curve or better technology all help the firm in becoming more competitive.
- Quality of the products should meet or exceed the customer requirements. With global sales, firms achieve economies of scale and with large production costs come down with quality remaining the same. Small manufacturers have to compromise on quality to reduce the price, a tradeoff.
- Communication and transportation technology have broadened the marketplace as products get known, are demanded and can be transported speedily with modern fast aircraft.
- Leverage-firm's/country's expertise like for India in the software technology, gets the right leverage for the firm in the global markets.

Given below are the restraining forces in the world market.

- Historical demand of the product in the local market.
- Competition from the countries own business enterprises.
- Management myopia: Firms may have shortsighted managers who consider that the profit from the country's market should be enough impetus and going global would be a waste of time and money.
- Organizational culture at times restricts operations overseas.
- Global barriers: Some countries do not encourage outsiders to come to their country and do business there.

Today, the global markets have progressed because the driving forces are more dominant than the restraining forces. Even then there are two different firms as given below:

1. In this firm the Marketing Manager decides the firm to be domestic in focus, vision and orientation while he keeps looking for opportunities.
2. In this firm the Marketing Manager focuses the firm for serving the global markets and in developing global strategies to compete with other global firms.

Let us discuss the economic, social and cultural environment of countries where the firms want to do business and see how they have an impact on the business.

The task of Global Marketing Manager is to recognize both the similarities and differences that characterize the economic, social and cultural ethos of the countries of the world and incorporate the perception into the market planning process while planning operations in those countries.

The firm must have a focus on its country's orientation. How is the country better than other countries? The firm may have an egocentric view to focus the areas where it is better than other firms of the world. It can also have similar polycentric view of its country, to focus on the areas where the country is better than other countries of the world. The best is, of course to have a geocentric view, with the dual focus, regarding the firms and country's superiority.

Expanding the theme further we see the following paradigm.

Ethnocentric focus of the home country—similarities in foreign countries/ dissimilarities in foreign countries to showcase the similarities and differences as competitive advantage.

Polycentric focus—home country is unique, locate the differences in foreign countries and either modifies the product as per requirements or use the difference as a competitive advantage.

Region-centric focus locates similarity in world region and plans sales accordingly.

Geocentric focus locates similarities and differences in home and host country.

Let us analyze the strengths of some of the countries.

USA buys superior products may be with high prices and top quality technology and

Latin America buys only from the people with whom they have solid relationships, good rapport. Quality becomes a secondary consideration. Contacts are built by the behaviour of the firm's people, gestures, words and posture.

In some countries, price and benefits of the product assume great importance. In fact, the firm needs to know, who are the customers in a country, what they want and what is important to them.

The economic environment of a country is a major determinant of market potential and opportunity. It is possible to identify distinct stages and formulate estimates about the type of demand that will be found in a country or market of a particular stage of economic development.

The vast difference comes when you notice the underdeveloped countries, the developing countries and the developed countries. Then there is agrarian society, and highly developed one. In each case the GDP, per capita income differs a great deal as follows:

- High-income countries with per capita income >$12000. There are 27 countries with population of 818 million
- Upper middle-income countries with per capita income between $2000 and $12000. There are 35 countries with population of 912 million
- Lower middle income countries with per capita income between $400 and $2000. There are 65 countries with population of 1.775 billion
- Lower income countries with per capita income < $400. There are 42 countries with population of 1.725 billion

These figures are given only as guidelines and should not be taken as sacrosanct.

In the 18th century, most countries of the world were having agrarian economy. It was only after the industrial revolution of the 18th century in Europe, which gave the world industrial economy, with assembly line mass production techniques and material wealth. Rich countries today have high productivity per worker, inasmuch that their labour costs are high too. Poor countries have low labour cost and lower productivity per worker. The following need to be addressed in selecting the markets.

- Population and income
- Number of households
- Climatic conditions
- Price negotiating culture
- Languages spoken

India with large population has good market potential. USA is a bigger market than Brazil. China has come up as a big market with its vast population. Russia as an emerging market provides opportunity to sell high tech products.

Cold countries have huge need of heating equipment while warm countries need air-conditioners and coolers.

Price has been an important factor in purchase decisions. In several countries, the method of price negotiations differ. Small to large gifts (read bribe) are norms in some countries. Inviting the customers of large potential purchase for cocktail parties is prevalent in some countries. However, the firms must know if it is good manners to invite ladies to such parties or not. In most courtiers it is advisable to hire a local guide who can tell about the customs of the country and translate the language with all its nuances so that no slip-up takes place. Forcing your own will does not necessarily succeed in business.

The task of the Global Marketing Manager is to identify similarities and differences that characterize individuals and cultures of the countries of the world, so that strategies, products and marketing plans are efficiently adapted to global markets.

The plans for expansion by firms should start by comparing, contrasting and analyzing the economic environment of different countries. Marketers should recognize that the economic environment is but one of the several influential factors for analyzing the global market. The culture and social environment need to be considered as well.

Product

The first method used in the global market is selling the same product as sold in the local market. Managers have to find customers for the product. Mercedes is one example where the product sold the world over is the same, but in this case also, depending on the country left-hand drive or right-hand drive cars are sold.

Most products in Japan have to take into account the fact that Japanese population's height is averagely less than that at other places. The following matrix shows how it works.

Promotion	Do not change product	Adapt product	Develop new product
Do not change promotion	Same product as local market product	Product adaptation	New product invention
Change promotion	Modify communication/ advertisements	Dual adaptation	New product invention

Supermarkets have been opened in India with some variations, with emphasis on high-end market with plenty of leisure time. Going to even less developed countries like some African countries some more innovation may be required. In some countries feminine body exploitation, could be permitted in advertising but in most countries it will not be allowed. Some countries prefer some specific colours, like the Muslim prefer green and the firms must keep it in mind. Advertising mostly needs local colour and touch, use of local models and festivals for timing the advertising efforts.

Price

Firms have to careful in pricing the product in different countries. Import levies, currency rate fluctuations, grey markets and price escalations are areas, which need careful consideration of the firm. Some of the methods used for price fixation are given below.

- Worldwide same price: Not really practical if the firm is marketing in both rich and poor countries.
- Prevailing market price: Adapt the price at which local vendors are selling the product.
- Modified prevailing price: If the export firm can charge higher price due to its better brand equity it should sell at a higher price as price gets equated with the product quality. Hence, if the firm charges low price or the same as the local vendor price and its product is superior the customers will put it in the same league as the local product.
- Cost plus pricing: It is adapted when the product is far superior and there is no competition worth the name. As there is no basis of competitive pricing, the firm can charge higher price on the basis of its cost to make and sell by adding extra amount by way of price of quality and brand equity.

In case of a country going through inflationary phase price increase can be resorted to at regular intervals.

Distribution Channels

When the product is manufactured in one country and sold in another country, the firm selling it has to consider globalization of channels. The firm may have its marketing centre for both local and export sales in its own country. Later on, it may start its export marketing office in either the country to which export is being made or in some third centrally located country. The distance and freight need to be taken into account. The marketing set-up would take shape as given below.

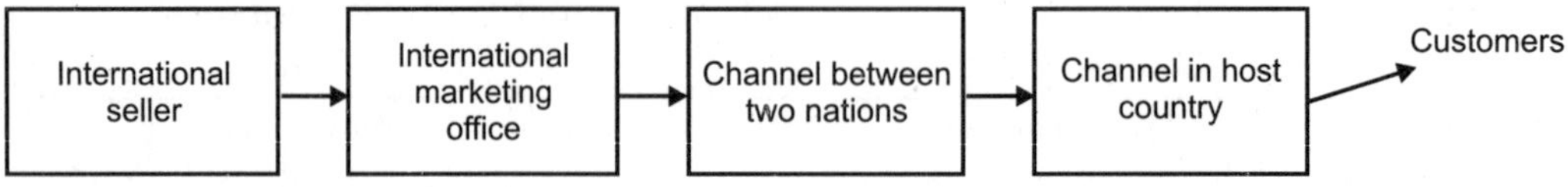

For finding the best channel within the host country, it is best to have a market survey done, because for different products it could be quite different.

Exceptions can be if the firm has world monopoly of the product. In the seventies of the 20th century one firm in the area of electronic components had such a monopoly and the customers were coming to India to buy the product, at the firm dictated prices and distributing in their country on their own.

The first step taken by firms normally is starting exports to designated countries. For the purpose they need to have an export sales department with one Export/Global Marketing Manager. As the business increases, the firm starts offices in host countries as well. Experts who arrange for market surveys, appointment of distribution channel members, market information system, made these offices.

Advertising and Promotion

For global marketing, the firm has to decide to have one of the following plans for advertising and promotion.

(i) Global strategy where the same advertising and promotion works for the entire world market. Pepsi circle of blue and red is recognized all over the world.

(ii) Multi-domestic strategy where the firm allows each country's local management to plan their own advertising and promotion most suited to local conditions, like what Lever Brothers do.

(iii) Hybrid strategy where the firm keeps the global perspective and yet alters the advertising and promotion to a limited degree. Most firms change the models in their advertisements. Japanese advertisements are better appreciated with Japanese models.

Market Globalization

Firms usually start marketing their products in their own country, the domestic market. Once established as a known brand and accepted supplier of goods they need to diversify their markets and the first step in that direction is exports to another country. Excess production, which cannot find market in the country of origin, is the starting point of exports. Later on firms do take up special production of goods for exports. Some others build an export bank (inventory) to avoid any clash with the demands of domestic market. Firms have to realize that the product, which is considered giving value for money and fulfilling customer's needs, must do the same in overseas market.

Once the firm wants to get established in the export market, it has to understand the business environment of the foreign country. The four Ps of host country Product, Price, Placement and Promotion may not have the same relevance outside.

In prehistoric times, the city-states traded through barter system. One state had one product while the other had some other product and they both needed the product, which the other had. The same type of advantage in tradable product in one country over the other works well even today, except the scene is much more complex with several countries, myriad of products having global access.

In India exports are firm's imperatives due to following reasons:

- Partial convertibility of rupee, which gives foreign exchange to exporters they need for their imports for production

- Need to achieve economies of scale of production for lowering costs and making prices competitive for exports too.
- With MNCs getting a foothold in India, firms need to have greater markets, which India cannot provide.
- Intangible benefits are, bettering of product quality, improvements in communication systems
- Upgradation of technology
- Cost reduction due to large-scale manufacture
- Utilization of human resources like in IT sector where India has a large workforce.
- Globalization of Indian brands

Let us discuss the negative factors of going for exports, which are as follows:

- Low image of the country as a supplier of quality goods. This is gradually changing
- Firm's culture, which does not give the required fillip to exports
- Inexperience of global business and the fear of the unknown
- Cultural differences in nations
- Entry barriers in some countries, their governmental controls and in some cases like the USA, quota system for exporting to that country (e.g. textiles imports into the USA)

There are some common factors as given below.

- Balance of payment between trading nations
- Stability of their currency
- Transportation costs
- Infrastructure status
- Quality control plans in each country and how these manifest in global trade
- Trading blocks like Euro, NAFTA, ASEAN
- WTO the world body that regulates global trade and settles trade disputes.
- Political instability in some regions
- Economic upheavals of the far east, Japan

Cultural Aspects of Global Business

It is widely believed that culture is not inherent but is learnt. Culture guides people to respond to situations and since it has been learnt, it is difficult to change. Marketers need to find some common reference point between cultures of different countries, because it is the culture of the country, which defines behaviour, norms and reactions to outside stimuli given to its people.

The home country objectives of business are dependent on its cultural ethos and transposing them on other country would need defining the cultural ethos of that country. If the marketers try to impose their country's culture on the other country, it may complicate the issue and hence own country's cultural bias must be taken out while formulating objectives of business for other countries. There may be, however, products which have universal appeal and they would not need any such action.

Product innovation: In one country the product could be introduced as an innovative product while it may be already in maturity stage in some other country. Product acceptance in new countries takes the following steps:

- Product knowledge or awareness which comes from advertising
- Interest in the product makes prospective customers to obtain more information about the product.
- Judgment to the value of the product is made at this stage
- Next step is the trial stage when the customer tries out the product before adopting it.

The rate of adoption of product depends on the following considerations:

- Competitive advantage of the product and also the country from which it is coming like low cost labour, balance of payment situation, currency rates.
- Acceptance of change: Some countries like the USA need to change their product all the time while countries like Japan and India prefer to stay with the old products unless some thing of great interest comes along.
- Ease of usage of the product and its compatibility with other products in use.
- Ease of trial helps in making sure of the product usage.
- Availability of information when needed is vital for customer trying to make a change.

A major difference in culture can be seen in the culture of the USA and Japan. While the USA has individualistic management style, Japan's management is based on group decisions.

The following table shows the differences in the two cultures:

Japan	USA
Formal indirect business	Direct informal business
Prolonged bargaining	Hard bargaining
More stability in jobs	Top management shifts
Bargain is a long drawn-out process	Persistent bargaining

Global marketers must take the cultural factors into account to succeed in their business.

Global Market Research

The secondary data available for different countries are not compatible and its comparison can pose problems. Consumer expenditure in Germany is taken from turnover receipts and in the USA, household surveys and production sources also add to the information base. Global market research has to take multiple countries into account and consider each country's unique market situations. In low profit markets a major research could prove expensive. In many underdeveloped countries, data availability is scarce and not reliable.

Global research needs the following rules:

- Ask yourself, what information do I need?
- Where can I get it—files, library or database?
- Why do I need the information?

- When do I need it?
- What is the money value of the information to me?
- What would be the cost of ignorance?

Start with secondary research by using libraries, online database, trade associations and government publications. Find out from foreign embassies about the information available from their countries. Crosscheck piece of information from several sources.

Survey research: It is conducted by using a questionnaire and asking questions from potential customers. The questionnaires should be simple, easy to answer and record. Questions should be clear and to the point.

The research should give the following information:

- Demand analysis is dependent on country's gross national product, per capita income. Low-income countries are more on core products like food, clothings. With high-income countries heavy industries start emerging.
- Income elasticity of demand can be found out both for consumer and industrial products. Basic necessities do not have much of income elasticity, while luxuries demand change with income changes.

Country's entry barriers are listed below and these will confirm whether or not market is conducive for entry.

- Government regulations regarding foreign firms
- Low infrastructure like telephones, power, roads railways and ports
- Poor availability of raw materials
- High cost of money, borrowing rates
- High rate of import duties

Global Monitory Fund was created under the auspices of the United Nations Organization. It is the body, which regulates smooth to compensate for balance of payment deficits. SDRs are assets allotted by the IMF on the basis of country's GDP and share of world trade.

Foreign exchange is the currency sold or bought in the foreign exchange market. The transaction takes place as given below.

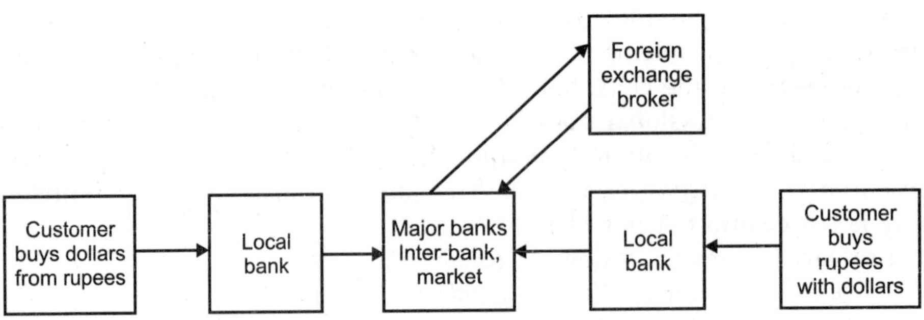

Local banks' major tasks in the global business are handling money. The most common form of money transactions is the Letter of Credit LC. LC can be of the following types:

- Revocable LC with recourse
- Revocable LC without recourse
- Irrevocable LC with recourse
- Irrevocable LC without recourses
- Part shipment allowed or not

Organization for Exports

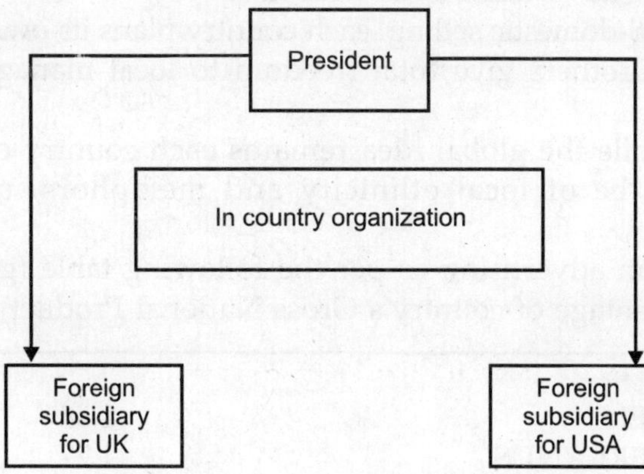

Another Alternative

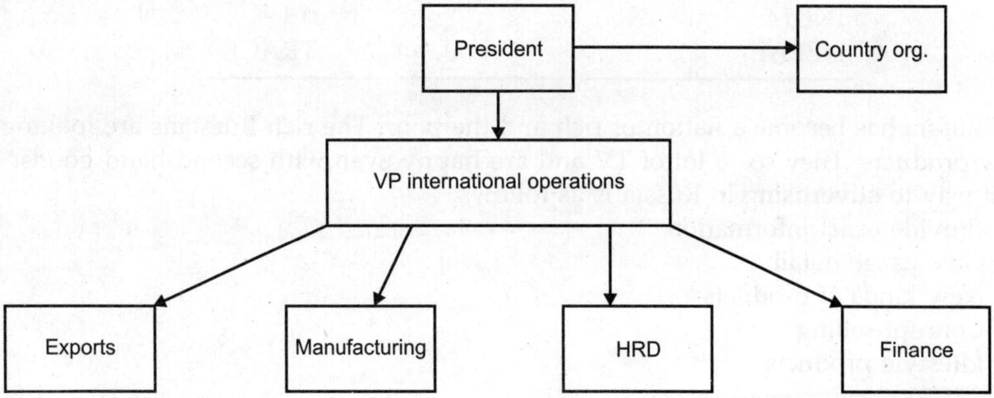

Global Communications: Advertising in the global market must take the country's cultural ethos into account. For example, in Islamic countries, green is the preferred colour. In China, yellow is the sacred colour and it should be used for only holy products. White is the colour of purity in the west while in South Asia it is the colour of mourning.

In UK all advertising is allowed unless not forbidden; in Germany all advertising is forbidden unless allowed. In Italy everything is allowed even if it is forbidden and in Belgium no one knows what is not allowed.

Advertising takes three forms in the global market as given below.

1. Global
2. Multi-domestic
3. Hybrid

In global advertising one campaign is planned and used globally wherever the firm is selling the product. Mercedes is a typical example as the same car sells without any modification and same advertising goes with it.

In contrast, in multi-domestic selling, each country plans its own campaign according to its culture. Lever Brothers give total freedom to local management regarding the campaign.

In hybrid plan while the global idea remains each country can change to suit its market. Models can be of local ethnicity and metaphors, understood by local population.

Countries spend on advertising as per the following table (giving the advertising expenditure as a percentage of country's Gross National Product).

USA	2
SWEDEN	1.88
NETHERLANDS	1.77
UK	1.74
SWITZERLAND	1.59
AUSTRALIA	1.37
INDIA	0.3
NEPAL	TRACE

Russia has become a nation of rich and the poor. The rich Russians are looking for new products. They see a lot of TV and are happy even with second-hand goods. The best way to advertising in Russia is as follows:

- Provide exact information
- Give usage detail
- New kinds of products
- Concept selling
- Lifestyle products

In China outdoor advertising is used. For product demonstrations Chinese want to see the TV ads. Testimonials by experts are favoured too.

While selecting an advertising agency, following needs to be considered:

- Indian agency with foreign collaboration or foreign agency with office in India
- Some countries go by nationalistic approach like in Canada it is a good idea to appoint a local agency. Local agencies provide the subtle nuances of local culture and language as also goodwill of the target market.

Marketing Channels

In order to decide the most effective channel, the firm must consider the market segment it wants to cater to and the product positioning in the market. Channel selection should reflect firm's strengths and competitive advantages. In the beginning it is correct to use similar channels as already in use by the competition. Distributors should be selected on the basis of their experience with similar products, commitment to the firm's objectives and financial and human resources for the task. Trainability of their staff in selling the product is useful. If they can provide after-sales service, it would be an added advantage.

The distributors normally appoint retailers, but initially it is a good idea to approve their appointment to ensure long-term profitable association with them.

For industrial products the firm should look for technically oriented distributors. They will then be able to supplement firm's salesperson's efforts in a positive way.

Following graph gives the relative importance of advertising and personal selling, either by firm's salesperson or distributors.

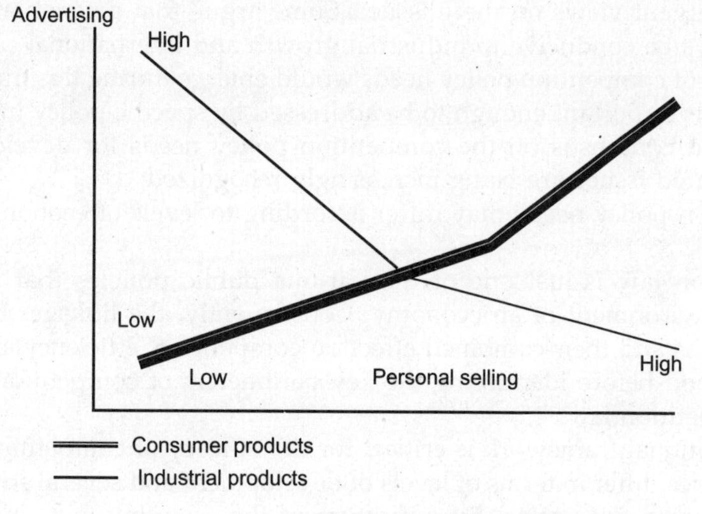

In most developing countries, the age-old distribution systems are valid as given below:

- Sole distributors
- Area distributors
- Dealers
- Agents
- Stockists
- C&F Agents
- Retailers
- Firm's own shops
- Franchisee outlets
- Super stores

In developed nations distribution through new channels like the Internet, teleshopping, personal door-to-door selling are gaining popularity.

Countries in Economic Transitions

Several developing countries referred to as *economies in transition* are generally characterised as having highly concentrated industries, large state-owned sectors, and inefficient firms operating in markets insulated by trade barriers. While many of these countries have adopted policies of trade liberalization, de-regulation and privatisation, a question arises as to whether market forces can be further strengthened. Others suggest that of liberalization international trade is sufficient to promote competition. While some others argue that even if competition law is considered desirable in the abstract, the probability of improper enforcement, misuse of bureaucratic power or regulatory capture is so high in developing and transition market economies that the expected costs of such legislation outweigh the possible benefits a competition (anti-trust) law. And whether such strengthening of market forces will result in higher economic growth? There are divergent views on these issues. Some argue that promotion of competition may not always be conducive to industrial growth and international competitiveness.

What kind of competition policy needs would emerge during this transition process? Are these needs important enough to be addressed by specific policy initiatives? While there is limited consensus on the competition policy needs for developing countries, three inter-related issues are being increasingly recognized:

Competition policy needs may differ according to levels of economic development of a nation.

Competition law is just one of the various public policies that impinge on the competitive environment of an economy. Consequently, the linkages between various policy initiatives and their combined effect on competition, efficiency and growth need to be understood before identifying the key parameters of competition policy and the scope of competition law.

The institutional framework is critical for the efficacy of competition law.

The countries differ in terms of levels of development and several structural features. These include size and sector diversification of the economy (e.g., importance of the service and manufacturing sectors), status of the financial markets, levels of concentration across industries, role of multinational corporations (MNCs) and state owned enterprises (SOEs, or PSUs-Public Sector Undertakings) and the degree of openness (import/export penetration). These countries also differ in terms of past and current policy regimes. While some of them have liberalised their policies in recent years, the extent of such liberalisation (e.g., deregulation, privatisation, trade liberalisation, openness to foreign direct investment, FDI etc.) differs across nations. Besides, not all of them have gone through the structural adjustment programmes.

Given the differences across countries and the three general issues raised above, this paper pools together the analysis/information contained in the seven country reports and papers to gain insights into the links between economic development and competition policy. In order to do that it focuses on two questions:

How the structural and policy differences affect competition policy requirements?

Given these requirements, what are the emerging substantive and administrative needs of competition law?

Socioeconomic Profile and the Developmental Context

It is evident that the socioeconomic factors differ significantly in terms of population size, size of the economy, per capita incomes, human development, industrial structure and exposure to the world economy. Are the competition policy requirements the same across these countries? On what parameters they should differ? Some key socioeconomic aspects of the countries are summarised here to highlight the importance of the development context of competition policy.

Some Structural Features

Apart from the differences in size (in terms of population and income), which varies significantly across countries a few interesting differences need to be highlighted:

In all nations, except South Africa and to some extent Zambia, agriculture is an important sector. However, even among the remaining countries, contribution to GDP varies a great deal; it is as high as 48 per cent in Tanzania and as low as 21 per cent in Sri Lanka.

The tertiary sector is the most important contributor to GDP in all countries and has improved its share during the 1990s. This sector has gained at the cost of agriculture and manufacturing. For example, the tourism sector is very important in Kenya and Tanzania.

During the 1990s, the relative decline in the manufacturing sector has been most striking in Zambia where it fell from 32 to 11 per cent. The manufacturing sector was most thin in Tanzania. Moreover, only India and South Africa, the two relatively large economies, can claim to have a diversified manufacturing sector.

Information on the levels of concentration (in distribution of assets and market shares in different industry groups) is sketchy but it seems to be high in most countries.

Role of FDI and Cross-border Mergers

Apart from exports and imports, another important aspect of an economy's 'openness' is the role of cross-border mergers and acquisition (M&A) activity and foreign direct investment.

All countries have seen cross-border M&A activity in recent years. While in terms of absolute values of these transactions, South Africa, India and Pakistan are way ahead of the others, as a proportion of GDP, these transactions seem to be quite important in Zambia and South Africa and not so much in India.

Cross-border M&A activity by local firms is somewhat significant only in South Africa and to some extent India.

As in the case of M&A activity while quantum of inward FDI flows & stock is significant only for India and South Africa, its share in investment and GDP is high in Zambia, Pakistan, Sri Lanka and South Africa; the share in India is actually the least.

Trade Barriers

Firms must understand the trade barriers, which can hamper their business as follows:

(a) Tariff barriers: These are created by the host country's government to give impetus to local production. There are three types of tariff barriers as given below.

  (i) Ad-velorem: This import tax is levied on the basis of the cost of import as a percentage of the cost.

  (ii) Specific duty is charged for nations given special treatment due to treaties or other factors like poverty prevailing in the country.

  (iii) Compound duty is charged which takes into account the above stated duties, the ad-valorem and the special duty.

(b) Non-tariff barriers: are also employed by countries in order to keep global competition to the acceptable levels, which are as follows:

  (i) Anti-dumping restrictions: USA and some European countries have anti-dumping laws, which restricts nations from the east to export there only up to certain quantities as laid down in the law and no more, while these countries can export anywhere whatever quantities they like. As such the law is totally biased in favour of the developed nations. The ostensible reason for the law is that some nations like Japan export their goods to the USA at less than its fair value, undermining the local industry.

  (ii) Textile quota from developing countries has been fixed as per the multi fibre agreement or through the VER or Voluntary Export Restraints where nothing is voluntary accept its name.

  (iii) Direct and indirect subsidies: Government favours its country's industry by offering cash benefits, in some form or the other. Indian government was doing the same till the open regime took over in 1991. For example, French Airbus is subsidized to make it competitive as far as Boeing of USA is concerned. It is heard that Kuwait government provides free or subsidized fuel to its global carrier, the Kuwait Airlines.

Summarizing the above the following are the major models of competitive strategies in the global trade:

- Working on imperfect competition with the help of the governments by using quota system or subsidies to keep the prices to their levels of benefit.
- Product swap based on differentiation needed in the market. For example, India could export Bajaj scooters and import Hurley Davidson motorcycles.
- Firms' work on economies of scale of manufacture to gain cost advantage.
- Production spillover: This can give firms advantage as then they can amortize their fixed costs on the local business and keep exports prices lower to meet competition.
- In case divestment is not possible and there is demand in the overseas markets firms can leverage their production to meet that demand. Certain government regulations are, at times, in the way of divestments and at times the product may be a support product, which helps the firm in selling one of its major brands.

The firm has to take a decision about going overseas, where it has to take the following into consideration:

1. The number of countries to be decided—2/3/4 at a time. To find out if there are commonalties in the markets of these countries or are they totally dissimilar in nature. This information would be of use while planning country specific marketing strategies.
2. To understand the comparative distance of the countries and the available logistic support for transportation of goods to the countries.
3. To understand special market needs that help in omitting the countries not favourable for the firm's products and other Ps.
4. To verify the assumptions made about the market in the initial shortlisting stage.
5. To do market segmentation and decide the most appropriate segment suited to the firm.
6. To understand the actual needs of the selected segment, the benefits the segment customers are looking for in the products of the firm.
7. The actual size of the market (this should be as accurately assessed as possible with the help of data, records available and a primary survey to be conducted by experts in the field, who are familiar with the market).
8. To know the competitors, both the large as also the small ones, their strengths and weaknesses. (do a SWOT Analysis)
9. To look at the competitor's 4 Ps; are they based on global multi-domestic or hybrid strategy.
10. To plan the firm's market share and profit margins, both on a short-term and long-term perspective.
11. To understand the countries currency, its fluctuations over the past three years.
12. To know the situation regarding the Balance of Payment between India and the other countries.
13. Use Mckinsey's 7S model to understand firms 7S namely—Structure, Skills, Style, Systems, Strategy, Shared Values, and Staff.
14. At this stage the firm has to plan its 4Ps for the overseas markets.
15. Next, the teams are formed and given targets to achieve with responsibility and accountability
16. As the business starts, the firm has to place a control mechanism in place to ensure that the targets are met or corrective steps can be taken on the initial default itself.

Global Trade

Most of the global trade depends on merchandise export and import. The countries want that their exports overall should be greater than their imports. This gives them edge over the countries, which are importing from them as the balance of payment remains with them and they remain net foreign currency earners.

India had till 1991 a close door policy and a lot of export from the country was channelled through government agencies like, STC, MMTC, and ET&T. The imports were restricted and exports were subsidized. There was a lot of emphasis on import substitution and for creating favourable balance of payment in respect of most countries and overall.

However, the country has realized now, after 1991, that the ways to gain competitive advantage and with its help improved balance of payment position are as follows:

1. Acquiring competitive advantage through product differentiation, improved methods of production for better productivity
2. Efficient use of available resources, bringing down cost of production, borrowing of money at lower interest rates, training of workers for improved productivity, better purchase plans, including Just in Time concept.
3. Country's core competencies should be considered not just that of the firm. For example, Japan has developed competencies in the area of electronic goods, cars and watches and India has core competency in the area of software development. It is a good idea to use these competencies for gaining competitive advantage in the selected export markets.
4. The business between the two countries should run on the following lines: (a) Better employment in both the countries, in one for manufacturing and in the other distribution and marketing areas (b) Economics efficiency in both the countries (c) Division of gains between the two countries.

To reiterate, Indian firms have the following advantages and disadvantages in respect of exports:

Advantages

- Low cost labour
- High tech workforce
- Leadership in software development
- Availability of raw materials
- Large local market, which helps in test marketing and standardization of products

Disadvantages

- Poor image of the country as supplier of quality goods
- Product quality non-standard ISO standards and BIS, are doing a lot to improve the situation
- Most firms have very little experience of exporting, which becomes a drawback in uncharterd routes of exports.
- A small number of unscrupulous exporters give the country a bad name.
- Rupee has been losing its value against the American dollar, which makes Indian products attractive to the foreign countries and yet the foreign exchange addition is only nominal.

SUMMARY

The global business is conducted in the following manner (firms use one or all the methods given below)

Exports	Home country	Goods/services	Host country
Licensing	Home country	Technical know-how	Host country
Franchising	Home country	Management technology & brand	Host country
Joint Ventures	Home country	Investment along with host country, Technology, Management and materials	Host country part finance
Wholly Owned	Home country	Capital know-how Subsidiaries	Host country CBU, SBU

Questions for Discussion

1. Discuss the advantages and the export imperatives for Indian firms in post-liberalization era.
2. What should be exporting firm's considerations in selecting countries for exports?

CHAPTER

3

Global Business Environment

Introduction

In dealing with different countries it is essential to understand their business environments before embarking on overseas business. There are cultural differences among nations as well as differences in economic levels, besides the political and legal differences.

There are great differences between political and legal systems between countries and MNCs have to formulate and implement their strategies taking these differences into account.

The role of the political system is to be the cohesive force in the society. The two opposing systems on the political horizons are democracy with people's participation in the running of the government and totalitarianism where a group of people or even one person wields the political power. In democracy, citizens enjoy widespread freedom, especially in the areas of political rights and civil liberties. Managers have to deal with several forms of government approach to business and stability of the governments in different countries. They must have the foresight to influence and respond to government action and any stimuli provided by it. Managers must also learn the ethically correct behaviour and operations for each country they operate in. At times law may not provide the guidelines in this regard.

There are several types of economies in the world, with many differences between them. These differences affect management decisions in significant manner. In market economy countries' individuals have the power to allocate control and distribute through their actions the economic resources. Incidentally planned economies the government does it. However, in the twenty-first century most countries are headed towards market driven economy and are succeeding in reaching there in varying degrees and these imbalances provide the challenge to the global business manager of today. Key factors that influence the MNC decision-making process are the country's economic growth, privatization, inflation, balance of payment between countries and external debt.

Countries with the high growth rates in their economy are able to exploit these human and natural resources most efficiently. On the other hand, the developing nations like India provide large market potential (more especially since the west nation markets are saturated with products and are having mostly replacement market). These countries are showing strong economic growth, investing in them would help in further developing the market, notwithstanding the risk factor involved due to political instability in some countries.

Let us discuss the economic differences and the ways of dealing with them.

Economic Business Environment

India became independent in 1947 and the then government of India with Mr. Jawaharlal Nehru as the first Prime Minister of India, decided that the country would have the socialistic pattern of society, with major economic developments to be in the hands of the government. The birth of the Public Sector Undertakings took place with a number of firms like, Bharat Heavy Electricals, Hindustan Machine Tools, Hindustan Steels coming into existence. Private sector was considered as having only unscrupulous people who wanted to cheat the government and the public. This resulted in the Permit License Raj, where the government bureaucracy started doling out favours in return of monetary gains. The Public Sector suffered from lack of accountability and undue interference from the political bosses. The bribery and corruption became so big that it is today the hydra-like monster rising its head higher and higher each day.

However, the realization came in 1991, that the country cannot live in isolation and it had to open up its economy. Globally two major changes had taken place. First was the destruction of USSR, which resulted in dismantling of communism from a major world area. At the same time the other major communist power China started going the capitalistic way in no mean measure. The only semblance of communism remains today only in Cuba. Till mid-20th century, there were two major economic ideologies, the American market based economy and the state controlled economy of the communist regimes. And then there was the third type, the mixed economy, which was practised in India among a few other nations. Mixed economy was meant to give equal impetus to the government and private enterprise. With this ideology, a new corporate sector was born, the joint sector, where both the private and the government were financiers of the project. This was started to get the government approvals quickly and then run the organisation on the lines of a private venture. However, the conflicting decisions by both the owners and tight government audit never allowed it to flourish as an economic force in the country.

Hence, it can be seen that the business organization matrix would look as given below.

	Private ownership	Mixed /joint ownership	Public or government ownership
Market control	Market driven private ownership	Market driven joint ownership	Market driven government ownership
Mixed control	Mixed control private ownership	Mixed control/joint ownership	Mixed control/ government ownership
Government control	Government control/ private ownership	Government control/ joint ownership	Government control/ government ownership

The government ownership of firms gave them tremendous leverage in getting business from the government, including a substantial price preference. In other words, a government owned firm would get an order for supplies from the government even if its prices are substantially higher. This led to extensive non-accountability factor as the price could be loaded with factors of inefficiency as also take care of any underhand dealings, which tended to increase the price. It should not be construed that such inefficiencies did not figure in the private ownership firms. Yet their numbers were a few and the accountability factor mostly took care of the inefficient and corrupt elements in the private sector.

Since, now we are truly in the age of market economy in practically the entire world, let us take a look at what exactly is market economy.

Market Economy of the World

Today in the 21st century, most countries are part of market driven economy. It is product quality, price, brand equity and availability of products, which play a major role in market dynamics. These factors have been given the celebrated name of four Ps. The product demand is also dependent on the market segment's business environment, like, demographic, social, cultural, political and legal factors. Competitive factors too play a major role in establishing business shares among the various players.

The factories churn out products, with the help of employees, raw materials and consumables and the employees are in a way buyers of the products. Employees work for wages and use the wages for making the purchases. (The products may be from one factory and buyers from another factory or any other discipline.)

Market economy brings the customer into main focus as he gets competitive products to choose from, competitive prices and firms vie with each other in product positioning and placement besides in communicating to the customers through multitude of advertising formats. The firms too are free to opt for certain markets, segments and channels of distribution. Thus, the interplay between buyers and sellers depends on the supply and demand situation and on the strengths of the firms. The strength comes from product quality, service to the customer and generation of brand equity.

Market economy can be best understood by comparing it with the closed economies of the communist world, where manufacturing is restricted by the government and so is the supply. We all have heard of the days of rationing in the Soviet Union. (In fact, even in India there was rationing of essential products till the first half of the last century.)

Market economy can come to a country only if the restrictions on production, rules to regulate the supply and purchase including imports of raw materials are not removed by the government and industry freed to take its own decisions in these matters on the basis of market needs. A look at the pre-1991 era is sufficient to understand the stranglehold the government had on the markets during the period prior to the reforms, as follows:

- For manufacturing any product firms needed a manufacturing licence from the government's ministry of industries.
- For foreign equity participation and technology transfer even more stringent approvals were required from ministry of industries and the RBI.

- For import of raw materials, a lot of approvals were required from the industry ministry and the Reserve Bank of India.
- The custom duty on most products was high up to even 300% ad-velorem
- Interest rates on borrowing was high.

Since 1991, with major changes in the industrial policy the government of India has tried to bring the country's economy in the market control. Yet a few more reforms are needed like full convertibility of money for the purpose.

For free economy the control of the government on business should be non-existent. The government's task should be to safeguard the interests of all its citizens. They should be free to choose their vocation, be it buying, selling, manufacturing, buying selling property and pursue it, as they desire without interference from the government as long as they do not do any legal transgressions.

In the communist regime, the entire production planning, raw materials procurement, doling out rationed quantities was centralized with the government. Seeing the growth and development of west, most countries of the erstwhile Soviet group have opted out of the central planning and now they are looking at joining the market driven economy.

Mixed Economies

In India, the mixed economy was created with the joint sector ventures, where the private and government were both partners. While such firms tried to get the best of both, i.e. easy government approvals and speedier decision-making process associated with the private sector. In the end, mostly they lost out on both counts as the government felt that their only responsibility is to control the activity of the firm, and the private partner felt that the government is interfering a lot.

Even in purely private firms there is an element of outside control in the form of directors on their board from the financial institutions and the banks that have financed the firm. Besides, there is the compulsory statutory audit by outside auditors. Despite these controls, the last few years have seen a large number of scams through either the equity market or through fake loan companies. It is in this context that the government of India is looking for checks and balances and has assigned the task to Securities and Exchange Control Board—SEBI.

The world over it can be seen that while in China there is greater degree of governmental control, Japan has lesser, where market forces determine the market dynamics. Some countries like Hungary, Taiwan are partly under free market with only some governmental interference, countries like Russia, Mexico are mostly not free. Likewise Cuba would be considered totally not free from governmental interference.

Products like power supply and telecommunication have remained in the government set up in most countries and today in India these products face competition from the private firms. This has created an era of competition, much to the benefit of the consumers and it has resulted in the streamlining process in the government firms in order to make them more efficient. Manufacturing and supply of defence equipment is usually the last of the product groups to come to the private sector, while in India, paradoxically, the defence services did not think twice while purchasing their products from foreign private firms.

The discussion on how much of governmental interference is good for the country's economic growth goes on eternally in most countries.

Developed countries like Germany, Sweden and France have low level of government ownership. They are highly taxed in the private sector and the money thus collected is used in welfare measures. In France, government ownership of business sector is greater as compared to the other two, like the telecom companies keep shuttling there between private and government ownership. Japanese system is based on government's influence on the private sector firms. Japan has been channelling the investment flow in the direction of their choice through setting targets and giving monetary incentives. Their Ministry of Global Trade and Industry guides the firms through strategic planning for investment and production with minimal controls.

The other dimension of economic environment deals with the fact whether the country is a developed one, developing or underdeveloped. UN and its subsidiaries have several plans for helping the poor nations and Indian firms must take advantage of the largesse offered to such nations by helping them come up in the economic order. It has been proven beyond doubt that countries, which opt for market economy, tend to grow economically faster than those which have not opted the same. China and India are typical examples of accelerated growth after they opened up to market based economy.

Politics plays a major role in the life of any country. Countries like the USA, Japan believe that in a democratic free market set-up customers are free thinking individuals who know what is best for them and they decide the fate of firms in the marketplace. There are no sops or financial crutches available to non-performers. It is therefore easy to understand that only the genuine firm, which believes in its product and is ready to provide customer satisfaction, is going to survive.

Countries which have been having totalitarianism as their political philosophy believe that firms should not be let loose to cheat the gullible customers and the restraints are provided by the governmental controls and interference in the shape of checkers, inspectors and auditors. Even France during its Socialists rule had taken over several of the country's private firms under its hold.

There are in fact no truly free economies as even in the US there are economic boundaries like the import quota system for textile imports from developing nations like India. Even the WTO is controlled by the dollar power, which restricts trade from developing countries through uncalled for restrictions and stringent product specifications. The other impediments towards free economic one world, are the trade pacts and trade zones.

It can be safely concluded that each country has its unique system of private and government ownership and control, depending on their system of governance, the status of the development process and their political situation. Therefore, it becomes imperative for firms entering foreign countries to understand the type of economic conditions prevailing in the overseas markets they plan to enter.

For the benefit of new entrepreneurs, it is necessary to put countries in economic zones. The competitiveness of countries in the global market depends on the following factors:

- Production and productivity
- Demand and its management

Production factors are based on the following:

- Capital resource
- Human resource
- Information resource
- Infrastructure
- Physical resource
- Management

Firms have to set up resourcing systems for the above in different countries, which would define the firms' production and its productivity.

Demand and its management would include home country's demand and its growth and global demand. The best way to ascertain the demands is through marketing research.

Classification of Countries

Countries are classified on the following basis:

- GNP–Gross National Product
- GDP–Gross Domestic Product
- Per Capita Income
- Quality of Life or Lifestyle
- Purchasing Power
- Macroeconomics Factors

Gross National Product is in essence the sum total of country's economic activity and can be defined as "the value of goods and services produced during the year from the country's resources", the actual manufacture could take place in the country or even outside.

GNP is the sum of domestic production plus the money received by residents from overseas on account of labour or capital investments by way of dividends reduced by the outflow of money made to non-residents.

Gross Domestic Product or GDP takes into account the entire domestic production irrespective of the fact that the production is from Indian resources or foreign. It describes the economic activities within the borders of the country.

The World Bank has, however, accepted the GNP as true representative of a country's wealth, for working on banks analysis for development plans in the country. Based on 1994 figures, the classification of countries on the basis of per capita income is given below.

Low income	$725 or less
Lower-middle income	$726-$2895
Upper-middle income	$2896-$8956
Middle income	$726-$8956
Huge income	$8957 or more

The low and middle-income countries are known as developing countries, while high-income countries are the developed ones. The classification have since been changed to include **Countries with Economies in Transition,** CEIT, like China, Russia and Cuba.

Per Capita Income

World Bank has categorized countries on the basis of per capita income GNP as given below (only selected countries have been included in the list). It will be noticed that with the exception of Australia and New Zealand, the rich countries are located in the northern hemisphere.

Rich counties per capita GNP $8956 or more	Upper middle per capita GNP between $2896-8955	Lower middle per capita GNP between $726-2895	Low income per capita GNP $725 or less
Australia	Argentina	Bolivia	Afghanistan
Austria	Brazil	Bulgaria	Bangladesh
Belgium	Chile	Croatia	China
Canada	Greece	Cuba	Egypt
Denmark	Hungary	Indonesia	Ghana
France	Korea republic	Iran	India
Germany	Malaysia	Iraq	Kenya
Netherlands	Mauritius	Jordan	Mongolia
New Zealand	Mexico	Korea dem. Rep	Myanmar
Spain	Oman	Lebanon	Nigeria
Sweden	Saudi Arabia	Morocco	Nepal
UAE	South Africa	Philippines	Pakistan
UK	Uruguay	Poland	Sri Lanka
USA		Russia	Zimbabwe

While the rich nations are only 20% of all the nations, they generate almost 80% of the world GNP. Countries in low income about 30%, bring in only about 5% of the world GNP.

Purchasing Power: World Bank believes that while GNP is a good indicator of country's wealth, it does not tell about the benefits accruing to the developmental work. Purchasing Power Parity tells about the purchase value of local currency in home country, against one-dollar purchase value in the USA. Purchasing power of local currency is compared to that of a dollar.

Lifestyle: It is measured by taking into account the following:

- Life expectancy
- Education levels
- Healthcare programmes

- Income and allocable surplus as purchasing power
- Welfare of women

As per 1996 surveys, the top 5 countries, which emerge as winners in these criteria, are the following:

1. Canada
2. USA
3. Japan
4. Holland
5. Norway

In a list of 174 countries, India ranks 135th, China 108th and Russia 57th.

In many countries while the wealth generation takes place, the rich are becoming richer and the poor remain as they were. Despite this most people in the world are satisfied with their lot and believe that they are living in a world, which is better than the world in which their parents grew up. However, they also believe that their children will be living in a world, which would be worse than today's world. India's philosophy of contentment under any circumstances has left many citizens so occupied with their miserable existence that they know nothing better.

Pakistan, on the other hand, has a lot of petro-dollars coming via the gulf, which has given their middle class a better standard of living than their counterparts in India. However, the war hysteria in Pakistan does not allow the extra wealth to be of good to the country as they use it for keep honing the war machinery.

With the opening up of the country's markets to the world, the customers now have a choice of different brands and the urban markets are replete with durable goods of global standards.

Macroeconomics Factors

Developing countries have their GDP distributed on the following lines:

1. Agriculture–30%
2. Industry–30%
3. Manufacturing–25%
4. Service–15%

For a developed country, the distribution is as given below.

1. Agriculture–2%
2. Industry–32%
3. Manufacturing–22%
4. Service–66%

The nations from affluent group are more service oriented. Most of their requirements are met with imports as with high labour costs they cannot produce goods economically as compared to less developed nations. Hence, the stress goes to service industry, which caters to the recreation needs of the population. This is directly related to the quality of life in these countries.

The communist theory was equal distribution of whatever wealth is existing, while market economy looks at increasing the wealth and believes in its distribution as per individual efforts in producing the wealth, which would indirectly make everyone richer than their existing status.

Economic Growth

The business and economic activity in any country depends on a stable government, low inflation rate and high growth rate. India is aiming at 6 to 7 per cent growth each year. Similarly, other developing nations can plan growth rates and by 2020, 60% of the world GNP could be from the today's developing countries. The rich nations want to invest in high growth countries like China, Malaysia, Mexico and the poor nations like India, Pakistan miss the FDI (Foreign Direct Investment). With the new industrial policy India has started getting FDI, yet more of it is definitely required. It is hoped that with stable government and increase in reforms for inviting FDI, there would be substantial improvement in FDI. Today, India gets about 10% of the FDI as compared to what China gets.

Inflation

Inflation is the measure of country's cost of living, interest rates, exchange rates and it involves the political and economic system of the country. It is the consumer price index variation over a period of time. Inflation can cause increase in interest rates to offer real interest on interestable assets, as also for slowing the economic development rate to fight inflation.

CHAPTER

4

Country Evaluation

Scanning the entire world for selecting the right country for doing business is an expensive and time-consuming exercise. Companies seldom get the resources to exploit all the opportunities available in the world. Companies, therefore, need to learn methods of finding out the right markets, countries to sell and to locate manufacturing to cater to those markets. The combined focus would have to be made to locate both the similarities and the differences that complement the existing operations.

Companies planning global business must plan strategies for going in a sequential manner from one country to another for allotting resources and entering a new country. These companies should become aware of the tools for comparing and rating different countries. Thus, they can get the promising and profit making opportunities. They should also avoid getting into expensive detailed scrutiny to survey a wide spectrum of countries. Market size, ease and matching areas of operations and geographic proximity, language and similarities in buying situations in the market are some of the parameters. Besides government interference, country's view on outside companies and more especially its expatriates should be the deciding factors, to enter a country or not.

Other variables include the following areas that need significant understanding by the companies planning to enter another country:

1. Do the business requirements of the country match with company's capabilities, policies
2. Company size is adequate for the business
3. Company has the requisite technology for the country
4. The country allows high percentage of ownership to outside country companies
5. The country allows easy remittance of profits
6. Costs, resources, infrastructure and transportation is manageable

Besides the company must look at the country where the business certainty can be expected rather than going to a country where there is uncertainty. Political stability is one good criterion to work for. In some countries product copying is a norm rather than an exception. Companies should avoid such countries; otherwise its first move advantage would get eroded in no time.

On the financial side, countries promising higher liquidity should be preferred even at the cost of lower returns.

Political risks can be apprehended by understanding the past historical patterns, where experts could be requested to analyze the current scene by looking at the level of frustration among the citizens that would provide for the instability factor of the government.

Given below is a matrix to judge country attractiveness along with company's strengths.

Competitive	Strength	High	Medium	Low
	High	Invest/grow		Dominate/divest
	Medium		Individual plans	
Country's Attractiveness	Low	Individual plans		Harvest/divest

The companies have to decide when they should go for diversification plans and when they should plan for consolidation and concentration. They should go for concentration when the following is happening:

1. Sales response is on the increase
2. Markets are on high growth path
3. Sales are stable
4. Competition entry is a long way off
5. There are spin-offs of sales on other products of the brand

The companies should plan for concentration due to the following reasons:

1. When the need for product adaptation is high
2. Communication, advertising needs to be adapted to local needs
3. Economic scales in distribution are needed
4. High levels of controls are required
5. There are several business constraints

In some countries reinvestments become necessary for survival there. Local managers would not recommend divestment easily.

Once the necessary information is available, decision tools can be used to rate the countries in a predetermined strategy of diversification or concentration.

Companies' must therefore understand the importance of planning strategies for sequencing the penetration of countries and committing resources. They must learn the tools for comparing and rating countries, besides making diversification and concentration plans. In the beginning of expansion plans, companies can respond to opportunities, as they unfold themselves. Afterwards, expansion may not be able to take advantage of all the opportunities. At a later stage, the company may have to select between diversification and concentration to go to many countries quickly and then build them up slowly or enter one or just a few countries and build them up quickly.

MNCs Impact on Global Business

The impact of the entry of MNCs is difficult to assess due to different and at times conflicting influences on different countries' objectives, variables that intervene which make the understanding of cause-effect relationship difficult. There are also major differences in the way the MNCs operate. The companies therefore, must learn to understand the separate interests of MNC stakeholders. There can be impact of MNCs on the economies of the country, as also political and legal impact of the MNCs. MNCs have stockholders, employees, customers and the society at large as their major stakeholders.

Between an MNC and a country, in global business, the chances are that both the country and the MNC may both win or both may lose. At times one may gain and the other loses. When both gain, they may disagree on the distribution of the gains. All the countries hosting MNCs want most benefits.

The economic effect of MNC can be measured in terms of the change in the Balance of Payment status between the two countries. To work it out net exports increase, net reduction in imports and net capital inflow can be added. Mostly, in the beginning Balance of Payment remains positive for the host country and minus for the home country. This trend gets reversed later on. In such a situation the home country can restrict the outflow of investments while, the host country may establishes repatriation restrictions and place controls on asset valuation of the MNCs and therefore prefer to invite debt instead of equity from the MNC.

MNCs have growth and economic effects when they use unemployed or underemployed resources. Home country tends to gain in such an event through improved efficiency and capital inflow due to repatriation of profits. However, home country loses out on job exports as has been happening in the USA. Host country, on the other hand, gains new jobs and technology. Host country's loss comes when the MNC replaces a local company and obtains the best of the country's resources including human resources. They can also be responsible for the demise of local entrepreneurship.

MNC investments are supposed to add on to the domestic interments. However, MNCs bring with them, besides Foreign Direct Investments (FDIs), they also bring the latest technology, styles and brands. Local companies do not have comparable finance arrangements, managerial skills and outside markets. However, if the local companies can acquire technology through transfers and management skills they can succeed in real growth levels for the country, rather than exploitative growth from the MNCs.

While balance of payment can be a gain for the host country, the MNCs may not give benefit to the country in terms of growth and employment, as they may bring their own expatriates and instead of reinvesting in the host country, take away the profits they earn.

Host country at times considers the MNCs as the instruments of their home country governments. At times they could be too powerful and independent to be able to play one country against another. If the MNCs are weak, they could start toeing the host country government's line.

The political and legal impact on global business could become strong under certain situations like, trade restrictions with South Africa during their apartheid rule. Besides, there is the antitrust law in the USA. If the MNCs start to control the host country's key sector industries, they may influence the host country's economy and even politics.

Bribery has become a way of life in most countries. In the USA the government allows companies to make payments to the political parties, while most other countries do not allow such payments.

Political worries about the operations of the MNCs are mainly about the fear that they may be used as foreign policy instruments of the home country or the host country or they may not be under the control of any government. MNCs create conflicting situations of interest with their stakeholders like cross-national problems. They do have influence over the Balance of Payment between the countries, growth and employment. The MNCs can influence on both political and legal stands across home and the host countries.

Global Business and Diplomacy

MNCs activities can be influenced by the idea of their home country government's intention of improving their position with the host country and this can be termed global business diplomacy. In this connection the host countries need to understand the relative power or strength of the two countries, the process involved is bargaining and the possibility of home country's involvement in such bargains. These ideas lead to multilateral and consortium plans for strengthening such influences. However, there is usually the problem over the Intellectual Property Rights between countries.

The bargaining power of countries depends on the need felt by one country for the assets of the other country. Country's assets can be considered the markets, land, technologies, funds, labour and the political stability. Company's assets are its technology, productivity, funds, R&D, capital and its trained manpower. Bargains are made for controlling ownership or controlling interest with a large local ownership.

In the bargaining process companies may accept to get foreign exchange deposits, levels and number of jobs, exports, local inputs, control of transfer price of the imports into the host country from the home country. Besides there may be an agreement on the induction of expatriates and having joint ventures. MNCs can negotiate with force if they are stronger in the global business and enjoy good brand equity worldwide.

Bargaining process in the global business gets affected by the differences in the following ways:

Misunderstandings because of language diversity; evening the same language different countries may have different meanings of one phrase. Cultural nuances can create confusion in the mindset of outsiders. Even professional background could limit emotional sensitivity. In certain countries decision-making is basically a group process like in Japan. In some countries people get argumentative. In most countries when two unknown persons meet, breaking the ice remains a problem. Besides, there is always the dilemma in most countries about the supremacy of engineers vis á vis managers.

Companies need to use negotiations to determine the terms and conditions under which they may operate in a foreign country. The terms can be understood mainly by the relative need of the company to operate in a country or the country's need of the company.

In the global business home countries' governments get involved, when their MNCs operate in a host country. The MNCs need to understand the "Global Standards of Fair Dealings". Some countries have used military force and coercion to make inroads in other countries. Others have applied trade pressures, including withholding of accepted aid and using their power over global financial institutions against the country where they want to do business.

Countries can have multilateral and consortium approaches to have smooth global business. They can use the following organizations for the purpose:

- Global Chamber of Commerce
- Global Court of Justice
- Consortium of countries like the Euro, NAFTA

It must be noted that the judgments given by the Global Court of Justice are ignored.

Public Relations in the Global Business

Countries and companies in the global business must plan their PR exercise for each country they plan to operate in as given below.

1. Countries should plan building country's brand equity through advertising campaigns, fairs through embassies and overseas trade offices
2. Companies should advertise that they are good corporate citizens in their home countries
3. They should advertise their code of conduct
4. They should advertise the support given by them for social causes
5. They should keep consulting the local interested parties
6. They should work out a mutually acceptable ownership-sharing plan
7. They should involve local management to the extent possible.

MNCs must avoid conflicts over the Intellectual Property Rights like, industrial patents, trademarks, inventions, besides artistic property like books, computer programs. Some countries are known for widespread piracy, where the government provides little anti-piracy protection.

Developed countries have in the past forced through military action and coercion that the other countries accept even the unreasonable terms of their investors. Today, however, aid is being used as bait to developing countries, as also the threat of trade sanctions. There is, however, no government with the authority to enforce global agreements.

Summing up, companies must learn the following before getting into the global business:

1. Comparative strengths and weaknesses of home and host countries
2. The bargaining power including flexibility of approach and behaviour patterns
3. Home country involvement like military action, coercion, calling for sanctions
4. Multilateral, bilateral agreements and consortiums
5. Conflicts over intellectual property rights

Political and Legal Business Environment

Governments are run on three basic structures, the legislature, the bureaucracy and the judiciary. Besides the political parties play their role in either running the government or sitting in the opposition as the watchdogs. The major difference in governance comes from the form of the government the country has adopted, democracy, dictatorship, monarchy or constitutional monarchy.

Firms planning global business have to keep scanning both the domestic and global environment. In a democratic set-up, the politicians who are the elected representatives of the people play an important role in framing the industrial policy of the country. The suggestions and advice comes from the businessmen, industrialists, trade bodies, financial institutions, which help the government to look for alternative plans. Once finalized these plans are implemented and monitored by the political powers, bureaucrats, legislatures and the judiciary. The control mechanism of the government gives the feedback about the success of the plan and it is then suitably modified if required.

The socio-political plans of the country are based on the ideology of the political will and the aims and the objectives of the government. Countries with multi-languages, several religions, a variety of ethnic groups, have multifaceted ideology. India is a good example of diverse beliefs and yet having unity in diversity.

Democratic system ensures the following to the citizens:

- Freedom of speech, opinion, freedom of the press
- Elections of legislatures on the basis of adult franchise
- Limited time for elected representatives
- Independent judiciary
- Nonpolitical bureaucracy and defence forces
- Mostly transparent decision process

The success of democracy lies in fulfilling the above obligations to the citizens of the country in a fair and free manner.

The citizens are guaranteed the following in the democratic set-up:

- Freedom of press
- Equality of all the citizens before the law
- Personal social freedom
- Freedom from governmental apathy and corruption

India has seen coalition form of the government for the past few years. This may well become the way of governance in the country, and yet it suffers from the being indecisive on most government business and it carries wrong impression that the country is not yet ready for foreign investments.

In the parliament system India has followed the British tradition of having a lower-house, the House of Commons in UK and Lok Sabha in India, and House of Lords in UK and Rajya Sabha in India. The elections to Lok Sabha are on the basis of adult franchise, while for Rajya Sabha they are based on the votes of elected representatives of the federal states and the Parliament.

Following are the critical government functions that support the country's economic development:

1. Protect the liberty and welfare of the citizens of the country
2. Organize national defence, transportation and communication
3. Correct market anomalies
4. Deal with external problems like pollution

MNCs should take action as given below.

1. Recognize the problem they will face in the host country related to its government
2. Identify other players, institutions and individuals
3. Formulate strategies, objectives, alternative strategies and anticipated results of the strategies
4. Select the most appropriate strategy and then implement the same
5. MNCs need to organize political lobbies and grass root campaign

MNCs have to deal with different degrees of governmental intervention and with the stability factor of the governments. They must plan and implement political strategies to affect and respond to government actions. That is why, companies having a high degree of internal cohesion are better able to deal with the governmental environments where they operate.

As per legal systems of the world, UK and USA have the common law based on tradition, precedent and customs. Germany and Japan have civil law based on detailed legal code. However, Islamic law is based on Koran, Muhammad's sayings and consensus of Muslim legal communities.

Legal System

Under Islamic law no interest is paid while the bank pays the depositors a share of profits. There are also costs involving torts, which are part of wrongful actions, like in the USA 2.4% of the GNP that is only 0.6% in other developed countries. In some countries foreign lawyers are not allowed to operate.

MNCs have to understand the following while operating in host countries:

1. Something that is unethical may not be illegal
2. Law can be slow in implementation with emerging issues
3. Moral concepts are relevant most of the time
4. Laws are tested in the court of law

There can be legal justification for ethical behaviour, the law, however, may not have enough teeth to guide such behaviour.

Summing up the following has been covered in the area of government and legal environment that the MNCs face:

1. A range of political ideologies including democracy to totalitarianism
2. Management decisions and strategies have to take the political systems of the host countries into account.
3. MNCs have to develop and implement political strategies for each host country in which they operate
4. The three prevalent major legal systems are common law, civil law and the Muslim law that cover most countries.

In a democracy citizens expect and get wide ranging freedoms, in the political area and civil liberties.

Manager and the Political System

Business has to cope up with the governmental interference in its working as also, with the instability of governments, which has become part of many countries fate, more especially India. In a democratic set-up the government has to ensure that the citizens are free to do what they want, where they want to do it and how they want to go about doing it. Protection of human rights, people's welfare and correction of market problems, like entry or exit barriers, communication with the consumers about their rights are the duties of the government. The political process like bilateral treaties, conventions and trade zones are the areas, which the manager has to deal with. Therefore, it is important for the firm to understand the governmental laws, rules and regulations, which are applicable for doing business in that country. In each country, a number of governmental agencies are involved with global trade. In some countries, there are facilitating agencies in others there are policing organizations. For example in the USA, the following agencies look after non-agricultural exports:

- The state department
- The department of defence
- The department of commerce

The firms must plan their strategies for meeting the political challenges the host country throws at the firm. For this purpose, it must understand the particular issue, is it the ecological and environmental concern, protection of local industry through high import duties or the laws regarding hiring of the workforce. The firm should assess the actions of competitors on the issues, the success rate, the politically strong lobby, which is ready to take up firm's just cause with the government. Next the firm should plan its strategy, while keeping contingent plans ready in case of the first strategy misfiring due to any reason. Proper care needs to be taken while implementing the strategy with the planning process criteria kept in mind.

Legal Environment

Most countries follow a legal system that is either evolved there over time or it has been adopted from some theocratic decree. England is considered to be the oldest democracy and it has only an unwritten constitution, which works on precedents, tradition, custom and its usage. The law there is the Common Civil Law. In most countries similar civil laws have become prevalent. These laws are interpreted and enforced by the countries' judiciary. The common civil law has become the codified legal system; the codes form the basis of doing business in more than seventy countries of the world.

The other legal system is the theocratic system, which is followed by the Islamic countries of the world. It is based on the Koran, the sayings of Prophet Muhammad, writings of Islamic scholars and the legal communities of the countries known as the shariyat. In Islamic system, taking and giving interest to the borrower or giver of money is an offence. Business with these countries if it involves leasing or credit with payable interest should be eschewed as it may be punished under their law.

The law, in general, is divided as civil and criminal law. Till recently, bank check bouncing was only a civil offence in India. Now it has been made into a criminal offence and therefore bouncing of check could mean imprisonment for the defaulter.

The entire business law of countries the firms want to operate must be understood as ***"ignorance of law is no excuse"***. Of special interest could be the laws relating to patents, environmental issues, anti-trust laws, employment laws, investment and technology transfer laws, which must be fully understood.

Global Business and the Cultural Divide

> ABB is a Swiss firm, is a supplier of power plants, electric equipment in 140 countries of the world. They have a single value system across their business empire spanning the 140 countries. They believe that this has given them competitive advantage over the renowned firms like Siemens, Alcatel-alsthom, and GE.
>
> ABB has a concept of no geographic divide in the firm, it has only home markets, and they draw their strengths from their global entity. They have 500 managers who adopt to the local conditions and yet go by the global strategies of the firm. They truly believe in staying local while thinking global.

From the stone-age of the history of mankind, people have been living in societies, made of persons of different disciplines, work areas, but having a common link, which can be defined as their culture today. Culture is made up of their customs, beliefs and ways of doing things, which are done by most of them. The evolution of religions, concepts of family based on husband and wife and their children are some aspects of the culture as we see it today. The members of a society start having similar attitude, beliefs, values and concepts of a good life. Country's climate, religions can influence its culture.

Societies are formed with members of linked families besides religion, profession, political affiliations too form societal groups, where the members of one group tend to behave in similar manner under similar circumstances and given the same type of stimulus.

Firms from overseas hire persons from their host country, where they are operating. The compensation, competence rewards should conform to the local custom. In many countries, hiring is encouraged from the local areas in which the firm is based in the country. In India, the local factor is increasing taking roots in several states. For instance, the Karnataka government wants that firms operating in Karnataka should recruit persons from the state only as far as possible. Besides each country has its own conventions regarding family pensions, equal pay for male and female workers and retirement benefits. In certain countries there is government influence in recruitment of staff.

The attitude towards male and female workers is widely different in countries. India, China and some other eastern countries have a distinct preference for male workers. Islamic countries sometimes ban the recruitment of females except in medical profession and as teachers. In Japan too wives of workers are supposed to be staying at a distance from the workplace, unlike in the west, the USA or UK where the spouses of workers are invited to annual dinners and are encouraged to feel part of the firm's family.

Hiring and retiring age is different in countries. In some countries, age and experience is valued, while in some the youth gets all the benefits. In the US, an achiever gets the reward irrespective of his age and it is common to see young persons in the age group of 25 to 35 being promoted as CEOs of companies. In some developing countries, the youth or junior level executives are kept under tension in the belief that they perform optimally under pressure. In most countries, because of competitive situations, the workers have to be result oriented if they hope to advance in the firm.

A major problem in India and several other countries, both developed and developing, is that of loss of ethical values. The government officers, together with the firms have created a cover of corruption in the entire business world, and this is true in varying degrees in most of the countries. Going overseas, the dilemma of falling in line for getting the work done by paying hush money is great. However, firms must be ready with the consequences of being caught in the dirty game, which could mean the end of their sojourn in that country and much more, like arrests, penalties.

Language of countries can be of great importance while dealing with them. English has become the language of the business the world over, yet countries like France, Germany and Japan try to keep the business contractual documentation in their own language. Knowledge of languages, including the expertise in translating the document in English without loss of its subtle candor is of utmost importance. English is also having several versions, the American English; the Australian English are a bit different from the English spoken in the UK and in India.

The language subtleties can cause a lot of problems if they are not understood properly. In the US, if the product were to be sold at cost, it would mean without giving any discount, while in India it would mean selling without any profit.

Firms have to consider the cultural divide, which exists between their country and the host country and decide whether to adopt the host country's culture while doing business or stick to their own culture. They can adopt the following three policies in this connection:

1. Global
2. Multi-domestic
3. Hybrid

In global strategy, the firm can retain its home country's culture in the country they do business. The western countries from English- speaking areas do business and bring their own culture with them. The spread of western culture in India can be, to some extent due to the foreign firms operating in India. The popularity of jeans, other western attires, western music, discos can be attributed to this phenomenon. Managers working with global outlook are supposed to conform to the work ethics and cultural ambience of their home country. The American anti-trust laws bind American firms, anywhere in the world.

In multi-domestic strategy, the firm adopts its working to the culture of the host country. In India the Swedish firm of Bofors tried this by believing that the only way to get their work done is through the use of speed money and it backfired. Yet the local managers can perform better if they are given the freedom of going by the host country's culture *"Do in Rome as the Romans do"*.

The ideal situation is to adopt a hybrid culture, which is a mixture of home country's culture with that of host country. The Cola firms use the cultural ethos of the host country, like the local festivals to promote their products.

Americans are hard negotiators in business, but once the deal is finalized they believe in informality, including getting on to first name basis. In some countries of Europe like Germany, it would not be acceptable at all. Visitors to African countries are in for cultural shocks as the way the people dress, interact with foreigners is quite unusual. However, when a manager gets posted to the countries, he starts learning the ways of the host country and may after a while start enjoying the same. It is best to spend some time as a tourist in the country where business is to be conducted before actually shifting there. For the purpose of understanding, the main countries can be grouped as far as their cultural ambience is considered as given below:

English Speaking—Australia, UK, USA, Ireland, South Africa, New Zealand

Middle East—Kuwait, Oman, Iran, Iraq, Saudi Arabia, UAE

Far East—Singapore, Philippines, Taiwan, Malaysia, Indonesia, Thailand

North Europe—Denmark, Norway, Sweden, Finland

Middle Europe—Germany, Austria, Switzerland

Southern Europe—France, Italy, Spain, Portugal, Belgium (with Latin influence)

East Europe—Russia, Turkey and other CIS countries

South America—Argentina, Chile, Mexico, Brazil

For the sheer vastness and cultural diversities existing, the following countries have been singled out:

India, China for sheer size and inversal cultural diversity Japan, because of its unique culture, which defies clubbing with any group.

The main area of understanding a country's culture could prove to be its value system. "What the firms can do and cannot do in the country" must be fully understood and appreciated by not just the managers operating in the host countries, but more importantly by the home country decision-makers.

The economic level of the host country, at times dictates the work culture. In rich nations, managers can afford to take holidays, while in poor countries, workers have to earn on a daily basis to feed their families.

Political system has a bearing on the culture of a country. In democracy, right to work is there, but with the influence of worker unions, the right to strike work can become prominent, especially for foreign firms. Labour laws, negotiation rules are areas of complexity unless knowledgeable people are involved in solving the problems, when they arise.

Foreign firms can plan to go by the host country's cultural ethos, in such a state they must calculate the cost of adopting the culture. If green colour is a must for all products, it could mean realigning the entire range of product, packaging, advertising and promotion plans.

There are a few major cultural differences in countries. In Islamic countries the green colour is preferred over other colours. In China, yellow is the color associated with the Gods and it cannot be used for mundane activities. White, in most countries is the colour of purity and that is why the bride wears white. In India, however, white is worn by widows and by others at the time of mourning.

Given below is a checklist for understanding business environments of different countries:

	Home business of industrialized country	Global business of industrialized country
Language	One (mostly)	Many
Education System	Easy to understand and adapt	Problems in adaptation
Social, cultural ethical environment-values, attitudes, risk taking attitude, scientific methods at workplace	Homogenous	Heterogeneous
Social set-up	Similar	Different
Political	Country centred	Transnational
Legal	Uniform	Different
Sovereignties	Same	Different
Government policies	Same	Different
Economic development	Similar stage	Different stage
Economic system	Same	Different
Tax laws	Same	Different

For example, the HSBC Bank has been operating in several countries to be justifiably called the MNC Bank. It describes its business credo as follows:

"Never underestimate the importance of local knowledge, and adds:

To truly understand a country and its culture you have to be a part of it".

That is why at HSBC we have local banks in more countries than anyone else does. And local people staff all our offices around the world.

It is their insight that allows us to recognize the financial opportunities invisible to outsiders.

But those opportunities do not just benefit our local customers.

Innovations and ideas are shared throughout the HSBC network so that everyone who banks with us can benefit.

Think of it as local knowledge that spans the globe!

This type of hybrid mixing of cultural ambience has helped several MNC's in achieving their global objectives.

Each country has its typical physical, demographic and behavioural characteristics that symbolize the national identity and it may affect a company's method of conducting its business in the country.

There are differences in the physical attributes in societies that affect the way business is organized like, certain diseases may influence the pharmaceutical market. Life expectancy of population may differ widely giving different type of business potential.

Culture can be defined as "specified learned norms based on attitudes, values and beliefs". Most people would accept that there are cultural differences between nations, but they would not be able to segregate the same. By the time a child is ten-year-old he imbibes the basic family value system and it is difficult to change it. However, changes do take place through choice or by imposing it on the child. Religion is a strong catalyst for cultural changes. Besides a common language, common heritage helps in initiating cultural ethos among the country's populace. Culture is the sum total of learned norms based on values, attitudes and beliefs, which are prevalent in every society. Consumer behaviour, which affects business, can be traced to proximity with family and can be gender based. Besides, religion, politics and social groupings too have their impact on the individual behaviour.

Companies place different weights on their employees' career planning on their seniority or on their competence. There are different types of mindset in different countries over the career planning on the basis of the employees' gender. In Australia and in Canada women hold 40 per cent managerial positions while in Japan and South Korea it is only 5 per cent. In some countries the employees' age is considered associated with his wisdom, while some cultures give a lot more importance to the employee's attitude towards his family.

With regards to attitude towards work, in some countries if income increases, workload gets reduced. Japanese take less time off from work and are dedicated to their work. Some employees show eagerness to work for rewards for success, while there is no surety for success and it is hard earned. The Maslow's hierarchy of needs governs behaviours.

While in Belgium and France people are highly independent regarding self-employment, in Japan professors hold higher status than the doctors.

There are a few distinctive styles and behavioural practices as given below.

1. Some countries like those in the Latin America preferred an autocratic style of behaviour and this is confirmed by the fact that there were the dictatorships in some countries of that region.
2. In countries where there is a high degree of trust the management style has been participative.
3. In certain countries like Japan the culture has been of collective decision-making rather than individualistic.

What is considered as graduate study in the UK is the undergraduate level in the States. During communications silent language including distance between people communicating, their mindset on punctuality and their body language combined affect the behaviour pattern. Behaviour pattern gets focused by people's attitude on fatalism as compared to self-determination; idealism with pragmatism.

Behavioural practices affect business in every culture in different ways as different cultures give levels of importance to the role of gender, family, age, work, career success and self-confidence in different ways.

Differences in Global Culture

In the context of global business the company should build awareness of cultural differences, which can be classified as given below:

1. Anglo culture: in UK, Canada and the USA
2. Latin American culture
3. Germanic culture in Austria, Germany and Switzerland
4. Nordic in Denmark, Finland, Norway
5. Near eastern: Greece, Iran, turkey
6. Arab culture
7. Far eastern
8. Indian
9. Chinese
10. Japanese

In order to close the gap by having a reconciliation of differences, local or host countries participation is required. The company should use opinion leaders to achieve its objectives, besides find the appropriate timing for taking action with regards to recognizing and reconciling with the cultural differences.

The company must decide whether and to what extent it should adopt home country practices to the foreign environment or persuade people in the host country to try out something new.

Technological Environment

The level of technology in countries differs and is related to their economic development. Most technically advanced nations have their R & D organizations in many fields in place. Most of the developing nations either resort to buying the advance technology products from the nations possessing them or they buy the technology from them. In India such technology transfers or purchases from different countries have been in vogue for the last fifty years. The problems firms buying the technology have faced are listed below:

- Mostly old or outdated technology is sold to avoid direct competition
- With the technology manufacturing equipment is sold at a jacked up price
- At times even used or reconditioned equipment has been sold.
- There is a pressure on the firm buying the technology, for purchasing, Completely Built Units (CBUs) and Semi-knocked Down Units (SBUs), of the product under technology transfer for a period of time or for a given number.

This has resulted in firms going for reverse engineering of the product, where they buy a few pieces of the product from a number of global firms, cannibalize the products to see what they are inside and how can they be assembled locally. For this reason, it has been accepted by most firms owning the technology that they cannot hold on to the technology on an exclusive basis in the rapidly changing business environment and information blitz.

SUMMARY

Managers in host country must be able to focus on the governmental attitude towards foreign companies. They must learn about the tax laws, legal formalities and issues regarding laws governing employment.

Managers should have a good knowledge of the local customs, which affect consumer behaviour.

Cultures of countries are unique and firms appreciating this uniqueness would do well in the countries they operate. Technological advances, media avenues, retailing channels should be dovetailed to suit the country.

Managers have to learn that, unlike in their own country, the selling action is controlled by various factors, including economic levels, infrastructure facilities, transport, communication problems, which would be new to the outsider.

Globalization of business has brought a large number of MNCs into each country, creating severe competitive situations. Managers would do well to know the 4 Ps of competitors and plan their own 4 P strategy taking them into account. Product positioning, advertising and promotion, pricing and distribution channels need innovative approach to gain sustainable competitive advantage, which is the key factor in the firms' success.

Technological supremacy can give firms a headstart, but they cannot keep that advantage for long as in no time better ME TOO Products invade the market. Patents can create problems for copying firms but in a host country, the legal tangles can sap the profits in no time. Managers have to keep themselves abreast with the latest products to be able to ensure their own innovative products give them a headstart always.

CHAPTER 5

Global Planning and Policies

After the end of World War II, the nations of the world decided to start a monitoring organization to avoid recurrence of war and they formed the United Nations Organization.

The UN accepts the fact that globalization has brought about several advantages to the population of the world—faster economic growth, higher standards of living, new opportunities for global business, it has given impetus to global crime, terrorism, drug and arm trafficking, albeit unwittingly. UN is determined to make globalization an engine of positive change in the lives of people living in poverty and misery. It should not be used to take people in negative direction.

The UN acknowledges the fact that poverty and inequality are the breeding grounds of conflicts. The wars have claimed more than 5 million lives in the last decade. Once the UN can come up with conflict prevention ideas, peace-building activities would become the harbinger of wealth for even the poor nations, as the world would generate more wealth. The USA and UK led attack on Iraq has brought the UN into a bit of oblivion, but its developmental agencies must take initiative now to further the aims of the UN.

United Nations Organization, the UNO, since its inception tried to form political, commercial and socio-cultural bridges, between member nations. Its member bodies include, WTO, World Bank, UNDP, IMF, IFC, UNCTAD, Global Trade Centre, UNIDO provide the support needed by developing countries like India. It is, therefore, necessary to understand how these operate, to be able to take their advantage in business globally.

WTO

In order to ensure free trade between member nations UNO members formed a set-up, which *is supposed to* monitor, regulate and assist in trade between nations. It started off as GATT—General Agreement on Trade and Tariff. GATT was basically for trade in merchandised goods. WTO includes goods, services like global telephones and creative works, the intellectual property rights. WTO is a formal structured organization with its rules binding on its members. It is also for settling disputes between nations, with arbitration mechanism and an appellate body where nations aggrieved from the decisions of arbitration can appeal against the same.

While the GATT had 128 members, WTO has a bigger strength with nearly 140 members, more wanting to join the organization. WTO has its headquarters in Geneva, Switzerland. WTO has the following three tasks to perform:

1. Administer and police the existing and new Free Trade Zones in the world.
2. Oversee the world trade practices
3. Settle disputes

It was in 1995 that WTO came into existence.

Background

There were seven years of long fruitless negotiations, known as the Uruguay round of trade talks. Then the new Apex body WTO was formed which came in existence on 1 January, 1995 with the authority to make rules and regulations governing global trade and to enforce the same among the member nations. There were problem areas as given below.

- European union farmers got huge subsidies giving them extra edge over others in agriculture product global trade.
- Multi-fiber Agreement for trade in textiles was another example of managed trade.
- Removal of these and similar biases are planned by the WTO; it may however take some time before quota in textile trade is fully removed making it totally part of free trade.

For the developing nations, however, WTO has some negative aspects as, the trade, finance and development go hand in hand and, the developing nations need extra support for their growth. In fact, it can be seen that the developing nations are also large markets for the developed nations and therefore their development is in the interest of the developed nations too. It is imperative that level-playing field is created between the two, the developing and the developed nations with special emphasis for the weaker nations.

WTO needs to focus on the following:

Managed trade: While the objective remains of free trade, yet most nations have non-tariff bases trade barriers. These include, critical and almost impossible product specifications, testing methods and source verification of components and raw materials. Outsourcing from global manufacturers the essence of global trade is getting warped.

Free trade: While the trade may be free; does it also give a fair share of trade profits to the trading partners? Profits, employment, foreign exchange earnings, technology upgrades, production capacities, infrastructure development and building of institutions keeps the parity between rich and developing nations a dream only.

Market entry: Even within WTO regime, powerful nations have the facility to safeguard their interests while the weaker nations have no option but to follow the WTO rules. The best way for these nations is to accept the existence of WTO and then work to get the best possible advantage of its rules. Each market has some internal forces like the political set-up, level of liberalization of economy and its infrastructure. Developed nations have built such difficult paths for the entry of products from developing nations; product specifications being one of them.

Hence, nations like India need to take following steps to make themselves ready for global markets.

- Have clear goals and strategies
- Strong points as strategic options and correct assessment of bargaining power during negotiations round of the WTO meetings.
- Dynamic coordination between nations with similar ideas/problems.

Work on these has been going on and it needs to be intensified with a sense of urgency. WTO, it must be understood is here to stay and it would be prudent to get the best out of it. It is for everyone's benefit in the global trade. Nations should help improve competitiveness of its trade with help in getting better technology, better infrastructure support, and management. There could be assistance to domestic trade to enable it to compete with world players on a level playing field.

India, a member of the WTO, has to accept and honour its rules. India should therefore plan an integrated plan of complying with WTO rules. It could be done in the following steps:

- Help firms get better technology and management, organize state-of-the-art infrastructure support to make them competitive in the country and globally. Technology should meet with the best in the range available anywhere in the world.
- Remove internal hurdles for firms to prepare them for global competition
- Phase introduction of globalization and liberalization to give breathing time to firms adjust to global competition
- Help in strengthening antidumping institution and competition by identifying the areas of dumping, damage it is causing to the affected countries. Then, the reasons for dumping including industry capacity, financial muscle should be understood.
- WTO accepts the link between law and economics. Legal battles fought in foreign countries are expensive. Experts and consultants in the area of WTO should be established and they should be able to coordinate with their global counterparts.

World Bank

World bank is a group of five institutions; the Global Bank for Reconstruction and Development (IBRD), the Global Finance Corporation (IFC), the Global Development Association (IDA), the Multilateral Investment Guarantee Agency (MIGA), and the Global Center for Settlement of Investment Disputes (ICSID)

The aim of these agencies is to reduce poverty around the world by assisting the poor nations in their economic development.

IBRD

The bank provides loans to middle income countries and creditworthy poorer countries. The bank obtains 90 per cent of its capital by sale of bonds in global capital markets. In 1999, the bank committed $29 billion, lending for institution building, governance, economic policies and social protection got the bulk of the amount, mainly for poverty removal with support to the social sector. Total lending is of the tune of $300 billion.

IDA

IDA provides loans at very low rates to the poorest of the nations of the world. The bulk of IDA resources come from contributions from richer IDA member countries, who are asked to replenish their contributions every three years, and the loan repayments starts only after a grace period of ten years.

IFC

IFC is the largest multilateral source of loan and equity financing for private sector projects in the developing world. It helps the governments in creating conditions for flow of both domestic and foreign private savings and investments. It supports the role of market investors. It acts as a catalyst in the developing world to prove that investments can be made profitably.

MIGA

It helps foreign investments in developing countries by covering the non-commercial risks like political, through insurance (guarantee).

ICSID

It provides for dispute settlements through conciliation or arbitration between private foreign investors and the government of the host country.

IMF

The fund is meant to do the following:
- Assist in global monetary transactions and cooperation
- Promote exchange rate stability and proper exchange arrangements
- Help in establishment of multilateral payment system and elimination of foreign exchange restrictions
- Provide bridge loans for meeting temporary adjustments of balance of payments
- Offer concessional aid to low income member countries

UNCTAD

UNCTAD undertakes the following tasks:
- Scan the global economy and its impact on the development process
- Analyze the macroeconomic policies of the governments regarding cooperation between nations

- Understand the development challenges and successful experiences to dovetail them to developing countries and countries going into market economy
- Assist developing countries in their debt repayments
- Prepares a database and provides trade and development related information
- Help poor nations to integrate with the global economy

Global Trade Centre-ITC

It is the technical cooperation agency of UNCTAD/WTO for operational and enterprise oriented aspects of global trade development. It works with developing nations and nations with economies in transition to set up trade promotion plans to expand exports and improve their import operations.

UNIDO

It helps to improve the living conditions of people and promote global prosperity, by offering tailor-made solutions for industrial development. It associates with the governments, private industry to develop industrial capacities.

Market Globalization

Even as the USA has been propagating the idea of a world common market and free trade, it has also been forming Cartel-like organizations that are meant to protect the interests of member nations. Some of the trade blocks are given below:

Trade Blocks

European Union has been formed for integrating the Europe with respect to trade, within its members as well as for trade with the rest of the world. It has adapted a common currency for Europe, the Euro. It seems to become a precursor of the political union of the member nations. The following nations have become part of the European Union:

1. Ireland
2. UK
3. France
4. Germany
5. Portugal
6. Italy
7. Greece
8. Austria
9. Belgium
10. Luxemburg
11. Holland
12. Denmark
13. Sweden
14. Finland

Other nations even of the Eastern Europe including Russia are inclined to join the EU. The EU has become a structured organization and has the following bodies that govern and administer the EU.

European Union

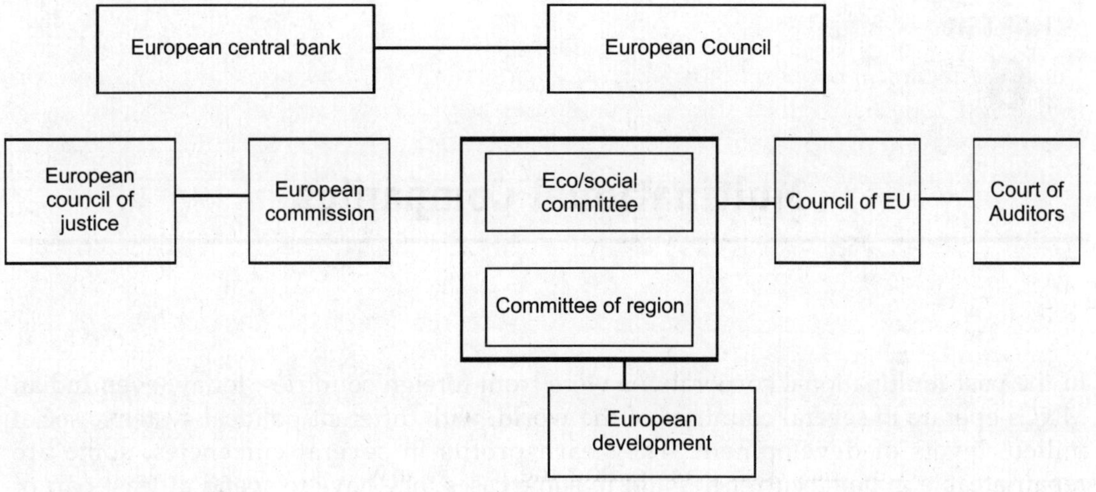

SUMMARY

Global Marketing Managers have to perform similar functions in home and host countries, except that in host country the business environment differs to a large extent and the managers must be vigilant in coping with the changing business scenario in the alien land.

Managers have to learn about the country's consumers tastes, buying patterns, income diversity and demand patterns, which could be fast changing due to technology changes and changes in income levels. Therefore, historical data could be misleading to the managers.

Managers have to ensure a product FIT with the consumers, which could entail product or package modifications. (Japanese homes have smaller refrigerators, which cannot accept the 200 ml Coke bottles.)

Managers have to relate to the stage of product life cycle and direct the firm's resources for the right products. This is important as a product could be in maturity stage in one country and be in growth stage in another.

Advertising, publicity, promotion plans all must be country specific, unless a product like the Mercedes is being sold, which is a world accepted product and can sell on global advertising plans.

CHAPTER
6

Multinational Companies

In the past multinational corporations were from foreign countries; today, even Indian MNCs operate in several countries of the world, with different political systems, social milieu, levels of development. They earn profits in several currencies, some are repatriateable in home currencies and in some cases they have to spend at least part of their profits in the host country. Global firms operate in one or two host countries from the home base; they may have a sales office or an agent in the host countries. Firms with global perspective operating in several countries with investment in marketing, production and even R&D can be considered true MNCs. They view the globe as their market place and target countries one after the other on the basis of priority, which is decided on the basis of the following factors:

- Geographic proximity
- Political alignments
- Economic zones and economic forces
- Product demand (without any changes in the product specifications)
- Technological advantage
- Price advantage due to economies of scale
- Firms have at least 20% of their assets overseas
- Overseas sales and business account for about 30-40 per cent of the firm's turnover
- Overseas factories could be just assembly plants, full-scale manufacturing units
- Overseas operations may be managed by host country personnel or even third country managers. To start with the top management stays with the home country personnel
- Global business starts as an offshoot in country business and then it moves across as an integrated part of the firm's operations.
- Products like retailing, banking are dovetailed to meet the specific needs of the host country, while cars, cokes, electronic products stay the same globally.

Countries like the USA have been advocating the free enterprise, no barrier business across the globe. Consolidating this thought and still focusing on the national interests, several trade zones have emerged in the world. MNCs are ready to take advantage of these zones and yet go beyond them to individual countries where they find comparable advantage.

In the 17th century, Adam Smith propounded the theory of absolute advantage of nations in business, which considered the fact that one country could produce a certain good better and at low cost as compared to other countries. He advised that the countries should manufacture those products only where they have the absolute advantage in manufacturing. Today, even if a country does not have absolute advantage, it can specialize in some products to gain competitive advantage in the global market. This could be gained through availability of raw materials, low cost labour, a good production base for achieving the economies of scale, technology and/or patents in their favour. More than anything else it is the will to go global, the mindset, which spurred the firms into becoming MNCs. Given below are the points, which add to the competitive advantage of the firms:

- Labour cost, infrastructure, availability of raw materials
- Product demand in the home country: If the demand is large and the customers are discerning regarding the product quality, the firm could have the advantage of low cost production having achieved the economies of scale, would have a good consistently high quality product and such a firm can create customer satisfaction in other countries as well.
- Home country's trained manpower, technology base, patents help the firms in the overseas markets.
- Effective and efficient policies, strategies, which are conducive to firm's global ventures.

Firms take the route to global business via the basic competitive advantage of technology, raw material availability, and trained manpower. Next the firms with innovative products, which have found a good marketing the home country, consider that they can be successful overseas as well. Firms, which have made considerable investments, plan overseas business to fully utilize the investment so that they can amortize the investment over large volume business, which may not be possible in the home country. Finally, once the firm becomes cash rich through global trade it plans venturing overseas through large-scale investments in manufacturing and marketing in the host countries.

Firms need to consider the following issues as they plan overseas business:

- Host county's economic development, per capita income, GDP futures, fiscal policies
- Host country's unemployment state
- Currency value
- Wage levels
- Nature of competition

- Influence of regional pacts and free trade zones
- Forms of the government, its stability
- Taxation levels
- Political ideology
- Money supply and interest rates
- Laws regarding foreign investments
- Trade regulations
- Government's attitude towards foreign firms
- Level of protection to local firms
- Technology import rules
- Power availability and costs
- Infrastructure like telecom, roads, transport system
- Social systems, values, languages, demographics, lifestyles
- Attitude towards foreigners

Before considering business options in other countries, the information listed above must be gathered from a known, reliable source.

Competitive advantage scan is done on the following lines:

- High brand equity worldwide, at least in the region the firm wants to start its business.
- Economy of scale in manufacturing
- Technological advantage through breakthrough and global patents
- Efficient market research capability in the host country to understand the business opportunities available there.
- Product like the Mercedes car, which sells by itself, just by its name
- Strong global management, especially the top man, who can make a big difference just by his personal knowledge of the host country, its market, buying habits of the customers and the language nuances.

Once the firm knows it has competitive advantage in another country, and its market is growing, the firm should invest in that country and grow. In case the market is growing and the firm does not have a competitive advantage, it should look for a niche market, find a joint venture partner or divest. In a country where the market is not growing and the firm does not have any advantage it should organize licence production or divest after harvesting. In the event of having middling advantage in a mildly attractive market the firm should plan selective market segments.

Selecting a JV Partner

When firms go overseas, they are new to the country, its financial status, social and cultural state, its political outlook and they find it useful to have a local partner who knows the country well and who can steer the firm through the initial problems. Many firms have found that the local partners have not been able to provide the kind of assistance they were looking for and the partnership does not flourish. The firms should not be in a hurry to find the partners, they should join hands only with like-minded firms, who share the same aspirations, have similar goals and who would take equal stake in the joint venture.

A fully multinational firm has the following attributes:

- Personnel selection on worldwide basis; manager of home country working with manager of a third country in the host country.
- R&D is having its wings in many countries with real-time coordination; they may be working on several parts of one project or several separate projects
- Sourcing of finance is not limited to home country and host country alone, but shares are floated in several countries.
- Manufacturing base is spread in several countries.
- Products are designed for global acceptance.
- Firm's structure is matrix or a mixed structure combing functions and SBU, and Matrix taking product range, functions and geographic considerations into account.

MNC Management

The host country management styles vary quite a bit ranging from totally authoritarian to high level of delegation of authority. Firms in countries like Malaysia and France are content to be ruled by managers. Some countries' firms want clear personnel policies about recruitment, promotions and stability like in Greece and Japan. Firms in countries like the USA and Canada want individual authority, delegation and accountability.

Most MNCs keep qualified and trained persons of the host country to man the second level of management ladder, keeping the top position for their own people. However, after the initial start up period, the expatriates tend to become a heavy burden on the firm as besides getting overseas salaries, home travel allowance, they get paid at home for maintaining their families. In case the families move with the personnel, then the expenses mount even further. Besides the firm may have to pay the local income tax also on behalf of the expatriates.

In order to avoid these problems firms like Unilever, IBM keep 95 per cent employees of the host country. These firms have accumulated huge amount of experience as MNCs. Several countries' governments insist that the MNCs must provide employment to the local people. These MNCs start training and orientation programmes to bring the locals in the mainstream of the home firm. Besides the locals being more attuned to the socio-culture ambience of the country are able to help the firm in planning customer communications better. Local managers, can become a hindrance when it comes to global thinking as they are concerned only about their country. A sound combination of locals and home country managers is found most useful. The trust building exercise with the locals takes time, which can become a negative factor if the firm wants to start rolling at full speed quickly. Daewoo Motors in India had some Indians in senior positions who were never part of the key decisions taken by the Koreans. The end results are there for all to see.

Firms can consider the global approach in filling key positions by getting the most suited person from around the world. European firms have adopted this principle; a Swiss firm had an Austrian director in Singapore. While this could prove to be expensive, but if the firm can find the right person, who knows the market, he could really offset the extra expense. Firms look for a person for their global operations who is sensitive to new cultural nuances, adaptable enough to accept changes and the resultant challenges, skilled to operate with a set of global team members, besides being strategically alive to the changing business environment the world over.

Management of host firm/subsidiary away from home country has become relatively easy with faster telecommunications and computer networking, emails as also faster of movement of people and goods through fast jets. Daily analysis of sales, payments received and made, changes in the business environments can be made without any time lag. Financial standings can be known through comparing the actual expenses with the budgeted figure, ROI with historical figures; however with global business margin should be taken to account for the host country's inflation and taxation rates.

Developing countries like India can find the entry of MNCs a double edged weapon; on the one hand, the MNCs bring in technology, finance and management expertise but they also pose a threat to the local industry. Repatriation of profits in foreign currency affects the host country's economy to a large degree (it is only a relative term as the MNCs have brought in finance in foreign exchange only.)

An MNC can be defined as a global approach to markets and production. These are of two categories, global and multi-domestic. There are external influences on IB of, physical, societal and competitive environments. The MNC operates in variety of external business environment and therefore its search for profitable markets is inhibited by different and confusing conditions in the foreign countries, with strong competition between nations, cross-national treaties, agreement and problems of ethics in different countries.

MNCs that integrate their operations located in different countries are the global companies and those operating in different countries and yet allow the foreign operations to act fairly independently are known as multi-domestic companies.

SUMMARY

An MNC has business spread in several countries, investments, production facilities marketing, and procurement functions in many parts of the world. MNCs plan multi-domestic strategy to modify to suit each country and then they go on to have global products. The management needs to have global management skills as also the mindset for operating globally. Firms look for global competitive advantage beyond the human resource, as these are now quite mobile around the globe. Copiers of the product, the ME TOO people who with a little expertise can bring a better product than the original, can dilute technological advantage. Competitive advantage can be gained by proper strategic planning and execution and by providing uniquely excellent service, which cannot be copied by the competition. Regular monitoring of business, general and competitive environment, host country's wage plans, tax laws, profit repatriation, study of free trade zones, all can provide the competitive advantage to the firm. Differentiated products, economies of scale of manufacture, technological edge and a top quality business team add to the competitive advantage.

CHAPTER

7

Global Trading Strategies

Governments seek to influence trade because of their own social, economic and political agenda. They are also under the influence of interest groups and at times conflicting objectives, like support of local industry as against getting new technology. In the developing countries, the rate of unemployment can be a big deterrent towards imports.

The economic reasons can be to provide employment, protect nascent industry, accelerate industrial growth and gain competitive advantage as compared to other countries. Some countries focus on strengthening core industries, as they want to remain a power in the region and maintain status quo. However, the import restrictions can lead to similar restrictions imposed by countries where the country may want to export. Import restriction can cause price increase of local products; increase in taxation and these should be weighed against the cost of unemployment. The other statement of helping local industry can provide it with economies of scale of manufacture and benefits of experience curve. Local industry can bring in faster growth than the agro-based economy, brings in funds through investments while economy stops depending on agriculture alone. Exports restrictions can cause increase in smuggling as it affects the world prices. It leads to use of substitute product and local prices come down as local supplies increase. Import restriction can decrease dumping to the benefit of local manufacturers. Foreign sellers are forced to reduce their prices.

Countries try to protect essential industries. They have to define the industries falling in this category, besides understanding the choice of alternative products and their political ramifications. Countries provide with non-tariff barriers as follows:

1. Subsidies to local sellers try to cover up market weaknesses
2. Custom valuations can lead to arbitrary increases in price valuation despite the fact that the invoice may have given the right price for imports.
3. Quota system as prevalent in the US regarding imports of textiles
4. The government may issue directives to its buyer to buy only local products

5. At times the importing countries may impose unilaterally strict and impossible standards of products

Global trade theory confirms the competitiveness of manufacture in a given location. It identifies the place where the manufacturing would be most efficient and it also explains if the local governments would allow free flow of trade between countries.

Global trade has been operative long before any trade theories were evolved. These theories are helpful today to MNCs in planning their operations. On the basis of trade theories, the firms would expect that the greater the dissimilarity between nations, greater is the trade potential between them. However, most of the trade occurs among nations having similar status. It is, however, believed that free trade results in the most efficient utilization of the resources of the world. While trade theories talk about cross-country benefits and cost, trading decisions are taken at the firm level only.

Countries want to influence trade for economic, social or political objective. A variety of measures are tried by them to balance conflicting objectives and appease various interest groups.

Political concerns are the main reasons for governmental interference in the global trade rather than economic factors. Political problems have led to serious conflicts within and among nations.

To augment their efforts, countries use the UN bodies like WTO and regional economic integration to reduce trade barriers on a multilateral basis and they agree on simplified mechanism for conduct of global trade. Trade liberalization on a global basis is difficult due to fundamental differences between nations.

One of the most important purposes of the governmental interference in trade is to secure and expand employment opportunities for the population. There can be the possibility of retaliation and the fact that both import and exports create job, it is difficult to determine the effect on employment of protecting an industry.

Trading worldwide is possible in those countries, which subscribe to free trade, at least to an extent. Most of the countries, however, have been giving lip service to free trade. The reasons for this non-subscribing to free trade are given below.

- As a boost to local business, which is saved of facing global competition
- When the country cannot provide the necessary infrastructure required by global traders
- When the country's political agenda does not match with free trade
- When the economic level of the country is low and the consumers are not able to afford anything beyond food and other items of dire necessity.

For these reasons, a number of trading models have emerged, and the firms select one or more of these models while going overseas, as follows:

- A single low cost product to be sold universally or a number of high value products to suit each country
- Special R&D efforts to keep adding innovative ideas into the products or waiting for the competition to bring a new innovative product and than with the help of reverse engineering bringing out a better alternative product (ME TOO Product, but better)

- Keeping to home country production for gaining economies of scale, because of additional export trade or outsource production from countries where there is a production cost advantage, due to either lower labour cost or cheaper availability of the raw materials
- Integrating with the host country business methods, ethics or maintaining the home country (the firm's own) standards. If it is the norm in the host country to sell the products on bargain counters, the firm has to decide to stick to their own distribution channels or vend through the bargain counters
- Product usage to be dovetailed to meet the local needs or imposing the home country usage. Daughnuts are eaten for breakfast in the west, while in Japan they are eaten as snacks. Daughnuts, therefore, started a chain of daughnut restaurants near railway stations, shopping malls.
- Outsourcing manufacturing operations to low cost labour countries can be counterproductive because of two reasons, one, the worker productivity may be much lower, increasing to the overall labour cost, two, the product quality may suffer because of the country's lower benchmarks.

The export and import trade of countries is governed by the trade policy the government of a country formulates to regulate the trade. These trade policies are then converted into trade by the firms in the following manner:

- With which countries they should have import export ties
- What product/s they should be importing and exporting to which country
- Whether these products should be fully manufactured in the home country or partly there and the rest in the host country
- Should the manufacturing be outsourced to a third country
- If the manufacturing is not in the home country, what quality control measures are required to be taken to ensure standards of quality are maintained

Global trade goes through the barriers placed by the governments of different countries, unless in some cases there are no governmental interference (in the global trade). Trade pacts between nations, both bilateral and multilateral have become the norm today, which govern the global trade to a large extent.

If, however, there were no such barriers, the trade would follow the natural route of comparative advantage between nations; the country having core competency in one area over the other country would be able to export to that country.

Trade between nations has been there from the last several centuries. From 1500 AD, when the nations were getting formed out of the city-states, tribes. The nations with gold reserves were considered rich and the balance of trade was equated by giving away of gold by the low exporting/high importing nations to the high exporting/low importing nations.

Today, the balance of trade means that if the country is exporting more than it is importing the balance is in its favour, otherwise it is not. In reality, the surplus nation is providing credit to the deficit nation and if this credit cannot buy goods required by the surplus nation from the deficit nation it can be harmful to the surplus nation.

Nations no longer work on the theory of absolute advantage of nations, the theory propounded by Adam Smith in the 17th century. The theory says that the country, which can produce a good at a lower cost than all others, can sell to the other nations.

The low cost of manufacture comes from the following factors:

- Economies of scale of manufacture where the fixed cost of manufacture remains constant while the total production increases. For example, if a firm is making 1000 cars per day and its daily fixed cost is Rs. 100,000 then the fixed cost per unit comes to Rs. 100. When the firm increases the production to 1200 cars per day, its fixed cost per unit comes to Rs. 83.33 this is on the premise that no new supervisor has been hired or the fixed cost has not gone up in any other manner.
- The firm uses robotics, which cut down on production time and cost, introduces new technology.
- Experience curve helps in reducing per unit variable cost. This reduction comes from the workers who gain experience working on the same equipment over the years and they reduce the rejection rate as well as the manufacturing time.

Besides, the absolute advantage of Adam Smith, firms and countries can achieve comparative advantage over each other. One country could be more efficient in automobile technology while the other could be an expert in computers. In such a case, instead of developing the skills not available with them, they could be exchanging the products.

Some countries enjoy a natural advantage over the others because of the following reasons:

- Availability of natural resources, like water, minerals
- Raw materials
- Climatic conditions conducive to manufacture of some products
- Trained and skilled manpower

Summarizing, the trade theory explains what can be produced competitively in a given location, where a firm may go to produce a given product efficiently and whether government policies may interfere with the free flow of trade between countries. The following are the eight theories of global trade:

1. Mercantilism
2. Absolute advantage
3. Natural advantage
4. Acquired advantage
5. Country size
6. Comparative advantage
7. Factor proportions
8. Product life cycle

Mercantilism

Countries wealth is determined by the gold as treasure they hold. Those countries, which export more than they import, tend to have a favourable balance of payment. Therefore, countries need to export in a greater measure than their imports bill. In neomercantilism, countries plan for achieving both social and political objective.

Absolute Advantage

A country's real wealth consists of the goods and the services it can provide to its citizens. If global trade was without any barriers, each country would specialize in those products where it has a competitive advantage. This theory was propagated Adam Smith in the 17th century.

Absolute advantage is achieved through specialization; when the labour force becomes more skilled and experienced. This results in no time loss in switching back and forth. Long production runs are conducive to improved efficiency.

Natural Advantage and Acquired Advantage

Natural advantage is due to country's climatic conditions, natural resources, and human resources. Acquired advantage is through technological advances, product differentiations and improvements in process efficiency.

Country Size

In most cases large countries are almost self-sufficient with large geographic areas, varied climates and natural resources. Even transportation costs vary greatly in large countries. Companies need long production runs for achieving economies of scale.

Comparative Advantage

A country should concentrate and specialize in those products and services it can produce or offer more efficiently, economically, rather than other products it can just produce.

Proportions Theory

Products, materials in relative abundance are cheaper than those in relative scarcity. Even labour, if skilled can become cost-effective. US exports can become more cost-effective due to highly skilled labour force as compared to labour cost of nations from where US imports as their skilled labour skills may not match with the skills of US labour.

Product Life Cycle

In the introductory stage, which is new to the country, (as against new to the company), the product offers innovation to the buyers. The market is in near monopoly state where sellers can charge skimming prices. They should, however, be cautious that competition can never be far behind as the company keeps generating high profits. In growth stage, exports can be started. Competition raises its head; foreign companies, MNCs join the fray, capital outlay increases as companies try to further innovate the product, services and other terms of business-like terms of payment, guarantee, warranty offered with the product. Dependence on trade partner keeps reducing as the product acceptance increases in the target market.

In the maturity stage of the product life cycle, product demand stabilizes, products are standardized and the production can move to less developed countries. In the declining stage demand of the product decreases, production remains in the less developed countries while the innovating countries become importers of the product from the less developed countries.

There are, however, exceptions as given below.

1. There are products like fashion garments, high technology electronic products where the rate of obsolescence is rapid. In such products the PLC is a short-lived phenomenon and companies must accept them as such.
2. Products can be easily differentiated. As soon as an innovative product is introduced in the market, competition brings out a ME-TOO product, which can be slightly better than the original one.
3. Luxury products like luxury cars, Mercedes, BMW become so unique that no differentiation is possible.
4. There are products where the transportation costs are high due to their volumes being disproportional to their weight.

Countries join hands with each other in trade partnerships due to geographic proximity, similarity in their cultural ethos, language similarity, and religious commonality and due to political affinity with each other. In some cases, countries become dependent on another country due to reasons of imports, exports, financing and transfer of technologies. Such dependence makes the country vulnerable, as it has to remain at the mercy of other country for its well-being in trade. However, if two countries are interdependent, then the mutual need makes the countries create level playing field. In case, a country is not interdependent on another country it can take its own decisions.

Competitive Advantage of a Country

Countries get competitive advantage when they find markets with demand of their products near their area of operations. Besides, they need the following:

1. The country is endowed with materials, human and technology resources.
2. Supporting or related industries are in proximity to lend support when needed.
3. Company's strategy, its structure can provide it with competitive advantage.
4. Company having excess production capacity.
5. Company having economy of scale in its production and experience curve for having low cost production.
6. Minimum fluctuation in product demand would lead to stable home country demand, minimizing risks in global trade
7. In case of importing the company can look for better quality supplies and by having multiple suppliers can reduce risks of failure of one supplier

From the trade theories the company can locate countries with greater dissimilarity for larger potential for trade. However, most global trade is happening between countries with great similarities. Trading decisions are, therefore, mostly taken at the company level, while trade theories talk about inter-country benefits and costs.

CHAPTER

8

Strategies for Exports and Import

In the 21st century global economy is growing and barriers of global trade are reducing. This has resulted in increase in the export and import trade between countries. And yet the developed countries are into Managed Trade, where these countries are placing artificial barriers like, heavy subsidies the government gives to their farmers, have set quotas for imports from developing countries.

For proper growth of exports, the following are required:

1. To understand the strategies for planning exports and imports
2. Locating the intermediate organisations for exports
3. Understanding the organization of export finance
4. Understanding counter trade

Exporting companies should start with making an assessment of export potential in the chosen countries/markets. They can then correlate the possible opportunities with the requirement of resources in the selected areas. They should get information about the countries from foreign government agencies, banks and financial institutions. Market selection can be done as follows:

1. Actively select the markets by using the marketing research techniques in the same market or similar markets located in the proximity of the selected markets.
2. Passively select the markets by responding to enquiries.

For formulating the export strategies, the following needs to be done:

1. Define both long-term and short-term objectives
2. Plan specific tactics for entering the market
3. Plan a detailed schedule of activities, deadlines focusing on results expected
4. Allocation of resources for the tasks
5. Determine the distribution channels, direct like, sales representatives, distributors, agents or indirect through host country importers

Besides, there are export marketing intermediaries given below.

1. Export management companies, which obtain purchase orders for a group of exports
2. Export trading companies which service the overseas buyers
3. Companies like the Japanese trading companies, which start by getting the raw materials and then find the export markets
4. Foreign freight forwarding companies, which arrange for expert licence where required, shipping and warehousing facilities.

Summing up, companies planning exports should work a good strategy by assessing the export potential in the selected markets through marketing research, obtain expert advice for the selected countries, select the markets, formulate the strategies by determining the 4 Ps, the product, its price, the distribution channels, direct or indirect and the best way of communicating with the market through advertising.

Export Financing

Companies have to understand the following while deciding about product pricing:

1. Currency of payment, its fluctuations: In case of highly fluctuating currencies, it is a good idea to insure the payments at known levels
2. Transportation, its costs: The alternative modes of transportation, sea, land, delivery time for each on average and the costs of each
3. Import duties in the host countries
4. Possible mark ups

Besides the companies should understand the best methods of receiving the payments for exports made, as follows:

1. Cash in advance
2. Bills of exchange used in commercial transactions like sight drafts or time drafts
3. Letter of Credit (LC) which should be irrevocable and confirmed
4. Financing receivables like Exim bank loans, guarantees, ECGC insurance

In counter trade the possibilities are of barter trade like what was happening between India and the USSR also known as Rupee trade. The other option is of offset trade where the exporters assist the buyers in earning the required foreign exchange for the imports.

Import Plans

Companies wanting to import should understand the following:

1. Procedures for imports like custom duties, customs brokers
2. Payments to be made by releasing the bill of lading or the airway bill for imports through air
3. Storage of imports
4. Long-term imports agreements for keeping price parity, quality assurance and ready availability

The price of the product, the method of payment and financing of receivables are the three important issues that relate to export financing.

Summing up, the companies need to know the main features of export and import strategies, the types of export intermediaries available, export financing, price, payment methods, financing receivables and methods of counter trade. Furthermore, for large companies export becomes imperative because large companies must export for increasing sales.

Collaborative Plans

Company getting into global business has to select the method of going overseas like exporting, joint ventures, franchising or forming a fully owned subsidiary. The decision would depend on the company's own experience, competitive factors, political, economic risks and the assets needed for the business. The choice would be made for the method with the greatest synergy with the company.

The company should understand the following:

The forms of doing global business, licensing, exporting, franchising, management contracts, turnkey operations, besides, the variables which decide the choice of operational method and the problems in managing them in foreign host countries. The host countries may have in place legal restrictions for overseas companies. They may be banning certain alternative methods besides, tax structures, antitrust regulations and limits of remittances of funds like dividends to the home country. The choice could be affected by the cost, external handling may become low in cost as volumes are small and if specialty company has excess capacity.

Variables that affect the choice are experience as greater experience leads to greater involvement. Competition changes the choice factor and the risks as external forms spread the risk and controls as internal handling means more controls and no sharing of profits.

Collaborative Strategies

The companies must understand that if their product meant for host country is complex and with high technology it is better to start marketing the product as sold in the home country. In case the company has got a good base in the host country or the economic standards of home and host countries are alike, the same product would suffice.

The companies have to accept that in the host country it has to offer rights to intangible property like trademarks, patents, copyright as the host country associate has to pay royalty to the company. Technology can be exchanged through cross-licensing, while the reasons for the licensing could be, if the strategic product does not form a part of the company's major product range. The problems featuring licensing procedure are given below.

1. Controls because of non- or low utilization of the licence
2. Poor quality of the product
3. Inviting future competitors
4. Maintenance of secrecy during negotiations before the agreement is signed
5. Determining the type of payment system like, fixed charges or usage based charges, value to give licence as compared to the cost to the company for providing the licence.

Franchisee Arrangement

Companies can offer franchisee arrangement to host country associate company. Franchisee arrangements are specialized forms of licence involving continuous inflow of capital by the franchiser into the host country's franchisee. At times there can be a master franchisee and under him subfranchisees too. The possible problems that face the franchiser are given below.

1. The host country does not accept highly standardized operations in the franchise.
2. If the standardization is of low level, it becomes less attractive in the host country.

Management Contracts

At times companies could get into Management Contracts especially when operations owned have been expropriated or they are in trouble. In such conditions, the host country gets technical as well as managerial expertise without the use of Foreign Direct Investment. The company can get out of the risk areas by joining hands with an insider, but knowing fully well that the insider could become a competitor.

Turnkey Operations

Construction companies in most of the cases use the turnkey operations. The contracts start with feasibility studies, and followed by study for means of protecting the contractor and the final bill is paid on satisfactory completion of the operations.

Summarizing the types of FDIs comprise the licensing, franchising, management contracts, and turnkey and the contract agreements, with equity participation, with or without controls.

Companies can obtain foreign technology by creating a monitoring unit for scanning the journals, databases. They can contract the research organizations and even start research projects with both foreign and local companies. They can establish their R&D operations in foreign countries taking their infrastructure and trained manpower.

Companies can plan global operations taking advantage of collaborative strategies with ownership shared with the host country companies. Such shared ownerships help with the advantages of better control of foreign operations and profits while the main disadvantages are the conflicts with local stockholders regarding payment of dividend and public disclosures on the company's activities. Shared ownership can be considered for quick expansion geographically besides spreading the research cost over larger base of sales. It helps in having the resources of both the companies complement each other. A cash rich company complements well with a technology rich company. In some cases, the shared ownership could be legal condition of entering a country. The company could have a larger voice in management of shared ownership due to its better brand equity. Companies can use equity as a control mechanism in shared ownership if remaining ownership is widespread and fragmented and voting rights stay with a particular class of shareholders. Joint venture's success depends on the compatibility of the sharing partners.

Foreign Contracts Management

The best way to manage the foreign contracts is to continuously monitor the performance besides understanding if the operation is ripe enough for takeover. The other important areas are resolution of conflicts and the disputes arising out of the contract.

Summing up, the companies have to employ different methods for different countries and for different products as the diversity increases; the task of managing and coordinating it becomes arduous and complex. Besides, working on collaborative strategies, the company has to include variables to be understood before selecting the operational form, the legal conditions, costs, competition, risks and problems associated with controls. The important forms of operation are licensing, franchising management contracts, joint ventures, turnkey operations besides wholly owned subsidiaries. Sometimes conflicts and disputes arise causing problems in managing the foreign operations.

The company has to decide regarding the proportion of resources it wants to offer to home management and to overseas operations. In this way, the company may have to plan separate types of forms in reference to internal and external activities and their handling by the company. The final choice of the form to be used in overseas operations should be based on company's corporate objectives. However, the choice involves trade-offs between the company's objectives.

Global Business Controls

The companies involved in global business have to understand the methods of controls in order to achieve their objectives. These controls should focus on planning, implementation, evaluation and modification or correction of strategies for achieving to the goals. Organizational structure and its culture help in making controls and success easy to achieve. They should lean the planning loop and complex possible organizational structures. They should decide the decision-making levels; centralized or decentralized location for making decisions.

Planning Loop

Companies have to intertwine the objectives with internal and external constraints. They should then assert the vision, mission, goals and objectives—the strategic intents. They should plan their strategies, implement them, place the control points in place and take suitable corrective actions when they miss out on their objectives in the given time frame.

The planning loop should focus on an analysis of the company's corporate resources, besides setting up the global corporate objectives. Next the host country's business general environments should be understood and analyzed by knowing the following factors as they have impact on the business.

1. Demographics
2. Social
3. Cultural
4. Political

5. Legal
6. Macroeconomics
7. Technology
8. Global

Besides, the company should understand the host country's competitive environment as applied to its products with the help of Michael Porter's 5 Force Model.

Next, the company should look for alternative strategies and then select the optimum strategy for best results in achieving the objectives. It should be followed with implementation plans and control points to check aberrations and errors in time to nip them in the bud. This would lead to reanalysis of the resource deployment and corrections in the same if needed.

The company should define the level of foreign operations and their relative importance for the company. Naturally, the more important operations would need higher management support and hence should have higher levels reporting by the foreign operations. They can plan to have a separate global division for the host country. The company can go for product or geographic grouping structure, within the functional home base structure. The company can plan on matrix structure with reporting to product, geographic and functional operations. The structure could be a hierarchy base one or of some equals working together for the common goals.

Decision-making Location

Centralized decision-making is usually through the top management of the home country. Most companies, however, have neither centralized nor totally decentralized decision levels. The selection of decision levels is based on the distance factor, levels of communication technology in the host country and the efficiency factors. The centralized decision level is preferred in case the movement of goods is global, where decisions must be made quickly and standardization is the key to success. In such cases the global competitive position takes precedence over country-by-country competitive position of the company.

Centralized decisions are preferred where the host country's conditions are similar to the conditions in the home country; the product is uniform and the decisions have far reaching importance for the company. However, it must be taken into consideration that centralized decision level may hurt the host country managers as they are then rendered as just implementers of the decisions with no role in making them and therefore can become a major de-motivating factor.

The level of decision-making should depend on the competence of individuals, the cost of wrong decisions the company has to pay at each level and the impact of the decisions on the company's performance in its totality.

Control Mechanism

Companies face difficulties in setting up the control systems, as the corporate culture of host subsidiary or joint venture could be quite different from the home country culture.

The timelines of reports is an important facet of the controls. Besides there can be the following problems the companies face planning for controls in the global business:

1. The difference in the standard operating ratios in different countries for comparing with the budget figures
2. Evaluation required for both the operating results as well as the host country managers, as some factors would be beyond their control.
3. Host country's companies that have been acquired may have managers with high level of autonomy in their operations.
4. Local controls may be difficult to remove when changing from multi-domestic to global strategy.

Besides the above there can be special situations needing a different planning process for the controls as given below.

1. Where the legal provisions and liabilities and taxation are different for subsidiaries and own branch offices.
2. Shared ownership with a company from the host country can create problems in deciding about control yardsticks and control points
3. The duality of operating forms, one for equity and the other of non-equity based would create special control problems.

Summing up, in the global business, controls are more difficult due to the following factors:

1. Geographic distances
2. Cultural diversities
3. Having different strategies for different countries in which the company is operating
4. Greater areas of uncontrolled areas
5. Problems of getting the right data
6. Rapid changes in both the general and competitive business environments.

Summarizing, the Planning Loop defines the company's strategic intents, its resources and their utilization, alternative choices of going for centralized or decentralized controls and decision levels.

CHAPTER

9

Strategies for Global Human Resource Management

Let us look at the present-day organization chart of some prominent firms

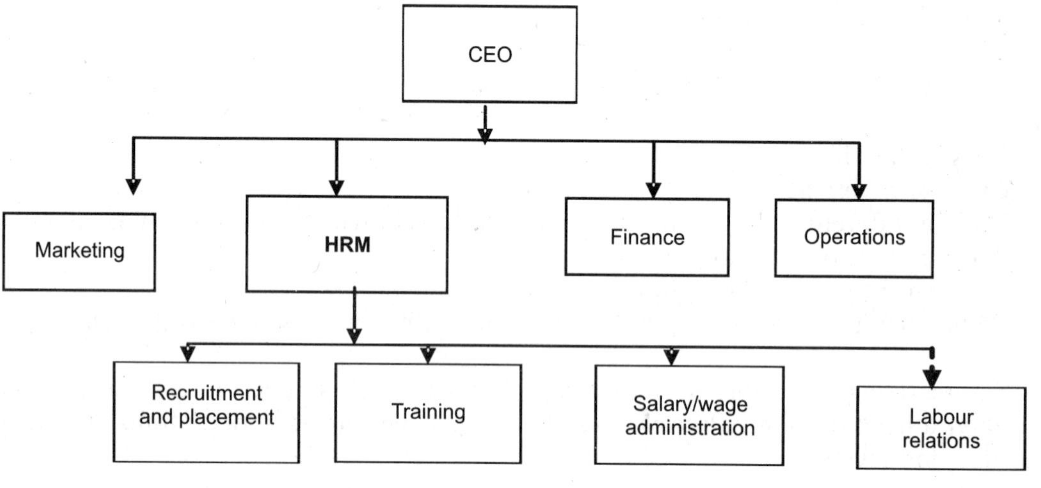

The CEO heads the organization and the departmental heads report to him, one of them being the head of HRD. The functions of HR are recruitment of staff, both white and blue collared. With the realization of the firms' dependence on successful functioning of the personnel, the firms have started giving HR function the importance due to it.

Deb Bilak of Buck Consultants says the following about the increasing importance of Human Resource Management in business, "HR people need to be involved with the pulse of the organization and the marketplace, and determine how they can influence the proper use of retention bonuses. Management might not be thinking about these things always."

Global Business Alternatives

In the global business there are a number of variations as given below.

- Home country has the global headquarters, with regional offices at the host country or countries.
- There can be marketing or outsourcing operations in third countries, which would need offices there.
- The HR activities could be centralized or given to the host country's management.
- In most cases, the senior or key persons are selected centrally at the home country and deployed in other countries
- These recruits could be from either the home country, host country or even a third country, depending on the requirements or specific needs of the person.

HRD Activities

Normal activities in a HRD are given below.

1. Recruitment of managers, supervisors, workers for each of the functional areas like, marketing, finance, operations, HR, legal and technical, e.g., R&D.
2. Training of the recruited staff
3. Staff positioning, depending on work needs and norms established on performance output
4. Performance reviews of the staff
5. Salary and wage management
6. Leave records and leave rules for the various categories of staff
7. Career planning, increments and promotions
8. Disciplinary actions as and when needed against the erring staff member
9. Administrative functions and record keeping
10. In the 21st century, the role of HR has widened, as the HR director is part of the top management decision group.

The HR function differs in the global arena because even a simple error overseas can become disastrous for the firm. Therefore of topmost importance is the recruitment of the right person for any given job.

Suitability Criteria for Staff

The following criteria are used to decide the suitability of the candidates:

1. Age
2. Qualifications
3. Technical skills required for the job
4. Experience in similar jobs
5. Experience of working in the host country
6. Knowledge of host country's language, culture, work norms, ethical standards
7. Candidate's own ethical standards (difficult to assess, should go by the previous employers' references)

8. Experience of any global work
9. Capacity for concentrated efforts for results
10. Capacity and ability for team work: This would include forming teams with home country employees, host country and even third country employees.

Country's Knowledge

For senior positions, knowledge of the following areas would be necessary:

1. Global host country's tax laws taxation period (January-December, or April -March like in India)
2. Host country's monetary system
3. Host country's borrowing interest rates
4. Host country's labour laws
5. Host country's laws relating to expatriates, their income tax, home leave payments
6. Education system for the children of home country's expatriates
7. Infrastructure, logistics and communication systems of the host country
8. Host country's language (could be optional in case of otherwise qualified candidate, because in most countries now English is spoken and understood at least in business dealings.) English has become the business language of the world
9. Host country's currency, its fluctuations and its parity with home country currency and with the US Dollar
10. Norms for Visa, work permits, travel within the host country and outside
11. Housing, weather, availability of essential items for daily needs (in ITI Mankapur near Gonda in UP the Alcatel France staff had to get even their food stuff flown in on a weekly basis from France)
12. Yardstick for paying salary and wages to employees
13. Medical facilities near the workplace and their costs
14. Insurance plans including accident insurance and medical insurance available in the host country
15. The governmental interference in business, recruitment, functioning of the firm
16. Ethical norms in the host government: The firm must have a policy of dealing with this phenomenon as steering away from the right path could prove to be very expensive to the firm.
17. Parity of salary with host country managers, could be difficult to achieve as the home country managers would get overseas allowances, education allowances, home leave payments, which would not be applicable to host country managers.

The firm has to understand that in another country the personal life of an employee gets disturbed and for this the employee has to be compensated with paid home leave and other benefits, like looking after the children's education, health if they are staying in the home country.

On the flip side, the salaries and perks given to the home country expatriates can become a sore point for the host country employees. Even technicians coming to India from affluent nations get far more pay than even the top managers of India do. Junior managers from the western countries come and stay in five star hotels, while even the middle level managers of the host country (India) cannot afford to stay there.

Most MNCs have training-cum-orientation programme for the managers being located in other countries, where the areas concerning the culture of the country, its language, currency, schooling, medical facilities are covered.

When the firms start global business, they place their own country's managers in place in the other countries. Gradually as the local managers learn the ways of the home country firm, local managers replace the expatriates. They prove to be more effective as they know the country well, as also they are lower in cost to the firm.

At times the home country managers are unable to perform in the host country, which leads to negative results for the firm and the losses are much more in size than the losses firms get in local markets. Additionally, once the firm loses its grip on the market it is difficult, time-consuming and expensive to regain the position globally.

Initially a lot of software export from India was in the shape of human beings; the software engineers were relocated from India to the USA, where they developed the software for the American firms. Thus, the American firms were able to get the best software people at a fraction of the cost of local American engineers. This resulted in lesser jobs for the local engineers. The government of USA had to force these firms in paying the expatriates the same salaries, as the locals would get. This stopped the body shopping from India and the result was that the same software got developed in India and was exported from here.

Summarizing the status of HR in today's business, we find the following:

1. Sending staff and managers from home country can be problematic due to different labour laws, economic differences, cultural variance. For specific skills people are sent before the host country persons can be trained in those skills.
2. Salary and wage can be different as also the productivity levels and norms
3. Working styles differ in most countries, which could result in friction between the home country management and the host country management
4. Host country priority with the home country top management.

To overcome these problems, most firms organize special training and orientation programmes before the employee is sent to the host country. The firms then try to locate the local talent, train them in the special skills and finally these people replace the expatriates. The local manager, if selected with care brings about economy (because he comes cheaper than his home country counterpart), can be more efficient as he knows the local conditions better.

The global organization of firms are shown in the chart given below.

CEO

|

Home Country Operations- Marketing-HRM, Finance, Operations, Legal

|

Host Country Management Country A, B, C— —N

The home country managers select the persons who manage the host country's operations and therefore report to them. The relationship between the two needs to be clearly delineated to enable the working plans; policies and methods are adopted from the general managerial ethos of the host country. The home country's 7 S model, containing—Style, Staffing, Systems, Structure, Strategy, Shared Values and Skills—may not be totally appropriate in the host country and the local management must be empowered to modify the model to suit the local conditions.

Home country management usually sends its best persons to look after their global operations. This helps the firm in establishing itself in the new environs quickly and well. These expatriates are more than welcome by the home country management and they usually get higher status on return as a reward for the good job done in the host country. Top managers in the home country watch each and every step taken by the managers posted in host countries. At times written guarantees are given to those posted out of permanency of their jobs in the home country operations.

7 S Model

7 S Model needs to be studied with reference to the differences and similarities of the 7Ss, in the home and the host country as follows:

Shared Values, Style, Staffing, Systems, Structure, Strategy, and Skills

Shared values are the higher level ideals, which the firm's promoters inculcate in the firm's employees. These values reflect the business ethics, work culture and human issues like, not just the medical benefits but much beyond that, taking hold of the sick employee or his kin for the best possible treatment, under any circumstances.

The divergence of shared values between the home country business and that of the host country business ethos needs to be fully understood and a bridge needs to be provided for spanning the gap. If home country business believes in age as hierarchy in promotions and the host country believes only in merit as the promotion criteria, a balance should be created to cover the divergence, like giving due weightage to age while taking merit points into account for promotions.

Style: Firms have work style differences as one firm could employ hands on training while other firm could give classroom training. One CEO could be friendly even with junior managers and other aloof. These differences can make or break a firm in another country, as the values—cultural and ethical do not span across countries.

Staffing: Some firms believe in promoting people from within the organization while others recruit from outside. In another country, outside could mean even from a third country. This works well if the business milieu of the host country is understood well.

Systems: It is said that in firms people do not work, it is the systems that work. There are the following types of systems in a firm:

1. Resourcing systems—human resource, finance and information resource systems
2. Accounting systems
3. Recruitment systems

4. Reporting systems
5. Control systems

In resource systems, the entire business dynamics comes into play, including the resourcefulness of the business promoter.

Accounting systems can vary from country to country and most firms working overseas like to maintain two sets of accounting records, one for the home country and the other for the host country, which should be in line with the practices followed in that country.

Recruitment of local staff should normally follow the pattern associated with the host country.

Reporting systems should be of two types, one for the home country reporting and the other for the host country.

Control system normally follows the firms' own systems as the entire success of overseas operations depend largely on this system. Control system delegates authority with accountability to the managers with catch points to ensure that they do not go berserk with power.

Structure: Organizational structure wields a great deal of influence on the firm's outcome. The hierarchy-based structure is accepted worldwide and yet flat organizations with lower levels of decision-making have become quite common. Virtual organizations and networking are also in the picture as firms are resorting to outsource a lot of their products, assemblies, sub-assemblies to cut down on costs. Global business has to accept the norms of the host country initially till they are ready to innovate and become more compact, streamlined and effective.

Strategy: The firms' strategies can be defined as its plans and policies and the action it takes in line with these plans and policies. As the business environment of countries is never the same, the plans and policies of one country would need to be suitably modified for them to succeed in another country.

Skills of a firm are part of its core competencies, as some firm may be good in electronics and the other in microbiology, while a third one in marketing. The home country skills need to be fine-tuned to be of significance in the host country.

It is only after a study has been made and the 7S scrutinized in all their dimensions can one hope for success in an alien land.

Global Information Exchange

As there is a physical distance between the home and the host countries, it is important to have good channels of information flow. While Internet, Fax, videoconferencing are available in several countries, the communication between the two countries must be clear, fast and confidential. In one country, leased telephone lines can be available. Similar facilities are needed globally too.

Home office has to communicate the policy matters, new product launches, promotional plans, all of which would be extremely useful to the competing firms. Therefore, confidentiality of communication is of utmost importance.

In several countries the language is not English, which makes communicating with them a lot more difficult. Business English has its own subtleties, besides some common-use words. It is a good idea to learn these terms.

Many firms keep their foreign subsidiaries in tune with the home office plans and policies and for this purpose they publish a newsletter giving an expose of their plans.

Translations in local languages can be a tricky problem as literal translation can rob the meaning from the matter. Only experts in both the languages can do a proper translation work and then it is worth the effort.

With the capital and technology flow worldwide, it is imperative that the Human Resources are kept on top priority for gaining and maintaining excellence in overseas operations.

Summary

Expatriate managers have the following tasks to perform in the host countries:

- Managing in host country with home country's expertise in management and with local work culture
- Maintaining technological excellence with local workforce
- Keeping high level government contacts
- Keeping high level of Public Relations through communications, including advertising and publicity.
- Understanding the consumer behaviour, his needs for products and more importantly, associated services and fulfilling the same
- Training and development of local managers, who would eventually take over the reins of the host country operations
- Understanding the business environment of the country, both the general business environment and the competitive business environment and the country's cultural ethos to be able to optimize results

Foreign Direct Investment

Direct investments made by foreign organizations are followed by their control on the concerned business. This becomes a cause for concern for the host government and the people. However, these investments are welcome especially in the developing countries if they bring progress and expansion for the MNC firm and the host country.

While direct investment overseas generally is acquired by transferring capital from one country to another, capital usually is not the only contribution made by the investor or the only means of gaining equity. Firms make direct investment overseas to expand markets by selling abroad or to acquire foreign resources. Firms with foreign investments tend to be more profitable and have more stable sales and earnings.

Direct investment, because of implied control permits firms to make decisions to maximize global performance. It also helps to serve global efficiency; however, countries distort movements by restricting the inward or outward flow, and by giving incentives for firms to locate within their boundaries.

Foreign Exchange

Domestic and global transactions differ in the use of more than one currency for global trade. The special checks and other instruments for making the payments abroad are referred to collectively as foreign exchange. It is important to know to understand the terms and definitions of foreign exchange and how the foreign exchange market operates for immediate and long-term transactions.

A key aspect of exchange of currency is its convertibility. Some governments impose restrictions to control access to foreign exchange, depending on their foreign exchange reserves. Global banking is the means for facilitating the flow of global transactions. It is the link between economies of the world. There is speculation in buying and selling of a commodity where activities contain both an element of risk and chance of huge profits. There is a general belief that currency speculators are destabilizing the world monetary system. Speculators may push the market in the direction it needs to go. In this case, by forcing governments to confront market realities, they may actually be contributing to long-term stability.

It is therefore important to understand how exchange rates are set and why the rates change, would help the MNC managers in making decisions that are dependent on those changes. There are three categories of exchange rate arrangement, according to the IMF, as given below.

1. Fixed rates
2. Limited flexibility
3. More flexible

If the arrangement does not reflect the real position regarding supply and demand of a currency, black market develops for the same. However, the major systems for determining exchange rates are, freely fluctuating rates, managed fixed rates and automatic fixed rates. Rates are affected by inflation, interest rate differentials and technical factors.

Balance of payment statistics, economic fundamentals and technical factors are used to predict exchange rate movements and fluctuates. After the II World War, it was though that a system of fixed exchange rates would help to bring stability and growth to the free world. It was, however, realized later on that system created rigidity rather than stability, and the system was restructured to allow greater exchange rate flexibility.

CHAPTER

10

Global Financial Plans

"It is good to have money, but it is even better to know how to organize it."

It is important to know the capital markets, cash management and financial risks for any company planning global business to help them in organizing finances in different countries. The main tasks of the finance officer of a company are the management of treasury and finance control. The finance function involves acquisition and allocation of financial resources to the company's various activities. The capital structure of a company is built through long-term loans, stocks (shares), and retained earnings. These assume greater importance in the global business due to the country specific factors on finance. The following need the attention of the finance officer in this regard:

1. Foreign exchange risks
2. Currency flows and country specific restrictions
3. Different tax laws and the differences in methods of calculating the taxable income
4. Debt equity ratio (it is finance officer's task to ensure that the company gets the capital at the lowest possible cost).
5. Dividend remission policy

Reliance of long-term debt increases the financial risks requiring higher rate of return for the investors. Foreign operations of companies have lower access to local capital markets making debts acquisition difficult. Local debt market is one of the sources of finance. Companies with access to hard currency find local debt and equity much easier than companies from non-hard currency areas. In such cases companies operating in other country get loans for their operations while host country companies can get loans from home country banks on a back-to-back loan planning.

Global Bonds

Several countries have a bond market for global finance that runs parallel to the domestic bond market, since for global business Global Finance Market is a good source of funds.

Companies can issue bonds in a foreign country to a group of investors. Several developing countries borrow money from global finance market by selling bonds. However, they have to pay a higher rate of interest because of the misperception in such investments from the rich countries.

Global stock exchanges like the American Stock Exchange or the Nasdaq—"National Association of Securities Dealers Automatic Quotation System. Nasdaq Stock Markets are one of the largest for trading stocks. However, for developing countries trading on Nasdaq may be subject to their government's approval.

Dow Jones Analysis group of daily and weekly indices of selected stocks and bond business are used as parameters for doing business in particular stocks. The firms of Standard and Poor indexes and ratios or averages are designed to measure the performance of finance market.

Foreign Bonds, Eurobonds and Global Bonds

Foreign bonds are sold outside the country of the borrowing company and they are in the currency of the country of issue, while the Eurobonds are sold in countries other than the one in whose currency the bond has been made. Global bond is registered in different national markets as per the registration requirements of each market.

Global bonds are useful way of obtaining finances because they help companies to diversify its finance portfolio from local banks and bond market and maturities not usually available in domestic markets.

Financial Centres

These are cities or offshore countries that provide large global currency funds. They offer a low cost source of finance for MNCs. They offer foreign currency like Euro for deposits and loans. At times these are intermediary or pass through markets for global loans. These could be for bringing economic and political stability and operate as efficient, experienced and reliable finance. They have good communication and support services; these could be operational or booking centres. Key offshore finance centres are in Bahrain, the Caribbean, Hong Kong, London, New York, Singapore and Switzerland besides others.

Internal Financing

Companies planning business expansion need to generate some of their own finances besides debt and equity. MNCs have diverse operations in different currencies and that makes the assessment of internal finance availability complex. Parent company can provide the seed capital as its share of equity. Following chart shows how the internal finance system operates.

There are several ways in which the MNCs can use internal cash flow to finance their overseas operations. They have to understand the local and corporate systems and their need for funds. Besides they have to lean the ways in which cash can be taken from associate companies and place in the central pool. After centralizing the cash they have to know its disbursement to various subsidiaries. While dividends are good source

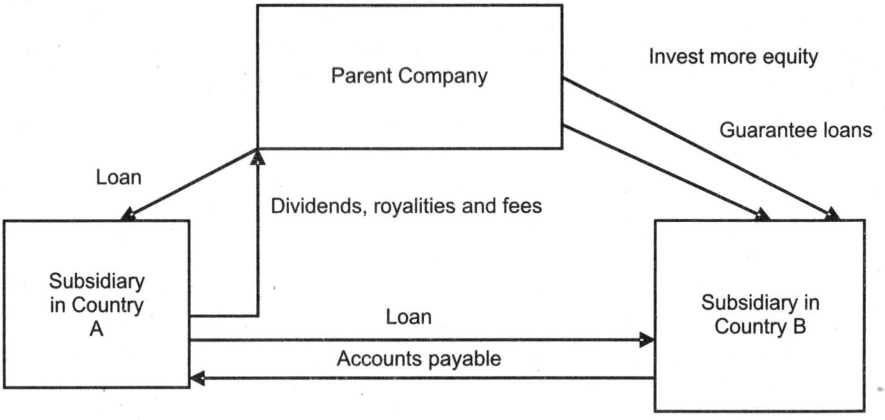

Internal source of working capital.

of inter-company transfer of funds at times the local government may restrict free flow of funds. While setting up cross-currency cash pooling system, several goals can be met like optimum use of funds, reduction in interest expenses while maximizing interest generation, reduction in expensive foreign exchange, swap transactions and inter-company transfers. These minimize paper work and centralize information for strict control, improved decision-making. Multilateral netting allows subsidiaries to transfer net inter-company flows to a cash centre or to a clearing account that disburses cash to net receivers. Coordination centres organize centralization of financial transactions including foreign exchange dealings, pooling and re-invoicing. Besides, they arrange centralization of administration, accounting, data processing and information systems. Advertising, insurance and reinsurance become part of its job, besides planning of other auxiliary services.

Financial Risks

Financial risks normally result from either inflation or currency fluctuations. It is better to understand the type of risk the company has to deal with, in the global finance. The nature of the risk, the conditions in which the risk becomes pronounced and how the company can preempt the avoidance of the risk factor. When the currency of a country becomes weak, or is devalued, inflation comes into play. Import restrictions, control on acquisition of funds, difficulties in getting credit terms and high interest rates all cause inflation. These can cause high levels of bills, receivables and longer credit periods disrupting the cash flow. At times the country's government tries inflation control through artificially established price. Price, as is known remains under the influence of competitive pricing, brand equity, production costs and at times government regulations. However, the company can offer a differentiated product, as a brand extension or in a different package to increase or decrease the price. Operating in high inflation country the company can increase the value of bills, payables, reduce the bills receivable value and invest or repatriate the excess cash generated. Risks arise when receivables or payables change in value due to changes in the exchange rate. When a company is operating in another country, the exchange rate weakening would change the intrinsic value of assets, bank accounts. Exchange fluctuation affects the inflow of foreign currency, imports of raw materials, components and complete built units.

The company needs to protect itself from exchange fluctuations by understanding the quantum of risk involved through an effective control system where detailed information on the fluctuations is available as they occur, and by using hedging strategies. Hedging requires deciding the importance of the different types of risks along with their criticality factor. Hedging would require balancing both assets and liabilities by managing the balance sheet. Besides the company can get into forward exchange contracts and currency options. The company can utilize local debts with local assets. Leads and lags of inter-company payments can be advantageous. If possible both receivables and payables must be paid or collected quickly. Depending on the currency forecasts payment should be made early or delayed to look for the company's advantage. Forward contracts can be used as insurance or currency fluctuations. The company needs to look at the following areas:

1. Payment to home country can be made as licence fees, payment for importing capital goods or materials and as dividends for equity investments.
2. Country's inflation rates must be understood in advance to prevent cash flow problems
3. Repatriation of profits to home country must be properly documented and recognized for maintaining transparency towards the host country's government and for obeying their laws.
4. Sudden exchange fluctuations must be considered as these can change the cash flow as well as the company's competitive position.

Accounting Systems

It is important for the companies in global business to understand the accounting systems for the MNCs as they operate in different countries. Decision process of MNCs starts with having timely and accurate information on the company's accounts and the taxation as prevalent in the host country. It is necessary to know about different currencies and accounting systems. Financial reporting differs in countries both in content and in presentation. The best way is to follow the accounting system according to the host country's established practices; also known as Generally Accepted Accounting Principles or GAAP. Each country's GAAP is different and yet the MNCs have to prepare their accounts in the manner required by the host country and also as per the home country's needs as they have to submit the accounts to the headquarters in the home country as well. Accounting focuses on locating, recording and interpreting economic business equations and therefore the accountant must know the objectives and the purposes of the accounting system. These help in taking investment and credit decisions, cash flow projections and an estimation of company's resources, resource need patterns and their deployment. The Global Accounting Standards Committee (GASC) sets the standards for accounting systems for companies. However, so far no generally accepted system has been finalized. The company's stakeholders like, creditors, investors, employees, suppliers, buyers and the government tax authorities need accounting information. Asset valuation differs from country to country and this is of special interest to investors of the company. Besides, the level of information that can be divulged and in which format is essential to the stakeholders. Normally the annual accounts and the balance sheet is the right platform for giving the information. The financial statement must be in the language understood by the stakeholder readers, must be in their currency, must provide the balance sheet, profit and loss account, cash flow, taxation and bad debts. The format of the statements must be in proper sequence and give readable numbers without any small print to confuse the readers. They must value the investors' viewpoint, as with the global integration of capital markets they need the information. MNCs are looking for capital outside the home country and unless their statements are investor-friendly they cannot get any finance. Foreign currency receivables and payables create plus and minus due to exchange rate fluctuations. The balance sheets must account for the profits and losses in the financial year of the accounting period to be of relevance to the stakeholders especially the investors.

Taxation of the host country defines the location of investments being made, the type of the new company, like a branch or a subsidiary and the method of transfer price to the buyers within the group companies. Some countries get into tax treaties to avoid double taxation by reciprocal reduction on dividend withholding and exemption on royalties and at times on interest payments from any taxation withholding.

MNCs have to take care of inflation rates, exchange rates; currency controls, taxation and duties and host country's requirements as they build their accounting reporting system.

CHAPTER 11

Global Business and the Governments

Host country government has to consider the following before given the green signal to foreign companies to operate in their country:

1. How would it affect their own country's industry and business?
2. How much it affects the rate of unemployment?
3. How far it will damage the growth of new local industries?
4. Will it on the other hand expedite industrialization process?
5. Will it improve country's global competitiveness?
6. Will it let the local industries grow with newer and better technologies?

It must be remembered that before 1991, India was almost a closed economy and it was indeed difficult for foreign companies to get into the country. The licence and clearance for foreign investments were big bottlenecks that foreign players faced while planning entry into India. It also meant that Indian business were finding it difficult to enter global markets. The Indian business was not even overtly interested in going overseas as the local market was increasing with only low level of competition. This lack of competition led to neglect of product quality as whatever was made sold at a profit. Technology upgrades were unheard of, as the customers were not even aware of better quality products and therefore accepted with a sense of fatality whatever was given to them. The case of Ambassador cars is well known. The car makers did nothing to upgrade the car in aesthetics or in technology while the world over better technology and better looking cars were on sale.

Most countries believe that outsiders may force their own businesses to move out, rendering thousands jobless. They forget that such policy can have retaliatory effect too, as other countries can stop the exports of their produce as well. Foreign companies are likely to bring in latest technologies and finance in foreign currency. The new technology may become a catalyst in nurturing countries exports and overseas business. In fact after 1991, India can also boast of a number of multinational companies of its own. With increase in exports countries get better balance of payment situation and it has a snowballing effect on the global business. If the country like India has the advantage of low cost labour, it can become a hub for global manufacture for a number of MNCs. Foreign exchange earnings start accumulating in the country that leads to improve standards of living for the country's population as the GNP goes up. Initially, the country has to provide for lower rates of customs duties, interest rates for borrowings for making it attractive for foreign companies to invest in the country. In India 1991 can be considered the watershed year, as in this year, LPG, liberalization, privatization and globalization of Indian markets and economy took place. Customs duties were reduced making imports interesting for the Indian customers; interest rates and taxation were reduced to make entry into the country more attractive. Besides, the Licence Raj ended and persons desirous of starting business could do so without taking any governmental approvals, as was the case prior to 1991.

With greater FDIs, country witnesses improvement in productivity, and with it demands of goods increases in cities and yet the agriculture may get a setback with less importance being given to it. With free markets emerging, companies plan manufacturing bases in host countries as they use labour at lower cost, lower transportation costs and gain the market. Foreign direct investments (the FDIs), help the host country in obtaining latest technologies, better managerial techniques and help in general improvement in the quality of products. It helps companies to start diversification plans; improvement plans and cost reduction techniques without compromising on product quality, as that is the only way to survive in the competitive market where foreign players are competing with the local ones. Country's buying capacity as imports is dependent on its exports. Low cost of labour in certain countries must be weighed along with the worker productivity to arrive at the true value of labour costs. With foreign technology and FDIs countries plan for sale in the country as well as exports. Several companies need to have foreign hubs for manufacturing outside the home country to cater to distant lands, to save on transportation costs plus making use of available resources like trained manpower, raw materials, infrastructure and low cost capital. Export restrictions may keep up the world price. Companies can find substitute products in the local market and keep the domestic prices low, while import restrictions can help the local manufacturers and avoid dumping by high volume low cost foreign manufacturers. At times foreign players are obliged to alter their terms of business including price reduction to make their products attractive despite the restrictions for importing.

Countries like to keep the manufacture of essential items within the local companies like the defence production. They can thus avoid their products from getting into countries not in favour and it helps in effectively creating their area of influence in the geographic areas. In times of crises like wars, such units become most useful. It is, therefore, important to define the essential industries to be kept strictly for local companies. Countries create their sphere of influence by offering technology, FDIs, aids and assigning some countries the MFN Most Favoured Nation status and finally regional economic zones.

Regional Economic Zones

The years from 1950 to 1960 can be considered a significant period for the major changes taking place in the world economics. Instead of competing nations, groups of countries formed economic zones to fight competition with those outside the zone, while the movement of goods within the zone became like that of movement within a country. Mostly geographic proximity was the cementing force for such zones. Beside, the consumer preferences, tastes were similar and physical movement of products was easy. At times common heritage, history, and societal norms were not very different. These zones offered inter-country trade with no tariff within; common external tariff and common economic growth plans. Monetary policies were made common to operate a rational economic base. These common zones had their impact on the political, economic and social systems of the countries. This resulted in transfer of resources from less efficient to more efficient producers of goods. However, in case of competition from outside the group, even less efficient producer was favoured to the outsider. With greater market potential in the zones, producers could reduce cost of unit manufacture through economies of scales and thus they became more competitive even outside the zones too. The zones are ready to follow WTO norms as well. The regional groups can be categorized as given below.

1. Free trade areas
2. Customs unions
3. Common market

European Union

The union has been planned to remove restrictions in free flow of goods, money and people. The union allows for standardization of economic policies among the concerned nations, besides planning a common external tariff. There is also a common transport policy in the union in 1962, the common agricultural policy was framed to promote proper earnings to producers and availability of food to the consumers. The European Commission starts the proposals for legislation, manages the compliances of treaties and implements the Union's policies. The European parliament is empowered to make the laws, look after the budgetary audits besides overseeing the implementation by the executive bodies of the countries. The parliament along with the Council for the union has the final authority in matters connected with the union. The union was not totally accepted as it created doubts about centralization of power, problems with new tax structure, shift of jobs and setback to small companies. It could result in competition becoming severe due to removal of barriers and due to companies going to enlarge their size with acquisitions and mergers for facing Japanese competition.

NAFTA or North American Free Trade Agreement

Since the US is the largest trading partner of Canada and Mexico, NAFTA was the logical extension of their informal union. It requires removal of all types of trade barriers, both tariff and non-tariff. It also requires liberalization on foreign investments. To get

lower rate of tariff, the goods must be from the North America. The local content must be 50% of the price. There is provision for safeguarding the Intellectual Property Rights of member countries and environment. Most trade between the US and Canada is free of any duty. NAFTA endorses conservation and protection of human health, the environment, encourages cooperation in these areas and organizes the spread of information on these areas. Trade between Canada and Mexico is relatively low and yet it is growing. NAFTA is meant to eliminate both tariff and non-tariff barriers between its partner countries. It streamlines the trade rules and regulations and looks at removing the restrictions on foreign investments. The population of the three countries is in the proportion of 1: 3: 8, starting with Canada, then Mexico and finally the US. Per capita income is roughly as given below.
Canada \$20 000
Mexico \$4000
USA \$26000

NAFTA believes in getting exporters specify the country of origin, as there is no common tariff between the countries. They want 50% of the product must be from the country of origin except in case of automobiles where it should be 62.5%. NAFTA provides for duty free imports and exports, protection of environment with a built-in provision in the commercial dealings, clear definition for investments between the countries and has built-in mechanism for settlement of disputes among the countries. This has resulted in having most trade between the US and Canada duty-free and it has kept the tariff between the US and Mexico mostly low.

Latin America

The countries of Latin America are keen to expand their markets. They are mostly targeting the US for their exports. The major Latin American trade group is the MERCOSUR. There is a plan to have linkage between the trading groups of the two Americas. MERCOSUR is meant to provide free trade access between the member countries.

ASEAN (Association of South-East Asian Nations) is a major free trade area in Asia.

Similarly, in Africa too, the following organizations have been formed for cooperation in trade:

1. Economic community of West African states
2. Organization of African unity
3. South African development community

Commodity agreements are meant to strengthen economic cooperation in stabilizing product supplies and increasing prices whenever required. These prices keep changing due to the changes taking place in supply and demand equations. The price changes can alter the exporting country's earnings, with demand shifts and price elasticity of demand. Countries can avoid these situations by keeping buffer stocks and having quota system for exports. These buffer stocks can be sold at prefixed prices. The commodity agreements become successful in the following manner:

1. Cooperation between the producer and the buyer
2. Strength of the producer
3. Commodity itself

OPEC

It is the Organization of Petroleum Exporting Countries, with Algeria, Gabon, Indonesia, Iran, Iraq, Kuwait, Libya, Nigeria, Qatar, Saudi Arabia, the UAE, and Venezuela as its members. The OPEC works taking into consideration the political and economic conditions of member countries, non-OPEC oil supplies, substitute products, demand and supply conditions, energy conservation policies of the governments.

SUMMARY

In the middle of the 20th century, regional economic cooperation idea started emerging. It started with having free trade areas, where there was no tariff discrimination. The cooperation between nations affected in a positive manner with more efficient resource allocation, production and reach to the consumer. Removal of protective regime helps the MNCs to operate on the basis of comparative advantage. EU, NAFTA, MERCOSUR are formed on the premise of regional cooperation. ASEAN has been formed for evolving economic cooperation in Asia SAARC has been on the fringe so far towards South Asia economic cooperation and it needs far more acceptance of individual member nations of the theory of regional coordination despite other political differences. Developing countries base their global business on commodity exports to augment their hard currency bank needed for their developmental activities.

CHAPTER 12

Global Investments

Making investments in other countries has become an important part of global strategies of companies wanting to conduct global business. Global investments have a direct effect on the economy of host country. Companies have to decide on the countries they should invest. They can also take to granting licence or making franchisees to start global business. Investors operating overseas try to get controlling interests that help them in happily giving the latest technology and other management assets. The companies making investments also do so on lower costs and with greater speed. The companies have to understand that the host country's unit would ultimately become their competitor in the world market. However, companies owning majority shares would consider the host country unit as their extension that helps in reducing time and transportation costs to the nearby markets. The host unit normally has a common corporate culture with the home organization. They run the unit with their own personnel who understand the company's objectives. Foreign Direct Investments (FDIs) are basic methods with which companies acquire other host country units.

Investors have two options, one, exporting finished goods on credit and second to invest in manufacturing facilities in the host countries. The impetus for investment comes from the demand and supply situation in the host country. The comparative costs in manufacturing like availability of lower cost labour; raw materials and host country's infrastructure are important parameters for making investment decisions. FDIs are meant as tools for the investing company for increasing their sales, or acquiring assets and reducing competition risks.

Investments are made when the cost of sending finished goods is high and the host country production capacity is not able to meet the demand. Investments are made outside when increase in production in the home country does not bring the requisite benefits of production scale. At times there are restrictions in host country for importing the products and it becomes imperative to make them. Investments can be made if the production costs are low in the host country. Other reason for investment comes from organizing vertical integration through the host country acquisitions where product rationalization can take place to suit the company. At times the host country's government offers investment incentives that can be made more attractive with low cost resources, labour and materials. Increase in customers and suppliers are the direct result of the investments. Host country manufacture can also help in fighting competition with other foreign players that manufacture outside the host country. Local manufacture competition is met with better management of resources, lower variable costs and better technology products.

As companies reach the economies of scale they can export large quantities with lower landed costs as they amortize the total costs over larger volumes. When companies have to use small-scale production, then it is better to have host country production bases as these reduce the transportation costs drastically. If imports are restricted by the host country, companies resort to local production to serve the host country markets. Depending on demand they can obtain economies of scale through local manufacture too. At times customers prefer locally made products due to national spirit, with better chances of faster service facilities and shorter delivery time. Home country advantage in costs leads to exports in several companies. These lower costs are the result of low cost manufacturing factors, company's size, transport costs and the productivity factor. As these areas keep changing the location advantage too keep shifting. In vertical integration of global business source of raw material, manufacturing base and the market could be in different countries. These integrations are usually supply chain oriented.

Companies go for acquisitions for vertical integration in the host country as it saves them the star uptime and it does not add extra capacity or competition in the market. However, if acquiring local companies is not possible they may set-up manufacturing unit in the host country.

Local successful companies are the ones that invest overseas. Such investments make the companies more successful even in the home country. FDIs are happening more in the developed countries as they have bigger markets, low risks and no discrimination against foreign companies.

Summarizing, it can be said that FDIs help companies in controlling the companies in a different country. The host country is apprehensive about the controls. Investments can be made via transfer of technology, equipment, personnel or even markets. Companies have to decide the economics of sale of goods through exports as against setting up production facilities overseas. FDIs help in gaining larger markets, acquiring resources, obtain access to raw materials or finished products. Outside production can be organized in more than one country with some components being made in one country and some others in different country, while the final assembly may take place at some other place.

Foreign Exchange

Foreign exchange covers the currencies and other instruments of payment denominated in currencies. Exchange rate is the number of units of one currency required to obtain one unit of another currency. Exchange rate transactions are done by commercial banks.

The world foreign exchange daily volume was $1.26 trillion in April 1995. At times a swap meaning the exchange of currencies is done with an agreement that it will be reversed in future. An option is the right but not an obligation to trade foreign currency at a fixed exchange rate. Futures contract fixes the exchange rate in advance and it is not as flexible as a forward contract. Trading in foreign exchange is happening twenty-four hours a day. The US dollar is the most widely used currency in the world for global trade. The foreign exchange market operates as given below.

Foreign Exchange Market

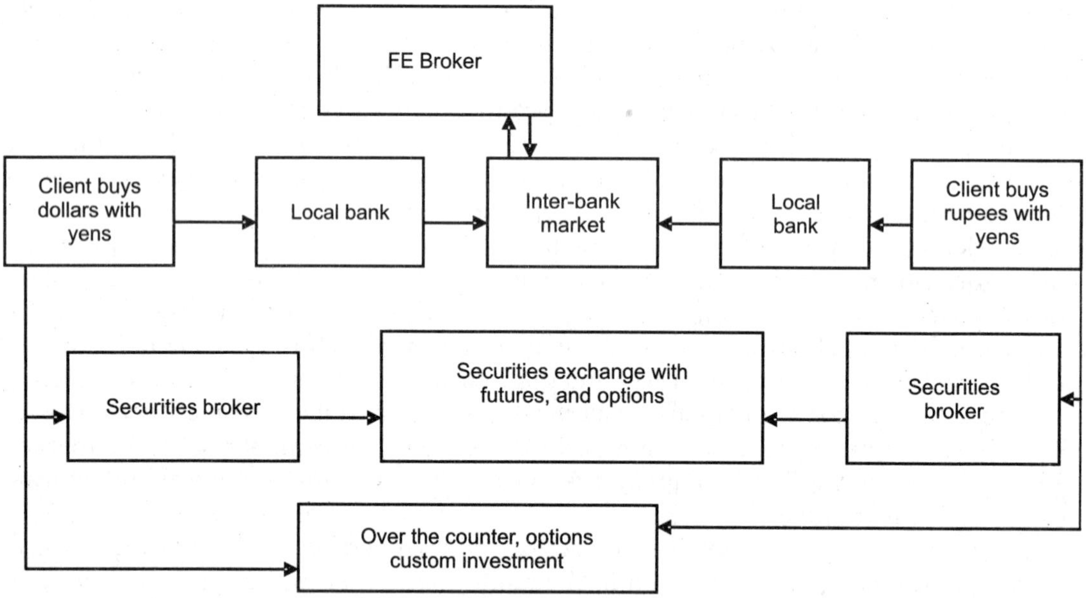

A company wanting to exchange currency has to work with a bank, a stockbroker on a securities exchange or an investment banker in the over-the-counter market.

Both residents and non-residents of a country can exchange convertible currencies. Hard currencies are fully convertible, strong and reliable. Commercial banks collect the foreign exchange and buy and sell the same.

Following are the three categories of exchange rate organization as per IMF.

1. Pegged exchange rate
2. Limited flexibility arrangement
3. More flexible arrangement

A country fixes the value of its currency to another currency or a basket of currencies in case of pegged exchange rate. In case of limited flexibility it could be either limited for a single currency or limited through cooperative arrangements. When the currency is totally floating as per supply demand ratio or because of frequent changes in currency's value it qualifies as more flexible arrangement. Black market emerges that follows the actual supply-demand situation of a currency. Demand for a country's goods, services and financial assets create the demand of that country's currency. At times the country's government buys and sells its currency in the open market to influence its price. Currencies are devalued and revalued by the governments when they alter their values in comparison to the currency of another country. The strength of country's currency depends on the rate of inflation as compared to the rate of inflation of the other country. With lower rate of inflation the country's currency would be comparatively stronger. The formula relating exchange rate to inflation is calculated taking into account. The exchange in terms of number of units of the domestic currency for one unit of foreign currency and the rate of inflation and the defining time periods. Interest rates of two countries are also defined as per the rate of inflation as the nominal interest rate in one country is lower than that in another country, the first country's inflation rate would be lower so that the real interest rates are equal. Exchange rate get affect with the confidence levels of countries and technical factors like availability of economic information about the countries.

Foreign exchange value assessment is crucial for global business and their forecasting is done on the basis of economic trends both the historical and the present trends. With the change in exchange rates companies have to view their existing price structure.

CHAPTER

13

Global Outsourcing: Collaborations and Controls

Organizing global business can be achieved in many ways, where the company could own the production and yet it could be either in home country or in the host country. If the production base is in the home country, then the global business is conducted by exporting goods to the host country. At the next level, the company can buy equity shares in host country's running company, which could be a wholly owned subsidiary, or partially owned unit or a joint venture. There can be no equity based arrangements like giving manufacturing licence to the host country's company, offering franchisee operations or just having management contracts or at times turnkey operations as given below.

Production at	Home country	Host country
	Exporting	1. Wholly owned operations 2. Partially owned with the balance widely held 3. Joint ventures 4. Equity alliances

Non-equity based arrangements in the host country are as follows:

Non-equity based arrangements	1. Licensing 2. Franchising 3. Management contracts 4. Turnkey operations

Companies like MacDonald's have franchisee operations within their home country; the US and have used the same method in their overseas ventures as well. At other times companies find it cheaper to get another company to handle their operations, especially if the operations are on a low scale and the franchisee company has excess capacity in production, manpower. Companies use strategic alliances to fulfil their global objectives.

Global Objectives

Company's global objectives can be surmised as given below.

1. Increase in sales volumes through geographic expansion
2. Acquiring new resources
3. Diversification, both vertical and horizontal
4. Reducing the risk of competitive actions

Each company has its core competencies and at times some products do not fit in the company's strategic plans. Such products can be given out through licensing to others, both in the country and outside. Companies may find the demand in one country not enough to justify its entry as other companies are also trying to get in there. Siemens of Germany and GEC of England joined hands to form GPT to operate in some other countries like India. Vertical integration helps in cost savings, while it needs to have resources and finances to manage complete value chain. However, these joint ventures may become difficult if the host country's government has placed legal entry barriers for the company. Some countries may have problems in foreign operating companies repatriation of profits earned in the host country. If legally permitted the collaborations can gain competitive advantage because of their size, economies of scale, technology, brand equity and better control of channels of distribution.

Collaboration Agreements

The collaboration types depend on the company's outlay allotted to its foreign operations and therefore there are trade-offs needed in some cases. Licensing would need lower foreign resource commitment than joint venture. If the level of competition is less, it would greater freedom for the choice of entry base in the global business. If the home country office of the company handles the affairs, it would amount to greater degree of control and no profit allocation to foreign unit.

Licensing agreements give rights to the licensees for a given period against payment of royalty to the licenser by the licensee. Patents, inventions process of manufacture is provided through licence agreements. Besides the licensee has the copyrights on the intellectual property like literary, musical or graphic designs. Licensee has access to methods, procedures, systems of the licenser. This helps the company to enter a market quickly at lower costs. Licensing agreements can have provisions for restricting the licensee on markets including exports, exclusivity of licence, production value limits, quality standards maintenance. There can be restrictions from the governments of both the countries, one of licenser and the other licensee. Level of competition can be the deciding factor too. In high technology products company has to assess the possibility of host country company's ability to absorb the technology.

Franchisee agreements differs as they provide for the use of trademarks of the licenser and continued update of technology and other assets. Franchisers try to ensure standardized products besides management systems. However, at times, these do not get the right reception in the host country. MacDonald's had to eschew the beef product line in India and redesign some of their products with local flavour.

Management contracts are made when the host country company is not able to manage efficiently and invites a foreign company to takeover its management. Turnkey operations are usually made by construction firms like the Japanese company that took up building the bridge on Yamuna River in Delhi.

Joint ventures need not be equal equity partnership. It could be formed with two companies from the same country join hands to form a joint venture to operate in another country. Long ago ESSO and Mobil had made joint venture known as Standard Vacuum Oil Company to operate in India and elsewhere. Foreign companies can join hands with a local company to enter the country like Daewoo joined hands with the DCM group to set up Daewoo motors. Before that DCM had a joint venture with Toyota Motor Company. Some companies can just take minority shareholding in the host country company to get a foothold for testing the markets before embarking on full-fledged operations.

Joint ventures are not always successful; as the partners do not give equal importance to the venture, have different objectives for it. At times they do not provide the venture with the required resources, directions and try to extract maximum benefits even when finances do not allow it. Cultural differences are hindrances in smooth running of joint ventures. Only with experience can the joint venture partners learn to evolve a separate operating method and organizational culture acceptable to both partners.

Global Business Controls

Major decisions taken by companies going overseas are the following:
1. Locations where decisions are to be made
2. Methods of gaining global competitive advantage
3. Reporting systems between home office and field offices in the host countries

Control on foreign offices is difficult due to the distance involved between these and the home office as communication and travel becomes expensive and time-consuming. When a company deals with several countries it has to understand the diversities of culture, economic levels, consumer behaviour between them. Besides, the host country's government formulates laws that support the local business. There are stockholders from the host country that have their own agenda. The business environment keeps changing rather rapidly in host countries for the company to be able to formulate a standard long-term plan. However, most globally operating companies use the following control process in their operations:
1. Country specific organizational structure
2. Levels of decision-making
3. Planning to include the control points and reporting systems
4. Special country specific areas

Controls are made by comparing the actual situations with the preplanned objectives on areas like sales, increases, and higher markups, amortizing fixed costs on larger volumes. Controls can be kept on resource acquisitions as the direct costs are reduced, tax advantages are gained, and complementary resources are acquired too. Objectives like diversification of markets and products can be seen from the control viewpoint. Objectives like reducing competitive strengths by obtaining the much-needed resources and depriving competition of the same.

Company's resources like cash flow needs for the present and in future need to be understood and compared for controlling the same. Profit and dividend plans, availability of capital and strength for borrowing additional capital are areas of study and control.

Company has to keep assessing the employees' general and product specific skills, special abilities, cross-functional operational ability, attitude for foreign operations, besides their ability for obtaining additional resources when needed and utilization of manufacturing capacity.

Company has to look for the adoption needed in products for the global markets, primary and secondary demands, full utilization of capacity, cost reduction through economies of scale and transport situation.

Company has to understand the business environment and its effect on areas like supply and costs in foreign trade demand patterns and cycles market share of competitors and the attitude of the society on the products.

Company has to understand the local tax laws, receivables and payables situation, meaning the credit to be allowed to buyers and the credit being given by the suppliers. Besides, the company should know if the buyers or the suppliers need to be financed. The host country government may also have their plans for fund usage, like a per cent to be spent on R&D.

Company should get the market data at a reasonable cost besides they should know the prevalent distribution system for the product. It is useful to know the level of competition and their market shares. It is good to know if there are governmental rules that fix the prices or the cost of advertising efforts. Company should understand the stability of the government and economic strength of the host country. They should know the country's attitude towards global companies and their products.

Company has to give its priorities on the value-added services like their locations, market geographic locations, its level of involvement in the host country operations, global or multi-domestic marketing, global moves and strategies, strategies on products and services for the specific market and priorities for these from among the possible alternatives.

Control points start with setting targets on sales, production and on costs and then comparing the actual figures with target figures. The control report should depict clearly the deviations in actual from the objectives. Company must keep its own or follow the host country's governmental laws on environment protection in their process and products. Wherever possible requisite corrective steps should be taken, in the control reports. Companies should maintain contingency plans for unknown eventualities.

Organizational Structures

The structures of an organization have a strong bearing on its success. Companies operating in the global markets have to decide whether they should continue with their existing structures set up for domestic management or they should reorganize it to suit the global business. Common structures in use are given below.

1. Functional structures
2. Strategic business units
3. Cross-functional structures
4. Matrix structures

Besides, there are the new concept structures as given below.

1. Networking structures
2. Virtual structures
3. Delaminated matrix structures

Simple Structure

In a small firm where the business is restricted to a small area, when there are only two to five people working it would have a simple structure as shown below.

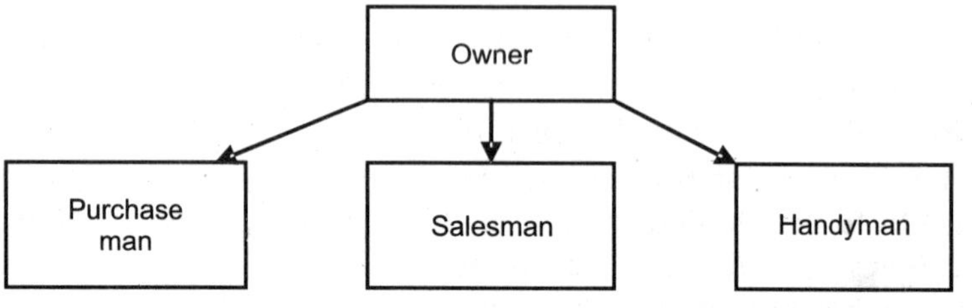

Many retail stores, repair shops, service units have this type of structure. The roadside dhaaba, hair cutting salons; photocopy shops are typical examples of simple structure.

The highlights of simple structures are given below.

- These structure make their operation highly informal, the supervision is done directly by the owner
- These firms could be flexible in their approach in decision-making and at times they could outbid bigger firms
- These structures could develop individual worker's personality, his creativity and individualism

The main drawback of the structure is that for its members there are no upward mobility, it reduces the chances of recruiting the right persons for the job. In one-man show the personal likes and dislikes, which could also change with the owner's mood, are used for hiring and firing and hence it could be unpredictable and irrational.

The simplest structure was found of a publishing house, which had only owner on its roles and the rest of the people are taken on contract basis, making it highly flexible and able to handle multifarious tasks.

Functional Structures

As business grows, in the range of its products, geographically selling in wider areas, it needs to expand its people base. When volumes are high, technology complex, only a few products, and vertical integration, functional structures are best suited. They encourage specialization in activities and skills. It provides for centralized decision-making. Most of the firms in India, before the advent of IT industry, have been operating in functional structure, which works around the different functions a firm has to perform, like marketing and finance. The structure on the lines of functions is given below.

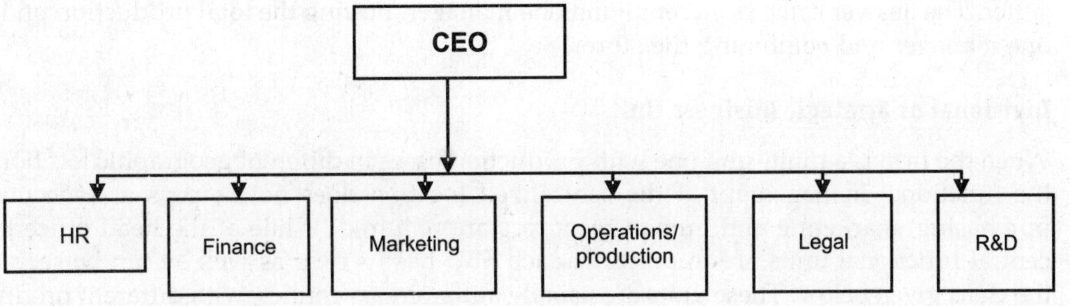

If the firm has to make centralized decisions, has work separation on the basis of departments, has high technical strength, and its expertise is critically costly and scarce, then the functional structures are the answers.

The main drawback of functional structures is the difficulty in coordination between the functions. Most of the functional heads consider their functions (departments) as their personal fiefdoms and their expertise as unique. They are loathe to share even the simplest of information about their operational areas, considering that knowledge is power they are just not interested in sharing power with anyone else; they feel that this way their value in the firm would go down. The answer to this problem is found in having cross-function liaison teams. Otherwise the firm has to change its structure.

The other problem faced by the functional structure is in finding appropriate methods of assessment of the performance of the different functional heads. It is not easy to have a common yardstick for performance of marketing head and the operations or HR head. Because of this lack of performance appraisal standard, the functional heads can get biased appraisals from the CEO. However, the HR experts have devised elaborate appraisal plans for equitable measurement of performance, being complicated they are hardly used.

The plus and the minus points of functional structures are given below.

Plus points	Minus points
Centralized decisions improve functional efficiency	Functional managers idea of superiority makes communications between the different functions difficult
Managers and technical persons are best utilized because they are focused on what they know best	CEO has to spend a lot of time in settling functional managers disputes, which they could utilize better for planning
Specialists improve coherence and control	Difficult to establish equitable standards for performance appraisals between the different functions
Functional career developments get priority as the training programmes are tailor-made for each functional area	Functional managers become narrow in their approach regarding the firm.

In an organization making two products, there were two production managers for each product; two separate raw material stores. The chasm between the two areas was so great that if one store had extra stocks of a component while the other starved of it the stock with extra stock would never part with it, though their production would suffer. The answer came from removing one manager, putting the total production under one manager and combining the stores.

Divisional or Strategic Business Unit

When the firm is a multi-unit one with production bases in different geographic locations, the functional management at the centralized location does not help as at each unit, purchasing, marketing and human resources are required. While at the head office the central functional units are in position, each SBU has its own as well as can be seen in the chart given below. These units are usually autonomous entities, with different product groups, which have little in common. They each have their own marketing, finance, human resource and operations, while in the head office there are directors for each functional area.

Similarly, the other SBUs have their own teams.

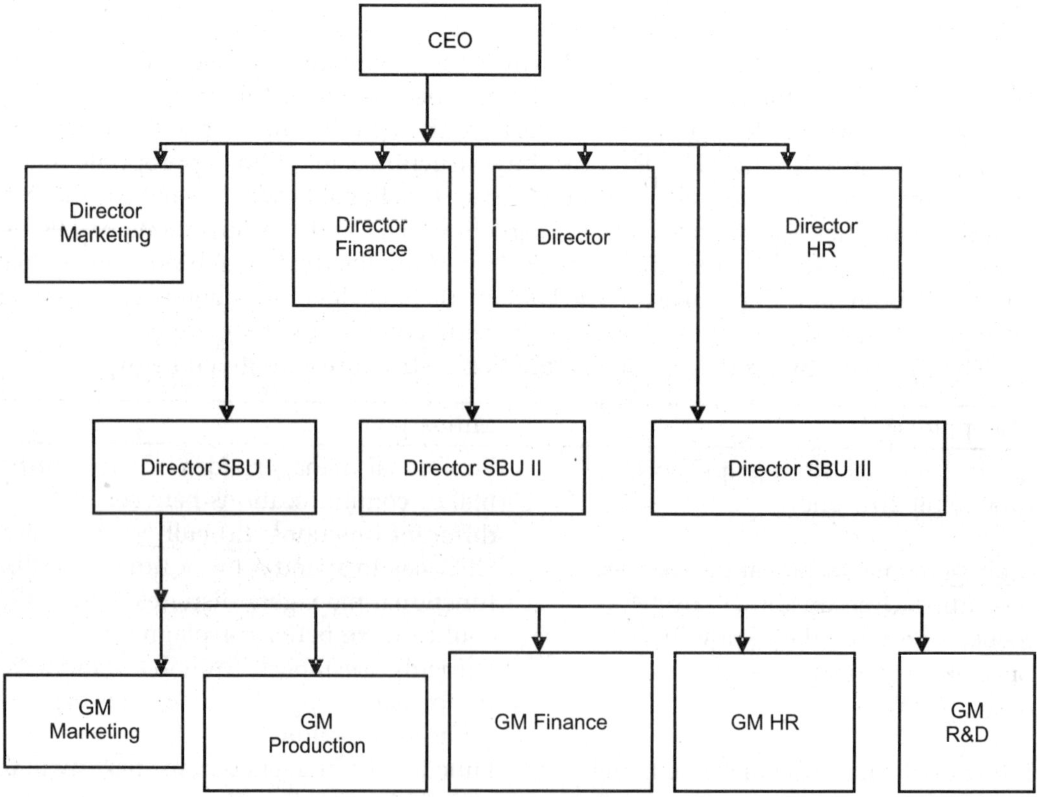

SBU structures work well when the products of the units are not closely related and they do not compete for the same business. In case of vertical integration, if one SBU feeds the other SBU then it helps the firm in avoiding transaction costs, as buying selling can be avoided. For keeping internal competition within the units, the firm can fix a transfer price. If the unit makes and sells to outside firms as well, there is a possibility of its customers fearing that the unit would give priority to its own unit, rather than to its competing firm. Such inter-unit sales could become counterproductive, as in the ultimate analysis the firm has to decide about its total profits and how much each unit is going to contribute to it.

While with the help of computers, inputting the relevant data the transactional price can be theoretically calculated; however, it is difficult to predict if this price would give the firm the profit it is looking for.

SBU units compete for the firm's resources. In this process, they try to jack up their actual requirements, as they fear that the management would surely reduce the actual money they will get.

The other major problem with SBU structure is that there is a lot of duplication of activities, and far too many people doing the same job. While one marketing department could sell the produce of all the SBUs, each unit wants to have one of their own. Furthermore, instead of the firm trying to obtain banks finance, each SBU tries for its unit, which could be a good thing for the firm, as the performance and reputation of one unit would not affect the others.

It is like the Parkinson's Law, you have one nodal person and soon he will build through hierarchy levels a force of fifty.

First there was one General in the army. He appointed four Lt. Generals, who all in turn appointed five Major Generals. The Major Generals appointed ten Colonels each and each colonel had twenty majors. Soon the country had an army of ten thousand people. This is how the Parkinson's Law works.

SBU structure has the following main characteristics:

- Relatively autonomous entities
- SBUs revolve around the products or markets
- Divisional competition is sub-optimal

The plus points and the minus points of SBU units are given below.

Plus points	Minus points
Functional areas commonality for different products brings conflicts, which are avoided in SBUs	There is a lot of duplication of personnel, operations, equipment and investments
Responses to market needs are quick as the autonomy helps in faster decision-making	All SBUs may not have the same brand image

Products and the markets get their due importance	Inter-unit competition (as the head of one unit may try to out do the head of the other unit to gain ascendancy in the corporate hierarchy)
Improves development of senior managers giving them better upward mobility options	Inter-unit sales may attract taxation; the price may be favouring one unit
SBUs have better operational control and head office gets time for strategic planning	SBUs may target the short-term goals and lose sight of long-range perspective of the firm.

Matrix Structures

They combine the divisional structure and the SBU structure. It tends to become participatory and suits the firms wanting a democratic culture. It may, however, lead to building of power structures as well. The main features of a matrix structure are as follows:

The structure combines two lines of authority, a vertical line for functional teams and a horizontal line from the different projects. Instead of projects the firms may have separate programmes, geographic divisions or even divisions. The project line provides for plans timetables, budgets and project administration, while the functional teams provide the expertise of the functions. The matrix structure is given below.

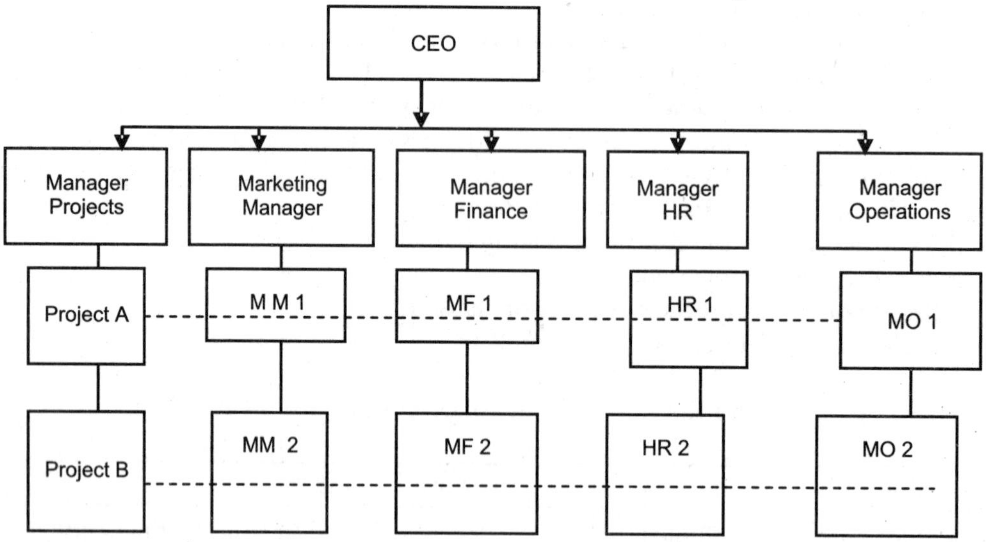

A Project Manager is in charge of all the different projects; here only two projects have been shown. With him there are people heading the different projects, who are supported by the nominated person from each of the department. These people, while they work for the designated project are also responsible to implement the project under the guidelines of their functional head. For example, MM1 reports to the marketing manager and also to the project head. This involves dual reporting, one to the project head and the other to the functional head. Construction firms handling many projects simultaneously and software project firms use the matrix structure.

The plus and minus points of matrix structure are given below.

Plus points	Minus points
Improves communications, flexibility and coordination	Dual reporting may lower accountability
Better utilization of resources	Power struggle and resulting conflicts
Synergy among teams improves market response time	Employees may compete rather than coordinate
Participatory decision-making improves morale of the teams	Time for taking decision may increase
Training and development of employees	Selection of functional employee may be opposed by the project team

Global Structures

Foreign operations of a firm would need a structure depending on their product portfolio, percentage of export sales in total firm's sale and the firm's external operations. Multi-domestic strategy focuses on the cultural and social ethos of the firm, while the global strategy operates on economic imperatives of the firm.

In a multi-domestic strategy, if global sales were low in percentage and if the product portfolio were large the firm would plan a global product division, and if the portfolio were small, the firm would opt for a global division. In case the sales percentage is high, and product portfolio was large the firm would plan a worldwide holding firm, and if portfolio were small, the firm would go for geographic area management.

For global strategy, if the product portfolio were large, and sales percentage low, the firm would go for global product division, and if the sales percentage is low and product portfolio small, the firm would go for worldwide functional structure. In case the portfolio is large and sales percentage high, the firm would accept worldwide matrix structure. However, if the sales per cent is high the firm should go for worldwide functional structure. The following table defines the global structures.

Product density	Multi-domestic	Multi-domestic	Global	Global
High	Worldwide product division	Worldwide holding firm	Worldwide product division	Worldwide matrix
Low	Global division	Geographic area	Worldwide functional	Worldwide functional
Product Density	Foreign sales % low	Foreign sales % high	Foreign sales low	Foreign sales % high

New Structures

The following new structures have emerged as necessities of changing business environments.

Horizontal or Flat Structures

In the vertical structures the customers have to interact with a host of people, starting from the firm's salesman, dealer or distributor, transporter and handler of goods, the bankers and any link in the chain could prove to be the weak link disrupting the entire operations rendering the customer at the mercy of some irresponsible person uncaring of the needs of the customer, which incidentally are also the laudable aims of the firm to keep the customer satisfied always. How many times have all of us encountered some such careless person and the firm remains unaware of the happenings at different levels, because of the layers of hierarchy surrounding the top management.

In order to obviate the problem the firms have to look at their Core Processes, which are as follows:

1. Product Development Process
2. Demand Management Process
3. Order Fulfilment Process

In these process segregations the customer orientation is kept in mind and both internal and external customers have to be involved with only one set of persons, in the firm. If the firm puts its structure around these, in the main, the customers would find it easy to deal with the firm. As it is the customer, who is the main purpose of the firm's very existence, the smoother the road for him to reach the firm the better. Firms spending huge amounts on advertising, promotion, on retail trade would not even make a minor impact on the firm's trade if the customers find the firm inaccessible to them, either physically or on the mental level.

In cross-functional structures as the customer interactions pronounce it is easier to let the customer help measure the firm's performance and the firm should pat its back only on getting a positive verdict from their customer groups, which is done through market surveys possible as exit shop polls. As there are tourist guides for major tourist spots, the customers should be guided gently by a knowledgeable person through the often-treacherous route to getting his products. This is truer for industrial customers and yet many consumer goods customers have failed to get any redress on their problems with the firm. As the cross-functional teams produce the results the reward system should be based on the team effort and rewards given to the teams and not the individuals. Teams should decide about the number of tasks they do, which do not add value to the customers and the teams should be encouraged to avoid such activities totally. This would help the teams to remain focused onto the value adding tasks, which would bring better and quicker results.

The entire process of order fulfilment can be one unit, which looks at the business from the customer's viewpoint. In such cases the structures revolve around processes rather than around functions. To make the structure a success, it is important to have a owner or a person responsible for the process and the sub-processes. There should be owners of cross-functional teams as well. All activities, which do not add value to the customers, should be avoided totally. It is necessary to identify the core processes of the firm from the cross-functional teams, other than the three mentioned, product development, demand management and order fulfilment process.

The structure helps in understanding the customer's viewpoint better and hence the customers can influence the firm's decisions. The structure helps in understanding the training needs of the employees, helps in proper budgeting from the customer's viewpoint, and adds value to the customers.

The IT industry has found the virtues of flat organizational structures and therefore they are oriented towards achieving their objectives.

Delaminated Matrix

The delaminated matrix is a structure in the experimental stage, yet it is felt that this structure would help the firm in achieving the state of organizational learning. In fact it combines two organizations into one. In this structure each manager looks after two areas, one functional area and one project area; same way even the workers shift between the project and the functional area. It becomes a real learning structure, where everyone is in the learning mode all the time.

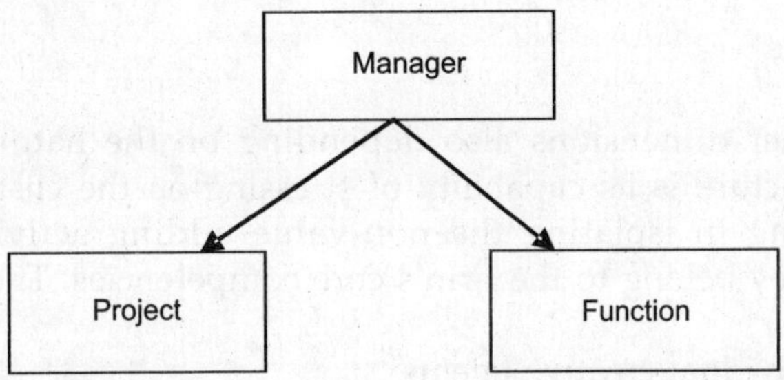

The structure separates the horizontal process from the vertical functions at the worker level. Workers, on the other hand, revolve between horizontal processes and vertical functions, giving them an exposure of both, improving them for higher positions in the firm. It provides for excitement and motivation to the workers. The structure is shown in the chart given below.

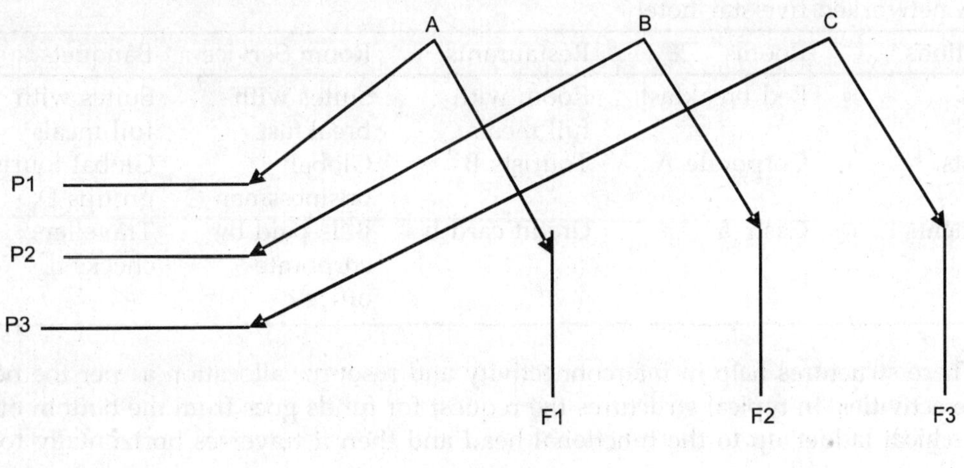

In the above A, B and C are the three managers and P1, P2 and P3 are three projects and F1, F2 and F3 are three functional areas. A manager looks after function F1 and process P1, and so on. As the manager is common for one function and one process, he can keep shifting his workers from process to function and vice versa, making the firm a learning organization.

It can be seen that a) functional structure is suitable for mature stable organizations, b) divisional or SBU structure for volatile environment, while the delaminated matrix for organizational learning.

A firm's formal macro-structure must be consistent with its chosen strategy.

Network Structure

The network structure becomes a three-dimensional structure as follows:

- Customer segment
- Time planning
- Facility usage
- Space and distance

There can be other dimensions also depending on the nature of the firm. The advantage of the structure is its capability of stressing on the customer value-adding activities, and helping in isolating the non-value adding activities which can be outsourced, unless they belong to the firm's core competencies. The advantages are as given below.

- Full scope for individual creative talents
- Motivation of employees
- Economic efficiency

The structure is being promoted through computer software and it would become reasonably priced soon enough. Communication and net service providers and freight and courier firms have used complex networking. The following gives an idea of a networking firm (a five-star hotel):

A networked five-star hotel

Functions	Rooms	Restaurants	Room Service	Banquets
Plans	Bed breakfast	Room with full meals	Suites with breakfast	Suites with full meals
Guests	Corporate A	Tourists B	Global businessman C	Global tourist groups D
Payments	Cash a	Credit card b	Bills paid by corporate office c	Travellers checks d

These structures help in interconnectivity and resource allocation as per the needs of the activities. In typical structures the request for funds goes from the bottom of the hierarchical ladder up to the functional head and then it traverses horizontally to the concerned person before it finally reaches the treasury and funds are released. This is time-consuming and at times distorts the information. In networking structure the information goes straight to the concerned person saving time. The information is given in need to know basis and nobody is deluged with a plethora of information not needed by him. An idea of networking structure is given below.

The capital, A,B,C,D refer to the type of guests and small a,b,c,d denote the payment methods in the hotel.

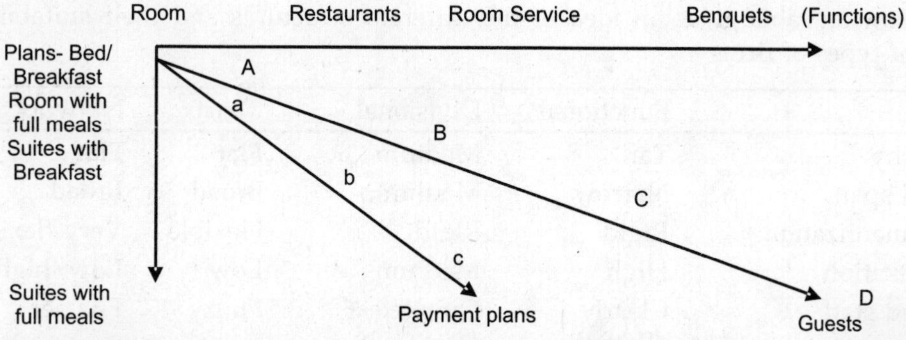

Virtual Structures

Once the firm decides to outsource some of its activities, it requires as much effort as setting up a new project. There must be synergy in the firm and outsource activity as given below.

- Both firms must be compatible in vision, business practices, language, employees background, profit perceptions
- Both firms must not be too dissimilar in size, as then the relative importance is sacrificed to browbeating by the big player.
- Both firms must accept the level of technology, which would be required.
- Business environment of both must be transparent to the extent possible; even then, the vendor's problems would come fully highlighted to their buyer and not his facilities. Vendor's suppliers credit would be to his privilege while his problems with the bank or with his source of materials would become the buyer's problems.

Firms farm out functions like the entire billing and collection, payroll, and hence while the function exists for the firm it is not directly with it. This makes for a virtual organization.

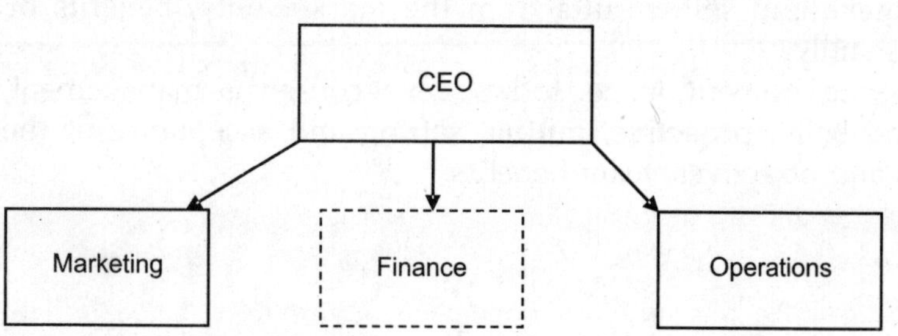

Organizational chart of a virtual organization is given below.

The firm has farmed out its finance functions to an outside organization. While the finance function exists it is not a part of the firm, and hence it makes that part of the firm as virtual. In India, Lotus firm had farmed out its finance accounts function to Price Waterhouse, as they found it cost-effective to do so.

Structures Suitability

The following table gives an idea of the different structures and their suitability for different types of firms:

	Functional	Divisional	Matrix	Network
Hierarchy	Tall	Medium	Flat	Flat
Control span	Narrow	Medium	Broad	Broad
Departmentization	Rigid	Rigid	Flexible	Very flexible
Specialization	High	Medium	Low	Low/high
Line and staff functions	Clearly allotted	Quite clear	Fuzzy	Fuzzier
Centralization	High	Medium	Low	Lowest/highest
Delegation of authority	Low	Low	High	Highest/lowest

The matrix and network structures have the advantage that they can be tall and flat at the same time, centralization along with decentralization coexists. The structures evolve from functional to matrices over time, taking the size of the firm, but this can happen once the technological and outsourcing areas are decided.

Firm's growth takes place due to the following reasons:

- Creativity, which can be curtailed by the leadership crisis.
- Direction except when experts start rejecting the same
- Delegation until management decides to hare greater controls
- Coordinating the activities till delays become prominent and ubiquitous
- Collaboration till there is nothing left to collaborate for, mostly changing mindsets

The growth stages can be seen from below:

First level of structures is the one with individual entrepreneur, informal structure, planning to make and sell, results from the market only, benefits or losses to the entrepreneur mainly.

Level in severe competition, i.e., today's level-consensus management, matrix teams, innovation and being proactive, mutual setting and acceptance of the firms vision, mission goals and objectives, team benefits.

Given below are the differences in flat and tall organizations.

Flat organizations	Tall organizations
Weak control system	High level of controls
Quick response to market needs	Greater distance between employees and the CEO
Several solutions to a problem possible	Standardized operations
High level of tolerance	Strict checks
For fast changing environment	For stable environments
Multi-skill planning	Specialized skills
Delegation important	Low level of delegation
Faster decisions	Boss's decisions
All pervasive information system	Information only with the power and authority
Low level of coordination	High level of coordination
Low level of supervision	High level of supervision
Low overheads	High overheads
Challenging careers	Power with a few
Pressure jobs	Low pressure jobs except for the top jobs
High rate of failures/employee turnover	Lower rate of failures
Unstructured work	Structured line of authority

Micro-Organizational Structures

Besides the macro structures, firms form micro or small structures for specific tasks and time durations. Initially they are formed as groups; with commonality of purpose, objective, the groups get converted into teams. In teams, there is joint responsibility and tasks are assigned to the team members. Care is taken to see that there is no overlap of work between members of the team. The process of groups getting converted into teams is an evolving one. The evolutionary process is given below.

Forming
Storming
Norming
Performing

As the groups are formed the members air the different views and opinions on the assigned responsibility and the meeting can become a little wild. As the members start understanding each other's viewpoint as also the objective for the team, the group gets converted into a team. The process is shown comparing the effectiveness of the teams.

Teams provide options to the firms to overcome the shortcomings of some structures, like the functional structure is not conducive to inter-functional interactions. Teams can perform the cross-functional tasks better. The teams are organized in the following

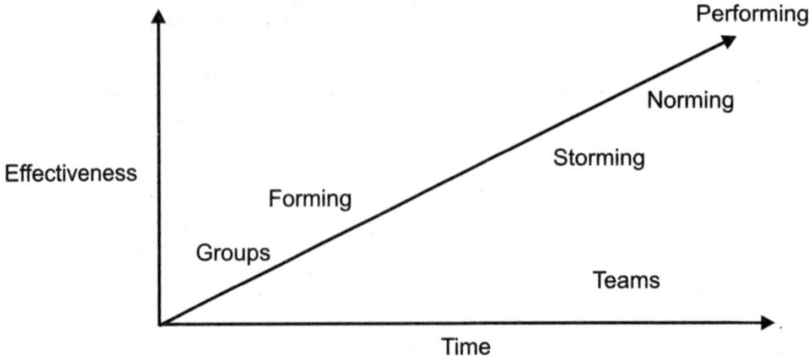

manner.

- Departmental teams: these are good for one task at a time only and after the task is completed they are disbanded. In these teams, one member of each relevant department is opted as a member, who brings with him his expertise relating to his department.

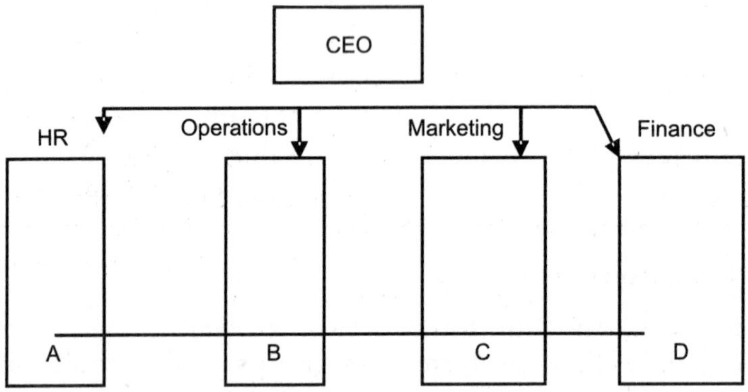

A, B, C, D are the members of four separate departments who have formed the team to perform one task like solving a discipline problem in one of the departments.

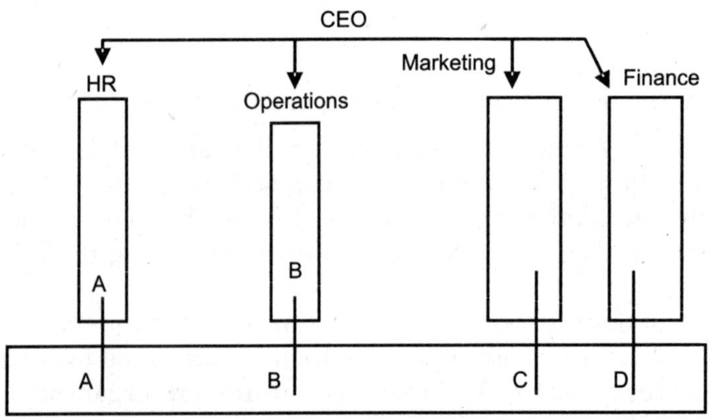

The liaison teams are given below.

The liaison teams are formed by taking one person from each relevant department A, B, C and D, who form a more permanent team to liaise between the departments, to sort out interdepartmental problems and keep smooth flow of relevant information in the departments. One team member says, D becomes the team coordinator.

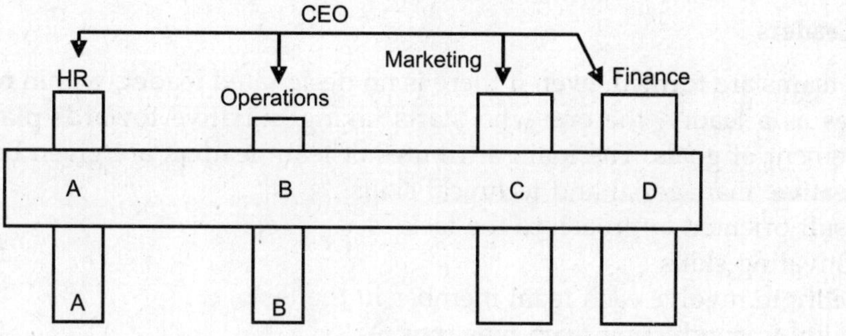

Project teams are formed as given below.

In project teams one member of each relevant department is taken out, placed in a separate location to work on a new project. These members usually leave the departments on permanent basis; once the project becomes a reality they become members of that entity.

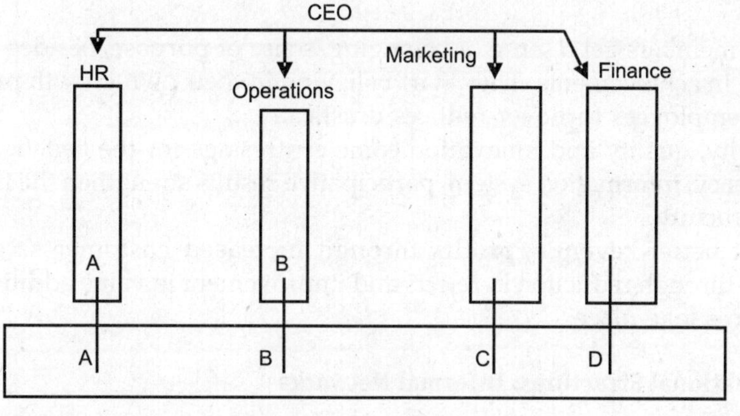

Independent teams are formed as given below.

In the independent teams people are taken out from the relevant departments and they remain in the teams never to go back to their parent departments. These are usually made for the purpose of intrapreneurship diversification.

Team Functions

The following are the tasks performed by the teams:

- Work allotment among the members by mutual agreement
- Periodic review meetings to plan action and coordination needed
- Locating problems anticipated in the team's work and seeking managerial support

in overcoming them
- Periodic reports and documentation for reference
- Planning actions to prevent time slippages
- Accepting critical appraisal from the management on the team's results and if required changing course to achieve goals on time

Team Leaders

As the teams are formed, even if there is no designated leader, within no time, someone emerges as a leader, the one who starts taking initiative towards planning action for achievement of goals. The main attributes of team leaders are given below.
- Creative, managerial and technical skills
- Result oriented approach to the task
- Motivating skills
- Ability to involve each team member in the task
- Ability in conducting team meetings
- Ability in solving problems faced by the team in the task through team discussion
- Ability to train team members if required
- Ability to admonish the members if required

When the groups are formed and they get converted into dynamic result oriented teams there are some other reciprocal changes, which take place in the firm as given below.
- The team members get a sense of belonging, sense of purpose, besides the challenges and pride in achievements. They start believing in their own growth prospects in the firm and employees turnover reduces drastically.
- Productivity, quality and innovation come centrestage for the benefit of the firm.
- Transparency, information system, participative results strengthen the firms processes and its structure.
- Firms get better revenue/profits through increased customer satisfaction, cost reduction through reduction in rejects and improvement in value addition in products and services take place.

Micro-Organizational Structures: Informal Networks

The informal networks are complementary to the formal structures and any management ignoring them would be doing so at its own peril.

These networks operate over office coffee sessions, lunch rooms and even during break times. These networks can be used effectively by the management for a variety of asks, which may appear difficult if the formal channels are used. Following tasks can be easily performed through them:
- Communication network to inform the employees of some changes taking place, like policy change, new supervisor
- For advising errant worker

- Giving technical information
- Giving sensitive information to select group to build their morale and confidence
- For building trust in employees

These networks do indulge in gossip mongering and yet they have their positive aspects too. To be most effective both formal and informal channels of communication should be used for optimum efficiency. It must be understood that employees of a firm play more roles in the firm than can be placed on the organization charts, macro- or even micro- structural charts. The production engineer can be on the quality management team. They wear several hats. Furthermore, due to levels of hierarchy, the two-way communication so essential for the success of the firm gets garbled most of the time. One example is given below.

Loss of communication in big hierarchical firms:

Problems from the shop floor sent to Assistant Manager numbering 10	AM finds 2 problems trivial and sends 8 to Deputy Manager	Dy M finds 1 trifling, sends 7 to the Manager
Manager accepts that only 5 need to be referred to the Dy GM	Dy GM brushes off 1 problem and sends 4 to the GM	GM reduces the problems by 1 and sends 3 to the MD
MD finds all the three as too simple, which should have been solved by different levels of officers and sends them to his secretary to be just filed.	Assistant Manager waits forever to get the answers to the problems	People at different levels do not attempt to solve any problem and they just pass the buck to the next in line above him

In formal groups the lack of effectiveness comes from miscommunication, something

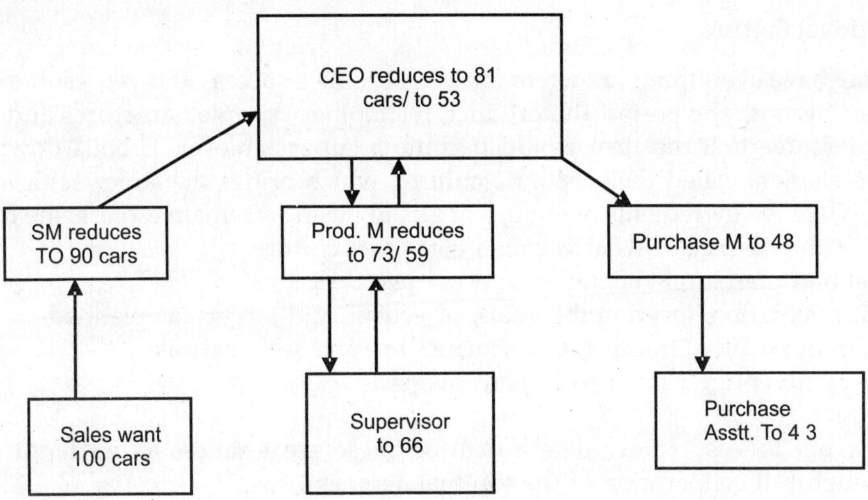

like children's play called Chinese Whispers as can be seen from below.

The reduction was only of 10 per cent at each stage and the person doing it, thinking that after all the requests are always jacked up rationalized it. In informal networks this error is totally eliminated as the information is exchanged face to face. There are the following major differences between formal and informal structures:

- Unlike formal teams where members are appointed by the management for specific tasks, the informal groups emerge, when like-minded people become friends, and the members join the informal groups of their own volition.
- While formal teams have a finite period of their existence, the informal groups are more permanent; they change only when some people leave the firm.
- Informal groups do not work through an agenda or any fixed objective. They handle multifarious functions as the problems arise in any area concerning their interests.
- Informal groups discussions go far beyond the firms activities

There are different types of informal groupings given below.

- Advisory, motivating groups, where firms official information is made available and is more effectively received than through the formal channels of communication
- Communication groups, which gels people as they can discuss their work related issues as also their personal problems
- Confidence building groups, when some vital information is given to the group it builds trust and motivates the group members.

Firms must, therefore not only acknowledge the existence of informal structures, but also help them in remaining healthy and vibrant, as a lot more can be achieved with their help. Transferring an important member of a group or moving out in any other way could prove counterproductive to the firm. New recruits must be admitted to the firm only if the management finds they would fit in the cultural patterns of informal groups.

Organizational Culture

A firm may have everything known to for it to become a success and yet result excellence slips away from it. The best of the product, technology, people, structures and systems do not guarantee that the firm would become a super achiever. It boils down to one intangible element called the corporate culture, which brings the super achiever tag to the firm. While the ingredients of culture in global business remain esoteric the following would give the essence of what is called corporate culture.

- Action and plan implementation and not just decisions
- Result orientation, meeting the goals, objectives and targets, as planned
- Faith in innovation, training, experimentation and self analysis
- Sense of adventure for venturing out overseas

It may not be easy to evaluate a firm on these areas unless an in-depth study is done through full cooperation of the top management.

Task Orientation

Firms believe in action, "Do it now", "Finish on time" are the buzzwords in the corporate circles. Besides, top managers also keep asserting that a) they believe in quality, b) they are market driven or c) They are technology driven. And yet the action with speed is the hallmark of values generated by the corporate culture. It transcends the boundaries of selection one from the different paths available for achieving the goals. It really defines the personal management virtues. Peter Drucker, the management guru has defined management as achieving things, which underscores the basic need of action, because without it nothing can be achieved.

Many firms in India believe that planning, conceptualizing thinking and evaluating are far better intellectual activities and they need greater attention. However, even if it is conceded, who would go to a doctor for treatment who has the degree but is not practising as a doctor. Strategies, plans, procedures and business philosophies are only as good as they appear after they are implemented. The Indian elitist manager believes that his work is acceptable only as long as it is concentrated on strategizing and planning. The role of staff functions like finance, administration and planning are accorded higher status than the mundane functions like manufacturing, marketing purchasing and logistics.

However, there are several successful Indian firms, which are action driven and they consider planning, evaluation and analysis as necessary adjuncts of the line functions. In successful firms time becomes the most important dimension in which success is measured. They do not believe in rationalizing failures; they would rather concentrate on the action to reach their objectives and goals. They are not even bothered about the deft handling of situations, skills displayed while negotiating a deal. A global organization's CEO circulated the copy of a ten million dollar purchase order sent by his travelling salesman enclosed with a scribbled note on a torn old envelope. The post-script said, "it is nice to receive orders enclosed with properly typed letters on the memo pads, however, I have enjoyed this order, because it shows the urgency of the salesman to reach us the order as fast as possible."

When the things are easy and going smooth, the managers are not even required. It is only during emergencies that the skill, acumen and resourcefulness of the manager comes into play and this happens only when such action oriented skills are part of the organizational culture. It is manager's job to find solutions to the tough problems and train his team to find solutions to problems related to their own areas of operation. This leads to a culture of transparency and experimentation at all levels; and in such cases failure of experimentation is not considered suicidal for the person doing the experiment. In fact, the failures of all experiments including those of the top management are discussed openly to ensure that such failures do not recur, and there is no adverse effect on the individual's future in the firm. In case the failure is attributable to lack of resource support by the management, the team member is supposed to bring it out much before the deadline to enable the management take corrective action. It is not enough to say that 'sorry it could not be done because I did not get xyz from the management in time'. If in the end the manager is not able to provide the resources, then it is he who takes the blame for failure and he does not pass it on to the team member. The team member employee has to relentlessly ask for, what is required to succeed and it would prove his drive for action.

Stress on Achievement

While in the Indian context, the ways of doing things are more important than the end results. They believe that as long as they have worked hard the other aspects of productivity and results would be automatically taken care of. People believe that they should be rewarded for their hard work and the poor results should never come in their way of success in the firm. They happily rationalize the exchange of results with hard work and several of Indian firms suffer from **work supreme even against results** syndrome. It can however be seen from the successful Indian firms that they are managing the results. The additional corollary to this theory is that while means are not supreme and only ends are a large number of firms to using unfair and at times illegal means to achieve their goals. This as they found in the not so long run is only counterproductive, as can be seen from the number of arrests of businessmen in the last decade on account of fraud committed by them.

Results come from resource mobilization, countering constraints and impediments, coordinating with internal and external agencies, which happens only if the manager is believes in action, is self-driven, innovator, organizer, planner and a motivator by example for others to emulate for achieving the results. The manager does not take credit for a windfall nor does he blame the employees for any shortfalls in results due to any unknown circumstances, like the act of God, recession. The firms believe that the output and results can define and assess the team's achievements, under the prevailing environmental conditions.

Self Analysis and Experimentation

Most firms believe that once they have achieved success using a particular strategy, plan, policy and methodology, they should stick to them and not think of making changes. However, in their thought process it is implied that the competitors would be just spectators in the marketplace, while the fact remains that the competition is ever ready to not only copy the success formula but also to upgrade it, which would leave the winners of the first race stranded. It is therefore imperative that even the most successful firms keep introspecting into their shortcomings to chart out new routes to success. The wise would question even the basic status of the firm like its structure, procedures, strategies, systems, style, the entire 7S Model and plan innovations, which would take the firm to greater heights. It is important for the top management to respect such innovations and even experimentations to support deviant views to motivate the innovators. Even persons playing the devil's advocate, questioning the wisdom of moving on the highly successful but beaten track should be encouraged or else the management remains surrounded by the usual sycophants, the YES MEN who ultimately do more disservice than good to the firm.

It is the person moving with the times who can keep modifying the winning model with innovation, foresight as also by learning from other firms worldwide. The firms, which become the benchmarks of excellence, have to keep raising the bar, upping the standards, which would be good not only for them but also for the competition and the marketplace too.

Changing the Firm's Culture

Each firm has its own shared values and beliefs and these form the culture of the firm. It can be described as, **"the way we do things around here"**! As people just walk around the floor of a firm they may find a lot of useful creative activities going around or they may find people just lazing about. Since these values are shared and deep rooted in the psyche of the employees it is an uphill task trying to change the culture of a firm!

Some of tried and tested methods of making successful cultural changes are given below:

- Understand and make a written statement on the existing culture.
- The time frame for making the changes should be kept flexible.
- Since the existing culture is also a shared one, employees would feel threatened if the effort for making the change were abrupt and confrontational in nature.
- If the top management has become part of the effete culture, it may be a good idea to replace them with management with a view for a different culture.
- While the firm's vision statement can do a lot for the success of a firm, it is not enough when cultural changes are needed. It is basically important to slowly but surely demolish the existing culture.
- In order to start the cultural evolution, it becomes important to take note of even small successes and then to get them spread out on the informal structure. These stories of success would start building confidence among the employees and would definitely bolster their morale. Creating stories of success and putting them before the informal teams would generate a snowballing effect.
- Each firm has some symbols, the logo, may be a mascot. If these represent a laid back culture and the firm wants to introduce a culture of dynamism, it may be a good idea to change these symbols and get new more vibrant and WIT IT symbols for the firm.
- Firms need to have patience and should wait till some tangible results can be seen. Perseverance becomes a positive virtue in this matter.

The most powerful type of change lever is the organizational culture. It determines what an organization would or would not do.

The management operate in the following manner if it wants to keep the firm's culture as it exists.

Work with logic, caution, in an orderly manner.

For changing the culture they operate with innovation, participation and creativity.

SUMMARY

Control of global operations is difficult because of distances involved and differences in country's cultures. Therefore, global plans should include analysis of the differences, and the basic environmental issues, operating plans and contingency plans.

The decision-making levels should depend on the competence of the people managing the host country offices. Both global and multi-domestic strategies can be considered depending on the local conditions, government regulations and host country's consumer behaviour towards the company's products.

Reporting systems from host country offices should be on the same patterns as the reporting systems used in the home country.

Organization structures are not considered change agents as they are in the background always, while they have a positive effect on making strategic changes in the firm. There are several forms of structures, each has its plus and minus points and each firm must decide about its structure from the viewpoint of the best fit in the times of making changes. However, for the day-to-day operations firms need to have the formal microstructures, the teams. Care needs to be taken regarding the interplay of team members to ensure the effectiveness of the teams. Each firm has informal groups, which can provide a vital link between the management and the employees as they inform, advise but also help in changing the firm's culture if it needs to be changed through the stable long-term network. The firm's culture should be action oriented, should support result-oriented action and should keep innovating, modifying even the successful formulas in order to remain in the top position they have carved for themselves.

Global business collaborations give the advantage of faster entry, lower entry cost, better utilization of company's core competencies besides it helps avoide certain types of competition. The collaborating companies can learn from each other, besides gaining location advantages of proximity of raw materials, markets and low cost labour. The company wanting to operate in host country may have to overcome problems like local legal issues and differences in business environments. Companies take their objectives, strengths into account in deciding the form they adopt in collaborations, be it licensing, franchising, joint ventures, management contracts or turnkey operations.

CHAPTER
14

Global Buyers

INTRODUCTION

At different times each member of the society is a buyer. And as a buyer people want to be known as sane and intelligent buyers. Buyer's skills come from an innate selfishness that when we are spending money, we should get money's worth. The term Value for Money is born out of this desire. To prove the rule, there are exceptions like people buying beyond their means when they have to impress somebody, like friends, fiancés. It is said that no one buys a product. They buy the benefits, which they derive from the product. If the benefits outweigh the cost the buyers have paid, then they have received value for money. Let us define customer value as follows:

- Total customer value: The sum total of all the benefits the customer is likely to derive from the product.
- Total customer cost: The sum of moneys the customer is to spend while selecting, buying, using and disposing of the product.
- Product perceived value: The difference of total customer value and total customer cost represents the customer's idea of the usefulness of the product.

The product purchase decisions are taken on the basis of the following:

- Product brand image/brand equity
- Buyer's usage value
- Value of the service provided with the product
- Intrinsic value of the product
- The above add up to total customer value of the product.

The other side of decision to buy comes from the following:

- Product price
- Product search expense
- Decision time delay costs

- Cost while using the product
- The above add up to total customer costs for the purchase of the product.

In case the buyer and the user are two different persons, there is likelihood of delays or wrong purchases. Personal choice of the buyer may be based on his own personal experience with the product or he may have some relationship with the seller. In such events, the sellers do well to establish relationship with the buyers and the users as well.

People do not buy products. They buy the benefits, which the product offers them. Therefore, after-purchase value of the product assumes great importance as only those products with high after-purchase value will be purchased repeatedly, which brings to the point of customer satisfaction from the usage of the product which is measured as follows:

- Actual benefit derived as compared to the benefit perception the customer had before the product was purchased.
- Benefits derived as compared to those obtained from a competitive product.
- Benefits get enlarged if the product costs are in consonance with the perceived benefits and in such cases the customers derive a sense of pride besides satisfaction, which in today's marketing terminology is stated as customer's delight.
- Customer's delight also comes from being known as an intelligent buyer among the peer group.

Product innovation, product differentiation, leads the buyers into the delight zone. As the competition is doing exactly the same thing, trying to win over the same segment customers, the firm which remains proactive to the perceived and even intangible needs of the customers, is the winner. In order to achieve it, firms must be in the market research mode all the time fathoming the customer, his mindset, likes and dislikes, the perception of product benefits. Product differentiation should, however, be made at those extra costs which can be borne by the market. There is no point in, as an extreme example, using gold wire in the television set instead of copper wire, because except for increasing the cost it will not improve the quality or even aesthetics of the product.

Sustainable Competitive Advantage

In order to achieve **Sustainable Competitive Advantage**, the firm has to constantly upgrade its product value to the customer and product delivery systems. Buyer's loyalty can never be taken for granted and therefore to ensure it the company takes the following actions:

- Differentiating the product, price, and distribution system and advertising promotion.
- Communicating the differentiation to the customer, "We know we are good, you should know it too."

Washing powder marketing looks like a battlefield where each player is trying to outdo the other by masking tall claims, "washes whitest" TV demonstrations, innovative use of the media, help in achieving one aim of getting trial use by the buyer. However, it is the real value of the product, which makes the customer buy it again.

In order to increase the market share, the firm has to take competitor's customers. It is of use to know that the value the competitor's customers are placing on the competitive products. Market surveys are conducted by firms to ascertain the perceived value of the product purchase both of their customers and those of competitor's. The results of the surveys assist in redefining the product differentiation, communication and service providing plans. These help the firms to keep upgrading the customer value of the products.

Satisfaction Survey: Firms need to know the satisfaction or dissatisfaction factors of the products with their existing and past customers. Following methods are used for the purpose:

- Personal interviews with those customers who were using the product earlier and have now stopped using the same, either they have switched to competition or stopped altogether. These interviews give an insight of the reasons and failure on the part of the firm in providing satisfaction. These apparent postmortems help rebuild the marketing strategies by improving service standards, terms of business like payment terms, and delivery systems.
- Surprise customers: Firms can send some unidentifiable customers who would give correct feedback about the service provided and customer care taken by the selling team. Such customers are part of many hotel chains who are interested to know the behaviour pattern of the service team when the top management is not there to watch the team in action.
- Complaint management: The firms who do not pay attention to the suggestions and complaints made by customers are likely to lose those customers. The top-most authority in the firm should attend to complaints, or at least they must be aware of the complaints. Suggestion boxes, complaint or assessment forms to assess the service being provided by hotels and restaurants are available in most places and they form a vital link between the customers and their satisfaction.
- Customer complaint and suggestion surveys: One telecom firm in India in the private sector is continuously on the customer's trail understanding, their varied and increasing demands, their dissatisfaction levels and they are able to find instant remedial measures for the same.

Pricing strategies can help in making the customers loyal. A value for money product stays with the customer and helps in making purchase decisions. Price changes, like lowering price can be helpful in penetrating the market. The inherent danger is the customer mindset, where many times a lower price product is considered to be having lower value.

Michael Porter has evolved Value Chain, a method for evaluating the customer value being built in the product through the management process. The Value Chain looks at the different functional areas of business from the customer's viewpoint, underscore the fact that if the customer is forgotten in any action or activity of the firm some value to the customer may be lost. The value chain is given below.

	A	Infrastructure					
	A	Finance					
	A	Human resource					
	A	Information					
Suppliers	B	In bound logistics	Operations	Outbound logistics	Marketing/ Sales	Service→	**Customers**

Note : A represents the Support functions and B represents the Primary functions.

As can be seen from the matrix, success of the firm depends on the way the activities of each functional area are conducted and coordinated with each other.

As an example, if purchasing department does not care to order the raw materials in time there will be delay in production and delivery to the customer. If the human resource management gets the wrong kind of person for operations, the quality of products may suffer ultimately affecting the sales and profitability. If the outbound delivery uses an ineffective transport system, there may be delays or even damages to the goods, hampering customer satisfaction. Each activity should be carried out and cared for as it is going to add value to the customer. If it is not performed well, it will take away some value from the customer resulting in loss of the customer to the firm, and the competitors are ever ready to grab dissatisfied customers all the time.

Service to customer is of paramount importance and this is one area, which many firms in India tend to neglect. To a customer, the firm's service is the only visible face of the firm. Therefore, the service must represent the firm correctly by involving the customer to the extent possible in the service delivery process showing the finer points like selection of transporter.

Michael Porter's Value Chain, as stated earlier, has a major drawback inasmuch that it does not render itself to cross-functional analysis in a firm. Hence, cross-functional work processes and teams lend themselves for better understanding on the total customer approach of the firm, which is given below.

- Defining new product: Firms keep bringing new products in the market. New products, which are brought out based on understanding of the market through marketing research, have better chance of success. The activities include, besides marketing research, technology through R&D, or purchase of technology (in some cases through Reverse Engineering Process, if it is not illegal).
- Production process: It includes purchasing, inventory management of raw material, components, semi-finished goods and finished goods with the Just in Time (JIT) technique for keeping current assets to a minimum, quality management with TQM.
- Marketing and servicing the customers: It includes continuous market research, distribution channels management, advertising and sales promotion, from getting the purchase order to supply and billing and finally getting paid for the supply. Next, the same order-to-payment cycle restarts.
- Service: The importance of the service to the customer can never be overemphasized as only the service provides the firm with Sustainable Competitive Advantage, as it cannot be easily copied.

Firms strive for profitable sales and growth. These come from customers who become loyal to the firm due to the satisfaction or delight they get from the product usage. Loyal customers normally buy more, accept new products from the firm, become spokespersons of the firm and take up advisory role in the firm's operations, like new promotional plan, new advertising campaign and some customers can be the part of Advisory Panel or Focus Group with the firm.

Understanding customer satisfaction for profiling the customer is therefore an absolute must in these days of severe competition.

Speedy complaint redress, complaint cause removal and complaint statistics are a must to survive for the firms.

Customers who are loyal to the firm must be retained as, over a period of time the firm's selling cost on such customers reduce as lots of activities become routine; the newsletter, direct mail promotional offers can be sent without having to bother about finding the new customers. They help the firm with word of mouth publicity in getting more customers.

A lost customer can become a major liability if he chooses to vilify the firm. Firms need to interview these lost customers and even if they become non-buyers of the firm's products they should remain friendly or at least neutral with respect to the firm.

The process of selling of the early 20th century has given way to relationship marketing of today as can be seen from the following.

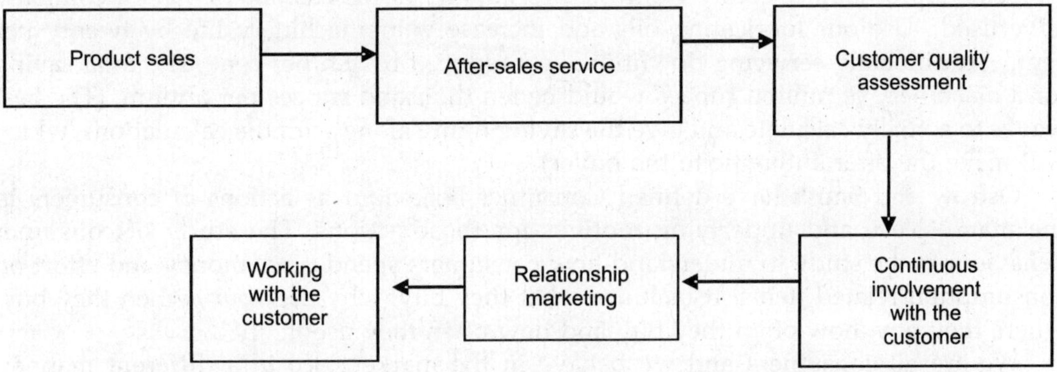

In the beginning of 20th century there was hardly any competition and sellers had to just place the product in the market and it was sold. Then came the fifties of the twentieth century and products, which needed service, were provided with after-sales service through service engineers of the firm. They also demonstrated the product if it was needed, informed the buyer's ways of optimizing the use of the product and methods of saving possible through the use of the product like lower down time.

In the third phase in the second half of the 20th century, customers were becoming quality conscious and the firms started quality control programmes in their manufacturing operations. From just testing the quality, the firms started checking the quality of purchased raw materials and components, and the quality of subassemblies inside the factories.

In the next phase, the customer became the focus of marketers and the products had to meet the expectation levels of the customer. The seller made phone calls after the sale was made to ask about the quality assessment and ease in usage of the product. However, as most products had little or no competition, manufacturers were in fact giving only lip service to improving product quality. A classic example is the Ambassador car. A new model of Ambassador was introduced with only minor change of putting ashtrays on the back door. After a few years, gradually the ashtrays were removed. Again to be reintroduced as a newer model. This game was obviously known to the customers but as they had little option, they had to buy the car. Only some bought a Fiat the only other option.

Relationship Marketing: It is the new mantra of marketing today. It works well only when the seller is able to overwhelm the customer with so much of importance that he cannot just think of going for competitive product. Newsletters, new product information, samples for trial, cultural activities invitations go a long way in building relationships.

Working with the customers: The seller does not leave the customer after the sale has been made. The seller keeps engineering support, maintenance support with the buyer to keep reassuring about the benefits he is going to derive from the use of the product. This is especially true of the industrial products like Power Plants, Air-conditioning units.

Seller's profitability comes from the profitability of his customers. An oil company advertised "Use our lubricating oils and increase your machinery life by twenty per cent." Additionally servicing downtime gets reduced by ten per cent. The total saving for a machinery of million rupees would be ten thousand rupees per annum. (The best way is to actually calculate and give the saving figure along with the calculations, which will make the offer authentic to the buyer).

Ostrow and Smith have defined Consumer Behaviour as actions of consumers in the marketplace and underlying motives for those actions. The study of consumer behaviour is the study to understand how consumers spend time, money and effort on consumption related items. It includes what they buy, why they buy, when they buy, where they buy, how often they buy and how often they use it.

We are all consumers and we behave in the marketplace in a different manner, sometimes logically and at other times irrationally. Study of consumer behaviour helps to predict with a high degree of accuracy how a particular person will behave under certain circumstances. This gives rise to more scientific approach to business communication.

Philip Kotler has designed a consumer behaviour model, which offers the variety of stimuli present for consumer for their decision-making for purchase action.

Model of Consumer Behaviour

Market stimuli	Other stimuli	Buyer Characteristics	Buyer Decision Process	Buyer Decisions
Product	Economic	Cultural	Problem Recognition	Product choice
Price	Technological	Social	Information Search	Brand choice
Placement	Political	Personal	Evaluating Alternatives	Dealer's choice
Promotion	Cultural	Psychological	Purchase Decisions	Purchase timings

Market stimulants: The main marketing mix factors, famous four Ps, Product, Price, Placement and Promotion can provide stimulus to buyers. We have seen in our lives how can a particular product just by being in the market makes us buy it. Listed below are influencing factors. Detailed discussions about the same will be taken up later on at the appropriate place.

Social Factors

Reference groups: They are the community leaders, religious gurus, professors, councillors and others.

Family includes, parents, children, grandparents, siblings, uncles and aunts.

Roles and Structures: Role of head of the household, the breadwinner in the family, which could be a new one, just husband-wife, or with small children, teenage kids, or grown-up children who have left the household, needs to be defined in the buying process.

Age and stage in life cycle: With better medical facility the average age of Indians has greatly increased. There is a large group of senior citizens. With lower rate of child mortality, the population of teens and preteens has increased manifolds giving rise to multitude needs and products to satisfy the same.

Occupation and economic circumstances: Standard of living of people differs because of the size of regular income as also on the occupation. A white collared worker would like to project an image of a well-dressed person as against a small businessman, who would not be bothered with appearances.

Lifestyle and psychographics are used to understand the mindset of people and for measuring and categorizing lifestyle.

Good resource people with financial backing.

Actualizers are those who have achieved their desires, who have become **somebody** i.e. gained recognition.

Fulfilled are the satisfied people.

Achievers are the people who have targeted their dreams and fulfilled them.

Experiencers are those who have gone through the struggle and come out successfully.

Low resource people with low finance
Believers are optimists who feel their time will come soon.
Strivers are hopefuls about their future.
Makers are busy people who are into nitty-gritty of making a success.
Strugglers are not so optimistic about their future.

Personality and Self-concept

People have physiological needs like food, clothing, shelter and psychological needs like need of love esteem and self-actualization. Maslow has propounded that people's needs follow a hierarchy, in terms of importance of needs and their place in the person's life.

Maslow's Hierarchy of Needs

Self-actualization A
Esteem B
Social Status C
Safety D
Physiological needs E

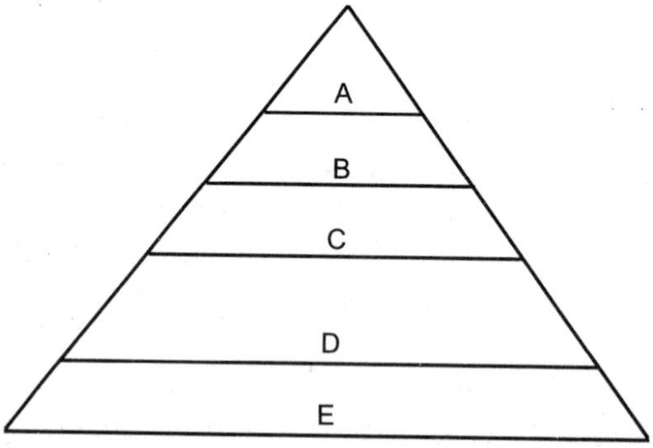

Perception means to select, organize, and interpret information in order to obtain a meaningful understanding for selecting and deciding in favour of a product.

Attitudes and beliefs: Attitudes are a person's evaluation of emotional feelings and tendencies for action towards some object or an idea.

Buying roles can be described as follows:

1. Initiator: The person who puts forward the idea of obtaining a certain product
2. Influencer is the one who gives his opinion about the suitability of the product
3. Decider is the one who has the authority to decide whether the product should be purchased or not
4. Buyer is the person who places the order
5. User is the one who puts the product to use

Thus, we can develop **Complete Buyer Behaviour** as given below.

- Believe in the product

- Develop attitudes
- Make thoughtful choice

Habitual Buying Behaviour

It can be seen from the following matrix

Major difference in brands	High involvement Complex buying behaviour	Low involvement Variety seeking buying behaviour
Less difference in brands	Dissonance reducing buying behaviour	Habitual buying behaviour

When, for example, the difference in brands is large like in cars and the involvement in buying is also more, the buying process becomes complex. Conversely, if the brand differences are low like in shampoos, and purchase involvement is low, most purchases are done on the basis of habit only.

Stages of Buying Decision Process

1. Problem recognition is defined by obvious or inherent need of the consumer.
2. Information search
3. Evaluation of alternatives
4. Purchase decision
5. Post-purchase behaviour

Sources of Information

Personal: Family, friends, neighbours
Commercial: Advertisements, salespersons, dealers, packages, displays
Public Sources: Mass media, consumer rating organizations,
Experiment: Handling the product, experiments, using samples of products like shampoo sachets.

Evaluation of Alternatives

Problem: purchase of a computer

Identify decision criteria is as follows:

1. Price
2. Manufacture/Model
3. Support
4. Repair record
5. Warranties
6. Reliability

Weightage to criteria allotted by consumer

Price 70, Manufacture/Model 60, Support 40, Repair record 75, Warranties 50, Reliability 70

Alternate choices: Wipro, LG, HCL, Compaq, IBM, Local Assembly

Now for each of these six computers, put weight, e.g., Wipro: Price 30, manufacture/ model 50, support 40, repair record 60, warranty 40, reliability 60.

As can be seen price weightage is inversely proportional to price. In other words, higher the price, lower the weightage.

Select the one where the numbers add up to highest. Then implement the decision, make the purchase.

Post-purchase behaviour comes from satisfaction, use and disposal after use.

Buying behaviour results from ethics in marketing as well. Marketers are required to sell products, which give value for money to the customers. Non-standard products, defective goods, prices that give wrong impression to the buyers (hidden charges like transport, taxes duties not mentioned in the beginning) short packing are some areas of unethical practices. Such deals can give only short-term small benefits and in the long run even if the law does not catch up, the customers eschew purchasing such goods and dealing with such marketers. In the bargain even good products of the marketer are discarded. A few examples will make the subject better understood by the students.

- Food items mixed with unhygienic wrong products like wrong non-food grade preservatives.
- Fake branded products
- Products like video and audio tapes which are pirated
- Quoting different prices to customers for standard products, unless quantity discounts are being offered.
- Advertising five star hotel when it does not have even three-star facilities
- Advertising contraband goods like liquor, drugs
- Cheating in annual **sales** where the prices are jacked up from original; then the discounted price still remains almost as original.

Incorrect or misleading advertising should be firmly avoided. It can cause untold harm including legal action, which has become one of the deterrents of such advertisements today.

Market Segmentation

Markets are such a heterogeneous place that unless we get to understand each part of it we remain ignorant of the market. There are people buying Mercedes cars and in the market people are buying low cost bicycles as means of transportation. Marketers of Mercedes communicate with the rich elitist class to sell their product. These people reside in certain section of the town; visit one club or the other, read a few business magazines like *Business India*, *Business Today*, and *India Today*. The cycle buyers go to cinema halls for low cost entertainment. Cycle sellers can show film advertising clips and slides to communicate to the segment. Both elite class and lower class persons would get the right message without too much clutter and in a language understood by them. Therefore, market segmentation helps both, the buyers and sellers.

Market segmentation is done on the following lines:

1. Geographic factors
2. Demographic factors
3. Psychological factors
4. Socio-cultural factors
5. Use related
6. Benefit segment
7. Combination of some of the above-mentioned factors

In India Tanishq watches have the following segment:

As the price starts from Rs. 20,000 to Rs. 1,25,000 high income, elite lifestyle, fashionable locality form the segment. Market communication, advertisement can thus be written in the language easily understood by the segment and placed in the media seen and read by them.

Geographic segment is for the region like south north-west and east of the country. Each region has its own peculiarities in customer needs and therefore consumer behaviour too is different for each. In each region, there are Metro large areas, large cities and smaller towns, besides villages. Urban semi-urban and rural divide provides a market segment.

Demographic segment is by age, sex, marital status, income, education and occupation.

Age segment is important as with growing population of senior citizens and a large teenage group, product needs for these segments are increasing. Healthcare products, vacation time products are needed for elder citizens. Teens need coffee bars, discos, and video game parlours.

Income separates people in their buying pattern and product groups. Marketers can decide to cater to one income group or the other, make products needed by them and then advertise in media most seen and read by them. Low cost ready-made garments for low-income segment can be advertised best on radio and local language press. Likewise Rolex watches for the rich segment can be advertised in Business magazines and TV Channels such as Star Plus.

Male and female customers have some specific products for each, like shaving creams for men and lipstick for women. With age the use of cosmetics change for women and marketers can make use of this change by offering products of their need. Young girls need cosmetics to enjoy mutual attraction with boys and for flirtation. Married women use cosmetics to keep their husbands happy and senior ladies use them to feel young.

Education and occupation segments: Customers who are well read would buy books of their interest. A professor of management would buy books on management.

Psychological/Psychographics segment: People's needs like shelter, food, safety, affection and self-actualization makes for different segments. These are the hierarchy of needs as per Maslow. The person who is self-actualized, graphics given below has different needs than others.

Psychological/psychographics segment divides customers around their mindset. People need ego boosting and certain products like fashion garments, designer watches and accessories make them feel good when they can have their heads in the cloud nine. Persons can be motivated to buy a car just because they have been selected to test drive it. Today's business executive is extremely busy and his/her involvement in buying daily need products is low. The target customer therefore is the buyer and not the user, may be the servant or some retired member of the family. The involvement increases with the value of purchase or some personal preference. "Please buy only Godrej Shaving cream for me" is a way in which the involvement manifests itself.

Socio-Cultural Segmentation

Family: In starting life the young persons are unmarried. They need household goods, like cleaning equipment, washing machine, cooking equipment, TV set.

Married couples initially need to go on honeymoon and later on according to their status and income needs keep adding up to car, house, and soon baby foods, diapers. Once the children grow, then music system, books, games and sports equipment are needed. As the children start their own life, the aging parents now alone again require, health products, medicines.

Society: Social groups originate from parity in income, occupation and education. Lots of purchases especially of consumer durables are made because the neighbour has purchased it. "Keeping up with the Jones" is the phrase used to describe this tendency of copying common in one social segment. Advertising based on targeting one social group becomes easy as the group members speak the same language, understand the same subtleties, the same comic situations and have the same attitudes and beliefs.

Cultural and subcultural segmentation: Our country boasts of unity in diversity. Cultural differences are quite pronounced as we travel from north to south, east to west. In the north for instance when guests are visiting offering them anything three in number is considered inauspicious, while in the south it is the done thing. Traditional women keep their heads covered in the north on auspicious occasions and in the south they have heads uncovered.

Subcultural segments come from areas like the north Punjabi culture with exuberant dances, music, extrovert lifestyle, as compared to Rajasthani segment, more conservative, traditional, although they also have their own dances and music. Each area in India has a fund of cultural heritage, which drives the segment members to behave in a certain manner. Durga Puja sees Bengalis buying dresses decoration material and the like.

With global marketing becoming important in India, cultural diversity around the world, has to be learnt. Simple things like favourite colours become important; cycles exported to Iran can come back to India if they do not come in Iran's favourite green colour. The subject will be discussed in detail in global advertising chapter.

Segmentation on the basis of usage: Imagine a person who buys a cell-phone and uses it only to see the number calling him and then goes to the nearest landline phone to call back. Another guy uses cell-phone the whole day, making STD and ISD calls to his foreign clients and collaborators. Or, a person stays in a five-star hotel only for one day in a year, eats out and just pays for the room rent of about Rs. 6,000 as against the person who stays at least for a week in a month, throws parties, uses the hotel facilities and his yearly bill exceeds Rs. 10,00,000. While it is understood that the customer is the king, we can now see that some customers are emperors, others are kings, some are princes, and yet others are just buyers. That is why to lure big buyers; firms have special treats for them, including the frequent flyer programme of many airlines, room upgrades of big hotel users. It may, however, be remembered that today's prince can become tomorrow's emperor and hence firms can ill afford to neglect to provide the best possible service to him.

Usage situation segment: Situational usage is prevalent for greeting cards, flowers, gift items that are given on occasions like Christmas, Deepavali and Eid. Card maker's gift suppliers focus their advertising effort towards the customers.

Benefit segment: People are looking for benefits all the time, like the calorie conscious person wants tasty food with low calories, and insurance people sell insurance promising life long benefits. In fact, the entire marketing is based on making customers aware of the benefits the firm's products provide as value for money and which are unique.

Demographic and psychographics analysis guides firms in their advertising communications by making them understand the following:

Who are our target markets?

What should we tell them?

Where this communication should be made?

Media too arranges such research and information so that firms know which media to use for which segment. In India, ABC gives the circulation figures of different publications and an idea of their readers. For TV, research organizations arrange for Television Rating Points (TRPs), which give area-wise idea of viewership of TV channels and their programmes.

Segmentation and its Usage in Advertising

To be of use to effective communication, the segment should be clearly defined. It should not be too small or too large, should be growing and should have access to advertising media.

Locating and identifying segments is easy for geographic or demographic segments. For psychological psychographics and user segments need market surveys with properly designed questionnaires and good reliable team asking questions, which are aware of the objective, methodology analysis and report writing.

For products like an expensive watch, segment in a town like Delhi would be in thousands, for Mercedes it may be in hundreds only. A segment for special type of trout safari may be too small.

The segment should be stable and increasing. Persons trying out new brands all the time are unstable buyers and cannot be counted for the segment.

Marketers have to communicate to the segment and availability of suitable and economical media becomes a necessity.

Motivation is the inner urge, which propels people to act. Seeing and smelling food people get motivated to eat while they may not be even hungry. Graphically it can be shown as on the next page.

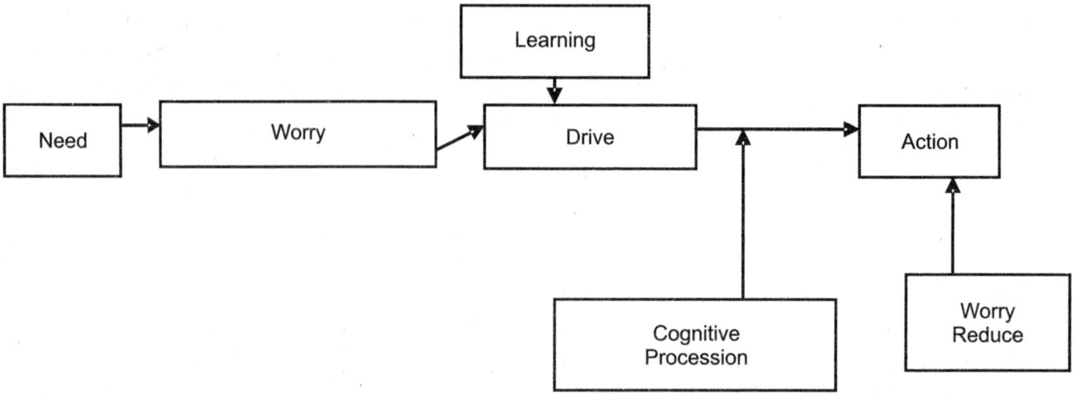

When the need is felt and till the time it is not fulfilled, the person suffers from anxiety and worry which forces him to understand the nature of the need and its fulfilment propelling him in to purchase action, which reduces his worry.

(From the *Consumer Behaviour* by Schiffman and Kanuk)

People have two types of needs, physiological, i.e., requirements of their bodies and psychological needs of the mind. Food, water, clothing and shelter are the primary physiological needs, and needs of power, self-esteem, affection, love are the secondary ones. A house may be the primary need but a bungalow where you can entertain guests becomes psychological secondary need.

Changing nature of goals and needs: When a particular goal or need cannot be fulfilled, a substitute goal emerges. Similarly, after fulfilment a new goal or need arises. In any case needs can never be fully satisfied. When a person becomes Vice President of a firm, he changes his goal to becoming the President. Product updates, newer technologies help the firms to use this **urge** as a springboard for launching innovative products.

Once the basic needs are fulfilled, people want to achieve higher goals. After getting a good house to live people would like to be community leaders.

As the saying goes, "Nothing succeeds like success", success gives extra fillip to people for going to higher level goals. Failure, on the other hand, make people redefine their goals, by either lowering the standard or taking a different road altogether.

Goal substitution occurs on non-attainment of goal. If you cannot buy Honda City car, buy a Maruti 800. Some people go into a dream world devoid of reality.

Non-achievement causes people to go into depression, which can result in behavioural changes like sulking and going into a shell, anger, rationalization of failure that is bad as it makes a person complacent, and frustrated.

Behaviour is oriented towards achieving personal goals. People have general types of goals and then they have product-oriented goals. *We will travel to the hills once I purchase my Ford IKON car* becomes a product and action oriented goal. We can see that everyone has rational and emotional motivations, with purely objective or subjective criteria.

Motivational Research is conducted as psychoanalysis of consumer's minds to understand, sometimes not so apparent reasons for their motives. The subconscious mind works for reasons of its own. Some product personality types have been profiled as a result of motivational research as follows:

- Baking: It conveys motherhood, feminity, love and caring; subconsciously the baking process is a substitute for the childbirth process.
- Ice cream is subconsciously associated with love and affection.
- Home maintenance kit: It is defining the man and machismo.
- Beer: It represents active alive people

Personality is the sum total of individual traits of character, bearing and behaviour. It allows us to fine-tune the differences among various people. With effort people can change their personality; from introvert they can become extrovert, from careless types they can become caring types.

Sigmund Freud developed the psychoanalytical theory of personality. He says that human personality consists of three overlapping areas—id, super ego and ego.

Id is the primitive animal-like instinct, which drives person's hunger, thrust and sex urges. Lots of advertising is based on using this animal force to advantage, and that is why female form is used to attract the males and vice versa.

Super ego is the mind's control on id, the animal instincts, so that people can live within social norms.

Ego is the balancing force between id and super ego helping people to keep to the right path between id's drive and societal norms.

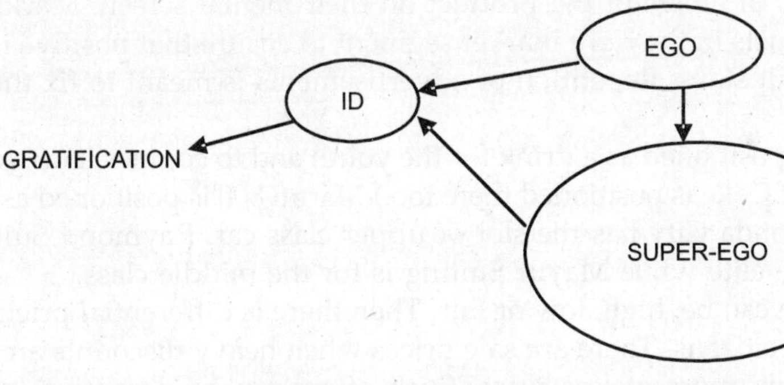

Freudian theory and brand/product personality: Some products are best represented by a celebrity, like Shah Rukh Khan can be called Mr. SANTRO, the car he is successfully advertising. He can also be named as Shah Rukh **Mayur** Khan when he personifies Mayur Suiting. Customers tend to associate the brands with the brand personality. Hence, marketers need to use a personality who can be fully identified with the product. Hrithik Roshan is promoting Coke, and yet as there have been many coke promoters, it is difficult to name Hrithik as Mr. Coke.

Personality theory of post-Freud People: Unlike Freud, other social scientists felt that motives cannot be confined to basic and sexual instincts. Social interaction and lifestyle too gives motivation to people to act.

There are four types of personalities as follows:

(a) Thinking and sensing types are rational, logical, objective and fast decision-makers

(b) Feeling and sensing types believe in their ownselves, are subjective and they consult others in decision-making
(c) Thinking and intuiting types take broad view, look for wider range of options and take decisions for long range of time.
(d) Feeling and intuiting types take broad view, are people oriented, take subjective decisions for long-time zones.

Karen Horney proposed that people can be classified in three personality types:

- Compliant types who seek company, want love and appreciation
- Aggressive types go against others and try to excel to gain admiration
- Detached types who remain away, want independence from interference and are keen to be solo winners

Let us discuss consumer materialism and compulsive buying. Materialistic people enjoy buying valuable goods and showing them off, which makes them egocentric and self-centred. They believe that their possessions would project their lifestyle and yet no possession gives them real satisfaction because the more you have, the more you want and there is no end to wanting. "My Swiss villa proves that I am a successful person."

Compulsive buying behaviour makes people buy things, which either they do not need or cannot afford. Sale offers, mail order people catch those people who are on a buying spree.

Consumers get an image of the product on their mental screen. Marketers have to position their products in the right market segment to ensure that positive mental image is formed and that it stays. Repetition of advertisements is meant to fix the product on the mind's screen.

Pepsi has been positioned as a drink for the youth and to counter it (as youth remains the biggest segment Coke is positioned there too.) Maruti 800 is positioned as the common man's car while Honda City has the slot of upper class car. Raymond Suiting is in the top position for the elite while Mayur Suiting is for the middle class.

Perceived price can be, high, low or fair. Then there is differential pricing like lower air ticket for senior citizens. There are sale prices when heavy discounts are offered, like save up to 50%, buy more at less price. Such offers can be deceptive, as the correct picture is not given to the consumers. While people feel happy at making purchases and acquiring products, if the price is the same as imagined by the buyer, then it does not give any pleasure. However, if the perceived price turns out to be more than the actual price then the transaction becomes interesting to the buyer. For example, buying a 200 litre refrigerator would cost the buyer Rs. 14000, and it costs him as much then there is no joy. In case the purchase price is Rs. 13500 only it gives mental satisfaction and pleasure to the buyer.

Most often, especially for consumer goods price and quality of a product get associated with each other and reduction in price can create doubts about the reduction in quality of the product. Similarly, product, country, quality and price are perceived by the customers as a package, as can be seen from below:

1. Made in the USA, best quality, high price
2. Made in Germany, solid in technology, medium price
3. Made in Japan, elegant, not sturdy, price quite high
4. Made in Korea, almost as good as from Japan, lower in price
5. Made in India, low labour cost, low price, inconsistent quality. (This perception is not correct any more but Brand India needs to be strengthened to overcome this perception.)

Price and quality relationship takes into account that each product has some service attached to it.

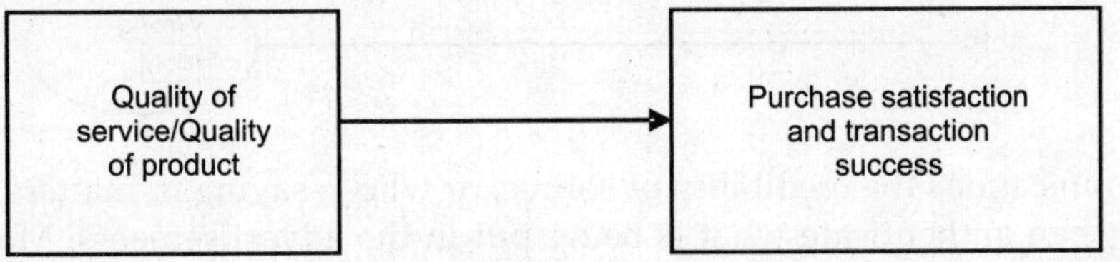

There are different types of consumers with unique personalities. There are consumers ready to experiment and they buy products in the introductory stage of product life cycle. Computer notepads, palmtop computers find a good market among this type of personality, who is always ready to innovate and experiment.

Dogmatic types have rigid behaviour pattern. When this type buys a new product it is contrary to their belief. Therefore, they have to be on the defensive and are uncomfortable with such purchases. They can be persuaded by authoritative, dramatic and dynamic advertisements, which help them overcome their basic negative attitude.

Open-minded consumers take to new products easily.

Social "type sets" - self-centred persons look for answers within themselves while extroverts are ready and at times eager to find out what their peers and seniors have to say, (**who says what** becomes important and a significant purchase decision tool).

Stimulation levels are important guides for consumer behaviour study. Some consumers lead a sedate life and minimum level of curiosity arousal is enough for them to become interested in the product. There are hard-core consumers who look for being shaken out of their slumber and for them heavy dosage of stimulation is needed. These persons can practically psyche themselves into the purchase mood.

Attitudes are predisposition levels people have towards a product or an idea. These positive or negative attitudes are based on earlier experience, odd remark heard from a known or even unknown person, from persons like salesmen connected to the product, the environment or mood in which the message about the product was given to the consumer.

Attitudes are normally consistent for a particular product. **If a thing is not liked, then it is not to be purchased**. Housewives may not even think of purchasing a twin drum-washing machine with the known benefits of single drum machines. At times attitudes change for reasons like, "let us economize" or non-availability of favourite brand in the shop visited and imminence of need. " Let us buy Godrej soap as Lux is not in stock." Such decisions for FMCG purchases are taken easily as the cost of replacement or repurchase is not heavy, unlike a consumer durable product like a car or TV, which cannot be purchased everyday.

Communication process is planned taking into account the target market segment and the mindset of the people of the segment. One communication model is given below.

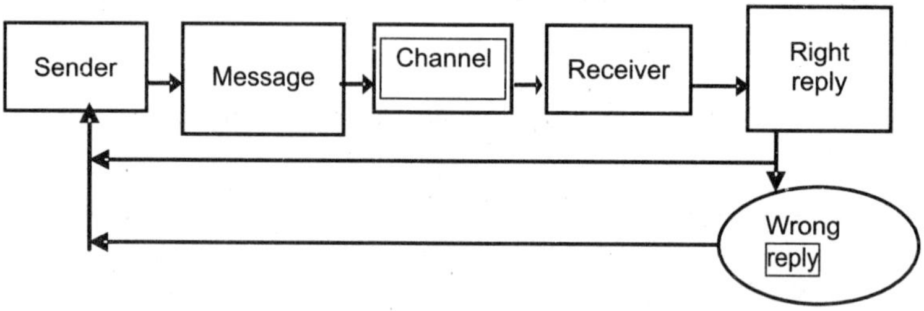

In communications the credibility of source, or who is saying it, matters a lot. Firm's brand equity can authenticate what is being put in the advertisements. Most firms use endorsers to talk about their products, which make the target segment believe in the product. Wrong endorsers can cause harm to the product or can have no impact rendering the advertisement useless. A top heroine endorsing washing powder may not have any impact as people know that she does not wash her clothes at all. When she endorses a beauty cream, people believe her.

Sender or source's credibility is important as it defines how or how much the receiver is going to believe it. **"Let us take it with a pinch of salt."** Such negative impressions come with unreliable senders of information. Use of endorsers becomes necessary in such cases. Source or sender has its own need for sending the message. How right is that need? For example, many firms resort to having **yearly sale** of their products. People want to know if it is a genuine sale, and if yes, why the firm is selling good products at heavily discounted prices? Is it that they have odd size unsold products, heavy inventory as their export order got cancelled, or, is it that the discounted prices are in fact the same as original? The firm increased the prices first and then declared the sale. Increase of prices was of 20% and discount offered is 17%. Such types of sales lose their impact in no time and bring bad name to the sale and to the sellers.

Personal involvement is the key factor on the interest the customer is going to have in understanding and correctly interpreting the message. Sachin Tendulkar will like to go through the exact specifications of the cricket bat, while a non-playing cricket TV commentator may just take no notice of the bat.

Moods of persons at the time they are receiving the message govern how well they will receive and accept the message. Watching a tragic sob story movie on TV would make people less willing to accept the positive aspects of a product. It calls for proper selection of media; sitcoms, news bulletins, and movie-based programmes are viewed on TV with a happy frame of mind, generally.

In order to monitor customer response to a message and its media pre-testing is done where the advertisement is shown to a select group of the market segment to gauge their reaction and get their feedback. In case of poor response, corrections in message and media can be made.

After the advertisement has been released, post-testing is done to find out how effectively the advertisement has met its objectives.

Persuasion strategy: For proper impact of the message, selection of the market segment to be catered to, creativity of the advertisement and objectives associated with the communication are key elements of strategy Some examples are given below:

- Housewife, family income Rs. 20,000 pm, urbanite, graduate would be reading, Femina, Cosmopolitan, Star Dust magazines, watching afternoon soap operas like, Saans, Santa Barbara, Dynasty
- College student's family income Rs. 40,000 pm would be reading sports, motorcycle and car magazines, listening to FM radio.
- Achievers, family income Rs. 80,000 pm, would be reading business magazines like Business India, Business Today, financial national and global newspapers and watching news on Star TV.
- Senior citizens family income Rs. 20,000 pm would be reading health and investment magazines, watching travel related TV programmes for enjoying vicarious adventure and thrills.
- Computer addicts would be surfing the Internet and the best media for communicating to them about software updates would be the web.
- There is always crossover in segments. For instance, for a person with monthly income of Rs, 10,000, a woollen suit worth Rs. 5,000 may be out of reach. However, he may buy it at least for his marriage.

Persuasion comes in the form of personal influence of some person who **counts.** In daily life, we communicate with other persons in social, political or business situations. A good communicator listens more than he/she speaks. When in doubt, we seek advice, or sometimes we get advice totally unasked for. In both cases, it is stored in the brain from where it can be restored at the time of purchase decision-making. We normally go to people whom we consider as more knowledgeable than us. These people are the **opinion leaders**. Buying a set of golf clubs it is best to ask the golf champion, rather than a layman. For cameras and films, the professional photographer, not the camera salesperson would be the best bet.

Opinion leaders being experts on their subjects can be trusted to give correct opinion on their subject of specialization. Marketers, on the other hand, would invariably give only the positive aspects of their products.

Several times customers seek only information, and sometimes they ask for advice. Can we trace which of the following statements of opinion leaders is information and which is advice?

1. Which is the best gent's shoe for formal wear? "In my view, Bata is still the best"
2. How to use the vacuum cleaner? "I use it once a week to clean the carpet, the curtains, the floors and the ceiling. You could do the same"
3. Where to take my Maruti for servicing in Delhi? "There is no better place than Competent Motors, my dear"
4. Where can I get a gift for my girl/boyfriend? "Try Giggles in CP and you will not go wrong"

As can be seen opinion-leaders are mostly "product" specific. You will not ask your milkman where to buy computer software. In case of doubt, people take second or even third opinion until they are satisfied by the opinion. People with set ideas, often stop after they have got an opinion, which agrees, to their own thinking. Such subjective opinions can be misleading resulting in wrong decisions.

Advertisers extend the theory of opinion leadership in advertising by using the **leaders as product endorsers.**

Self-image is the some total of a person as he thinks about himself and it is a guiding factor in purchase decision along with wisdom of opinion leaders. "What type of person am I? The image I project to outsiders, how people view my personality" make for the self-image. There are several types of self image:

- How people view themselves
- How they want others to view them
- How they would like to seen in the future

Self-image and products purchased has an interesting connection, as the industrialist buys Mercedes to project the self-image of a successful person. Actors and actresses want to look good and attractive to their fans and their clothes, makeup is meant to focus on that image. Marketers take advantage by using this concept while communicating to them.

Consumer perception is the consumer's view of the things including messages and stimuli seen/focused on him. These perceptions are given or acquired by visual stimulus, like seeing pictures of products in advertisements, hearing about the products from friends and looking the retail shops, point of purchase (POP), visual impact.

To heighten the impact, advertisers use sensational gimmicks including adventure sports, pretty women as sex objects to make the impact. The level of minimum stimulation, which can attract is called the **threshold level**. For two different stimuli the minimum difference, which becomes noticeable is known as JND, **Just Noticeable Difference**.

Weber has given the law, which stipulates that, "an additional stimulus equal to JND must be added for majority of people to perceive a difference between the resulting stimulus and the initial stimulus."

Car polish makers add some ingredients in the product that it keeps the lustre for a week as compared to competitive product where the shine lasts for four days. The danger in making it better, to the extent that the shine lasts for a month or even a fortnight, would increase the gap between purchases. Marketers and advertisers use the JND to good use in their **product development and advertising strategy**.

Subliminal perception considers even below the JND stimulus as psychologists have found that even such stimulus leaves an impression on the subconscious level and while it remains dormant it may manifest itself at the right time when product purchase is being considered. Years before a friend had said that the best TV set is from Sony and today finalizing the purchase it comes as bolt from the blue and the decision is made in its favour.

Hence, the decision process is based on the complex nature of human insights, which the marketers find ways to stimulate and bring to surface in their favour.

Marketing and communicating to the target market segment, of new innovative product calls for sustained efforts of advertising, personal selling and word of mouth appreciation of product for a period of time.

Market based new product, which the market considers as new. When Airtel Company introduced cellular phones in Delhi, they were new to the market, and consumers took it as such.

Consumer based new products are the ones which the consumers find totally new.

The **innovative or the new product** is seen by the firm as new to it and the firm becomes buoyant about it. The firm ignores the fact the product may not be new to the market as competitors may already have introduced the same.

Product innovation takes into account the features, which are unique to the product. One refrigerator manufacturer is claiming novel door cooling system, not available in other refrigerators.

The new product development can be on a continuous basis or on one-off base. Telephone industry has had both types of innovations as can be seen from the following table.

Discontinuous development	Dynamic continuous development	Continuous development
Telephone	Answering machine, voice mail	Auto-dialing facility, memory phones
Pager	Nation-wide paging, two-way paging, sports scores	Message displays, alarm clocks
Fax	Fax modem, mobile fax	Speed dial, delayed dispatches

Consumers look for **relative advantages** in each product. Also the expense of making change and product's compatibility with other products with the consumer too plays an important role in buying new products. For example, the modem and printer should be able to work with the computer before they are purchased.

Organizational Buying Behaviour

Organizations or firms involved in manufacturing goods purchase, raw materials and components needed in the manufacturing process. They also buy consumables like electricity, water and gases, which are consumed, in the manufacturing process. Such purchases by the firms have the following characteristics:

1. Fewer buyers but large quantity buyers
2. Close supplier and buyer relationship
3. Geographic concentration of buyers
4. Derived demand
5. Inelastic demand/fluctuating demand
6. Professional purchasing
7. Several buying influences

Firms produce large volumes of products and hence need large quantity of materials. An individual will buy a TV picture tube only as a replacement only if his TV set's picture tube has become defective. A TV set manufacturer will be buying picture tubes in thousands for putting them in the TV sets. Yet as compared to individual buyers, TV set manufacturers will be far less in number.

In most cases industries are established near the source of one or two major raw materials needed for manufacture. Hence, most industries are concentrated in that area. Gujarat has lot of cotton, which accounts for large number of textile mills in that region.

The demand of raw materials is derived from the plan of manufacture of products, which use the material. The tyre sale is dependent on the number of cars manufactured in a particular period.

For such intermediary products the demand remains inelastic over long periods of time with only marginal changes. However, it could also be grammatically changed in case the buyers find different usages of the product when the demand will increase. If the product becomes obsolete, the demand could just disappear, as happens often in fashion garments.

Purchase in such cases becomes a professional discipline. Depending on the value in money terms and also in availability terms, the importance is given to purchase decisions.

Buying situations can be classified as follows:

1. First buy is when a new firm makes the purchases or an old firm tries out a new product.
2. Re-buy takes place when a satisfied buyer buys the product again. This happens when besides the product other factors like firms after sales service, the buyer accepts behaviour of its sales people.
3. Modified re-buy is made when the manufacturer accepts customer's suggestions and product is suitably modified to suit the firm.
4. New task purchase depends on the launch of new products and is planned accordingly.

System for buying in the organizations consists of the following persons.

Initiators are the people who place the requirement of the product before the firm's authorities. In most firms, they would be either R& D persons or purchase executives.

Users are the people who define the product with specifications and would ultimately use it. They would be R&D engineers, production engineers.

Influencers are the people who influence the purchase decision, which brand; model to buy, from which dealer. These could be R&D managers, consultants.

Deciders are the authorized people who can decide spending of money for making the purchase. They are of the rank of general managers,

Approvers are the people with power of approving the purchase like chief executive officers and managing directors.

Gatekeepers are those who filter information and see to it that only relevant information reaches the decision-makers about the product. These could be receptionists, purchasing agents.

Consumer behaviour in organizational buying therefore becomes complex, with a number of persons involved in the decision-making. Therefore, unlike in consumer products the role of advertisement in organizational buying is limited to image building of the firm and providing detailed information to the buyers about the products.

Environment factors are also major influencers in organizational buying as follows.

Environmental factors	Organizational factors	Interpersonal factors	Individual	Business Buyer
Level of demand	Objectives	Interests	Age	-do-
Economic outlook	Policies	Authority	Income education job position	-do-
Interest rate	Policies	Authority	-do-	-do-
Risk of technical changes	Procedures	Status	Personality	-do-
Political and regulatory developments	-do-	-do-	Attitude for risks	-do-
Competitive developments	Organizational structure	Empathy	-do-	-do-
Social	Systems	Persuasiveness	Culture	-do-

Environment factors like market demand of the product influences the quantity of purchase as also purchase frequency.

Economic outlook of the country gives the information on the money supply situation, interest rates for leasing and it has influence on purchase decisions.

If the firms know that a **new technically superior** product is going to be available in the near future, they would not risk large purchased of materials.

Political environment deals with the political will which allows or restricts trading, like the anti-dumping laws of the USA.

If the market is swaying towards **a better competitive product,** the firm may make only cautious purchases.

If **the sociological changes force** the market towards decline, then also purchases get reduced. With the availability of packed wheat flour, no one is buying wheat and getting it ground in a mill.

Organizational policy changes, changes in hierarchy levels, promotions, procedural changes and systems could alter the purchase pattern of the firm.

Factors connected to individual members of a firm like inter-personnel relations, people's authority, personal interests, empathy with suppliers and persuasiveness of marketers are important for purchase decisions.

Organizational buying decisions are taken by purchase committee consisting of:

1. CEO, who only wants **the best in the line** product.
2. R&D manager, who wants the **state-of-the-art** product.
3. Financial manager, who wants **value for money**, economical products.
4. Purchase manager, who wants the usual product, to avoid **inventory** hassles.

5. Production manager, who wants no change in assembly process unless new product helps in major **cost reduction**.
   - Each one is a customer in his own right and his needs must be satisfied. It calls for communication excellence to put same points in different words to conform to their perception of need as follows:
   - To the CEO, "Our product is top of the line as can be seen from our specifications, which incidentally, exceed the specifications given by competition and you can see the testimonials from our national and global customers which speak for themselves."
   - To the R&D manager, "you have heard of the latest proven technology in microprocessors based on fibre optics, you can open the equipment and see it for yourself that we are giving you the state-of-the-art product"
   - To the finance manager, "our product pricing is based on volume business and that is why we can give you the price of our product with latest technology comparable to the price offered by competition for their older generation product."
   - To the purchase manager, "we believe that by the time our product reaches you, your old inventory would be almost exhausted and it would be easy for you to standardize on our state-of-the-art product, which we are sure would make you even more respected member of your firm."
   - To the production manager, "you would be able to reduce manufacturing time after the training we will provide to you people, thus reducing the cost of manufacture considerably. Besides, with reduction in quality problem, the firm will get a better brand image and after-sales service team would become practically redundant."

It would be necessary to test the product before making the claims as mentioned above.

Consumer behaviour and firms responses find that firms do take care of how the consumer will behave.

1. ITC Agro introduced their branded Atta, Health World first in the south India, as their study showed that south Indians are more quality conscious than north Indians in the matter of a product like Atta, in spite of the fact that the Atta consumption in the north is nine times more than in the south. Once the brand gets established in the south, they will move to the north as well with region specific brands and tastes to suit different palates.
2. Dwarka Men's Wear offering cool cotton trousers and shirts, chose the month of March 2000 to launch the product just before the onset of summer. They have successfully marketed their product in the West Asian and European markets.
3. Targeting their cell phones for the youth of the country, Ericsson have introduced FM radio in the phones which come in a range of bright colours to capture the fancy of the youth.

Consumer Behaviour-Positivism and Interpretism

Positivism—prediction of consumer action—Quantitative-consumer rationale, weigh alternatives. With market study, it can be predicted that x per cent customers would buy the product.

Interpretism—understanding consumer practices—qualitative-reality is subjective, each usage experience is unique, and research findings can be subjective. Cannot be generalized, like it is not easy to predict how many first buyers would go for repurchase of the product.

Attitudes play an important role in purchase actions and it is necessary to understand as to how they are formed.

- Direct experience from using the product, "the soap is too hard"
- Influence of family and friends, "Son, buy only Honda motorcycle, it is the best value for money"
- Direct marketing, Eureka Forbes salesman in your house, "see for yourself how easy it is to use the vacuum cleaner sir"
- Exposure to advertisements, wife to husband, "see the mixer grinder ad on the TV and you would agree it is the best value for money"
- Personality factor, "I cannot buy a motorcycle, only a car would do for me"

Attitudes - four functions

- Utilitarian function: brand utility
- Ego-defensive function: product enhances self-concept
- Value expressive function: consumer values, lifestyle are reflected
- Knowledge function: fulfilling need to know

Also, there can be a combination of several of these functions.

The task before buyers is one of resolving conflicting attitudes as given below.

Tasty v/s healthy food, pizza or fruit cream

Quality v/s price, Wipro PC or the assembled one

Sturdy v/s elegant, jeans or silk

The decisions are taken on purchases on the following considerations:

The Family

Economics

Emotional support

Lifestyle

Family socialization—manners, values, goals

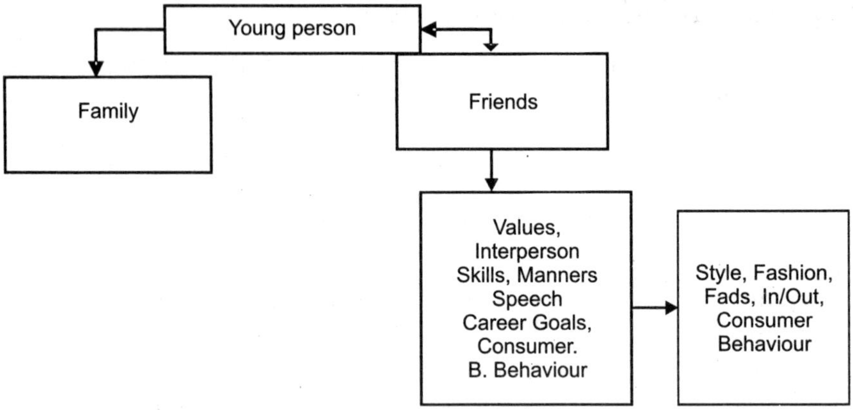

Family Consumer Roles

Husband/wife
Children
Teens

Family life cycle, where lifestyle keeps changing as can be seen from the following:

- Bachelor—mostly carefree
- Honeymooners—need affordable luxuries
- Parents—young children—need baby products
- Parents—teenage children—need teen fad products, like FM Radio
- Parents with children away from home, healthcare products
- Dissolution—old age homes

Feeling and Emotions

These can be measured on a scale. Let us try out a skin cream and get reactions of women after they have used the cream on a scale as follows:

A-like it very much—B-like it—C-nothing special—D-do not like—E-do not like it at all.

The survey can be done on the following parameters:

Skin felt	A	B	C	D	E
Relaxed					
Beautiful					
Tight					
Smooth					
Supple					
Clean					
Refreshed					
Oily					
Pampered					

Designing Persuasive Communication

- Proper market segmentation
- If product transcendent segmentation: umbrella messaging for all audience
- Good PR
- Media plan: consumer profile to match with media audience profile
- Each media is effective for some products, audience and advertising objectives
- WWW
- Overlapping audience

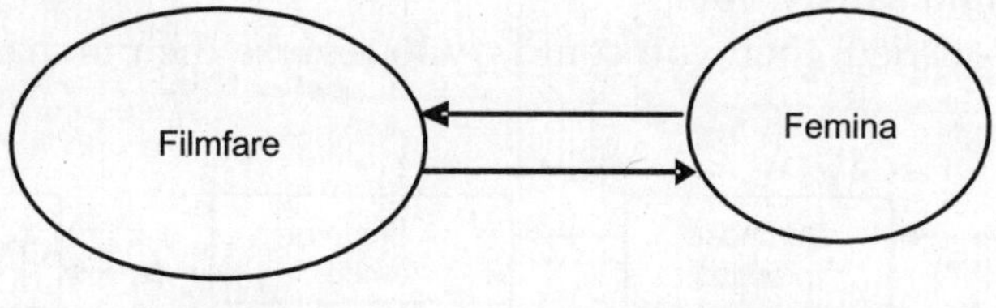

Some customers read Filmfare, other read Femina and yet other read both.

In advertising copy, it is important to think of the following:

- Copy appeal
- Copy length
- Endorsements
- Visuals
- Time limit offers
- Free trial offers
- Pricing

Example

You are the Marketing and Advertising Manager of Advance Stereo Systems with five competitors, Philips, Videocon, BPL, AIWA and Sony. Your market share is 3%. You have to increase it to 5% in one year. Discuss the following questions about market and its behaviour:

1. What cultural, social, personal and psychological factors influence the buyers most? What sort of research should be undertaken to know the buyer's attitude and behaviour?
2. What factors should advance focus on in their marketing plan?
3. What kind of marketing activities advance should plan to coincide with each stage of consumer buying process?

Plan your target market in Delhi, and look at the marketing mix factors for giving your recommendations to Advance MD.

Purchase Decisions Plan

1. Problem recognition: when the need tends to become acute
2. Information search: Personal—family, friends, neighbours, acquaintances, commercial-advertising, salesmen, dealers, packaging, displays, public source—consumer rating organizations, experiential-handling, examining, using the product.

3. Evaluation of alternatives with weightage given on parameters decided by you, cameras—size, weight, auto-focus, zoom, speed, price, hotels—location, cleanliness, atmosphere and price
4. Purchase decision: There can be a situation where after deciding to buy you delay or even cancel the purchase. Sometimes if people close to you have a negative attitude towards the product you may not buy it. Secondly, there may be a change in situation

Post-purchase decisions

The product could satisfy you.

If you are not satisfied, then you could try to reverse the purchase action. Or sell of the product.

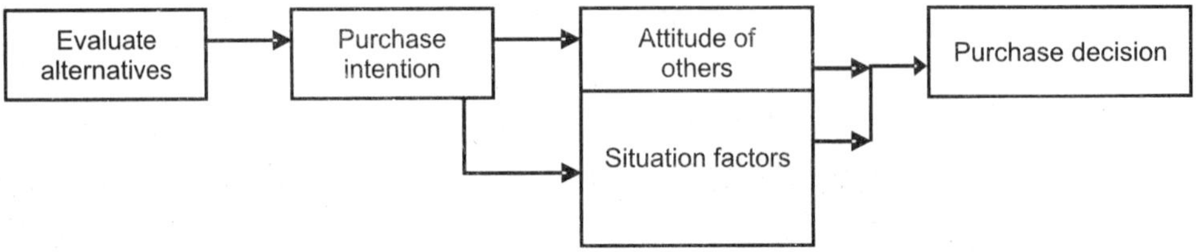

Let us discuss buyers in the developing countries purchases of some common FMCG products.

- Washing powder sells about 30% less than washing soap cakes.
- Toilet soap sells about fifty per cent of washing soap cakes.
- Electric bulbs sell six times more than the tubelights.
- Nail polish sells about the same as lipsticks.
- Leather shoes sell fifty per cent less than the casual shoes.

Product penetration in urban and rural developing countries is as follows:

S. No.	Products	Urban%	Rural%	Total%
1.	Tooth care	90	50	60
2.	Washing powder	100	90	98
3.	Tea	90	70	80
4.	Milk powder	9	3	5
5.	Butter	10	2	4
6.	Salt	100	95	97
7.	Chocolates	10	2	4
8.	Ice cream	25	10	14
9.	Shampoo	25	9	13
10.	Hair oil	90	85	87
11.	Wristwatches	45	20	28
12.	Talcum powder	45	25	30
13.	Lipsticks	22	12	15
14.	Nail polish	40	30	32

CHAPTER

15

Global Manufacturing and Operations

It must be understood that with every product there is some service involved and with every service there is a product. The ratio of product is higher in consumer durables, FMCGs; they usually need large manufacturing facilities and are capital intensive. The output in product groups can be measured and quality checks are easy to organize. Conversely the services are more intangible and perishable (you cannot carry the aeroplane seat with you on disembarking. An empty seat on the plane loses its fare and hence perishes.) The output of service cannot be placed under inventory. The customers are in close touch with the service provider, while in products the customer comes in contact only with the retailer. Service as a product is usually labour-intensive and its quality checks are difficult.

The MNCs have to decide about the location where the components would be made, subassemblies arranged and where the final assembly would take place, as these may not be necessarily at one location. The decision on these points are taken by taking the following into consideration:

1. Cost of labour, its efficiency levels
2. Cost of money supply
3. Availability of raw material and their costs
4. Infrastructure availability
5. Transportation costs to the markets and from the raw material components and subassemblies production areas.
6. Trust and dependability of the supplier group, company's own or outsourced
7. Level of awareness of quality requirements
8. Flexibility of activities
9. Level of innovative activities

Production efficiency would help reduce the cost of products, as it would cut down the rejection rate and the cost of rework. Raw material availability would help in saving time in their search as well as reduce transportation time. Without proper infrastructure the company would be handicapped in communications with the home country, with the suppliers, buyers, bankers and with the other stakeholders. Trust and dependability helps in building long-term associations with the host county organization for mutual benefit. As the company sells on its brand name that is singly characterized by the product and service quality it is imperative that the host country unit understands and remains focused on the company's quality requirements. As the market is not a static entity, the manufacturing unit must be flexible enough to react quickly to the demand from the market with a little lead-time as possible. While the company may depend on its home country R&D, it is an asset if the host unit is also prepared to modify the product to suit the market.

Once the country has been selected it becomes necessary to select a location along with the production scale. It would call for an assessment of the market needs of the areas or even countries the company wants to cater to, from the facility. The choice of process would follow once the size of operations has been decided. Companies in USA have found outsourcing as a viable option in case of several products, like shoes where starting from Nike to Adidas the US firms are getting the shoes made from some far eastern countries like Taiwan, Korea, Hong Kong, Philippines. They are getting software developed from other countries like India. This brings the companies to the subject of vertical integration, where either upstream or downstream products are added on to the manufacturing list. For instance, the car maker can take up making of car seats as well. The company can plan coordinating the activities of its various R&D activities that could be placed in home country besides some host countries as well. The manufacturing processes can be made uniform based on the home country's facilities or could be modified in host countries taking the level of manufacturing technology available there. Companies can decide to have manufacturing only in the home country for exporting from there to the markets worldwide. They could opt for independent manufacturing bases in different host countries, as per the market needs, logistics support availability. They can plan both global manufacturing as well as regional, to suit the market needs. Availability of raw materials, low cost skilled labour and low cost finance are other factors that guide companies to plan overseas production. Companies can shift manufacturing to countries where the technology is available at reasonable cost and/or the market is in close proximity. At times the home country governments provide incentives to outside companies for setting up manufacturing bases in their country to obtain technology, increase job potential and improve the country's GNP. If the company finds host country manufacture lower in cost even as compared to home country manufacture, they could import from the host country to sell in the home country.

A good example of such outsourcing can be seen from the British Raj in India when the raw materials from India like cotton, wool, and iron ore were exported to the UK, and after they got converted into finished products they were imported to India, giving the entire profit to the UK companies that were engaged in the conversion process. India suffered due to its political handicap of being a slave country.

Today, however, locating the manufacturing unit would depend on several factors as given below.

1. Cost of transportation of raw materials, components and finished goods
2. Import duties on components
3. Import duties on finished goods
4. Market proximity
5. Economies of scale possible
6. Risk of currency fluctuations
7. Availability of technology

The actual process of manufacture would depend on the levels of technology available ad the cost of labour in the host country. If the cost of labour is low, then the manufacturing process can envisage labour intensive and if the labour cost is high then it may be better to have lot of automated process with may be robotics involved. Cost and availability of land, availability of essential infrastructure like power, water, telecommunication, roads that are motorable, nearness of railhead, ports and airfield. Manufacturing layout normally takes a standard pattern that reduces backtracking of semi-finished goods and yet some of the considerations stated above can cause changes in the same.

A major issue in outsourcing remains the quality level of manufactured product in the host country. While quality is usually determined by the company's norms, the actual implementation and enforcement of quality standards have to be left to the host country units. Most companies keep their trusted quality assurance persons in the host country operations to maintain uniform quality standards with the home country production. Companies have resorted to theories of TQM, the **Total Quality Management** concept that empowers the workers to ensure maintenance of **Acceptable Quality Levels.** TQM as a process is meant to arrange manufacturing with zero defects. This saves on reworking expenses, besides improves on the cycle of manufacture, enabling lower lead-time for dispatches of finished goods. TQM process continuously improves the process of manufacture as the workers themselves keep experimenting for making improvements happen. Zero defects manufacture helps in lowering the manufacturing costs as the rework time is reduced to zero. Companies may have to invest in better technology manufacturing equipment that result in lowering defects, and improving the product quality. Manufacturing costs run into the costs of making plus the costs of defects, defective customer returns and cost of repairs. With zero defects the manufacturing costs have no element in it other than the cost of manufacture.

Hence, it can be summarized that TQM remove defects through continuous improvements at all levels of the organization besides manufacturing; it goes beyond to purchasing, sales, HRM and finance.

ISO 9000 certification appears essential today for non-European companies wanting to do business with Europe. The ISO series is about a company documenting their entire process and keeping records at each stage of their operation to show to interested persons that they are adhering to the process they have adopted for their operations. The types of ISO certification given are as follows:

1. ISO 9001: It is issued if the company has comprehensive and detailed standards for design, development, production, installation and servicing.

2. ISO 9002: It is issued for companies having standards on production and installation
3. ISO 9003: It is issued to companies focusing on final inspection of the products and testing.

Global Outsourcing and Manufacturing

Companies have several options, like getting components from other countries and assembling them in the home country for local consumption and for exports. Besides, the company and arrange components in a host country, assemble the product there, import into home country and other countries as well, as given below.

1. Outsourcing material, assembly in home country, host country/countries or both
2. Manufacture of components, assembly in home country, host country/countries or both
3. Product sales in home country, host countries/countries or both

Most companies prefer to use home country raw materials and components as it helps in avoiding problems of distances, political problems, currency fluctuation problems, tariff variations, and the problems arising out of dealing with different languages. However, companies keep looking at global sourcing to reduce costs and for improving the product quality. Finally, outsourcing should provide the company with cost reduction, quality improvements, increased access to global state-of-the-art technology and improvement in reliability and delivery process.

According to Ford motor company, they have an extensive global network for obtaining components needed in the two manufacturing facilities they have in Europe. For example, some of the components they get from the UK are, clutch, ignition, oil pump, speedometer, battery, steering wheel, fuel tank, glass and locks. Other locations they outsource the components are as follows:

1. Austria: tyres, radiator and heater hoses
2. Belgium: tyres, tubes, seat pads, brakes and trims
3. Italy: cylinder head, carburettor, glass, lamps, and defrost grill
4. Canada: glass and radio
5. Japan: starter, alternator, roller and cone bearings, windscreen washer pumps
6. Norway: exhaust ranges and tyres
7. Sweden: hose clamps, cylinder bolts, exhaust pipes, pressings and hardware
8. Denmark: fan belt
9. Switzerland: under chassis coating, speedometer, and gears
10. Holland: tyres, paints and hardware
11. United States: EGR valves, wheel nuts, hydraulic tappet and glass
12. Germany: locks, pistons, front disc, distributor, weather-strips, rocker arm, speedometer, fuel tank, cylinder bolt, cylinder head gasket, front wheel knuckles, rear wheel spindle, transmission cases, clutch cases, steering column, battery and glass
13. France: alternator, cylinder head, master cylinder, brakes, under chassis coating, weather strips, clutch release bearings, steering shaft and joints, seat pads and frames,

transmission cases, clutch cases, tyres, suspension bushes, ventilation units, heater hose clamps, sealers and hardware.

As can be seen, the company has, for certain critical components arranged for more than one source of supply, while their production bases are just two in Europe, in Halewood, UK and in Saarlouis, Germany.

The companies add foreign supplier to the domestic ones, for ensuring reliability of supplies. In some cases, the technical expertise may be available only overseas along with capacity to supply the components as per the company's requirements. Outsourcing overseas could allow the company to get better quality components, besides it could help in fighting competition from home suppliers base from where other manufacturers are also obtaining the components. It helps in opening up the global markets to the company. Moreover, if competition is outsourcing their components, the company should find out the economic viability of doing so and then plan its own offshore sourcing.

The companies have to take a stand on making the products or buying it for sales. At times some components could be made and some others could be bought out. Companies could go for vertical integration and get into manufacturing of the downstream components. The other option is to just buy them from outside suppliers. Outsourcing should be resorted to where the supplier has the advantage of economies of scale, better technology, have lower manufacturing cost structure or incentives for higher levels of production. Components that are critical should be outsourced with great care as it would bind the company to the source that could play truant by not supplying on time and pressurizing the company for better prices, cash payments. The quality management of the suppliers need careful scrutiny and at times may need imparting training to suppliers' engineers in proper testing methods and the value of TQM. When the suppliers can provide quality products, constantly upgraded technological innovations, economies of scales translated into price reductions the company can look for long-term relationship with such suppliers. At times when such a supplier has been found, the company would be tempted to vertically integrate the supplier in its own ambit. Else, the company can opt for long-term agreements, cooperation in technology upgradation, finance, manpower planning, management expertise for maintaining close contacts where the supplier feels almost one with the company. In such a scenario, the company can even change the components, their specifications and yet get the same at a low price, enabling the company to plan new models at competitive prices. The value chain can in a way become an arm of the company.

Companies have several options before they plan their purchase function. They can go in for totally local purchase when the controls are easier, time for obtaining supplies shorter and price negotiations can be conducted with relative ease, as the supplier is aware of the business ethos of the country. The companies can plan small supply sizes with lower cash requirements. And the latest "Just in Time" inventory management becomes more possible.

Next, the companies can selectively locate global component manufacturers, with the necessary qualifications to become suppliers. It could start as a one-off purchase deal and ultimately become a regular supply commitment from both the suppliers' side and the company. Finally, companies can plan global outsourcing strategies to obtain the benefits available in different parts of the world, like that of some country having better technology, other having low cost labour and yet another having easy availability of the required raw materials.

Companies use number of ways for getting overseas supplies, like involving the home office purchase department to do the job. They could use foreign subsidiaries or business units for selecting the suppliers most suited for their operations. Some companies that have global offices use them for organizing outsourcing in the countries they operate. The most advanced companies using global outsourcing in an integrated manner for worldwide operations. These centralized operations are most useful when the money value of purchase is high; the components are of strategic importance, including the value of quality and if they have high technology inputs. The companies can plan to obtain up to 70% of their requirements from one source. The supply agreements can be also on long-term basis may be up to five years. The purchase actions could be centralized from home office for keeping direct control on the vital purchases.

Inventory Management and JIT

Just in Time inventory management calls for supplies to be made in time when required for use and of good quality. Foreign sourcing becomes problematic when the companies are looking for JIT. Economies in transportation, distances, language and cultural differences are mainly responsible for the problems. JIT requirements constitute the following:

1. Understanding of shipment size and consequent shipment frequency
2. Company's policy on inventory management should be clearly understood by purchase people as inventory or current assets block company's cash reserves.
3. Lead-time required by the supplier for supply batches
4. Rejection rate of supplies and quality management of the suppliers
5. Means and methods of communication available with the supplier
6. Number of suppliers for a particular component, whether sole or multiple suppliers
7. Supplier's record of timely supplies
8. Supplier's approach to sudden changes in supply schedules
9. Availability of shipping lines, air cargos and their frequency

Uncertainties in shipment schedules cause inventory built-up increasing the costs. Ocean freight costs much less than air cargo but depending on the time schedule either option can be used. JIT usually creates a one supply source situation, that commits to strict supply plans and yet global supply base almost forces companies into keeping alternative supply source due to several imponderables associated with global suppliers.

Free Trade Zones

Free Trade Zones are promoted by certain governments where tariff payments can be delayed or totally avoided. In these zones, storage and manufacturing can take place without payment of any duty. Having a large inventory in these zones does not block money meant for paying the duties and taxes. These could be industrial parks or distribution zones.

Product Development

Companies operating globally arrange their product development and new product launches through their global R&D facilities that may be spread in several countries. The R&D and manufacturing units may be in different countries and yet they have to keep interacting for getting the right product as needed by the customers and that too at the lowest cost. Such designing of the products gets the nearest possible fit, as the demands and variety required by different countries can be quite different from each other. National consumer tastes, preferences and sophistication needs can be met only with across the national boundary research establishments.

SUMMARY

Production management is responsible for the conversion process that converts the raw materials and components into saleable products. As expertise of manufacturing, availability of raw materials and components, skilled labour for different products may be available in different countries, companies have to take the decision regarding the location of their manufacturing units. Proximity of markets, money supplies at low cost are major considerations in this regard, besides the host country's governments laws and attitudes towards foreign companies operating in the country.

Companies have to keep strict vigil on the quality of products being manufactured in other countries. Outside manufacture can take place through having joint venture with some local company. TQM, ISO 9000 are methods of improving quality and maintaining the same as per the customers' requirements.

Companies can start with home country manufacture and exports, followed by manufacturing facilities in other countries that can operate in the multi-domestic mode with autonomy. When the offshore manufacture is widespread in several countries, then the company can create global focus with regional emphasis on product designs for different country markets. At times only outsourcing of components can be done with one or two locations for assembling the same. Transportation costs play an important role in deciding the location of the manufacturing units. JIT inventory management in global outsourcing scenario becomes complicated as lead-time variations and transportation time can be the deciding factors. Worldwide R&D can help the MNCs in promoting the right mix of manufacture in different countries that could be catering to the needs of a vast variety of customers.

CHAPTER

16

Global Cultural Diversity

Cultural diversity is a fact of modern life and it exists now in practically all countries of the world. In addition to conventional elements such as race, religion and language, cultural diversity is accentuated by new factors including globalization, the breakdown of the traditional moral consensus, the emphasis on individual choice regarding issues like the place of religion in public life, family discipline, relations between parents and children, and other aspects of life today.

Cultural diversity is at the root of most conflicts, tensions and uncertainties in the contemporary world. Some have attributed the present "international insecurity" to the Clash of Civilisations whilst others advocate dialogue of religions and cultures to prevent such conflicts and bitterness. In 2001, the General Assembly of the United Nations adopted the Global Agenda for Dialogue among Civilisations and the UNESCO endorsed the International Declaration on Cultural Diversity.

A common assumption inspires both covenants. A multicultural society needs to find ways and means to accommodate diversity without losing its cohesiveness and unity. Two approaches are rejected. Assimilation which requires minorities to abandon their own distinctive institutions, cultures and values to merge into the prevailing culture is to be avoided. This way sociologically is unlikely to succeed and is morally untenable in view of the people's deep adherence to normative values such as religion.

Similarly, unbounded multiculturalism which entails giving up the concept of shared values and identity in order to privilege ethnic and religious differences presuming that a nation can be replaced by a number of diverse minorities is unacceptable.

Cultural pluralism values diversity and implements policies of inclusion that cater to the requirements of all groups. The sensitivities of the minorities as well as of the majority need attention. Fundamental rights and fundamental freedoms of all are to be protected. The rights of the weaker sections are particularly important in a society that respects cultural pluralism.

Intercultural dialogue is necessary both at the national and at the global levels so that contentious issues are resolved amicably. The more a nation harmonises differences at home, the greater is its ability to contribute to dialogue at the international level. The stronger the cooperation and goodwill among nations, the lesser the need to spend huge resources on arms and military strategies.

Education has a crucial role to play in providing ethical and spiritual value systems that facilitate understanding of other cultures and civilisations. The UNESCO Constitution begins with the words "Since wars begin in the minds of men it is in the minds of men that the defences of peace must be constructed." Education ought to promote tolerance, respect for diversity and friendship among peoples and nations.

Educational institutions must be provided with a learning environment which contributes to tolerance, understanding and respect for diversity. They should be protected from teachings that promote extremism, intolerance and violence.

India is home to diverse languages, religions, races and lifestyles. It is a vast country where questions of unity and diversity interplay. Yet, India emerges with an excellent record at managing diversity. This makes it possible to survive as a nation and to move ahead as the largest democracy in the world. The Constitution of India ensures that all citizens have equal rights and should have an equal opportunity. In particular, the principle of secularism enshrined in our Constitution is the best method to accommodate religious diversity and could be emulated across the world.

Types of diversity

Age gap between employees: The age difference between the youngest and the oldest persons holding directorship positions on the firms listed on the Bombay Stock Exchange is a gaping 79 years.

Recruitment of foreign national

Best found in IT sector and aviation industry.

Indian firms are now competing globally, and in the process, Indian firms are slowly becoming diverse. The best examples of cultural diversity in Indian organizations can be seen in the IT sector.

Infosys, TCS and Wipro are actively recruiting foreign nationals. Indian aviation industry has more number of foreign pilots than Indian pilots. Even some of the family owned businesses are slowly getting on to this bandwagon. A recent report from the Indian Ministry of Foreign Affairs shows that there are about 37,000 British working in India.

Caste based diversity: Indian society although is getting rid of this social stigma, but we can still find its recurrence in form of reservations as our government sometime talk about reservation for the socially deprived in the private sector. In such case, the employees of the firm who are from the general group feel the heat and then they react. Although the caste based diversity always doesn't hold good.

Linguistic Diversity

A vast majority of Indian firms are cultural mono types. They hire people from the same background—usually the same religion, religious subgroups and those who speak the language.

Not having a culturally diverse workforce will create a serious handicap for Indian companies when they plan to expand overseas—or even when they have to compete with foreign imports or MNCs.

In a multicultural society, the State cannot be identified with any religious or cultural group and it should either be neutral or even-handed in its approach to all such groups. Unity in diversity is the highest possible civilizational attainment. It is made possible through respect for choice in an atmosphere of mutual trust.

Managing diversity

A team leader must think about diversity as diversity of ideas and experience, not just race and gender. A leader needs to recognize the diversity of each team member and achieve unity of common goals without destroying the uniqueness of any person. The team leader must do this within the scope of the organization's resources relative to the growth of the team member.

Most problems in the workplace are not that people cannot do their jobs, rather it is that people cannot get along with others. The team leader should make efforts in effectively training soft skills. This includes such subjects as diversity, communication and people skills that allow people to understand each other and develop good team skills.

Every team member must not only be able to understand and work with all the other team members, but they must also want to. Embracing diversity is the first step to managing a truly diverse team. In order to facilitate this, team leaders should consider the following:

Develop an atmosphere in which it is safe for all employees to ask for help. People should not be viewed as weak if they ask for help. Joining weakness with strengths to get a goal or objective accomplished is one aspect of building great teams. One person's weakness should be another person's strength.

Actively seek information from people from a variety of backgrounds and cultures in order to develop a broad picture.

Include everyone in the problem solving and decision-making process.

Include people who are different than you in informal gatherings such as lunch, coffee breaks and spur of the moment meetings.

Create a team spirit in which every member feels a part.

A team leader enables the other members to be innovative as well as self-directed within the capacity of individual assignments and allows them to learn from their own, as well as others' successes, mistakes and failures. It is important to assure that each individual on the team has the opportunity to make the maximum contribution to the success of the team by doing the type of work for which he/she has the greatest opportunity for productivity and achievement.

Leaders have the task of using the other team members' diverse gifts, abilities, and skills to achieve the common goal without the unintended consequence of conforming to the characteristics the others on the team. This requires active management by the leader to ensure that diverse followers show respect and acceptance of the followers that are different in one way or another.

If team members do not accept others for what they are, they will be unable to use the abilities of each team member to fill in their own weak areas. Hence, the team effort develops knowledge and skill gaps that often lead to failure. Their only goal becomes the ones on their personal agendas while ignoring the needs of the team and the organization. Creating an environment that encourages diversity enables team members to accept every individual on the team and helps them realize that it takes a variety of people to become the best.

This kind of environment also enforces the need to rely on everyone within the team, no matter how different another person may be. These characteristics and experiences make a worker unique. Diversity occurs when the whole team sees all these unique characteristics, and realizes that workers are more valuable because of their differences.

Such a course of action usually results in an undemocratic backlash, support for extremist parties, populist leaders and anti-minority policies. It is morally unjustified as it does not accept the values and institutions upheld by society at large. Regions that breakaway from democratic societies hoping to achieve a larger measure of self-government are not likely to enhance self-government and may rather weaken it.

Global Organisation Structure

Managers in a global environment must consider not only similarities and differences among firms in different cultures but also the structural features of multinational organisations.

Between-culture issues: "Between-culture issues" are variations in the structure and design of companies operating in different cultures. As might be expected, such companies have both differences and similarities. For example, one study compared the structures of 55 US and 51 Japanese plants. Results suggested that the Japanese plants had less specialization, more "formal" centralisation (but less "real" centralization), and taller hierarchies than their US counterparts. The Japanese structures were also less affected by their technology than the US plants.

Many cultures still take a traditional view of organization structure not unlike the approaches used in this country during the days of classical organization theory. For example, Tom Peters, a leading US management consultant and co-author of *In Search of Excellence*, spent sometime lecturing to managers in China. They were not interested in his ideas about decentralization and worker participation. Instead, the most frequently asked question concerned how a manager determined optimal span of control.

Multinational company: More and more firms have entered the international arena and have found it necessary to adapt their designs to better cope with different cultures. For example, after a company achieved a moderate level of international activity, it often establishes an international division, usually at the same organizational level as other major functional divisions.

For an organization that has become more deeply involved in international activities, a logical form of organization design is in the international matrix. This type of matrix arrays product managers across the product departments. A company with three basic product lines, for example, might establish three product departments (of course it would include domestic advertising, finance and operations departments as well). Foreign market managers can be designated for, say, Canada, Japan, Europe, Latin America, and Australia. Each foreign market manager is then responsible for all three of the company's products in his or her market. Finally, at the most advanced level of multinational activity, a firm might become an international conglomerate.

Dominant Themes of Contemporary Designs

The emphasis on productivity through people that was energised by Thomas Peters and Robert Waterman Junior in the 1980s continues in almost every aspect of contemporary organisation design. In addition, Peters and Austin further emphasized the importance of staying in touch with customers at the initial stage in organisation design.

These popular contemporary approaches and the four dominant factors argue for a contingency design perspective. Unfortunately, there is no "one best way." Managers must consider the impact of multiple factors, the structural imperatives, socio-technical systems, strategy, changing IT, people, global considerations, and a concern for end users on their particular organization and design the organization structure accordingly.

Universal approaches— top organization design attempts to specify the one best way to structure organizations for effectiveness. Contingency approaches, on the other hand, propose that the best way to design organization structure depends on a variety of factors. Important contingency approaches to organization design centre on the organizational strategy, the determinants of structure, and strategic choice.

Initially, strategy was seen as the determinant of structure: the structure of the organization was designed to implement its purpose, goals and strategies. Taking managerial choice into account in determining organization structure is a modification of this view. The manager designs the structure to accomplish organizational goals, guided by an analysis of the contextual factors, the strategies of the organization, and personal preference.

The structural imperatives are size, technology, and environment. In general, large organisations have more complex structures and usually more than one technology. The structures of small organizations, on the other hand, may be dominated by one core operation technology.

The structure of an organization is also established to fit with the environmental demands and buffer the core operating technology from uncertainties and environmental changes.

Organization designs can take many forms. A mechanistic structure relies on the administrative hierarchy for communication and directing activities.

In the socio-technical systems view, the organization is an open system structured to integrate two important subsystems: the technical (task) subsystem and the social subsystem. According to this approach, organizations should structure the task, authority, reporting relationships around the work group, delegating to the group decisions on job assignments, training, inspection, rewards, and punishments.

The task of management is to monitor the environment and coordinate the structures, rules, and procedures. Ideal types of organization design were derived from a framework of coordinating mechanisms. The five types are simple structure, divisionalized form, machine and professional bureaucracy, and adhocracy. Most organizations have some characteristics of each type, but one is more likely to predominate.

The most important consideration in designing and organization is the fit among parts of the organization.

MNE/MNC Activities

Home government feel they neglect home social issues due to their foreign business
Host countries fear the economic dominance of large MNCs
MNCs have to look after their stakeholders' interest to thrive
One country's decisions may not apply in other countries
Management decisions
Locating manufacturing base
Acquisitions and operations
Market need to be targeted
Profit plans and deployment
Host country partner benefits, both benefit or both lose.
If both benefit profit share out?
Host government's benefit/profit

Global Core Competencies

International experience
Manufacturing
Marketing research
Marketing
Purchasing
HRM
Organization of finance at low cost
Host country government relations

International MR

Host country product demand fluctuations, seasonality
Price sensitivity of demand
Type of competition—monopoly, oligopoly, stratified competition, perfect competition
Knowledge of channels of distribution and media for advertising
PR, Publicity, Promotion avenues

Experience

Companies get confidence as they go overseas
International business not possible sitting at home
Knowledge of host business environment essential
Knowledge of competition vital for success
Manufacturing
Home country manufacturing experience helps in host country plans
Purchasing, logistics, inventory control easy
TQM or other quality programmes easy to organize
Material sourcing possible from home, host or even third country
PURCHASING
Market scan for RM and components
International purchase price negotiations
Purchase from home, host or third country
Purchase product quality and consistency of supply
EOQ, inventory carrying costs
Transport and time-cost analysis
HRM
Host country's laws regarding expats
Minimum wage act in the host country
Home/host country's policies on recruitment, training, compensation, working hours, work ethics
Labour laws in host country
Host country insistence on a minimum number of host country employees
Finance
Availability of funds with banks, financial institutions
Interest rates
Rules regarding home country funding/repatriation of profits
Third country finance and their interest rates
Blocking period on borrowed money
Accounting systems
Host country government regulations
Host country's stand on market economy/globalization
Host country taxation policy
Host country policy on expat firms
Host and home country government's relations and mutual trust
Language, customs, cultural differences
Host government's take on home country's product quality

Global Manufacturing

Labour cost-efficiency levels
Cost of money—its supply position
RM and their costs

Infrastructure
Transport
Suppliers
Quality
Flexi-activities
Innovation
Locating manufacture
Transport cost of materials and FGs
Duties and taxes
Market proximity
Economies of scale
Currency fluctuations
Technology availability
Outsourcing
Materials only
Manufacture of components
Products for sale in home, host and third countries
Outsourcing by Ford
Tyres and radiators–Austria
Tyres seats, brakes–Belgium
Glass and radio–Canada
Starter, bearings–Japan
Locks, pistons–Germany
Alternators, master cylinder–France
Inventory
Shipment size, frequency
Low current assets
Lead-time of supplies
Rejection rate
Communication systems
Number of suppliers per item
Timely supplier record
Sudden change acceptance by supplier
Availability of shipping lines, frequency

Global Fin Markets

One of the most significant aspects of financial globalization has been the extremely rapid expansion of international liquidity. The enormous increase in liquid assets available to international market participants is worrisome for several reasons: it erodes central banks' ability to exercise monetary control; it triggers potential inflationary pressures that could easily be triggered if expectations change; finally, it facilitates the opening of speculative positions and may cause the quality of credit to decline. These last two channels can create instability in the financial and real markets.

A financial market is a mechanism that allows people to buy and sell trade financial securities (such as stocks and bonds), commodities (such as precious metals or agricultural goods), and other items of value at low transaction costs and at prices that reflect the efficient market hypothesis.

Fin Markets

Financial markets have evolved significantly over several hundred years and are undergoing constant innovation to improve liquidity.

Both general markets (where many commodities are traded) and specialized markets (where only one commodity is traded) exist. Markets work by placing many interested buyers and sellers in one "place", thus making it easier for them to find each other. An economy which relies primarily on interactions between buyers and sellers to allocate resources is known as a market economy.

Fin Markets

In financial markets facilitate:

The raising of capital

The transfer of risk (in the derivative markets)

International trade in the currency markets

- and are used to match those who *want* capital to those who *have* it.

Typically a borrower issues a receipt to the lender promising to pay back. These receipts are securities which may be freely bought or sold. In return for lending money to the borrower, the lender will expect some compensation in the form of interest or dividend.

Capital Market

Capital market consists of:

- Stock markets which provide financing through the issuance of shares and enable the subsequent trading thereof.
- Bond markets which provide financing through the issuance of bonds, and enable the subsequent trading thereof.
- Commodity markets, which facilitate the trading of commodities.
- Money markets, which provide short-term debt financing and investment.
- Derivatives markets, which provide instruments for the management of financial risk.
- Futures markets, which provide standardized forward contracts for trading products at some future date; see also forward market
- Insurance markets, which facilitate the redistribution of various risks.
- FE markets, which facilitate the trading of foreign exchange.

International Liquidity

In the period between 1991 and 1994, which was characterized by the stagnation of cross-border interbank flows in conjunction with the economic slowdown in the industrial countries, a total of $170 billion flowed out of Japan towards other industrial nations and Asian offshore banking centres. The latter played a major role in intermediating flows at the international level, borrowing funds from Japan and redirecting them to other industrial countries and the emerging economies.

International Liquidity

Studies conducted by the Bank of Italy's research department have analyzed this phenomenon, focusing on the multiplication process of cross-border deposits to evaluate its stability, implications for monetary control by central banks and the risk of inflation.

The analyses found that the international multiplier is broadly stable for cross-border deposits, which make up a small share of the money available to households and firms. They, therefore, pose a limited threat to the stability of prices through the traditional channel whereby excess money leads to inflation. Alongside this relatively reassuring conclusion, however, the studies revealed important risks in two other areas.

INT LIQUIDITY

In the period between 1995 and 1997, global interbank activity expanded rapidly, characterized once again by net outflows from Japan. During this period, however, the banking system of the industrial countries (excluding Japan) played the role of intermediary in the reallocation of flows, having made loans to offshore centres that were nearly equal to fund-raising from Japan ($50 billion). The flows to emerging economies were enormous: $150 billion to banks and $130 billion to non-bank agents. Large capital flows (around $100 billion) were recorded in favour of non-bank agents located in offshore centres, among which some non-bank financial intermediaries such as hedge funds are also probably included.

STAGNATION

The stagnation recorded between 1991 and 1994 is attributable to a variety of factors : the cyclical weakness of the world economy, which not only had direct effects but also was accompanied by a deterioration of the credit standing of many banking groups and, in some countries, by a large fall in prices of securities and real estate; and the contraction of international activity by Japanese banks, which is also linked to the collapse of Japan's financial and real estate sectors at the end of the 1980s.

ASIAN FIN CRISES

- Following the outbreak of the Asian crisis in the first half of 1998, there was a generalized contraction in banks' gross international exposure; the year as a whole witnessed sizeable net capital outflows from offshore centres towards banks located in Japan and other OECD countries (around $190 billion) and a sharp reduction in loans to both banks ($53 billion) and non-bank borrowers (around $30 billion) in the emerging economies.

- An analysis of flows broken down by the nationality of the intermediaries' parent company.

JAPANESE BANKS

In the four years from 1991 to 1994 the significant contraction in the balance sheets of banks resident in Japan was paralleled by one in those of banks of Japanese nationality engaged in cross-border business. The latter's repayments of liabilities were mainly to other banks ($455 billion), whereas the reduction in their assets involved both claims on other branches of the group and claims on other banks ($227 billion and $354 billion respectively); activity with non-bank customers kept growing, with banks of Japanese nationality granting $140 billion of fresh funds.

Global Value Chain

Asian corporate strategies play a great role in the development of Asia, but their limitations are also the limitations to Asia's growth. Asia's great success in its export-led manufacturing strategy was attributed historically to Asia being monsoon economies, where the seasonal nature of rice farming led to Asians being culturally adept at working together in rice fields and in the dry season, skilful at weaving and other handicrafts, so that the agricultural labour force adapted quickly to assembly-line manufacturing. Of course, forward-looking government policies to open up to foreign manufacturing, the attention to social infrastructure and education helped to equip their economies to copy, learn and then slowly move up the value chain.

Value Chain

Japan's export-led manufacturing strategy was successfully imitated throughout East Asia and in the famous flying geese formation, the four Dragon economies (Taiwan, South Korea, Hong Kong and Singapore) followed by four Tigers (Malaysia, Thailand, the Philippines and Indonesia) rapidly formed the global supply chain. China did not emerge as an export giant until the early 1990s, but today forms the core of the supply chain by sheer size and market capacity. No regional corporation with global ambitions can ignore its China strategy.

Asian corporate and economic strategy had a fundamental flaw. In mobilising savings to invest in manufacturing, East Asian governments typically protected the services and distribution sectors, so that the financial sectors were not well developed. The result is that trade surpluses generated from manufacturing exports remain largely intermediated via Western banks and the financial centres of London, New York, Hong Kong and Singapore, rather than through domestic capital markets.

You look at value chains, you discover that there are three key parts – the manufacturing, distribution and trading side. A T-shirt could cost less than US$1 to manufacture, but the distribution, marketing and trading costs will take more and more margin, so that the final product could be sold for more than US$20–US$100 depending on the design, branding and quality. You can imagine how much profit the cotton farmer gets from his sales of raw cotton.

Supply Chain

The downturn raised challenges with some traditional distribution channels and some were forced to slow investment in technology.

Good performers are ahead of the curve in both areas, as they are with finding new market opportunities for existing products where the major costs have been incurred and the upside can be especially profitable.

Supply Chain

China is a market of vast potential but it is also a complex market with significant variation. And companies have often completed similar analyses to conclude that urban centres on the western seaboard are the most attractive targets.

But a "Beijing, Shanghai, Hong Kong" entry strategy may take you directly into competition with most of your competitors. There are 49 cities in China with population in excess of one million. Some companies are therefore exploring "tier-two" urban entry strategies to build critical scale to reinforce the approach to larger markets.

Which markets will be the most important in the short, medium and long term?
Is your analysis of the new market as deep as it needs to be?
Where have your competitors gone and how have they progressed?
What is different about your approach?
Have you explored all the possible routes to achieving your goals?
What is your time horizon for entry?
How developed is your thinking for the post-entry phase?

Capital Budget

Capital budget (or investment appraisal) is the planning process used to determine whether a firm's long term investments such as new machinery, replacement machinery, new plants, new products, and research & development projects are worth pursuing. It is budget for major capital, or investment, expenditures.

Many formal methods are used in capital budgeting, including the techniques such as

- Accounting rate of return
- NPV: net present value
- Profitability index
- Internal rate of return

Transfer Price

Transfer pricing refers to the pricing of contributions (assets, tangible and intangible, services, and funds) transferred *within* an organization. For example, goods from the production division may be sold to the marketing division, or goods from a parent company may be sold to a foreign subsidiary. Since the prices are set within an organization, the typical market mechanisms that establish prices for such transactions between third parties may not apply.

The choice of the transfer price will affect the allocation of the total profit among the parts of the company. This is a major concern for fiscal authorities who worry that multi-national entities may set transfer prices on cross-border transactions to reduce taxable profits in their jurisdiction. This has led to the rise of transfer pricing regulations and enforcement, making transfer pricing a major tax compliance issue for multinational companies.

CHAPTER

17

Countries of the Globe

The information given about selected countries should be useful to the students in understanding certain social cultural aspects. Once the company has selected the country or countries where it wants to do business, it has to organize marketing research that would provide more authentic information. Such information would also be latest for the company to use it in its dealings in the concerned countries. The information provided in the below is only indicative of what to expect in the countries.

AUSTRALIA

Introduction

Australia has a population of almost 20 million people. The great majority of the population is located in a few major urban centres. The large majority of the population (93%) has a European heritage, primarily English. The predominant language of the country is English with Christianity the largest religion (75%). The aborigines are indigenous to Australia, and are thought to have canoed to Australia from South-East Asia some 30,000 to 50,000 years ago. Australia is a very friendly and open culture. However, tourists overuse "G'day" the informal "hello". The Australians expect one's work to speak for itself, so they are not impressed with your position, title, or status. Don't arrive in town wearing the latest status symbol to announce how important *you think you are.*

Dress code: Men wear a conservative dark business suit and tie; women may wear a dress, or skirt and blouse, for business. Informal clothing is appropriate when not attending business functions. Casual pants are fine for men, but women are rarely seen in pants. Men should not become physically demonstrative with another man, or wink at a woman. Do not give the "thumbs up" sign, or use a crooked index finger to call someone over. Both gestures are considered offensive. Being punctual is critical. Maintain good eye contact during meetings and conversations. Single, male passenger using a taxi should sit in the front seat. Gift giving is not a common practice in business. You may bring a small gift of chocolate, wine or flowers if invited to someone's home. When paying for a round of drinks, do not pick up the tab out of turn, and make sure to pay when it is your turn. Should you approach a line/queue, go to the end/back and wait for your turn. Do not litter. English is the spoken language, shake hands when meeting and when leaving.

Women may greet other women with a kiss on the cheek. You may present your business card when introduced. However, you may not receive a business card from an Australian, as they do not always use them. Australians are friendly and open, but directness and brevity are valued. Opinions are respected, and opinionated discussions are entertaining. Be an active listener, and ask if you do not understand something in the conversation. Do not hype yourself, your company or your information. Sightseeing and sports are good conversational topics. Afternoon tea is about 4:00 pm. Tea is between 6:00 - 8:00pm and is an evening meal. Supper is a late night light meal or snack.

BRAZIL

Introduction

Brazil has a population of 146 million people concentrated on its two hundred miles of east coast.

Over 90 per cent of the people live on 10 per cent of the land, and over 15 million live in Sao Paulo and Rio de Janeiro. Brazil's ethnic composition is 55 per cent European descent (primarily Portuguese), 38 per cent a mixture of cultures (African, German, Japanese, Amerindian, and so forth), 6 per cent African, and only 1 per cent Amerindian. Brazil is a multiparty federal republic. The president is both the chief of state and the head of the government. There are two legislative houses: an 81-member Senate and a 503-member Chamber of Deputies. Portuguese is the official language, although some of the population speaks Spanish, Italian, or various Amerindian languages. There is no official religion, however, the predominant religion is Roman Catholic (about 90 per cent of the population). Some 16 per cent practice Afro-Brazilian religions that combine tribal and Catholic beliefs (Spiritual Catholics) and Evangelical Catholics make up 9 per cent. Protestants, Judaism, Buddhism, and other religions account for less than 9 per cent. Nearly 50 per cent of the population is under twenty years of age.

Despite massive economic problems, Brazil is often regarded as a potentially rich country with a strong industrial sector, large agricultural production, and rich natural resources. An example of its potential for efficient utilization of resources is its processing of sugar cane into ethyl alcohol for fuelling 1.5 million Brazilian cars. Three-piece suits carry an "executive" connotation, whereas two-piece suits are associated with office workers. The colours of the Brazilian flag are yellow and green. Avoid wearing this combination in any fashion. Touching arms and elbows and backs very common. The O.K. hand signal a rude gesture in Brazil. To express appreciation, a Brazilian may appear to pinch his earlobe between thumb and forefinger. Flicking the fingertips underneath the chin indicates that you do not know the answer to a question. Make appointments at least two weeks in advance. Never try to make impromptu calls at business or government offices; be prepared to commit long-term resources (both in time and money) toward establishing strong relationships in Brazil. This is the key to business success. Casual about both time and work. Customary to arrive ten to fifteen minutes late for an appointment. Never start into business discussions unless your host does first.

Midday is the normal time for the main meal. A light meal is common at night, unless entertaining formally, American coffee is a mere shadow of Brazilian coffee. Expect to be served small cups of very strong coffee. In Brazil, restaurant entertainment prevails versus at home. If entertained in the home, it is polite to send flowers to the hostess the next day, with a thank-you note. Giving a gift is not required at a first business meeting; instead buy lunch or dinner. Purple is the colour of death... don't send purple flowers. Toast: Saude or Viva (Sah-OO-Day, VEE-va).Tipping: *jeito* (means, "you do a favour for me, and I'll do a favour for you"). Money rarely changes hands. Handshaking, often for a long time, is common. Shake hands for hello and goodbye; use good eye contact; when leaving a small group, be sure to shake hands with everyone present. When women meet, they exchange kisses by placing their cheeks together and kissing the air. First names used often, but titles important. Music and long, animated conversation are favourite Brazilian habits. When conversing, interruptions are viewed as enthusiasm. Brazilians enjoy joking, informality, and friendships. Portuguese is the language of Brazil. Good conversation topics: soccer, family, and children. Bad conversation topics: Argentina, politics, poverty, and religion.

CANADA

Introduction

Canada has a population just less than 30 million people in a country twice the area of the United States. The heritage of Canada was French and English; however, significant immigration from Asia and Europe's non-French and English countries has broadened Canada's cultural richness. This cultural diversity is considered a national asset, and the Constitution Act prohibits discrimination against individual citizens on the basis of race, colour, religion, or sex. The great majority of Canadians are Christian. The predominant language in Canada is English, with French being primary in the province of Quebec.

The Italian language is a strong third due to a great influx of Italian immigrants following W.W.II. Canada's three major cities are distinctively, even fiercely different from one another even though each is a commercially thriving metropolitan centre. Montreal, established in the 17th century and the largest French city outside France, has a strong influence of French architecture and culture. It is a financial and manufacturing centre and seaport, with the majority of Canada's European exports and imports coming through its harbour. Toronto, another major financial and commercial centre, is filled with office towers and not historic buildings. It has a great number of people living in and around the central business district. The downtown district does not "close up" when people leave work.Vancouver, nestled at the base of the Coast Mountains, is the financial, commercial, agricultural, and industrial centre of western Canada. Its harbour and mountains make it one of Canada's most picturesque location. Consequently, West Vancouver is the most densely populated urban area and has the highest income per person of any municipality.

Visitors should plan for a very cold climate, especially during their winter. Men should wear a dark conservative business suit with tie, especially in cities. Build a wardrobe based on classic lines (selecting suits with a traditional lapel width, and ties staying within a traditional width range), with conservative colours of navy and gray, and shirts in white and light blue. Women should wear a conservative business suit or dress, especially in cities. Select your clothing with classic lines and colours in mind. Navy, grey, ivory, and white are the basics to work with. New or trendy clothing is a poor choice. Older, classic clothing that is clean and neat is more valued. Choosing quality, natural fibres for your wardrobe will give you this look. Quality leather shoes are important to completing this look. Rural areas are less formal, but stay conservative in your wardrobe. Casual attire is appropriate when you are not working. The "V for Victory" sign is an insult if your palm is facing yourself. If you must use this sign, face your palm outward.

Visitors must be punctual for meetings and appointments, as promptness is valued and always maintain a reserved demeanour, and follow good rules of etiquette. Traditions and gracious manners are part of the culture, even in more rural areas. If you travel to different cities or areas, pay attention to local customs. By being observant, you will respect the pace and nuances of each area. Do not eat while walking in public. Plan your time so you can stop in a café or restaurant to enjoy your snack. Gifts are not routinely given. If you do give a gift when you arrive or when you are leaving, make it a modest one. A lavish gift, though accepted, would be frowned upon. Gifts *are* given to celebrate finalizing a negotiation, a contract, or a project. Gifts for the office, a nice bottle of wine or liquor would be appropriate. Taking a business associate to a nice meal or an evening sporting event, play, or symphony is always a nice gesture. Invitations to private homes are rare. Occasionally, in the western provinces, you may be invited to someone's home. If you are invited, you may take candy, flowers, or liquor to the host or hostess. Wait for your host to start a business conversation during or following a meal. Traditionally, business is not discussed during dinner; however, this is slowly changing. Personal space and body movement or gestures differ between the English and the French provinces and cities. In English areas, body movement is minimal, there is rarely touching other than handshakes, and personal space–how close someone stands–is about two feet. In French areas, people stand closer together, people will frequently touch, and gestures are more expressive. Use a firm handshake with good eye contact when meeting and leaving. Both French and English areas use and expect a firm handshake. Men will wait for a woman to extend her hand for a handshake. French Canadians will shake hands more frequently, even with a subsequent encounter the same day. Others may just nod or smile at a subsequent encounter on the same day. Use a person's title if he or she has one. Otherwise, use Mr., Mrs., Miss and the surname. English is spoken in most of Canada. French is spoken in Quebec, and some area of Nova Scotia and New Brunswick. French Canadians may use their first name when talking to you on the telephone, but will generally use their full name when meeting you in person.

Be open and friendly in your conversation. If you are naturally reserved in your behaviour, you will appear confident and credible. If your natural tendency is large sweeping arm gestures, restrain yourself when meeting and talking with Canadians– other than with French Canadians. French Canadians stand closer and are more demonstrative when talking. For French Canadians, print all material in French and English. Don't be boastful, and don't overstate your product or service's capabilities. You could implicate your company in a legal situation.

CHILE

Introduction

Chile has a population of nearly 14 million people with almost 5 million located in the capital city, Santiago. It has an ethnic composition of 95 per cent mestizo (of mixed European and Indian blood), 3 per cent Indian (mostly Araucanian), and less than 2 per cent are solely of European descent. Because of the geography of the area, the country has experienced a large degree of isolation and, as a result, is more ethnically homogeneous than most of South America. The Republic of Chile is a multiparty republic with two legislative houses, the 48-seat Senate and the 120-seat Chamber of Deputies. The president is the chief of state as well as the head of government. The official language is Spanish, although English is spoken by well-educated business people and in tourist centres. There is no official religion, however, approximately 78 per cent identify themselves as Roman Catholics, and about 13 per cent are Protestants. There is a large number of people that consider themselves atheist. Chile is the world's longest country - north to south.

Chileans have a renowned reputation for achievement in many cultural fields. Literature, social science, and fine arts are considered prestigious areas of study. Family respect and loyalty are primary concerns in Chile, even taking precedence over business responsibilities. Chile has a stellar track record for global trade. As an exporting nation, Chile competes with countries beyond its Latin American neighbourhood. The 1996 World Competitiveness Report published by the Global Institute for Management Development in Lausanne, Switzerland ranked Chile 18th out of the 49 most competitive economies in the world. It exports more than 3,800 diverse products to more than 170 markets worldwide. Men customarily wear dark blue or grey suit, a light shirt, and a conservative tie. Bright colours and flashy fashions are not suitable, nor are wearing anything on the lapel. Men should note that when a woman enters a room, the polite gesture is to rise and be prepared to shake her hand if she offers it. A seated woman, however, need not rise nor is she obliged to offer her hand. Chileans converse in close proximity to one another. Maintaining eye contact is necessary to show interest and sincerity. At a meal, keep your hands above the table at all times. Holding the palm upward and then spreading the fingers signals that someone is "stupid". Slapping your right fist into your left open palm is considered obscene. Do not raise your right fist to head level, as this is a Communist sign. Prior appointments are necessary. In business, punctuality, respected. Meetings should start and end on time. Have business cards printed with English on one side and Spanish on the other. Present cards to everyone in a meeting except secretaries. Business entertaining generally is done at major hotels and restaurants. Light conversation is customary before business discussions. Don't serve wine with your left hand. Wines, especially white wines, are a national treasure. Proper table manners are important.

Women have advanced in professions in Chile, more so than in most other Latin countries. However, they will be at a slight disadvantage because of the *machismo* ethnic that continues to exist. Gifts are not expected in business until the relationship is a close one. Chileans do not bargain in either stores or street markets. It is illegal to sell something and not issue a receipt. With first introductions, a handshake is the custom Male Chileans may greet each other with hearty hugs, with women customarily kissing each other on the cheek. Titles are important and should be included on business cards. Address a person directly by using his or her title only. A Ph.D. or a physician is called *Doctor*. Teachers prefer the title *Professor*, engineers go by *Ingeniero*, architects are *Arquitecto*, and lawyers are *Abogado*. Persons who do not have professional titles should be addressed as Mr., Mrs., or Miss, plus their surnames. In Spanish these are Mr. = *Senor*, Mrs. = *Senora*, Miss = *Senorita*.

Most Hispanics have two surnames: one from their father, which is listed first, followed by one from their mother. Only the father's surname is used when addressing someone. Good conversation topics: families, children, Easter Island, history. Bad conversation topics: politics, human rights, 1988 grape export scare.

CHINA

Background

For centuries China stood as a leading civilization, outpacing the rest of the world in the arts and sciences, but in the 19th and early 20th centuries, the country was beset by civil unrest, major famines, military defeats, and foreign occupation. After World War II, the Communists under Mao Zedong established an autocratic socialist system that, while ensuring China's sovereignty, imposed strict controls over everyday life and cost the lives of tens of millions of people. After 1978, his successor Deng Xiaoping and other leaders focused on market-oriented economic development and by 2000 output had quadrupled. For much of the population, living standards have improved dramatically and the room for personal choice has expanded, yet political controls remain tight.

China has Communist government but now they are trying to come to market economy. Its capital is Beijing.

National Holiday

Anniversary of the Founding of the People's Republic of China, 1 October (1949).

Legal System

A complex amalgam of custom and statute, largely criminal law; rudimentary civil code in effect since 1 January 1987; new legal codes in effect since 1 January 1980; continuing efforts are being made to improve civil, administrative, criminal, and commercial law.

Executive Branch

Chief of state: President Hu Jintao (since 15 March 2003) and Vice President Zeng Qinghong (since 15 March 2003)

Head of government: Premier Wen Jiabao (since 16 March 2003);

Legislative Branch

Unicameral National People's Congress or Quanguo Renmin Daibiao Dahui (2,985 seats; members elected by municipal, regional, and provincial people's congresses to serve five-year terms) *elections:* last held December 2002-February 2003 (next to be held late 2007-February 2008) *election results:* per cent of vote - NA; seats – NA

Judicial Branch

Supreme People's Court (judges appointed by the National People's Congress); Local People's Courts (comprise higher, intermediate and local courts); Special People's Courts (primarily military, maritime, and railway transport courts)

Political Parties and Leaders

Chinese Communist Party or CCP [Hu Jintao, General Secretary of the Central Committee]; eight registered small parties controlled by CCP

Location

Eastern Asia, bordering the East China Sea, Korea Bay, Yellow Sea, and South China Sea, between North Korea and Vietnam

Climate

Extremely diverse; tropical in south to sub-arctic in north

Natural Resources

Coal, iron ore, petroleum, natural gas, mercury, tin, tungsten, antimony, manganese, molybdenum, vanadium, magnetite, aluminium, lead, zinc, uranium, hydropower potential (world's largest)

Environment—Current Issues

Air pollution (greenhouse gases, sulphur dioxide particulates) from reliance on coal produces acid rain; water shortages, particularly in the north; water pollution from untreated wastes; deforestation; estimated loss of one-fifth of agricultural land since 1949 to soil erosion and economic development; desertification; trade in endangered species.

Geography–world's fourth largest country (after Russia, Canada, and US); Mount Everest on the border with Nepal is the world's tallest peak.

Religions

Daoist (Taoist), Buddhist, Muslim 1%-2%, Christian 3%-4% *note:* officially atheist (2002 est.)

Languages

Standard Chinese or Mandarin

In late 1978, the Chinese leadership began moving the economy from a sluggish, inefficient, Soviet-style centrally planned economy to a more market-oriented system. Whereas the system operates within a political framework of strict Communist control, the economic influence of non-state organizations and individual citizens has been steadily increasing. The authorities switched to a system of household and village responsibility in agriculture in place of the old collectivization increased the authority of local officials and plant managers in industry, permitted a wide variety of small-scale enterprises in services and light manufacturing, and opened the economy to increased foreign trade and investment. The result has been a quadrupling of GDP since 1978. Measured on a purchasing power parity (PPP) basis, China in 2003 stood as the second-largest economy in the world after the US, although in per capita terms the country is still poor. Agriculture and industry have posted major gains especially in coastal areas near Hong Kong, opposite Taiwan, and in Shanghai, where foreign investment has helped spur output of both domestic and export goods. The leadership, however, often has experienced-as a result of its hybrid system—the worst results of socialism (bureaucracy and lassitude) and of capitalism (growing income disparities and rising unemployment). China thus has periodically backtracked, retightening central controls at intervals. The government has struggled to (a) sustain adequate jobs growth for tens of millions of workers laid off from state-owned enterprises, migrants, and new entrants to the workforce; (b) reduce corruption and other economic crimes; and (c) keep afloat the large state-owned enterprises, many of which had been shielded from competition by subsidies and had been losing the ability to pay full wages and pensions. From 80 to 120 million surplus, rural workers are adrift between the villages and the cities, many subsisting through part-time, low-paying jobs. Popular resistance, changes in central policy, and loss of authority by rural cadres have weakened. China's population control programme, which is essential to maintaining long-term growth in living standards. Another long-term threat to growth is the deterioration in the environment, notably air pollution, soil erosion, and the steady fall of the water table especially in the north. China continues to lose arable land because of erosion and economic development. Beijing says it will intensify efforts to stimulate growth through spending on infrastructure—such as water supply and power grids—and poverty relief and through rural tax reform. Accession to the World Trade Organization helps strengthen its ability to maintain strong growth rates but at the same time puts additional pressure on the hybrid system of strong political controls and growing market influences. China has benefited from a huge expansion in computer Internet use. Foreign investment remains a strong element in China's remarkable economic growth.

Railways

Total: 70,058 km *standard gauge:* 68,000 km 1.435-m gauge (18,668 km electrified) *narrow gauge:* 3,600 km 1.000 m and 0.750 m gauge local industrial lines *dual gauge:* 22,640 km (not included in total) (2003).

Highways

Total: 1,402,698 km *paved:* 314,204 km (with at least 16,314 km of expressways) *unpaved:* 1,088,494 km (2000).

Ports and Harbours

Dalian, Fuzhou, Guangzhou, Haikou, Huangpu, Lianyungang, Nanjing, Nantong, Ningbo, Qingdao, Qinhuangdao, Shanghai, Shantou, Shenzhen, Tianjin, Wenzhou, Xiamen, Xingang, Yantai, Zhanjiang (2001)

COLOMBIA

Introduction

Colombia has a population of approximately 33 million with an ethnic composition of 58 per cent mestizo, 20 per cent European, 14 per cent mulatto, and the remaining of African descent (living on the north coastal areas), and mixed African-Amerindian. Pureblooded Amerindians now constitute only 1 percent of the population. The Republic of Colombia is a unitary, multiparty republic with two legislative houses: the 102-seat Senate and the 161-seat House of Representatives. The president is elected to a single four-year term and cannot succeed himself. The president is both chief of state and head of government. Spanish is the official language, however, some Amerindians speak only their native languages. Many business people understand English. The vast majority of Colombians (95 per cent) are Roman Catholic. The Colombia constitution guarantees freedom of religion.

For dress, formality increases as you move inland. It is important to adopt conservative business attire inland. Suits in dark colors are preferred. Women should dress conservatively and modestly: a suit or dress Colombians stand closer together when conversing than North Americans, however they engage in less physical contact during conversation than other South Americans. Colombian women will often substitute the gesture of holding forearms for a handshake. Colombians indicate that someone is stingy by tapping their fingers on their elbow. Avoid putting your feet up on a table or other piece of furniture. Women visitors should be especially sensitive about making any glance or gesture that might be considered flirtatious. Schedule business appointments in advance. Punctuality is relaxed; although as a foreigner you are expected to be on time.

Have business cards printed in English on one side and the translation in Spanish on the other. Present the card with the Spanish side facing your Colombian colleague. Business people prefer relaxed conversation before business. Lunch is the main meal of the day and a popular choice for a business meal. Typically, the person who has initiated the invitation will pay for a meal in a restaurant, although you may have to fight for the cheque even though you have issued the invitation. Let the host make a toast first, then you might wish to make on. Handshaking the customary greeting in business; don't rush it. Colombians take a long time in greetings; they feel it conveys respect for the other person. Among friends, expect the *abrazo*, or embrace. Titles are important and should be included on business cards. Address a person directly by using his or her title only. A Ph.D. or a physician is called *Doctor*. Teachers prefer the title *Professor*, engineers go by *Ingeniero*, architects are *Arquitecto*, and lawyers are *Abogado*. Persons who do not have professional titles should be addressed as Mr., Mrs., or Miss, plus their surnames. In Spanish these are Mr. = *Senor*, Mrs. = *Senora*, Miss = *Senorita*. Most Hispanics have two surnames: one from their father, which is listed first, followed by one from their mother. Only the father's surname is used when addressing someone. Bullfighting is popular; don't make negative comments. Good conversation topics: history, culture, soccer, coffee, gold museum. Bad conversation topics: drug traffic, politics, and religion

COSTA RICA

Introduction

Costa Rica (meaning "rich coast") has a population of 3 million in which 95 per cent is of European (including some 7 per cent Mestizo—mixed European and Indian blood), 3 per cent black or Mulatto, 1 per cent East Asian (primarily Chinese), and 1 per cent Amerindian. About 51 per cent of Costa Ricans live in urban centres. Costa Rica has developed and maintained a stable democratic government. They are a fiercely democratic culture with a belief in peace through negotiations. The government is a unitary multiparty republic, composed of a president, a unicarneral legislative assembly made up of 57 deputies, and the Supreme Court of Justice. The President is both chief of state and the head of the government, holding only one successive four-year term of office.

The people of Costa Rica are politically active and proud of their government. Election voting is mandatory for anyone over 18 years old.

The official language is Spanish. Creole is also spoken. English is widely understood. Roman Catholicism is the official religion. However, various evangelical Protestant sects have been growing. In recent years, Costa Rica has nearly become synonymous with the term "ecotourism." Costa Rica has a higher number of lawyers per capita than any other country in Central America.

Business dress: Men should wear a conservative dark suit. In warmer climates, a jacket is optional. Women should wear a dress or skirt and blouse. Women never wear pants. Costa Ricans are much more formal and serious than other Latin Americans. Therefore, keep jackets on during business meetings. Local people bathe frequently because of the heat, and guests are expected to bathe at least once daily. Making a fist with the thumb sticking out between the middle an index finger is obscene. This gesture is known as the "fig". Don't put your feet up on any furniture except items expressly designed for that purpose. Fidgeting with your hands or feet is considered distracting and impolite. Costa Ricans are by far the most punctual people in Central America.

Since Costa Ricans allow themselves only a limited time for their midday break, everyone is expected to be on time for a business lunch. Most business entertaining takes place in the evening, since lunch is the main meal of the day. Spouses are welcome at business dinners. Gifts frequently exchanged on all kinds of special occasions. If you are invited for dinner to a home, bring flowers, chocolates, scotch, or wine. Do not bring calla lilies; they are associated with funerals. Have business cards, proposals, and other material printed in both English and Spanish. Handshaking is the common greeting. *Abrazos* (embrace of good friends) is not as common as in other Latin countries.

Titles are important and should be included on business cards.

Most Hispanics have two surnames: one from their father, which is listed first, followed by one from their mother. Only the father's surname is used when addressing someone. Costa Ricans call themselves *Ticos* (TEE-kos) Politics is freely discussed because of the stability there. Good conversation topics: children, history, art. Bad topics: any personal criticism, religion.

ECUADOR

Introduction

Ecuador has a population of approximately 11 million people with an ethnic composition of 65 per cent Mestizo (mixed European and Indian blood), and 25 per cent Amerindian. Along the north coast lives a small black minority. The population is evenly split between urban and rural residents. The Republic of Ecuador is a unitary multiparty republic. It has a single legislative house, the National Congress. The president is both chief of state and head of government and serves a single four-year term. Spanish is the official language; however, some Indians speak only Quechua. Many business people understand English. The vast majority (95 per cent) of Ecuadorans are Roman Catholic. The Ecuador constitution guarantees freedom of religion.

Ecuador is South America's second largest producer of oil. The drop in oil prices since 1982, plus an earthquake in 1987 that crippled the country's main oil line, forced Ecuador to temporarily suspend interest payments on its foreign debt. Ecuador resigned from OPEC in 1992, stating that the cartel failed to benefit smaller oil producers.

For dress, formality increases as you move inland. Inland, business dress should be conservative. Men should wear dark suits and women should dress conservatively and modestly – a suit or dress. Ecuadorians stand closer together when conversing than North Americans. It is considered impolite to yawn or point at others in public. Nervous, repetitive movements (toe tapping, knee jiggling, thumb twiddling, and so forth) should be minimized – Ecuadorians find them annoying. Make appointments about two weeks in advance. Have business cards printed in English on one side and the translation in Spanish on the other. Present the card with the Spanish side facing your Ecuadorian colleague. Lunch is the customary time for the main meal and is the usual business meal. Ecuadorians are used to alcohol with lunch. Women should note that while it is acceptable to drink wine, Ecuadorians are not accustomed to seeing a woman drink whiskey or other hard liquor. If a businesswoman wishes to pay for an Ecuadorian man's meal, arrangements should be made ahead of time, otherwise the man will refuse to let her pay. If you are given a gift, be very effusive in your thanks. Fine wines and liquors make good gifts. Avoid lilies and marigolds, which are used at funerals. Let the host make the toast first, then you may wish to make one. Handshaking is common when arriving and when leaving. Men friends embrace and women friends kiss.

Titles are important and should be included on business cards. Address a person directly by using his or her title only. A Ph.D. or a physician is called *Doctor*. Teachers prefer the title *Profesor*, engineers go by *Ingeniero*, architects are *Arquitecto*, and lawyers are *Abogado*. Persons who do not have professional titles should be addressed as Mr., Mrs., or Miss, plus their surnames. In Spanish these are Mr. = *Senor* Mrs. = *Senora* Miss = *Senorita*.

Most Hispanics have two surnames: one from their father, which is listed first, followed by one from their mother. Only the father's surname is used when addressing someone. Relations with neighbour Peru have always been strained. Famous parts of Ecuador are the Galapagos Islands. Good conversation topics: family, culture, and history. Bad conversation topics: politics, U.S. political influence.

EGYPT

Introduction

Egypt, officially Arab Republic of Egypt, is a country in north-eastern Africa and south-western Asia. The land of the Nile River, Egypt is the cradle of one of the world's greatest ancient civilizations and has a recorded history that dates from approximately 3200 BC. Although modern day Egyptians are usually lumped together with "the Arabs" due to their language and Islamic traditions, this is not completely accurate. There is a truly Bedouin Arab grouping within Egypt, who are still largely nomadic tribal people living in isolated oases and roaming through the country's vast desert regions. Many Bedouin Arabs reside in the Sinai Peninsula and along the Red Sea coast, across from Arabia. Foreigners are expected to abide by local standards of modesty, however, do not adopt native clothing. Traditional clothes on foreigners may be offensive. Most of the body must always remain covered despite the heat.

A jacket and tie are usually required for men at business meetings. Men should wear long pants and a shirt, preferably long-sleeved, buttoned up to the collar. Men should also avoid wearing visible jewellery, particularly around the neck. Women should always wear modest clothing in public.

High necklines, sleeves at least to the elbows, are expected. Hemlines, if not ankle-length should at least be well below the knee. A look of baggy concealment should be the goal, pants or pant suits are not recommended. It is a good idea to keep a scarf handy, especially if entering a mosque. Space relationships among members of the same sex will be much closer than North Americans and Europeans are comfortable with. Egyptians will tend to stand close and moving away may be seen as a sign of aloofness. On the other hand, men and women stand farther apart from each other than is the custom in United States and Europe. Only the right hand should be used for eating. Throughout most of the Middle East the left hand is reserved for bodily hygiene. Try not to sit with your legs crossed. Showing the sole of your shoe is considered an insult to another person.

Tapping the two index fingers together is considered a crude gesture meaning, "Would you sleep with me?" It is common to smoke in public. Be considerate to others present and offer your cigarettes. While dining it is considered impolite to eat everything on your plate. Leaving food on your plate symbolizes abundance and is considered a compliment to your host. Names are often confusing. It's best to get the names (in English) of those you will meet, speak to, or correspond with ahead of time so that you can find out both their full names and how they are to be addressed in person. Arabic is read from right to left and books or magazines start at what would be the last page. Nearly all Egyptians speak Arabic. Most global business people will speak English, French or both. Frequently appointments are interrupted by phone calls and visits from friend and family. Business cards should be printed in English on one side and Arabic on the other. Documents should carry two dates, the Gregorian (Western) date and the Hijrah (Arabic) date.

Professional titles should be addressed as Mr., Mrs., or Miss, plus their surnames. In Spanish these are:

Mr. = *Senor*
Mrs. = *Senora*
Miss = *Senorita*

Most Hispanics have two surnames: one from their father, which is listed first, followed by one from their mother. Only the father's surname is used when addressing someone. Good conversation topics: history, geography, culture, families. Bad conversation topics: local politics, religion.

ENGLAND

Introduction

England is one of four distinct regions of the United Kingdom, which also includes Wales, Scotland, and Northern Ireland. England's population is approximately 47 million. It is important to note that the Scots, Welsh, and Irish are not English, and are often offended when referred to as such. Additionally, citizens of the U.K. do not consider themselves European. Unfortunately, they are usually grouped as such, due in part to their membership in the European Union.

The English are very proud of their heritage and history. Along with their contributions to the world of today, several famous writers came from England. Some of the most famous are Shakespeare, T.S. Eliot, and Chaucer. This century, England has seen many influential daughters and sons. The Beatles, Winston Churchill, and Queen Elizabeth II have all played a tremendous role in England's presence in the modern world. Business attire rules are somewhat relaxed in England, but conservative dress is still very important for both men and women. Dark suits, usually black, blue, or grey, are quite acceptable. Men's shirts should not have pockets; if they do, the pockets should always be kept empty. Additionally, men should wear solid or patterned ties, while avoiding striped ties. Men wear laced shoes, not loafers. Businesswomen are not as limited to colours and styles as men are, though it is still important to maintain a conservative image. Always be punctual in England. Arriving a few minutes early for safety is acceptable. Decision-making is slower in England than in the United States; therefore, it is unwise to rush the English into making a decision. A simple handshake is the standard greeting (for both men and women) for business occasions and for visiting a home.

Privacy is very important to the English. Therefore, asking personal questions or intensely staring at another person should be avoided. Eye contact is seldom kept during British conversations. To signal that something is to be kept confidential or secret, tap your nose. Personal space is important in England, and one should maintain a wide physical space when conversing. Furthermore, it is considered inappropriate to touch others in public. Gifts are generally not part of doing business in England. A business lunch will often be conducted in a pub and will consist of a light meal and perhaps a pint of ale. When socializing after work hours, do not bring up the subject of work. When dining out, it is not considered polite to toast those who are older than yourself. "America and Britain are two nations divided by a common language" *George Bernard* was once quoted as saying. In England, English is the official language, but it should be noted that Queen's English and American English are very different. Often, ordinary vocabulary can differ between the two countries. Loud talking and disruptive behaviour should be avoided. One gesture to avoid is the V for Victory sign, done with the palm facing yourself. This is a very offensive gesture.

FRANCE

Introduction

France has a population of approximately 58 million people and is the largest West European country. France does not have an official religion, but the majority of French citizens are Roman Catholic. France is home to approximately 4.5 million foreigners, many are from other European countries or former Communist countries. Education is of great importance to the French. This is demonstrated by the fact that the educational system is almost free of charge from the primary school through the Ph.D. level, for French citizens.

The French are very conscientious of their appearance. Dress conservative and invest in well-tailored clothing. Patterned fabrics and dark colours are most acceptable, but avoid bright colours. French businessmen do not loosen their ties or take off their jackets in the office. Women should also dress conservatively. Avoiding bright or gaudy colours is recommended. Women should also avoid any glitzy or overpowering objects, such as flashy jewellery. Punctuality is treated very casually in France. France is a highly stratified society, with strong definition and competition between classes. The French handshake is brief, and is accompanied by a short span of eye contact. Always shake hands when meeting someone, as well as when leaving. French handshakes are not as firm as in the United States.

The French have a great respect for privacy. Knock and wait before entering into a room. Additionally, do not "drop in" unannounced. Always give notice before your arrival. Business can be conducted during any meal, but lunch is best. Avoid drinking hard liquor before meals or smoking cigars between courses. The French believe this permeates the taste buds, compromising the taste of the meal. Gift giving is left to the foreigner's discretion. Good gifts to present include books or music, as they demonstrate interest in intellectual pursuits. French is the official language in France. If you do not speak French, it is very important that you apologize for your lack of knowledge. Most individuals in business speak English. The French have a great appreciation for the art of conversation. The French frequently interrupt each other, as the argument is a form of entertainment. Be sensitive to the volume of your voice. Loud voices are known to offend everyone. Eye contact is frequent and intense, and can often be intimidating.

GERMANY

Introduction

The Federal Republic of Germany has a population of 81 million people. Germany's religions are split evenly between Roman Catholics, who are concentrated in the southern part of the country, and Protestants, who are found in the northern region. Germany's economy ranks as the largest in Europe, and the third largest in the world, behind the U.S. and Japan. The decision-making process in Germany is much slow. Be prepared for the process to take much longer, as there is often a "hidden" group of advisors and decision-makers that must approve of any transaction that is to occur.

Germany recently went through a unification process, bringing the east and the west together. Today, there still continues to be sensitivities between the two regions, as the eastern region struggles economically and technologically to catch up with the west. Business dress in Germany is very conservative. Businessmen wear dark suits; solid, conservative ties, and white shirts Women also dress conservatively, in dark suits and white blouses.

Chewing gum while talking to someone is considered rude. Germans are strongly individualistic.

The German thought process is extremely thorough, with each aspect of a project being examined in great detail. This process is often very time-intensive. Germans do not like surprises. Sudden changes in business transactions, even if they may improve the outcome, are unwelcome.

German citizens do not need or expect to be complimented. In Germany, it is assumed that everything is satisfactory unless the person hears otherwise. Punctuality is necessity in Germany. Arrive on time for every appointment, whether for business or social. Being late, even if it is only by a few minutes, is insulting to a German executive. In business situations, shake hands at both the beginning and the end of a meeting. Additionally, a handshake may be accompanied with a slight bow. Reciprocating the nod is a good way to make a good impression, as failure to respond with this nod/bow (especially a superior) may get you off to a bad start. When being introduced to a woman, wait to see if she extends her hand. Business is viewed as being very serious, and Germans do not appreciate humour in a business context. In business meetings, age takes precedence over youth. If you are in a group setting, the eldest person enters first. Germans keep a larger personal space around them, approximately 6 inches more space than North Americans do.

German is the official language. Approximately ninety-nine per cent of the population speaks German. However, there are several different dialects in the various regions. Germans love to talk on the telephone. While important business decisions are not made over the phone, expect many follow-up calls or faxes. Germans guard their private life, so do not phone a German executive at home without permission. Titles are very important to Germans. Do your best to address people by their full, correct title, no matter how extraordinarily long that title may seem to foreigners. This is also true when addressing a letter.

INDIA

Introduction

India is officially called Republic of India (Hindi *Bharat*), is located in southern Asia and is a member of the Commonwealth of Nations. The current leadership of India is implementing sweeping changes to encourage global business in India, from privatization to the liberalization of trade. Men are generally expected to wear a suit and tie for business, although the jacket may be removed in the summer.

When dressing casual, short-sleeved shirts and long pants are preferred for men; shorts are acceptable only when exercising. Women wear saris, salvar suits or modern dress of business suit. Hindus do not eat beef and Muslims do not eat pork. There are more than twenty major and three hundred minor languages spoken in India. The official languages are English and Hindi. English is widely used in business, politics and education. Titles are very important. Always use professional titles.

INDONESIA

Introduction

With a population of almost 200 million people on 13,667 islands, Indonesia is the world's largest archipelago located between the continents of Asia and Australia, and between the Pacific and the Indian Oceans. Only 35% of the population lives in urban areas, but there are more than 30 cities with 100,000+ population. Plus, five cities have a population of over 1 million. They are Jakarta, Surabaya, Bandung, and Semarang, and are all located on Java. To truly understand the socio-political culture in Indonesia, one needs to understand Java.

Although the population has a significant Malay heritage, it is also diverse with over 300 distinct cultures residing within its borders. With each culture comes a unique language or dialect; however, Bahasa Indonesia, the common language of the country, unites everyone. In tourist areas and population centres English is the most commonly spoken second language. Though the large majority of Indonesians follow the Islamic faith (85%), the intensity of their observance for their faith varies due to the large diversity within this nation. Christianity is a distant second (10%). One important historic note is the strong sentiment against the Chinese. Keep this in mind and be sensitive to this reality. Indonesia is a gracious culture that is polite. Wanting to be agreeable and never wanting to embarrass another, the native language Bahasa. Indonesia has 12 words that "say *yes* but really *mean no*.

An umbrella is an essential wardrobe component in rainy season (September–February). High heat and humidity require packing enough clothing to always appear clean–fresh. You may have to change your clothes several times a day to maintain this look. Men should wear coat and tie until appropriate to dress more casually. Follow the lead of those you are meeting with. Men generally wear dark slacks, long sleeve and light coloured shirt, and tie (no jacket)." Lounge suit" requires men to wear a business suit. This term may be included on an invitation. Men may find in a very casual business office that a short sleeve shirt and no tie would be appropriate. Women must always cover their upper arms when wearing a casual blouse. Jeans may be worn for very casual, but never shorts for men or women. Even though the climate is warm and humid, proper attire even for very casual appearance will always dictate your choice of clothing. Do not crook your index finger to call someone over. This gesture is offensive. Do not put your hands into your pockets when talking to someone. No physical contact between men and women is made in public, except a possible handshake.

Be on time for any meetings. The meetings traditionally start late, and your Indonesian business associates will probably arrive late. However, you are expected on time, and should never make any comment about the meeting starting late or any person arriving late.

Never stand with your back to an elderly person or a high-ranking official. As you enter a room be aware of the people who will be in that room with you. Always rise when your host/hostess enters the room. Leaving food on your plate signifies you are impolite; so eat all the food you are served. Only use your right hand for eating, when touching someone, or handling money/papers. Talking is impolite while having dinner. Conversation is reserved for before or after the meal. Never show the soles of your feet/shoes or touch anything with your foot. Never touch another person's head; this includes a child's head (such as a pat on the head). Never eat while walking in public, or chew on a toothpick. Yawning in public is inappropriate (cover your mouth if you must yawn).Remove your hat and sunglasses when going indoors. Gifts, though small, are frequently given. Gifts are not opened when given. This practice shows the recipient is gracious, not greedy.

Religion/culture dictates specific rules for appropriate gifts. Muslim, Hindus, and the Chinese culture each have rules regarding food, alcohol, and other items. Make sure your gift is not offensive to the person you are giving it to.

Chinese may politely refuse a gift three times before accepting it. When the gift is accepted, tell the recipient how happy you are with his or her acceptance. Do not give gifts of alcohol or pork. This would also include perfume since it is made with alcohol, and any leather product made from pigskin (Muslim). Do not give gifts containing beef or items made of cowhide (Hindu). Do not give gifts or pictures that show dogs. They are considered unclean. On Chinese New Year, give children and people you frequently deal with, who are not government employees, a gift of money. The money must be an even number of new bills, and presented in a red envelope (Chinese). Do not give a knife, scissors, clock, handkerchief, or straw sandals (Chinese). Do not give a gift that numbers four or shows a crane or stork. In selecting the gift and the gift-wrapping paper stay away from the colours white, black, or blue (Chinese). A gift of an umbrella means you do not want to see that person again (Chinese). Shake hands upon greeting and leaving, and always use your right hand. The handshake is limp and lasts 10-15 seconds. For religious reasons (Muslim and Hindu) men and women do not touch in public in this culture. Women do not offer a handshake to an Indonesian man. However, should a man extend his hand, always shake hands. Some Indonesian men may follow western business rules in a business setting. Address each person using his/her title plus full name. A title may be an honorific title or an academic title. Rank and status is very important in this culture.

One important honorific title is for Muslims who have made a pilgrimage to Mecca. *Haji* is the title for a man, *Hajjah* is for a woman. Mr., Madam, Mrs. or Miss is used if a person does not have a title. A man is addressed as *Pak* (Mr.) or *Bapak* (Sir). A lady is addressed as *Ibu.* People are normally called by their first name, as in Mr. Robert or Miss Susan, rather than using their last name. Married Chinese women keep their maiden name. *Selamat* means peace and is a traditional greeting. "Yes, but" means *no* when someone is speaking to you. Never allow your voice to get loud, whether in anger or joy. Expressing anger in public through tone of voice, loudness, or body language is always inappropriate. Do not use red ink when writing, or having printing done (Chinese).

ITALY

Introduction

Officially called the Republic of Italy, Italy is located in southern Europe, and has a population of roughly 58.2 million. Italy has much to offer its citizens and visitors. Surrounded by the four seas of the Mediterranean, Italy is famous for its coastline activities. Italy also has a mountain range with elevations over 13,500 feet for the skiing and hiking enthusiast. Italy has no official religion, though the majority of Italy's citizens are Roman Catholic. The Vatican City, the home of the Pope and the Roman Catholic Church, is located within the city of Rome and is considered a separate state completely. The Vatican has its own currency, flag, and stamps, although Italian money can be used.

Fashions and fashion design are trademarks of Italy. Therefore, in the business world, good clothes are synonymous of success. Men should ideally wear fashionable, high quality suits. Shirts may be coloured or pinstriped, and they should be paired with an Italian designer tie. Women dress in quiet, expensive elegance. Slacks are generally not worn by either sex. Quality accessories such as shoes and leather goods will make a good impression with the Italians. Italian history has played a crucial role in the modern business world. Some of their contributions include banking, insurance, and double entry bookkeeping. "Time is money" is not a common phrase in Italy. Foreign businessmen/women should be punctual for business appointments, although the Italian executive may not be. Handshakes are common for both sexes, and may include grasping the arm with the other hand.

Do not expect quick decisions or actions to take place, as the Italian bureaucracy and legal systems are rather slow. Italian companies often have a rigid hierarchy, with little visible association between the ranks. It is common for everyone to speak simultaneously at Italian gatherings. This applies to business meetings as well as social events. Do not exchange business cards at social occasions; but it is the norm at business functions and meetings. Italians often have two different business cards, one with business credentials for formal relationships, and another with personal information for less formal relationships. Italian cards are often plain white with black print. When entering a business function, the most senior or eldest person present should always be given special treatment.

When invited to someone's home, bring gift-wrapped chocolates, pastries, or flowers. Never give an even number of flowers. Also, avoid giving anything in quantities of 13, as 13 is considered to be bad luck. If you bring wine as a gift, make sure that it is of excellent vintage, as many Italians are wine connoisseurs. Italian is the official language, although there are many diverse dialects. English is spoken by many businesspeople. Avoid talking about religion, politics, and World War II. At social gatherings, it is considered insulting to ask someone you have just met about their profession. Good conversational topics include Italian culture, art, food, wine, family, and films.

JAPAN

Introduction

Japan has a population of approximately 125 million people packed tightly into a rather small geographic area. The official language in Japan is Japanese. Japanese is spoken only in Japan. The literacy rate in Japan is very close to 100 per cent and 95 per cent of the Japanese population has a high school education. Japan's form of government is parliamentarian democracy under the rule of a constitutional monarch. The Prime Minister is the chief government officer. The dominant religion is Shinto, which is exclusive to Japan. However, the Japanese have no official religion. Culturally, the Japanese tend to be somewhat introverted in their ways. They generally are not receptive to outsiders. When conducting business in Japan, relationships and loyalty to the group is critical for success. The Japanese tend to be rather direct in their questioning of foreigners. You may be asked personal questions such as how much money do you earn or how large is your house?

Those who dress according to their status or position impress the Japanese. Dress to impress. Men should wear dark conservative attire. Business suits are most suitable. Casual dress is never appropriate in a business setting. Shoes should be easy to remove, as you will do so often. Slip-ons are the best choice. Women's dress should be conservative. Little emphasis should be placed on accessories. They should be minimal. Women should not wear pants in a business situation. Japanese men tend to find it offensive. Women should only wear low-heeled shoes to avoid towering over men. A kimono should be wrapped left over right to do otherwise symbolizes death. Remember the Japanese phrase "The nail that sticks up gets hit with the hammer" when considering your choices for attire in Japan.

Avoid using large hand gestures, unusual facial expressions and any dramatic movements. The Japanese do not talk with their hands and to do so could distract your host. Avoid the "OK" sign; in Japan it means money. Pointing is not acceptable. Do not blow your nose in public. Personal space is valued. Because the Japanese live in such a densely populated area, they value their personal space. A smile can have double meaning. It can express either joy or displeasure. Use caution with your facial expressions. They can be easily misunderstood. The Japanese are not uncomfortable with silence. They use it to their advantage in many situations. Allow your host to sit in silence. The word for toasting is kampai, pronounced 'kahm-pie'. When toasting, the glass is never left unfilled. Drinking is an important part of Japanese culture. It is a way to relieve business stress. Never pour a drink yourself; always allow someone else to do it for you. Most business entertaining is done in restaurants or bars after business hours. Often-in *karaoke* or "hostess bars." Businesswomen should not attend "hostess bars." Let the host order the meal and pay. Business may be discussed at dinner during these events. Japanese rarely entertain in the home. If you are invited to the home of your Japanese host, consider it a great honour and display a tremendous amount of appreciation. If you are invited to a social event, punctuality is not expected. It is the custom to be "fashionably late." If you do take your host out, insist upon paying. The Japanese will refuse but insist. They will prefer that you choose a western-style restaurant when entertaining them.

Key phrases to learn are "itadakimasu" at the beginning of dinner, and "gochisou-sama-deshita" at the end. It is polite to use these phrase and it will show your host that you have enjoyed the meal. "Sumimasen" (excuse-me) is a very useful term to add to your vocabulary along with the phrase "kekko desu" (I've had enough). It is perfectly acceptable to slurp your noodles. Doing so will exhibit your enjoyment of your food. To do otherwise, indicates that your meal was not a pleasant one. Do not openly display money. It is rare to see it given from person to person in Japan. It is important to use an envelope to pass money. Tipping is not expected. Gift giving is very important both business and personal gifts. Style is tantamount. The gift itself is of little importance, the ceremony surrounding it is very important. Always wrap gifts. The selection of the wrapping paper is critical. Do not give anything wrapped in white as it symbolizes death. Do not use bright colours or bows to wrap the gift. It is better to have the hotel or the store warp the gift to ensure that it is appropriate. Do not surprise the recipient with the gift. Give your host some warning during the evening that you intend to give them a present. Give the gift with both hands and accept gifts with hands.

Generally, gifts will not be opened in your presence. If your host insist that you open the gift do so gingerly. They take pride in gift wrapping, show that you appreciate the effort. Do not give gifts in odd number or the number four, as odd numbers are bad luck and four sounds like the word for death in Japanese. Gifts should be given at the end of a visit. Do not admire anything belonging to your host too closely. The Japanese strive to please; you may be rewarded for your admiration. The most popular gift giving occasions in Japan are *oseibo,* which falls at the end of the year and O-*chugen* that falls during the middle of the year. Good gift ideas include top choice beef, fruit and alcohol such as brandy, quality whiskey and Bourbon along with excellent wines. They also appreciate gifts from high-end departmental stores like Saks and Neiman Marcus. The Japanese frown on open displays of affection. They do not touch in public. It is highly inappropriate to touch someone of the opposite sex in public.

In Japan, business cards are called meishi. Japanese give and receive meishi with both hands. It should be printed in your home language on one side and Japanese on the other. Present the card with your home country language side up. The card will contain the name and title along with the company name, address and telephone number of the businessman. In Japan, businessmen are call "sarariman." A sarariman who does not have a business card is not considered a vital individual. Take special care in handling cards that are given to you. Do not write on the card. Do not put the card in you pocket or wallet, as either of these actions will be viewed as defacing or disrespecting the business card. Upon receipt of the card, it is important to make a photocopy of the name and title of the individual in your mind. Examine the card carefully as a show of respect. In a business situation, business cannot begin until the meishi exchange process is complete. The customary greeting is the bow. However, some Japanese may greet you with a handshake, albeit a weak one. Do not misinterpret a weak handshake as an indication of character.

If you are greeted with a bow, return with a bow as low as the one you received. How low you bow determines the status of the relationship between you and the other individual. When you bow keep your eyes low and your palms flat next to your thighs.

The business card should be given after the bow. This is very important to remember. In introductions use the person's last name plus the word san that means Mr. or Ms. The Japanese prefer to use last names. Do not request that they call you by your first name only. If you are uncertain about the pronunciation of a name, ask for assistance. Understand that the Japanese prefer not to use the word no. If you ask a question they may simply respond with a yes but clearly mean no. Understanding this is critical in the negotiation process.

MEXICO

Introduction

Mexico has a population of almost 88 million. The ethnic composition of the country is 60 per cent Mestizo (a mixture of Indian and European), 30 per cent Amerindian, 9 per cent white, and 1 per cent others. Mexico is a federal republic. Spanish is the official language of Mexico, although over 100 Indian languages are also spoken. English is widely understood by educated people and in urban centres. There is no official religion, but almost 90 per cent of Mexicans are Roman Catholic. Protestants account for around 5 per cent of the population. One must know a person before doing business with him or her, and the only way to know a person in Mexico is to know the family. Personal relationships are the key to business success. In order to make this connection intermediaries are used.

It is critical, especially for a high-ranking meeting, to use a person who is known to the Mexican businessman or woman you are meeting. This is your "business family" connection, the person who will introduce you. This person is the bridge that builds the trust necessary to do business in Mexico. Mexicans are warm and gracious. They embrace the *manana* attitude, and do not embrace the time-is-money mentality of many other cultures. The old Mexican saying is that "North Americans live to work, but Mexicans work to live!" Respect their sense of time and traditions. If your natural tendency is to speak quickly or you have a forceful or sharp tone of voice, become aware of how you are coming across. Become sensitive to the pace and tone used in Mexico. Otherwise you will destroy a relationship with your caustic tone and behaviour. Men should wear a conservative dark suit and tie. Your wardrobe should include suits that have classic lines and tailoring in gray or navy, and white or light blue shirts. A white shirt is more formal and should be worn when the formality of the meeting dictates. Men may wear pants and a light shirt for casual. Standing with your hands on your hips suggests aggressiveness, and keeping your hands in your pockets is impolite. Mexicans may not make eye contact. This is a sign of respect and should not be taken as an affront. Men shake hands upon meeting and leaving, and will wait for a woman to be the first to offer her hand. Women may shake hands with men and other women. Many times a woman may pat another woman's shoulder or forearm, or kiss on the cheek. Long-time friends may embrace, and after several meetings you may also be greeted with an embrace. Punctuality is not rigid because of the emphasis on personal obligations. The best time for appointments is between 10:00 a.m. and 1:00 p.m., with late afternoon a second choice. Business lunches, rather than dinners are the traditional form of business entertaining and are usually prolonged affairs, beginning between 2:00 and 3:00 p.m. and lasting three to four hours, with little time being devoted to actual business. Lunches are an essential part of business to establish a personal relationship. Working breakfasts are also popular, meeting at 8:00 or 8:30 at your hotel, and usually lasting two hours at the most.

Conversations take place at a close physical distance. Stepping back may be regarded as unfriendly.

Mexican men are warm and friendly, and make a lot of physical contact. They often touch shoulders or hold another's arm. To withdraw from this touch is considered insulting. Giving gifts to business executives is not required. Small items with a company logo (for an initial visit) are appreciate. Secretaries do appreciate gifts. If giving a valuable gift, such as perfume or a scarf, present it on a return visit. A man giving it to a female secretary should indicate the gift is from his wife. Gifts are not required for a dinner guest, but will be appreciated. Good choices are candy, flowers (sent ahead of time), or local crafts from home. When giving flowers: yellow – represent death, red – cast spells, and white – lift spells. Do not give gifts made of silver, as it is associated with trinkets sold to tourists. Women should not invite a male counterpart for a business dinner unless other associates or spouses attend. Also, Mexican men will graciously attempt to pay for a meal, even though you are hosting it. A professional way to host a meal is to dine or lunch at your hotel. Pre-arrange to have the meal added to your hotel bill. Tipping is appropriate for services provided. Wages are often so low that workers depend heavily on gratuities for their income. Pay for store purchases by placing money in the cashier's hand, rather than on the counter. Refrain from using first names until invited to do so. Titles are important and should be included on business cards. You may directly speak to someone by only using his or her title only, without including the last name. *Doctor* is a physician or Ph.D. *Professor* is the title for a teacher. *Ingeniero* is an engineer. *Arquitecto* is an architect. *Abogado* is a lawyer. People without professional titles are addressed using Mr., Mrs., or Miss and his or her surname. *Senor* is Mr., *Senora* is Mrs., and *Senorita* is Miss.

Hispanics generally use two surnames. The first surname listed is from the father, and the second surname listed is from the mother. When speaking to someone use his or her father's surname. A married woman will add her husband's father's name to the end of her name, usually shown as *de (name)* when written. This woman would be formally addressed as *Senora de (name)*. In speaking to this same married woman less formally, you would simply say *Senora (name)*. Do not use red ink anytime you are writing someone's name. The traditional toast in Mexico is *Salud* (Sal-UUD).Mexican's use a "psst-psst" sound to catch another's attention in public. This is not considered rude. Mexicans refer to people from the United States as North Americans. Good conversational topics are Mexican culture, history, art, and museums. Never discuss the Mexican-American war, poverty, illegal aliens, or earthquakes.

NEW ZEALAND

Introduction

New Zealand has a population of slightly less than 4 million people with most living in the key cities. The large majority of the population (89%) has a European heritage, primarily English. Therefore, English is the predominant language and Christianity the largest religion. The Maori, a Polynesian people who were the earliest inhabitants of New Zealand make up the remaining population.

There is little racial tension between the Maori and the predominately European/ English people. Though Maori and Europeans freely intermarry and have similar ways of life, each maintains its identity, so social and cultural aspects remain distinct for each group. The standard of living is high, and their literacy rate is 100%.

The state provides extensive social services for the welfare of its citizens, and has one of the most comprehensive healthcare programmes in the world. Adding to their quality of life is the nation's geographic location and size. No one is more than 75 miles from the ocean and the climate encourages outdoor activities. This nation actively participates in hiking, fishing, sailing, and competitive sports. Although New Zealand is often mentioned in the same sentence with Australia, New Zealanders do not appreciate this mutual reference, as they are an independent nation. This country was very forward thinking. Not only did these people believe in individualism, they created the environment for it to thrive. They also understood their obligation to the people who worked to establish and maintain the society. In 1893, this British Commonwealth gave women the right to vote, and in 1898, established an old-age pension, the first Commonwealth member to do so. If you are walking down the street and see two people *pressing noses,* they are Maoris using their traditional greeting. The Maoris are also highly regarded for their tattooing art.

When conducting business in New Zealand, you want to dress conservatively and tending toward a more formal look. Men should wear darker coloured suits with a conservative tie. To maintain formality, a white shirt would be worn. Women should wear a suit, a dress, or skirt and blouse with a jacket. Umbrellas and raincoats are necessary most of the year because of the climate and rainfall. The climate is temperate, not tropical. A medium weight wool gabardine would be a good choice of fabric for your basic wardrobe. When not involved in business meetings and activities, your wardrobe may be casual. Do not use the "V for victory" sign while in this country. Always be on time or early for all appointments. Punctuality is part of the culture. "Fashionably late" is not an option in this country as most social events start on time. Maintain a reserved, formal demeanor, especially when first meeting someone. Take your lead to become more relaxed by following the behaviour of your New Zealand hosts. Normal business hours are Monday – Friday 8:30 am-5:00 pm and Saturday 9:00 am-12:30 pm. Talking is minimal while you are eating a meal. The conversation will occur before and after your meal. Dinners are reserved for social interactions only; therefore no business is discussed at these occasions. Lunch is used for business conversations. Boisterous behaviour is always inappropriate, even when you are drinking. Pace yourself to maintain the proper reserved and polite behavior. Afternoon tea is between 3:00-4:00 pm. Tea is between 6:00-8:00 pm, and an evening meal is served. Supper is a snack served much later in the evening. A tip may be refused, as tipping is rare. Entertaining is frequently done in a person's home. A small thank you gift of flowers, chocolate, or whisky may be taken to the host and/or hostess. Cover your mouth if you must yawn, and do not chew gum or toothpicks in public. Ask permission before you attempt to photograph someone. The official language is English. When meeting someone, and when leaving, use a firm handshake with good eye contact. Good eye contact means looking into the other person's eyes when shaking hands, not looking down at your hand. The eye contact is maintained during the handshake. You are not staring at the other person, but showing genuine interest in meeting or seeing the person. Men generally wait for a woman to be the first to extend her hand for a handshake. Women do shake other women's hands. Use your same firm handshake with good eye contact. When you are meeting someone, say "How do you do?" A more relaxed greeting, such as "Hello", is reserved for the meetings after you've had the opportunity to get to know the person. The people are reserved, but always very warm and polite when you meet them. Address a person using his/her title, or Mr., Mrs., Miss plus the full name. Honesty is the best policy. Don't hype your product or service, and don't be a braggart.

Do not allow your voice to get loud. Maintain a reserved manner. Politics, sports, and weather are good conversational topics, and may be hotly debated. In order to be a good conversationalist, stay current and informed on critical topics. One in particular is New Zealand's "nuclear free" zone. Avoid confusing or comparing New Zealand with Australia, as they are two distinct countries. If you are not familiar with New Zealand, spend time before your trip to learn about the history and culture.

PANAMA

Introduction

Panama has a population of 2.4 million people and is one of the smallest countries in Central America. Its ethnic composition is 70 per cent Mestizo (a mix of Indian and European), 14 per cent West Indian, 10 per cent European, and 6 per cent Amerindian.

Panama is a multiparty republic, with a president, two vice-presidents, a cabinet, a unicameral legislative assembly serving 5-year terms, and a supreme court. The President is the head of state and the head of the government. The official language is Spanish. Because of the extensive U.S. influence, most Panamanians are bilingual in Spanish and English. The majority of the people (94 per cent) are Roman Catholic, although Panama has no official religion. There are also small numbers of Protestants, Muslims, Hindus, and others. Conservative business suits are appropriate for men. Panamanian businessmen in higher positions wear suits; others wear camisillas (a lightweight, open-necked shirt that is not tucked inside the trousers). Women should wear a dress or skirt and blouse. Women should avoid wearing any kind of revealing clothing. Have business cards and other material printed in Spanish as well as English.

When dining, the host usually sits at one end of the table with the guest of honour at the other end. Foreign businesswomen should always include spouses in invitations to business dinners. Gifts are not normally exchanged when entertaining. Handshaking is the custom; old friends embrace. Titles are important and should be included on business cards. Address a person directly by using his or her title only. A Ph.D. or a physician is called *Doctor*. Teachers prefer the title *Professor*, engineers go by *Ingeniero*, architects are *Arquitecto*, and lawyers are *Abogado*. Persons who do not have professional titles should be addressed as Mr., Mrs., or Miss, plus their surnames. In Spanish these are: Mr. = *Senor*, Mrs. = *Senora*, Miss = *Senorita.*

Most Hispanics have two surnames: one from their father, which is listed first, followed by one from their mother. Only the father's surname is used when addressing someone. In business, conversations begin with much small talk. Good conversation topics: family, hobbies, basketball, and baseball. Bad conversation topics: former Canal Zone, race problems, and politics.

RUSSIA

Introduction

The Russian Federation has over 150 million people, and covers an area of greater than 6,592,800 m^2. The country has gone through many changes in recent years, as communism ended in 1991. At that time, the U.S.S.R. as it was called, separated into independent states. This separation ended the communism reign that had lasted from 1917 to 1991.

After the break up of the old Soviet Union, fifteen new independent states emerged. This number, however, is ever changing as boundaries are continually being modified. Negotiations with Russians often involve flared tempers. During negotiations and meetings, temper tantrums and walkouts often occur. Businessmen in Russia usually wear suits that are dark and well tailored along with good dress shoes. A businessman's wardrobe demonstrates the individual's image as a professional. Men often do not take off their jackets in negotiations. Do not stand with your hands in your pockets. This is considered rude. Women dress rather conservatively, avoiding overly flashy or gaudy outfits. Women should always cover their heads when entering into any Russian Orthodox Churches. Skirts should be worn rather than pants. When attending dinner in a citizen's home, casual dress of slacks and a nice shirt without a tie are appropriate. As a foreigner, you are expected to be on time to all business appointments. However, your Russian counterpart may be late, as this may be a test of your patience. Do not expect an apology from a late Russian, and do not demonstrate any kind of attitude if your business appointments begin one or two hours late. This may also be a test of your patience.

Social events are more relaxed. It is acceptable for foreigners to be 15 to 30 minutes late. Patience is an extremely important virtue among Russians; punctuality is not. "Glasnost", which means new openness, and "perestroika", the restructuring of the economy, are common topics of conversation in Russia. Russians are known as great "sitters" during negotiations, this demonstrates their tremendous patience. The U.S.S.R. was officially an atheist nation in the days of communism. Now, however, participation by the citizens in religion in increasing. Many citizens are practising Protestantism, Islam, Russian Orthodoxy, and Judaism. Some hard-line Russians still view compromise as a sign of weakness, and often refuse to back down. To these individuals, compromising is bad business. As a foreigner, you should realize that "Final Offers" are often not actually the end of the negotiations, and that often times the outcome will be more beneficial and attractive if you can hold out. There is a Russian term meaning "connections" or "influences". It is extremely difficult to do business in Russia without help from a local. To help with this, gifts, money or other items are often a good idea when doing business in Russia. If attending dinner at a family residence, it is appropriate to bring a gift, such as a bottle of wine, dessert, or a bouquet of flowers. When shaking hands with someone, you be sure to take off your gloves, as it is considered rude not to. When attending any formal engagements such as the theatre, it is appropriate to check your coat and other belongings at the front door of the establishment.

Do not show the soles of your shoes, as this is considered impolite. They are considered dirty, and should never come in contact with any type of seat (like on a subway or bus). Be sure to have plenty of business cards with double sides of information. One side should be printed in English, the other side in Russian. Be alert and open to taking a drink or having a toast, as refusing to do so is a serious breach of etiquette. Russian is the official language. Speaking or laughing loudly in public is considered rude, as Russians are generally reserved and sober. Many Russians speak English, as it is often taught beginning in the third grade. Russians are highly literate, and have almost a 100% literacy rate. Good topics of conversation include peace, the current changes taking place in Russia, and their current economic situation.

SOUTH AFRICA

Introduction

South Africa has a population of approximately 40 million people. Three-quarters of its population is black (African) and approximately 15% is white (European). The rest is a mixture of white, Malayan and blacks whose ancestors were of Asian descent. There are six major ethnic groups in South Africa: Afrikaner, Coloured/Cape Malay, Bantu, English, Chinese and Indian. There are 11 official languages in South Africa.

Most South Africans speak English and Afrikaans, which is derived from their Dutch heritage. South Africa has a democratic government. Nelson Mandela, the current president of South Africa spent 27 years in prison for the formation of Operation Mayjibuye, a revolutionary plan. South Africa is considered the industrial giant of Africa. It is a substantial resource for minerals including gold, silver, copper and diamonds. South Africans of urban cultures generally wear western dress. Dress well in public, it will be expected by your South African host. African women wear a sari. Gift giving is not the norm in business. Do not present gifts with the left hand. Use both hands or the right hand when giving and presenting gifts. Gifts will be opened upon receipt.

Business meetings can be held over lunch or dinner in a good restaurant. Meals at the home of a white South African will include a barbecue by the pool—called a braaivleis (Afrikaans for roasted meat) or braai. The handshake is the most common greeting. There are a variety of handshakes between ethnic groups. Use titles and surnames to address people. Appointments should be made starting at 9 a.m. Do not rush deals. South Africans are very casual in their business dealings. Business cards have no formal exchange protocol. South Africans prefer a "win-win" situation.

SAUDI ARABIA

Introduction

Saudi Arabia is a monarchy in south-western Asia, and occupies most of the Arabian Peninsula. If you are not a Muslim, you may not enter Saudi Arabia without an invitation and you may not leave without an exit permit. Visitors to Saudi Arabia are subject to the same rigorous Islamic law as Saudis. It is not uncommon for Westerners to be imprisoned for possessing illegal substances such as alcohol, pornography, pork or narcotics. Thieves still have their hands amputated and capital crimes are punished by public beheadings. Never show bare shoulders, stomach, calves and thighs. Visitors are expected to abide by local standards of modesty, however, do not adopt native clothing. Traditional clothes on foreigners may be offensive. Despite the heat, most of the body must always remain covered. A jacket and tie are usually required for men at business meetings. Men should wear long pants and a shirt, preferably long-sleeved, and buttoned up to the collar. Men should also avoid wearing visible jewellery, particularly around the neck.

Women should always wear modest clothing in public. High necklines sleeves at least to the elbows are expected. Hemlines, if not ankle-length should at least be well below the knee. A look of baggy concealment should be the goal; pants or pantsuits are not recommended. It is a good idea to keep a scarf handy, especially if entering a mosque.

It is common to remove your shoes before entering a building. Follow the lead of your host. Alcohol and pork are illegal. In the Muslim world, Friday is the day of rest. There are several styles of greetings used; it is best to wait for your counterpart to initiate the greeting. Men shake hands with other men. Some men will shake hands with a woman; it is advisable for a businesswoman to wait for a man to offer his hand. A more traditional greeting between men involves grasping each other's right hand, placing the left hand on the other's right shoulder and exchanging kisses on each cheek.

The left hand is considered unclean and reserved for hygiene. Avoid gestures with the right hand. Do not point at another person and do not eat with the left hand. Men walking hand in hand are proof of their friendship. Try not to cross your legs when sitting. Never show the bottom of your feet. The "thumbs up" gesture is offensive. Gifts are not necessary, but appreciated. Avoid admiring an item too much, your host may feel obligated to give it to you. When offered a gift, it is impolite to refuse. Women in Saudi Arabia are not permitted to drive vehicles. Do not discuss the subject of women, not even to inquire about the health of a wife or daughter.

Sports are an appropriate topic. Names are often confusing. It's best to get the names (in English) of those you will meet, speak to, or correspond with beforehand. Find out both their full names and how they are to be addressed in person. Communications occur at a slow pace. Do not feel obligated to speak during periods of silence. "Yes" usually means "possibly". Your Saudi host may interrupt your meeting or conversation, leave the room and be gone for 15 to 20 minutes for the purpose of his daily prayers. At a meeting, the person who asks the most questions is likely to be the least important. The decision-maker is likely a silent observer. A customary greeting is *salaam alaykum.* Shaking hands and saying *kaif halak* comes next.

SPAIN

Introduction

The Kingdom of Spain has a population of 39.2 million people, and is 194,992 m^2. The majority of citizens are raised Roman Catholic, and family values are extremely important in Spain. The Spanish lifestyle is more relaxed than many other nations. For example, many businesses are closed between 1:30 p.m. and 4:30 p.m. for a siesta, allowing families to get together for a meal. Punctuallity is only taken seriously when attending a bullfight. Men still hold the majority of positions within companies. A woman lawyer is a very rare occurrence, and it is very unusual for a woman at any level in a company to be making a career for herself. When attending a business dinner, be prepared to stay up late. Most restaurants do not open until after nine o'clock, and often do not get active until around eleven! Also, while Spanish is the official language, Spain's Castilian dialect is different from the Spanish that is spoken in Mexico. This is often confusing to travellers, as the same words can have very different meanings between the two languages.

The Spanish dress more formal than many other Europeans. In Spain, it is important to project good taste in apparel. Business attire includes well-made, conservative suits and ties. Avoid flashy colours, as it is not popular to stand out. Shorts are not usually worn in public. If you pull down on your eyelid in Spain, you are insinuating to "be alert" or that "I am alert." In Spain, crossing your fingers has several good meanings, usually things such as "protection" or "good luck". This is a nice gesture to be friendly. The family is the most important thing to people in Spain. Time is very relaxed. It is wise for foreigners to be punctual, but Spaniards do not put a great emphasis on time themselves. The Spaniards often consider deadlines an objective that will be met if possible, but do not become overly concerned if the deadline is not achieved. Although many Spanish businesspeople speak English, it is a good idea for foreigners to have all of your materials printed in Spanish. Business cards should be two-sided, one side having English and the other side containing Spanish. When presenting your business card, place the card with the Spanish side facing your Spanish colleague. Much like Mexico, business in Spain is often obtained as a result of personal relationships.

While the relationship building process takes time, it is imperative to gain such relationships if you are to be effective in Spain. Also, you must be very selective when choosing your Spanish representative, as it is extremely difficult to change to another person. Be prepared for chaotic business negotiations. Often numerous people will be speaking simultaneously. Men who are close friends will often exchange a hug. Women who are close friends usually meet and part with a small hug and a kiss on each cheek. Negotiations are usually an extremely long and arduous task, so do not be in a rush to close a deal in Spain. Dining is usually associated with establishing business relationships in Spain, so be prepared for your business associate(s) to join you at any or all of your daily meals. Dinner is usually served after 9:00 p.m. so you may want to take full advantage of the siesta and get in a nap. Spanish is the official language of Spain. There are several regional dialects of Spanish. Dialects can include Catalian, which is usually spoken in eastern Spain, and Gallego, which is popular in the northwest. Each dialect has different pronunciations and spellings. Additionally, the native language of the Basque region is called Euskera. It is not a form of Spanish, and its origins are unknown.

A large portion of your communication will take place over lunches and dinners. They are an extremely important part of business life in Spain. During business negotiations, rules and systems are only used as a last resort to solving a problem. During business meetings, doors are usually kept shut. Business colleagues often dine together, but different ranks within a company do not mix.

TAIWAN

Introduction

The Taiwanese migrated to Mainland China starting in AD 500. Taiwan has a population of approximately 20.5 million. The official language is Mandarin Chinese. Most businessmen speak and understand English. It is governed by a multiparty republican system. Taiwan is often referred to as Nationalist China. Although the Taiwanese practise a variety of religions the culture is strongly influenced by Confucianism. Taiwan has a very young population. Almost 55 per cent of the population is under thirty. Conservative dress for men is changing rapidly to a more open style, due largely in part to the younger staff. Women should dress conservatively as well with a simple skirt and blouse. Causal activities should reflect a modest dress. Appearance should be neat and clean. Winking is inappropriate in any situation. Do not touch another person's shoulders. Do not touch anyone's head particularly the head of someone's child. Children are held in very high regard in Taiwan. Do not touch or point at anything with your feet, they are considered dirty.

Business relationships are based on respect. Meet face-to-face if possible. Elders make the decisions. Always include a senior executive in meetings. Women are rare in business in Taiwan but this is changing rapidly. Candor is not appreciated. Divide topics into segments for presentations. Direct presentations are made to the senior ranking individual. Have all new products registered and or patented to avoid copying. Translate all written documents. Subtlety is key. Modify tone and volume as not to appear loud. Do not visit a home without an invitation. Do not discard food from your mouth back into your bowl.

Good topics during dinner include art, family, and Chinese sightseeing. Gift giving is common practice in business. Good choices are items with your company logo on them for your first visit to Taiwan. Give and receive gifts with both hands. Gifts will not be opened in your presence. Food is a good gift. Avoid giving knives, scissors or cutting tools as they symbolize the cutting off of friendships. A nod of your head is an appropriate greeting. Handshakes are for casual meetings and introductions. Bowing slightly is a good way to show respect with your hands to your sides and your feet together. Women rarely shake hands but this is changing. Business is becoming more westernized and men now shake hands. "Have you eaten?' is a standard greeting. It is more of a rhetorical question. Always wait for introductions. Punctuality is of great importance in Taiwan.

UAE

Introduction

The United Arab Emirates is considered one of the Gulf countries (Bahrain, Kuwait, Sultanate of Oman, Qatar, and the United Arab Emirates). They are located on the Arabian Gulf - it is important NOT to refer to it as the Persian Gulf. When holding business meetings in the United Arab Emirates, some foreign businesspeople suggest holding the meeting in the lobby of an global hotel rather than in an office. The advantage of this is that there will be fewer people wandering in and out of the meeting. Also, your counterpart's willingness to come to you demonstrates a true interest. You will also have access to refreshments that may be more to your taste.

Visitors are expected to abide by local standards of modesty, however, do not adopt native clothing. Traditional clothes on foreigners may be offensive. Despite the heat, most of the body must always be covered. A jacket and tie are usually required for men at business meetings. Men should wear long pants and a shirt, preferably long-sleeved, buttoned up to the collar. Men should also avoid wearing visible jewellery, particularly around the neck. Women should always wear modest clothing in public. High necklines sleeves at least to the elbows are expected. Hemlines, if not ankle-length should at least be well below the knee. A look of baggy concealment should be the goal, pants or pantsuits are not recommended. It is a good idea to keep a scarf handy, especially if entering a mosque. Avoid admiring an item to an excess, your host may feel obligated to give it to you. When offered a gift, it is impolite to refuse. Often shoes are removed before entering a building. Follow the lead of your host. Alcohol and pork are illegal. There are several styles of greetings in use, it is best to wait for your counterpart to initiate the greeting. Men shake hands with other men. Some men will shake hands with women, however, it is advisable for a businesswoman to wait for a man to offer his hand. A more traditional greeting between men involves grasping each other's right hand, placing the left hand on the other's right shoulder and exchanging kisses on each cheek. The left hand is considered unclean and reserved for hygiene. Gesture and eat with the right hand. Do not point at another person. In the Muslim world, Friday is the day of rest. Do not cross your legs when sitting, showing the bottom of your shoe is offensive. The "thumbs up" gesture is offensive. Gifts are not necessary, but appreciated.

Do not discuss the subject of women, not even to inquire about the health of a wife or daughter. The topic of Israel should also be avoided. Sports are an appropriate topic.

Names are often confusing. It's best to get the names (in English) of those you will meet, speak to, or correspond with. Learn both their full names and how they are to be addressed in person before you meet. Communication is slow; do not feel obligated to speak during periods of silence. "Yes" usually means "possibly". Meetings are commonly interrupted by phone calls and visits from friends and family. The person at a meeting who asks the most questions is likely to be the least important. The decision-maker is likely a silent observer. A customary greeting is *salaam alaykum*. Shaking hands and saying *kaif halak* follows.

USA

Introduction

The population of the United States is over 250 million people of mixed races and heritage. Although the population is predominantly of European descent, the country has been a welcoming beacon to immigrants from virtually every country and culture in the world. English is the predominant language, although languages from many foreign countries are spoken within cultural enclaves throughout the U.S. The majority of Americans (U.S.) are Christian. The United States of America consists of 50 states governed on a federal level, as well as a state level. Laws are written at both levels, and when doing business in the United States one must make sure to meet the requirements mandated by these laws. The country is very litigious so legal resources are available and specialists can be found to assist with any transaction.

The culture and geographic location of an area will influence how business is done. Traditionally, the East Coast is more conservative and formal in their dress and manners than the West Coast. That is not to say a West Coast meeting carries any less importance. The climate and lifestyle are just more relaxed, which is reflected in the pace and informality. The U. S. was founded on the work ethic that good, honest, hard work is rewarded. Because of this work ethic, time is money and punctuality is highly regarded, so a cellular phone *can* save the day when automobile traffic in a major city causes unexpected delays. Business suit and tie are appropriate in all major cities. Wear dark coloured business suits in classic colours of grey and navy. For an important formal meeting, choose a white dress shirt, for less formal a light blue shirt will still give you a conservative appearance. Women should wear a suit or dress with jacket in major cities.

Wearing classic clothing and classic colours of navy, grey, ivory, and white will ensure you give a confident and conservative appearance. Casual clothing is appropriate when not attending a work related meeting/dinner. Clothing, whether formal or casual, should be clean and neat in appearance. Men may generally wear jeans or khaki pants with a shirt for casual attire. Women may wear comfortably fitting slacks with a casual shirt. Wearing jeans or shorts, even in a casual setting, may be inappropriate for the city. It is better to err on the conservative side if you are not sure.

Business conversation *may* take place during meals. However, many times you will find more social conversation taking place during the actual meal. Business meetings may be arranged as breakfast meetings, luncheon meetings, or dinner meetings depending on time schedules and necessity. Generally a dinner, even though for business purposes, is treated as a social meal and a time to build rapport. Gift giving is discouraged or limited by many US companies. A gracious written note is always appropriate and acceptable. Should you give a gift, it should not appear to be a bribe. An invitation for a meal or a modest gift is usually acceptable. Should you be some place with a line or queue, go to the end and wait for your turn. Do not use or chew on a toothpick in public. Many public places and private homes do not allow smoking. In some areas laws have been passed to prevent smoking in public places.

Offer a firm handshake, lasting 3-5 seconds, upon greeting and leaving. Maintain good eye contact during your handshake. If you are meeting several people at once, maintain eye contact with the person you are shaking hands with, until you are moving on the next person. Good eye contact during business and social conversations shows interest, sincerity and confidence. Good friends may briefly embrace, although the larger the city, usually the more formal the behaviour. Introductions include one's title if appropriate, or Mr., Ms, Mrs. and the full name. Business cards are generally exchanged during introductions. However, they may be exchanged when one party is leaving. Ask permission to smoke before lighting a cigarette or cigar. Due to health concerns, you may or may not be given permission.

VENEZUELA

Introduction

The population of Venezuela is 20.2 million with an ethnic makeup of 70 per cent mestizo, and the rest - Spanish, Italian, Portuguese, Arab, German, and African. Only 2 per cent of the population is pureblooded Amerindian. The capital of Caracas has approximately 3.2 million people within its city limits. Venezuela is a federal multiparty republic, with a president who is both chief of state and head of government. The cabinet, or Council of Ministers, has twenty-six members. There is a bicameral congress, composed of the Chamber of Deputies and the Senate, and the Supreme Court represents the judiciary. Elections are held every five years.

The official language is Spanish. English and a variety of Amerindian dialects are spoken. There is no official religion, but the vast majority of people are Roman Catholic (96 per cent). In Venezuela, there are two generations with distinct differences doing business. The older generation will want to get to know you personally first, rather than your company or firm. The younger generation may have been educated in the United States and will typically want to relate more to your business dealings or company, rather than to you personally.

Dress for men is conservative – dark business suits of tropical weight wool. Fashion is very important to Venezuelan women. Women should pack their best business clothes and one cocktail dress. People tend to stand very close together when conversing. Venezuelans often touch each other's arms or jacket during conversation. Posture while seated is important; avoid slouching.

Business people are punctual and small talk is minimal. It is good practice to follow up morning appointments with an invitation to lunch.

Have business cards printed in English on one side and Spanish on the other. Be sure your position is clearly indicated and present your card immediately following an introduction. Unlike lunch, dinner is for socializing, not for business. Businesswomen should be aware that going out alone with Venezuelan businessmen may be misconstrued. The two senior executives should sit facing each other. When dining, wait until everyone is served before beginning to eat. Guests rarely sit at the head of the table.

Good friends hug and women kiss cheeks. Avoid dominating the conversation. Venezuelans like to be in control. Titles are important and should be included on business cards. Address a person directly by using his or her title only. A Ph.D. or a physician is called *Doctor*. Teachers prefer the title *Professor*, engineers go by *Ingeniero*, architects are *Arquitecto*, and lawyers are *Abogado*. Persons who do not have professional titles should be addressed as Mr., Mrs., or Miss, plus their surnames. In Spanish these are: Mr. = *Senor* Mrs. = *Senora* Miss = *Senorita*. Most Hispanics have two surnames: one from their father, which is listed first, followed by one from their mother. Only the father's surname is used when addressing someone. Good conversation topics: business, art, literature, and history. Bad conversation topics: local unrest, inflation, and politics.

CASE STUDIES

CASE STUDY 1

Alcatel Global Strategy

Large firms have to opt for either the centralized or decentralized way of management. In fact, they believe that centralization or decentralization could coexist in a large firm like theirs. These states could reflect the profitability and growth of the firms.

Decentralized firms become autonomous bodies, which take most of their decisions themselves. Only a few decisions, which may have major impact on the firm's overall performance, are taken at the corporate level. The centralized decision-making firms can be equally guilty of taking vague, or delayed decisions. Both these states of affairs are having retardation effect in progress of the firm. The best way is the middle path, which works a fine-tuned balance. It provides flexibility on the organization chart and yet, it promoted interaction between the strategic corporate planners and the operational managers.

Alcatel was born out of merger of two telecom giants of Europe, the CGE-*Compagnie Generale d' Electricite* and ITTs telecom wing, creating the world number one company in the area of telecom. The promoters of Alcatel wanted a vibrant pulsating entity, which would be the front-runner in telecom in the world. They were not interested in merely merging to combine the two balance sheets of the firms which had different work style, different cultural ethos and yet they had a common desire to succeed as Alcatel.

The Chairman of the merged firm Alcatel set the following guidelines for the firm:

- Believe that the merger, (unlike several other mergers) had to succeed.
- Speed of action was the key to gaining credibility for Alcatel.
- Get rid of weaknesses in each of the firm's constituents.
- In one year maximum put every thing in order, which was a tall order with more than 1,25,000 employees, overlapping product lines and operations in more than 100 countries.

As speed was the essence of success, it was decided to take good enough decisions, rather than wait for optimized solutions. Take a decision and then stick to it. It was never easy to convert the managers running their business successfully to change to the new ways of doing things, just because the directors wanted it that way. Alcatel did not need to break the psychological barriers. The sudden shock of merger did the job of *unfreezing* the firm. In the process they could put the best of both organizations together in the new entity.

Alcatel have five main product groups as follows:

- Public switching
- Transmission
- Business systems
- Cables
- Network engineering

Alcatel board of directors meets once in six weeks to discuss and decide on precisely the following key areas:

- Acquisitions and mergers
- Product development
- Overseas markets
- Key appointments and promotions

This demarcation of powers has left the confusion out of the top management. It has also given greater responsibility to unit operations managers. Alcatel works with the matrix organization structure, with half of the executive committee members having dual responsibility as product group head and operational manager. Thus, the product group decisions are taken by people with direct interaction with customers and competitors as operational heads. This also helps the dual role person as he can mobilize resources for products he wants to market. Conflict of interest due to duality of roles has the benefit of at least having the person's interests automatically known.

Pre-merger qualms: The CGEs French managers did not want to share the markets, they considered as their own with outsiders and the ITTs. US managers were reluctant to be brought under the European controls.

From September 1986, till end of 1986, Alcatel spent in negotiating the merger deal with their ITT counterparts. During this period they understood their business, and their people, which greatly helped in starting the merged organization, Alcatel from January 1987. In filling senior posts the board is making great efforts to keep the French bias out of the selection process.

The Alcatel Way: Under their People Plan, Alcatel has installed genuine commitment in their 250 senior managers who are primarily responsible to implement their central strategy. In return, the board looks after their career plans to ensure they reach the top echelon of the organization.

In the new Alcatel regime, business strategy cannot be fragmented in any way, despite the fact that an HQ staff of half the size of former ITT staff, the HQ is handling twice the volume of sales.

From the start the board understood the *unfreezing* of attitudes and that it had to be countered by strong planning and financial disciplines.

ITTs system was of five-year planning; but the budget targets were revised often as they discussed it in monthly meetings. Managers not performing well would downsize their targets and enjoy the euphoria of having done well when in fact the contrary was true. Alcatel has started with yearly unalterable budgets to which the managers have to offer their commitment. There is also a five-year strategic plan within the guidelines of product groups and the executive committee.

Alcatel is described as a European business with global objectives and now in the 21st century it can be recognized as a global business that happens to have its roots in Europe. It has succeeded because Alcatel framed its strategies well and without losing time. In March 1987, the board decided that as big players dominate the world telecom market, and it wanted to project a strong image, wherever possible, its operating units in the world would add Alcatel to its name. Local objections were easily removed by massive investment in image building which local units could never dream of doing.

Task for the students: What are the main features of the merger, which made it successful. Do you think they could have done something more or differently?

CASE STUDY 2

International Automobile Giant Ford Cars

Indian car market is singled out because of its cost competitiveness. The product should be designed to cover the costs and compete in the price sensitive market. Cars should be tough as the Indian roads are bad, terrain rough. The temperatures go high needing air-conditioning, at least in medium cars.

The Indian buyer is like buyers anywhere in the world, they know what they want. Urban India is characterized by the following:

- English literacy
- Internet literacy
- Well connected with the world with Internet

Customers know what is available anywhere in the world and they want it but at prices they can afford to pay. They are looking for *value for money* products. Customers are fully conscious of quality and latest technology in the world market. They do not go for technological advancements unless they know their benefits to them. As far as car's quality is concerned they do not know beforehand, but once they use a quality product they stick with it and they become the most demanding customers in terms of quality in the world.

Indians have a great sense of value when Ford brought out their Ikon car, with a superior feeling that matches with the demand of Indian customers, they could justify its purchase. In the mid-car segment Ford was launched in 1996, with quality and customer service as its USPs. They have found that Indian customer is sophisticated, well informed and has the upper hand. With several players, including Maruti's Esteem, Opel Astra, Honda City, Mitsubishi Lancer, Fiat's Palio, cars crowd the market and in its true sense it is a buyers market.

Market trends: Small and mid size cars are going to be sold in large numbers in India for quite some time. In the first instance buyers go for small cars as they are easy to manoeuvre in crowded roads, easy to park. Next, when they can afford, they go for mid size cars. That is where Ford's dealer network scores over others, with its strong customer bonding. Even during recession, Ford could sell its Escorts car fairly well, in contrast to competition. How they succeeded in launching Ford Ikon despite recession is the story given below.

THE FORD IKON STORY DIRECTLY FROM FORD

Introduction

In its category, the Ford Ikon has captured the mindset of car lovers and critiques alike. This document is a summary of the series of activities which were carried out to achieve the main communication objective, "a launch that never ends" spread over a period of nine months, the communication was present in the entire spectrum of the media—TV, Print, to ground events and the Internet, supported by timely and full of impact press releases. All this to ensure that the potential car buyer will drive straight in to our car dealership!

Market Situation

The future of Indian car industry is brighter than ever before, with growth rate of 19.2%. Cars grew from 1998 to 1999 by 27%. The customers have a good choice both in the small cars segment and also in Ikon segment. Hyundai Accent, Opel Corsa and other cars are on the anvil.

Ford Ikon Car - Fords Philosophy

We aim to be the leading consumer company in the field of automobiles, says Ford's President Mr. Jac Nasser. The car has the NEW EDGE design with excellent power and acceleration and luxurious interiors. Ford Ikon is the JOSH Machine, a car with the spirit and enthusiasm to take you anywhere you want to go, in style.

Customer Profile

Our customer is a **full of life person**. He wants to lead a richer life than previous day. It is this desire to continuously better his position and quality of life that drives him.

Positioning

In India ford is perceived as a warm, approachable, large-hearted company. And Ford Ikon has been positioned for such large hearted persons, the Zinda Dil, who are full of energy, exuberance and adventurous spirit. Therefore, the company is staffed with people aggressive go-getters, aided by dealers who believe in giving their best. 'Play Hard and Work Hard' is their motto.

Competition

Maruti Esteem–Market leader, under threat from new, better quality cars. Largest dealer and service network.

Fiat Siena–World-class market accepted car, needs to improve production and dealer network.

Hyundai Accent–Strongest competitor to Ikon.

Honda City–Top end of the segment car, interiors need to be improved.

Opel Corsa–GM is positioning the car in the low-end of mid size segment.

Ford Ikon expects furious growth and competition in its segment in coming years and is fully prepared for action and is confident of storming into the battlefield and emerging victorious.

Communication Objectives

- To execute the most *impactful* car launch in India
- To re-launch Ford brand in India through Ford Ikon
- To communicate the positioning of Zinda Dil
- Add dynamism to Ford's inherent quality of safety, security and trustworthiness.
- To sum up, we say 'The Launch Never Ends!'

Series of activities planned are as follows:

1. On ground activities like, Early Consumer Reveal, Road Shows, the Name reveal, the faces behind the Ikon campaign
2. Continuous positive press releases in main publications
3. The launch plan included all forms of media, like Press, TV. Outdoor, Cinema, Direct Marketing, Joint Promotion and the Internet.

With powerful engine, both petrol and diesel, the car is good for city start-stops and also for long drives. Ford's "New Edge" Styling and high gloss paint make heads turn. Its luxurious interiors, seating comfort are best in the class. With large luggage boot and QualityCare philosophy behind Ford's service makes owning a Ford Ikon a totally hassle-free experience.

The Ford Ikon is a "Josh Machine" every way you look at it.

Plant Inauguration

On 19th March 1999, Rs. 1,700 crore plant was inaugurated in Chennai, in the august presence of the Chief Minister and the governor of the state and top officials of Ford.

Objectives

Dedication of this facility to the people of India as well as reiterating Ford's commitment to contributing to India's future.

Media Used

Main line–Press, All India.

Name Reveal

The name of the Ford's new car—the Ikon was revealed to the press at a conference in Mumbai. Hosted by Ford's senior people, it was really a showcase of the Zinda Dil attitude of Ford India Ltd. The highlight of the evening was the revelation of the name to the Press through a taped recording.

Time period–May-June 1999

Press Ads

Objective–The objective was to reveal the name in an interesting manner and also to create a sense of anticipation with these ads. The three ad series in dailies and magazines (all run in a single day) revealed some of the distinct parts of the car as a tear away in the visual. The ads highlighted the fact that each feature of the car makes it a distinctive car.

Cinema

Cinema as a medium was used in Delhi to reveal the name to the public. The commercials were run in the theatres in Anupam PVR for one month.

Partial Reveal Campaign

Objectives

- To do a partial reveal of the car to arouse interest in the Ford Ikon prior to the Autocar reveal.
- The objective was also to portray the Zinda Dil spirit that is going into the making of the Ford Ikon.
- Focus on the mood of optimism and the sheer positive feeling that is prevalent amongst all the people who are involved in making the car—the Ford employees, the dealers and the suppliers. The car partially hidden by photographs of happy people in a work scenario contributed to expressing this feeling of optimism.

Result

The campaign succeeded in creating immense curiosity among leading auto-journalists, who in their magazines tried to create the final shape of the car from these ads.

Time frame–July-August 1999

Media: Business daily, magazines

Early Consumer Reveal

Objective

1. To build up excitement around the car, when the first cars are available at dealerships for display, and generate positive hype around the car
2. To serve as a filter, in a time of no media activity
3. Get a prospect database

   Time frame: September-October 1999

   Advertising used:

- Direct Mail: inviting the dealers and customers
- Press Ads: teaser ads in black and white
- Press Ads: black and white-final
- Dealership Decoration Material: Streamers
- Dealership Decoration Material: Banners
- Training Material: Six Position Selling Guide
- Training Material: Dealership Product Guide
- Product Flyer
- Give: away Poster
- Technical Specification Stands at Dealerships

The New Ford India Website

Objective

On August 1999, Ford India Limited launched an informative and interactive website accessible at the address www.india.ford.com with the objectives of

- Sales lead generation
- Increase interactivity
- Develop relationships
- Extend loyalty programme
- Build the brand

The new website, designed on the latest Flash Animation Technology, is a visual treat for net surfers. The site provides in-depth and up-to-date information on Ford and its products. At the same time it allows the surfer to provide feedback. This site has been revamped to make it animated, colourful and easy to use. This new website will also provide links to Ford's international brand. It allows access to global Ford Motor Company site (www.ford.com) and a chance to visit Ford's international racing site. Constant updating with latest information on Ford is expected to be a highlight of this site.

Timing–August 1999 onwards.

Ford World Issue 6

Objective

To provide the Ford customers and hot prospects, a special preview of the Ford Ikon before the display to the public of the car.

Timing–August 1999

Quality Care

Objective

To launch the Quality care programme–an umbrella under which the customer is assured of value during every encounter with the company.

Timeline–August 1999

Launch Communication

Objectives

- To build to a crescendo the communication across all media to coincide with the order taking for the car and its subsequent launch.
- To communicate the various aspects of the Ford Ikon that made it the ultimate **"Josh machine"**

Timeline–October-December 1999

Media used:

- Television
- Mainline Press
- Direct Mail
- Outdoor
- Point of sale material at the dealerships

Ford Invitation Golf

Objective

- To associate JOSH with this high profile corporate sport and to increase visibility amongst key corporates and professionals in important markets.
- Capitalize on the opportunity to showcase the Ford Ikon prior to its launch.
- To develop a relationship between Ford and the Corporate customer

The result:

The target audience got a sneak preview of the Josh Machine that greatly influenced the word of mouth publicity.

Time frame–October-November 1999

Continued Media Presence

These started with Dealer Recruitment advertisement

- The Josh machine seeks like-minded dealer in New Delhi.
- Objective was to keep the josh machine top of the mind with the consumers and create awareness of the complete Ford Ikon range, an Ikon for everyone.
- To take leadership stance vis-à-vis competition in the consumer's mind
- Time frame–March-April 2000
- Media used press, brochure
- Paint chip stand and flyer
- New product brochure
- Sales training module
- Product video
- Plant video
- Mahendra Holiday Resorts joint promotion

Direct Marketing

Ford World

Objective

To communicate to existing Ford customers and prospects about the auto show and the other events.

Time frame–February 2000

Accessories

Flyer and selling guide

Quality Care

Press Ads and Sticker Pads

Making of an Automobile Brand

Serendipity—fate, chance, karma all work only when your own efforts are discernibly concentrated and strong. Defining serendipity became the mantra at, both the agency and the FORD Company. Let us try hardest and achieve, leaving nothing to chance and we are sure, chance, fate will be on our side.

Market scenario was as given below.

- No choice in buying cars to More Choices—does it add to confusion among the customers?
- Acceptability criteria changed as quality became the basis of selection of cars
- Honda and Opel enjoyed high brand equity

Key Discoveries for Ford Brand

- Ford was synonymous of Escort-Ford. Escort cars were the only Ford cars popular in India
- For several decades Ford was accepted as a trustworthy and reliable car
- Ford builds cars that are engineered for India, safe and sturdy
- Ford cars are dependable
- Ford cars were not known to be exciting cars
- Ford was known as an American company

A visceral understanding of the customer was undertaken to get to the key customer insights and it was considered that the psychographics segment for Ford Ikon would be **Full of Life**.

After exhaustive survey of 1200 car owners, two broad classifications emerged.

- The enthusiasts
- Non-enthusiasts

Six clusters in Mumbai and Delhi emerged as follows:

Driving Enthusiasts	Driving Non-Enthusiasts
Starting out small–20%	Contented conformists–17%
Affluent People–13%	The Upper Crust–4%
Full of Life–20%	Life without Spice–26%

The key discoveries on the customer's were as follows:

- The customer belongs to the FULL OF LIFE segment.
- He is young, in early thirties, and has a successful career
- He is well travelled, aware of the latest trends and technologies worldwide. He will not be taken for a ride
- He wants to show that he has arrived and his car plays a key role in that
- He is a driving enthusiast and his car is an important possession for him.
- Brand and price are important considerations for him
- The customer may belong to erstwhile refugee family with "spirit of flamboyance"
- The customer is a positive thinker, "I can do it, must do it and will do it.
- The customer also believes in "If you have got it flaunt it"

The product strategy, which followed from the customer profile, is as given below.

- Preferred car was with three-box structure, unlike Maruti 800, the two-box car
- The car should be built for India
- The car should have international looks—to give it a new edge
- Ford should lead from the high end, as per what Ford learnt from their Escort model
- The car should be **freshened up** constantly to keep up the excitement

The following positioning of different cars were found:

- Esteem–Driving pleasure
- Honda City–Power and Technology
- Siena–?? (Safety)
- Accent–??
- Corsa–Technology

In view of the above, the following positioning strategy was formulated:

- There was the temptation of calling the car as "Engineered for India"
- Of Iconising the Ford Ikon
- The temptation of calling it a "Value for money car"
- And arriving at a Brand Vision

With respect to brand, we sought the answer to the following question:

What does the Brand offer to the customer?

The large hearted, generous spirited, hard working, can do must do and will do company

The search of Brand Vision established that customer desires, smart-working, can-do, must-do, well-do attitude

Hence, the Brand Vision emerged as given below.

Zinda Dil

Exuberance

- Living life king size
- Gregarious
- Big hearted

Ford Ikon's personality can be described in the following manner.

Brand Vision

Why do people find me appealing?

"I represent everything that is contemporary in Ford—From the "New Edge" styling to the powerful engines. I am being launched for the first time in the world in India.

What is my personality?

"Progressive, contemporary, full of life, work hard play hard"

Who do I appeal to?

"Young, successful males, who are full of life"
Firm believers in "Work Hard, Play Hard Ethic"
Big on life, driving enthusiasts, love socializing

What relationship do I have with them?

I am their friend. To increase their excitement. I never say no, because they never say no either.

Why am I different?

I am more than just sheet metal and four wheels. I am contemporary and exciting. I represent an attitude, a way of life.

How do I express myself?

I am colourful, confident and bold. Everything I do is youthful, energetic. I appeal to the heart more than the head.

Brand Idea

Josh

- The Brand has youthful energy
- It has passion
- It is full of enthusiasm
- Its reactions are spontaneous and it provides an emotional high to its owners/users.

The Communication Plan

Following were the discoveries in the research done prior to the campaign:

So far the communication had been conservative, feature led and product focused. The communication idiom has been changing in the marketplace. The car had become a personality statement for the owners. A tone change was required in Ford communication—from Test cricket to One day international, from laid back to vibrant and dynamic communication.

The communication imperatives can be described as given below.

Planning communication in an integrated manner across the varied communication channels, the period needed for gestation being nine months. The other imperative was THAT THE LAUNCH NEVER ENDS, to sustain the excitement in the post-launch period.

Creating a Blockbuster Campaign

The creative task was to imagine how the customers really visualize communication. For this purpose, it was decided to treat Press as Billboards—bring JOSH through Ikon's looks. The attitude of JOSH had to be planted in the TV Ads to cut through the clutter of advertisements on TV.

The launch events were used to build JOSH theme and it was spread through road shows in 44 cities across the country.

Taking JOSH forward

Josh being an emotion and sentiment, it had to be reinforced through peer group endorsement of the decision of purchasing the Ikon. Reviews from experts were used prominently in the AD campaign. The drive to maintain JOSH through attitude and emotion was relentlessly pursued. The campaign was based on thrill, intoxication and exhilaration.

The Excitement Grows

The need to sustain the JOSH was met with strategic launches of car variants. The following versions were launched:

- 1.3 CLXi–move up to the JOSH zone
- Rally Sport–for the racer in you
- Exi–a sign of success

Even with these variants, the communication of JOSH was not diluted as the JOSH tongue-in-cheek attitude was carried through even in tactical advertising as can be seen from the following:

- An event lead Auto Show
- Airline promotion–targeting the high fliers
- The 1.3 car Road Show–into new markets
- Resort Promotion–a new contact opportunity with the customers
- JOSH Karting–was meant to spread JOSH among the corporate

Reinforcing JOSH through Ownership

Once a customer has purchased the JOSH Machine he has to be pampered by the company. It is done through continuous contact programme with interaction with Ford World and Theater Premiers.

Furthermore, a periodic feedback is obtained from the owners about their ownership experience.

Let us analyze where does JOSH fit. Here come the JOSH FITS.

- Objective: To associate JOSH clearly with excitement, fun and 'IN" things
- Strategy–To create branded properties on TV, with events at happening places like Djinns
- The results:
  - i. "Josh action cuts' on AXN
  - ii. "Extreme JOSH" on Discovery Channel
  - iii. "Top Gaana' on MTV

Josh in the New Media

Integrated communication was achieved by the use of new media available today as follows:

- www.india.ford.com–which is the website of the brand
- Mirror marketing activity
- Innovate, Innovate, Innovate
- Ikonnect 2home.com
- Autoshow on the web
- Launch of the Sxi
- Customer conversations
- Car care tips, driving tips

The Results

- Largest selling car in its segment in the first month of the launch itself
- Cumulative sale from the launch till date highest in the segment
- Josh the most recalled brand property amongst any automobile advertising in independent research

Sales percentage of different brands of the segment are given below for the years 1999 and 2000.

Sales percentage	1999	2000
Maruti Esteem	37	22
Opel Astra	6	4
Honda City	20	13
Ford Ikon	4	21
Cielo	7	3
Mitsubishi Lancer	16	12
Fiat Siena	7	3
Hyundai Accent		15

Ford Ikon Report Card

Ford Ikon holds its own amongst other more established players.

Purchase consideration importance given to various factors while buying a car.

Cars proud to own	100
Cars full of life and vitality	91
Good value for money	90
Stylish	90
Family cars	85
Safest cars	81
Better drive than others	80
Solid built	78
Comfortable	75
Quality car	74
Low running cost	32
Especially designed for India	74
Confidence car	75
Brand	99

The statement given below gives the value judgment of different cars in the time frame January to June 2000.

Largest selling car in its segment in the first month of the launch.

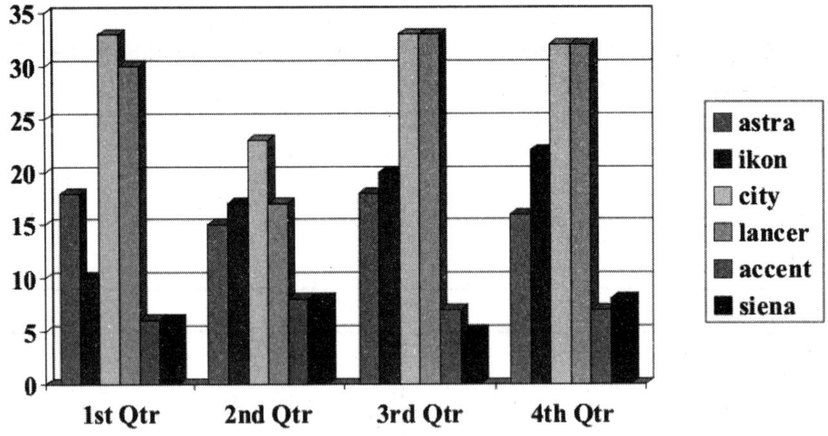

CARS YOU WOULD BE PROUD TO OWN

Tasks for the students-analyze the strategy adopted by Ford, and give your recommendations for keeping pace with Indian competitive environment.

CASE STUDY 3

The Chrysler Turnaround

Through the 1970s, Lee Iacocca was the trusted friend of the top man of the Ford Motor Company Henry Ford and CEO of Ford. Lee and his wife and Ford and his wife were seen partying together as the spouses too had a great rapport. At that time Lee got an offer from Chrysler to join them as their CEO, but due to the friendship with the Ford, he rejected the offer. In 1977/78, however, the relationship with Ford started souring and Lee was sacked by Ford on ego issues. By this time, Chrysler was in real bad shape and they welcomed Lee with great expectations.

Chrysler was the third largest automobile firm in the world, with a reputation of building tough sturdy cars. Unfortunately, with one bad model, the firm started slipping down. The Chrysler scenario in 1977 is described below:

- One million cars called back to the factory for retrofitting due counter serious safety hazards
- New fuel efficiency and emission norms of the government of the USA required the firm to invest $7.5 billion for getting new tools to do the job
- Cash flow was threatened
- Bankruptcy was round the corner due to the firms inability to service the huge debts

For 1978, the financial situation is given below.

- 1st quarter loss $120 million
- 2nd quarter earnings $30 million
- 3rd quarter loss $160 million

Most of the directors of Chrysler were recommending that the firm should declare bankruptcy. Some had faith in Lee and on the day the 3rd quarter results were declared the directors also confirmed the appointment of Lee Iacocca as the new CEO of Chrysler.

The automobile market of 1970/80s

Henry Ford had stuck on to the T model Ford car. He believed that, " if the product is selling well as it had done from its inception why change it?" He also did not budge on the colour issue and wanted all his cars to be black, despite the pleadings of several of his lieutenants.

General Motors, albeit a late start had come to the forefront of the car market, with their new design cars in different colours, shapes and sizes. GM were in fact the number one firm in the world for all products in terms of assets.

Chrysler faced the following problems:

- poor product quality
- drop in sales
- suppliers had become arrogant as they were not being paid in time
- customers felt they can take full advantage of the situation
- Chrysler UK was doing better but being so far off, and with only 15 per cent of Chrysler business could not be depended on rescuing it from disaster.

After joining Lee analyzed the situation and planned his strategy for bringing Chrysler around in five years. He made some top level changes, threw out the dead wood, the incompetent and non-believers of future success of Chrysler. He brought some of his top associates from Ford, who had mutual trust with him enough to leave Ford to join a declared sick firm. He found the scenario as given below.

- He needed money for R&D to bring out better cars commensurate with Chrysler's earlier image of building good sturdy cars
- Bank overdrafts had hit the limits and they were not interested in backing Chrysler any more
- Suppliers, car dealers and some senior executives had recommended that Chrysler should declare bankruptcy
- Lee kept persisting that Chrysler would find a solution to its problems.

He arranged marathon meetings with the bankers, who were aware of Lee's reputation, but seeing the Chrysler's plight decided against giving any loans to the firm. Unruffled, he went to Washington and met some of his senator friends, who agreed to help. (There were a few senators totally opposed to any help to Chrysler.) His senator friend prevailed on the bankers, who agreed to consider giving the loan on a specific stipulation that the US Government guarantees the loan.

Lee decided to meet the President of the USA, and on his intervention, the US government agreed to give the requisite guarantee on some difficult conditions like the following:

- Chrysler would reduce expenses
- Get some capital of its own
- Defer payments even further to their suppliers

At this juncture it was the sagacity, statesmanship and discipline, which Lee possessed, was of great importance to Chrysler. He took the following actions in order to meet with the loan stipulations:

- Lee cut down his own salary to $ one till good times are back at Chrysler, and the loan had been repaid
- With his immense persuasive power he made other managers to work with full force and vigour at half the salary
- Lee met all the suppliers personally and after he had explained the position they agreed to deferred payments while continuing the supplies
- Lee arranged some loans from private placements from his friends and completed the compliance of the US Government loan guarantee

Lee got the money, invested it in R&D. The new product was test-marketed and the sales boomed! Repayment started and was over in three years, two years in advance banks volunteered to give further money as required by Chrysler.

Chrysler was truly on way to becoming a force to reckon with in the automobile business again. It could ward off the competition from Japanese cars for quite a while.

CASE STUDY 4

The Gillette Edge

Gillette's Vision is of being a world class firm with world class people, products and brands.

The firm's mission is to be a global leader in products marketed by them.

They operate in 200 countries with manufacturing facilities in 56 countries.

The firm's core businesses are given below.

- Blades and razors–GILLETTE, 7O'Clock, Wilkinson Sword
- Batteries–Duracell
- Personal grooming products–Braun, Silkipel razors for women
- Oral care products–Oral B
- Writing Instruments–Parker, Paper mate, Waterman

Strategic Marketing Plan for success:

Gillette makes a five-year rolling plan, which is reviewed three times a year and modified as required. Every six months sales forecast is made.

Philosophy of Gillette can be summarized as follows:

1. Keep introducing new products and fifty per cent of their business must come from products, which have been introduced less than 5 years ago.
2. Technical superiority in every product and they consider competition as a spur for customer retention.

Gillette's game plan is as given below.

- Keep the user/customer at the centre of activities,
- Provide improved products – gain increased net sales
- Have pricing options by improvement in products
- Gillette considers the following as their key growth areas:
    1. Value addition in existing products
    2. New product speedy launches

3. Distribution network
4. Display and merchandising
5. Advertising and promotion
6. They keep a close watch on standard direct costs and post marketing expenses, which can be considered as controllable overheads
7. Synergy for efficiency and effectiveness
8. Profits through IT driven TQM and people's involvement

Gillette has developed a marketing strategy for facing recession in the market. They view the impact of recession on the different segments of the market as follows:

- Consumers–their demand reduces for non-essential articles and they switch to value for money products
- Trade–they suffer from inventory blockage of non-essential products and they end up with heavy stocks of a variety of products
- Firm–it loses customers as also trade/distribution channels who show little interest in the products

Gillette's policy for marketing during recession is that of PAUSE! They believe in operating in the following manner:

- Basic marketing strategy does not change
- They organize better management of resources and plan tactical moves
- They provide value addition; when consumers downgrade, Gillette provides added value to the product; they reinforce the advertising messages; improve the product package
- They arrange new product launches to increase user share and also upgrade the users

The result so far has been that Gillette has grown even during recession.

Task for the students: Is the firm justified in upgrading their products and charging more when the customers are finding it hard to pay their existing prices? Discuss their policy for success.

CASE STUDY

5

Citibank in India

To Indians Citibank has been representing car loans providers and that too in a rather government-like arrogance; you pay up or else! Obviously, this situation is hardly conducing to a service sector, where competition is abounding and on the increase. Considering these facts the management of Citibank took two major decisions as follows:

1. Pay greater attention to their entire product range, especially the banking by individual customers (so far they have been emphasizing on the corporate sector only).
2. Become user-friendly to cater to the Indian masses, instead of just to the elite segment.

With the legacy of the Second World War, the mindset of Citibank personnel has been clogged with rules, regulations and red tape mentality. Innovations by Citibank staff have been frowned upon, albeit at times seeing their use they were adopted. The superiority complex which has been the bet noire of the bank employees has to change per force as the Indian economy is trying to walk tall as compared to the world economy.

Under the above stated conditions the bank has to redefine its vision, which reads today as given below:

The vision of Citibank in India is to be the preferred, innovative one-stop provider of financial services. Innovation is critical. It does not mean that you have to be number one in every activity, in every product, all the time. But you must demonstrate over a period of time that by and large you are an innovator because that is very attractive to a customer, be it a retail customer, a corporate customer or a small or medium enterprise. One stop is where we should be able to provide anything by way of products or services - both globally and locally provided. The advantage we have is that, Citibank is a large local bank with a large global network.

Citibank has realized globally that if they want to grow quickly, they have to plan a mix of customers from consumer banking and corporate banking. They would still keep pampering the blue chip firms while focusing on the retail banking. The bank is expecting a growth of 20-25 per cent in the consumer-banking sector.

The thrust on consumer banking started in 1985 when the bank brought out products like, car loans, credit cards, ATMs, 24-hour Citibank, mortgages and Internet banking. The bank believes that it has changed the service benchmark in the banking sector in India.

Consumer banking stress is really manifesting itself in the bank. Earlier the consumer needed Rs. 3 lakhs to open an account in the bank. Today, with Suvidha schemes the minimum deposit is only Rs. 1000. Under the scheme, the customer is encouraged to use the bank's ATM, phone or Internet and he need not visit the bank at all. The bank found out that each visit of a customer costs the bank as front office expenses, against which the bank charges Rs. 100 for each of the visits by customers.

Looking at their corporate clients, the bank decided to match their Suvidha strengths with their corporate clientele. The bank offers to the corporate client employees the Suvidha facility. The employees can get three times their salary as loan and there are several other benefits too. They are also into insurance package with the assistance of LIC of India for these employees. Thus, the bank is readying to provide one-stop financial solutions across the corporations and their employees.

Suvidha scheme being a non-branch banking is also necessary because as against State Bank of India's 9000 odd branches the Citibank has only 20 branches in the entire country. They are also planning to provide more ground facilities with increased branch network to 65, adding 5 each year. The reason for expansion is, the need to have a presence in different segments, to be fully effective, to be seen not only as an upscale bank but for the masses too. However, while reach is important in retail banking, there are different avenues of increasing the banks presence with the mass clientele. For consumers the bank has basically two segments, Suvidha and the branch banking for upper middle and upper class customers.

The new strategy to widen its base the bank is as follows:

- Greater emphasis on retail trade through Suvidha schemes
- Offering Suvidha to employees of their corporate clients
- Non-branch banking through ATMs, Internet and telephones
- Increasing the number of branches of the bank
- Increase in product portfolio to suit different market segments

Besides, the bank is augmenting its facilities for the non-resident Indians, who can avail of its expertise for investments through the bank's worldwide branches. Besides the bank's leadership in NRI accounts, it also leads in the credit card segment, despite severe competition.

The bank has been feeling the pinch of rapidly lowering of interest rates, while the banking sector is stuck with large non-performing assets, each bank is trying to have a certain number of corporate clients and they feel that their success would come from lending to retail customers. They believe that consumer banking products from bank accounts, to credit and debit cards and to consumer lending have huge growth potential, especially with the lowering of age group as the youth is not averse to debts.

Threats perception of the bank comes from dismal performance of the corporate sector in the past few years; the growth of 5.6 per cent is mainly due to increase in agriculture and service sectors. Besides the competition has increased manifold in the last decade. With the restrictions on opening new branches by the RBI, the bank's strategy is to differentiate, innovate and segment the market to their advantage. The segments the bank are seeking are the following:

- Traditional corporate sector, which accounts for 50 per cent of the business, but is growing slowly at the rate of just ten per cent.
- Financial institutions; banks, FIs, Mutual Funds, Insurance Companies
- Emerging local corporations in this segment Citibank is looking at only the suppliers and customers of blue-chip firms.

Citibank feels it is way ahead of other foreign banks operating in India. However, it is not complacent and is using its product portfolio management and market segmentation strategies to say ahead.

Some of the Citibank's financial and other statements are given below.

Citibank's financial picture in crores of rupees for the years 2001 and 2002 (March ending).

	2000-2001	2001-2002	Change %
Interest income	1910	1755	9
Other income	803	530	52
Net profit	325	285	14
Deposits	15,242	14,052	8
Advances	11,385	9,325	22
Investments	6,007	5,603	7

Citi-Group in India

Name	Equity I crores	Activity
Citicorp financial	280.2	Hire purchase, loans, leasing, treasury and venture capital
Citicorp brokerage	31.5	Debt broking and underwriting
Citicorp Maruti finance	100	Hire purchase and loan finance for Maruti cars
Citifinancial retail services	5	Hire purchase and loans on consumer durables and personal loans
Citifinancials insurance services	0.05	Distribution of insurance products
Associates Indian holding company	231.6	Investment arm of the bank

Task for the students: Considering the fact that Citibank is a foreign bank working in India under certain constraints plan their growth strategy after analyzing the banks strengths and weaknesses.

CASE STUDY 6

Toyota – with Stakeholders

The question Toyota asks its employees is, "what are we working for, who are we working for? Is what we are doing, what our customers want us to do for them? Do we really meet their expectations? In other words, we need to hear what they think about us and what they feel about us."

The above statement from Toyota outlines their philosophy of business, which is to meet the customers' expectations of a strong safe eco-friendly car.

Global Market Scene–1999

Global automobile industry is undergoing rapid changes in response to the maturing markets of the world. The main characteristic is the emergence of the consumers as the leaders and trendsetters rather than manufacturers. The change has been hastened by the rapid usage of information technology by the consumers, as they can now access the information instantly around the world through Internet.

Global Responsible Citizen

The main factor of consumer driven markets is customer's expectations that firms are responsible members of both global and local communities. In response to these new expectations, Toyota, a leading global car maker and the world's third largest auto maker, is investing heavily in the research and development of technologies to reduce the impact of cars on the environment and increase passenger safety. Toyota shares the consumers' concern for the environment, and are committed to being an energetic leader in the development of eco-friendly technologies, and providing customers with exciting high quality products in markets worldwide.

As a result, the Toyota R&D came out with the following vehicles:

- Prius: The world's first mass-produced hybrid car, with reduction by 50 per cent of fuel emissions and fuel consumption as compared to same size conventional cars.

- Yaris and Echo for the north and Latin America Africa Asia and Middle East displays Toyota's ability to create global trends.

Developed using consumer feedback from around the world, it has been an instant hit in every market it has been introduced. Its trendy compact design and class leading standards of fuel economy and value meet Toyota's criteria to satisfy today's consumers.

New marketing initiatives utilize exciting new media.

With the fast adoption of information technology dramatically changing the development and marketing of new cars, Toyota's inspiring approach to marketing reveals a fresh new image for Toyota. At the heart of the vision are innovative new marketing initiatives to aim of getting closer to the customers, to enable Toyota to better meet changing consumer needs and expectations, Toyota expresses its goal "we need to understand our customers better, leveraging the opportunities provided by their access to the latest information technologies to give our customers around the world better products and services."

From the globaltoyota.com Internet portal to Internet radio to entertaining on site car culture, venues that dispense car related information; his marketing initiatives utilize the latest information technologies to connect the contemporary consumers,

www.globaltoyota.com at the heart of Internet access.

Toyota has moved boldly into the new media used by the increasing number of today's consumers, especially the Internet. To ensure customers around the world have easy access to all things about Toyota on the Internet, it has created its own dedicated global portal of www.globaltoyota.com. Further, rationalization of information on the Internet includes links to Toyota website in individual countries around the world, which provide local marketing news and contact information.

Studio Toyota

Studio Toyota is a state-of-the-art virtual information centre that focuses on Toyota's activities in different regions of the globe. Visitors can look at the latest cars, pick up and download information and they can play games in the Toyota territory.

Within the global, portal is the studio Toyota an exciting virtual environment where visitors can pick up and download hot news and vehicle information, and enjoy real-time games and entertainment. It allows consumers to spend as much time as they like checking out the latest cars. It also enables Toyota to track what consumers are interest in and get instant feedback via email.

Exploring the New Dimensions of Internet Radio

Toyota's sponsorship of the innovative new medium of Internet radio leverages. Toyota's currency with early adopters of leading edge technologies. The world's first truly global radio station is a great way to connect with the young, aware consumer around the world. Internet radio will use streaming technologies to deliver live radio with the latest news, music views from around the world, to only PC connected to the Internet. In the near future, digital, audio satellite net broadcasting will enable drivers to listen to Internet radio in their cars.

Getting Close to the Customers with New Generation Showrooms

Toyota's multimedia amusement space mega web on the Toyota waterfront is a good example of the real-world initiatives Toyota is creating to capture the attention and generate loyalty among both young people and families. This exciting venue has been an instant success with Japan's trend conscious consumers since it opened in 1999 mega web welcomes average of 18000 visitors to its 15000 m^2 of interactive displays every day, who come to enjoy a great days entertainment.

Activities of mega web range from designing cars using CAD graphics workstations through to test drivers of every Toyota vehicle currently available and encourage consumer feedback, giving Toyota customers service representatives valuable insights into individual customer needs.

The experience gained at mega web could form the base of similar ventures around the world. Another innovative concept for reaching customers on site is le Rendezvous Toyota, on the famous Champs Elysees in central Paris. This new Toyota centre aims to establish a unique and high profile presence for Toyota in the important European market. It combines a cultural gallery featuring a changing calendar of events, a show case Toyota and Lexus brands, and on information centre in interactive multimedia environment.

Toyota world of wildlife foster environmental preservation around the world.

To create awareness for the fragility and beauty of our natural world with the widest possible audience, Toyota is sponsoring **Toyota World of Wildlife** TV series known as TWOW. This new marketing initiative includes underwriting the development of TWOW series and distributing it to the TV broadcasters round the world. The 26 episode series explores our natural world, using stunning photography to reveal little known mysteries and wonders of nature.

Ready for the 21st Century

Brought together the diverse range of innovative marketing activities highlight Toyota's desire to stake a new image for itself in this century. In doing this, Toyota is extending the range and appeal of its products to a new generation of global consumers and ultimately crating new levels of consumer participation and satisfaction. At the heart of these innovative marketing activities lie the question that Toyota asks its employees," they believe that they should not merely ask WHAT, but also begin to ask HOW? How we will meet the challenges that we face.

Task for the student: Do a SWOT analysis of Toyota. Do you agree with their initiative on wildlife? Give reasons in favour of your arguments. Do you believe that Toyota can be termed as a stakeholder's corporation? Give your reasons for your belief.

CASE STUDY
7

Hershey Chocolates Edge

Hershey and Mars stand out as two major firms in the US competing for the $15 chocolate market. Besides they had impressive overseas business. In 1990, when Iraq attacked Kuwait Mars were on a selling spree to the Saudi Arab. Despite the war Mars were determined to sell their chocolates. Mars met the US Army Command that their chocolates were as essential in the war as the arsenal. Mars with its refrigerated trucks could supply the chocolates to scattered US troops over a million square miles in the Saudi deserts. On getting the approval Mars started loading chocolates ice cream onto barges heading for the Gulf. And then competition raised its head like the waking up of a sleeping python.

Before the gulf war it was Hershey who was supplying chocolates to the US military and was known as their chief chocolate maker. Hershey had started supplying chocolates to the army during the First World War. They had convinced the army that their high energy chocolate rations would sustain soldiers when they had nothing else to eat. To produce Field Ration D the Hershey factory was operating twenty-four hours a day seven days a week churning out millions of Ration D bars. When the war ended Hershey had become a household name and buying its chocolates was considered a patriotic act. Now in 1990, it was not to give up the tag of main army supplier of chocolates so easily to Mars.

Hershey started developing a new chocolate bar aptly named the Desert Bar, which could withstand temperatures up to 60°C. In order to replace Mars as a supplier to the army they proclaimed that their desert bar melts in your mouth and not in sand. However, as Mars was now well entrenched in the army with continuous supplies of their heat resistant chocolates and when the Pentagon floated a tender for 6.9 million non-melting chocolates in 1991, Mars won it.

Not to lose hope Hershey filed a strong protest with the army brass and employed three best lawyers to assert that the Desert Bar was far superior to the Mars product. Next four months saw a bitter war of words between the two firms. The final verdict went in favour of Mars.

Genesis of the Chocolate Giants

Milton Hershey was born in 1857 of poor parentage. Educated up to fourth standard Milton, at the age of 14 joined a well-known confectioner as apprentice. As he discovered he had a flair for concocting chocolates he started chocolate business with $150 of borrowed capital. With a lot of ups and downs in which time he had to close shop twice, undeterred he started making caramels; with two copper kettles, 100 kilos of sugar and some molasses he set up his shop. He made caramels, his mother and sister wrapped them and he paddled them in the town. This time he achieved success and as he grew he bought four factories to increase his production and there was no looking back for him. At 33 Milton was a wealthy man. Leaving his business to his managers, he and his wife started travelling to Europe. In 1903, on one of his trips he got the idea of building his personal utopia. He bought 500 acres of land in Pennsylvania, where he built an industry based village, a modern American community "where the things of modern progress all centre in the town that has no poverty, no nuisance and no evil". The town was built around a factory, which produced milk chocolate.

The connection between chocolate and romance is universal. Casanova used it with champagne for romance. It has become the hallmark of today's Valentine day. In 1907, a new chocolate was named Hershey's Kisses and the firm became associated with the product and today even after 100 years Hershey means chocolates the world over.

Milton gave his employees the best of the houses, insurance benefits, built schools for their children and a large modern community theatre. He built homes for poor orphan children.

In 1916, Hershey and his friend William Murrie made a wager that William could sell more chocolates than Hershey could make. Murrie did what he promised and joined Hershey as president of the chocolate firm. For the next 50 years he remained Milton's right hand man.

In 1933, a young man, Forrest Mars came to the Hershey town as his firm was into making Milky Way, a popular nugget bar covered with chocolate from Hershey. Mars met Murrie, who by that time had become disgruntles with his stay at Hershey, as he saw no way of his taking over Milton's place. Lure of partnership and good opening for his son Bruce made the offer irresistible. Forrest named the new firm Mars and Murrie and in 1941 it opened its business.

Earlier Mars put chocolate malted milk in a chocolate bar and created a strikingly different product compared to competition. The new Milky Way was an instant success and it was much cheaper to make.

With M&M in existence and Bruce with him Forrest felt he can do much better but was disappointed the way Bruce was not able take the work pressure. Finally, Bruce had to leave and Forrest bought his minor shares.

Forrest had a big inheritance, which he used for takeovers till 1964. When he got total control. He downsized his grand offices and sold the firm's helicopter. He increased the salaries by 30 per cent. His managers were getting three to four times more than other firms offered. In return he expected them to work 12 to 14 hours a day. He offered a bonus to punctual employees. Superior quality, perfection in products and cleanliness were his bywords.

To improve communication he made his staff sit in the open with the juniors surrounding their seniors. He cut down on paper work; there was no need for office memos, office meetings. He believed in result-oriented work environment and backed the winners. Forrest was so quality conscious that he bought his products from retailers to check on their quality. On slight mistake in the M indenture on the chocolate the manager had to get up at 3 in the morning to go to the plant to investigate how the error occurred, for fear of being fired.

Forrest had considered Hershey as his friend, but the next generation was taking over, his son did not take Hershey as anything except a competitor. In 1966, Hershey was selling chocolate worth $150 million and Mars sales were worth $90 million. Till mid-1960s Hershey was not having any marketing and advertising and Mars took full advantage of this situation. In 1973, for the first time Mars overtook Hershey in sales. The marketing blitz of Mars was backed by aggressive sales force, the best in the industry.

In 1981, Hershey tied up with Universal Studios in Hollywood called Hershey after Mars had refused them to use their product in the film shoot. Hershey agreed to it on condition that he would be able to use the film to promote his product, which was agreed to. Advertising was organized in displays cases in 600 cinema halls across the country. Hershey worked overtime to meet the increased demand of its chocolates. Mars had rejected the offer perhaps because of the change in its leadership in 1973. Forrest's children took over the reins from their father. Unlike the father the younger generation was not interested in buying firms to expand to increase market share as they believed in building their own, and hence they lost many opportunities. This decision denied them business in the US but it increased their worldwide businesses.

Tasks for the students: Do a SWOT Analysis of both Hershey and of Mars; how their business plan changed over a period of time and how each tried to gain superiority competitive advantage over the other and with what success.

CASE STUDY 8

The Samsung Saga

In the 1990s, Korea was still reeling under the Asian money crisis and its prime firm Samsung had also been affected by it. The firm decided to undergo strategic changes to overcome the problems they were facing.

The Samsung change was from being a technology driven firm they wanted to become a market driven firm.

At the time of restructuring the firm was firmly of the view that the old model, which had served them for so long was not right any more. The firm was looking for a new model and hence receptive to change. From its inception it had remained a proud firm, which could do no wrong and which was keen to replace its main rivals the Japanese firms in the top slot of the world market. The crisis of the 1990s had been quite a shaking experience for the firm.

The change model worked in the following way:

- From a firm of lifetime employment it became the firm with the best available people
- From chasing market share the model changed to value creation and profitability
- The firm now wanted to become differentiable and the one providing unique value for money to the customers
- The firm had to have better than competitors understanding of the marketplace
- The firm needed to be innovative for creating products and also marketplaces
- The firm was looking for new thought process, systems and new set of skills
- The firm had to build on creating brand equity and using R&D for new product development
- And finally they needed a new marketing formula in 2000. By 2001 it became a truly global brand strategy

To have a brand strategy the firm needed great products for sustainable competitive advantage and profitability. The thrust came from the firm's leadership from the 1980s in digital technology being leaders in digital displays and digital wireless. From technological viewpoint the firm was at par with the competition. Taking advantage of the early adapters young age people, who were open to new ideas and were changing to digital, created a vacuum in the marketplace, which was conducive for a new brand to be built.

Samsung seized the opportunity by concentrating on wireless digital phones, digital audio, MP3 and video DVD and digital personal information management, thus digitalizing homes mobile and offices.

The Marketing and Advertising Strategy, which followed laid stress on the single brand **Samsung,** instead of several brands they were focusing on earlier, when each country manager was on to his own advertising (55 marketing agencies worldwide.).

Samsung established a single brand, a single brand strategy and one global agency. Added to this they had single central budget and uniform brand theme.

Samsung found the process of change getting into rough weather, because while the top management were committed to the change the juniors were not and they felt uneasy that the brands they had been marketing have disappeared and now there is only one brand. A master brand requires major investment in terms of money, manpower and planning, but if succeeds only if the brand is basically strong. The brand must meet the technical criteria and needs of the customers and the customers must trust it, for it to work. In the ultimate analysis it is the brand, which carries the entire firm.

On the upside the switch from analogue is fast worldwide including in India, where the youth are all on to the digital sounds.

The product philosophy of Samsung can be described as follows:

- Consumer response for their products should be just "WOW"! Products should have an emotional appeal to the customers.
- Product should be user-friendly and technology must support this simplicity of the products.

The mission of Samsung is to make leading edge digital products available to more and reduce the digital divide.

Tasks for the students–write an imaginary dialogue between the CEO of Samsung and their junior executive explaining the reasons for the change of their strategy from being multi-domestic to planning global strategy. Do you think Samsung had the right strategy for overcoming the nineties financial crisis or they could have done better? Suggest your alternative plan for Samsung.

CASE STUDY 9

Japan a Case Study

Japan in the last sixty years may not have forgotten the defeat in the Second World War, but due to the indomitable spirit of its populace it has come out a winner in the business world, with extremely high growth rate as compared to even its victors. Pre-war Japanese products in India were not considered as of good quality. "Oh! It is a Japanese product" were the derisive words used for the imports from Japan. How this dramatic change took place makes an interesting case study. Japan has no natural resources, is plagued with recurrent earthquakes has very little land and is made up of several islands. Its culture is age old and people are bound by traditions. The transformation from a laidback eastern tradition bound country into a modern fast moving dynamic business potentate has left most theorists and philosophers agape with wonder.

After the war was over and Japan became an ally of the powerful USA, who incidentally took over the country's defence, a fact, which left the Japanese ready to concentrate on nation rebuilding activities. To create wealth for the country, business and industry were the most important planks and they went into these areas with full vigour. This time around the Japanese wanted to drop the tag of poor quality suppliers. For this purpose, they invited business gurus from the USA who toured the country giving their inputs in quality improving techniques. Quick on the uptake, the Japanese improved on the teachings of the gurus and came out with the Quality Circle Programme, which has revolutionized the business world over. Over the last sixty years, the Japanese innovations in the field of business and industry have underscored even the success of the giant the USA. Some of their strategic decisions and innovations are given below.

- Understanding the value of money blocked in inward inventories introduced to the world the Just In Time—JIT—plan for saving of cost to the tune of ten per cent in having virtually no inventories. JIT works well if there is close partnership like cooperation between the firm and the supplier. In turn it becomes useful to see that the supplier is also having JIT from his suppliers. Such a chain can account for large sums of money being released for the purposes of development and growth.

- Zero defect production came about with the help of TQM and Quality Circle programmes. Firms could eliminate the final product testing and could disband the entire set of engineers involved in the testing process. This led to higher production, lower rejections and savings of raw material and manpower and reworking costs. This made the Japanese competitive in the world.
- Suppliers seized to be necessary evils who never supplied on time gave defective products and always wanted higher prices for their products. Joining hands with suppliers and making them almost their partners, helping them in their JIT and quality programmes gave the firms and the supplier's confidence in each other. The firm has been able to reduce costs by eliminating suppliers assessment for each order placed on him. It has also helped in reducing the time to bring new products in the market. New materials are available from the partnership sources without delay.
- Japanese innovation of small teams, the quality circles, which manage continuous incremental improvements in the firms processes to create low cost and high profit system.
- Japanese firms bring about technological cohesion by using different technology together as tech-fusion as a paradigm shift in the product development areas. Hybrid technologies like opto-electronics mechatronics.
- Japanese firms believe in cross-functional teams and flexible structures in problem solving areas. Product development process time period has been greatly reduced in view of the market demands and shortening product life cycles.

Japanese firms believe that if the employees are fully motivated, enjoy job satisfaction and teamwork, they can create better organizational processes and work with total dedication and this is achieved through well-structured programmes like quality circles. Quality circles are engaged in the processes as follows:

1. Problem finding action
2. Problem solving function
3. Solution action plans
4. Feedback loops
5. Integrated responsibility
6. Study of the environment to avoid pitfalls

Problem finding goes down the firm's ladder as even the lowly worker is expected to locate problems, so that they can be nipped in the bud and the need for finding solutions does not arise. Also if the workers find the problems and solutions to the problems, it would be easy during implementation.

Problem solving leads to finding solutions of the market needs, new products and services; solutions to quality problems, process problems and product differentiation plans of existing products to bring sustainable competitive advantage.

Using new ideas in the existing processes the firm arrives at solutions implementation. Most Indian firms do not want to have workers trying to find out the solutions for their own workstation problems, as they consider them unworthy of taking important decisions and they believe that only top managers are capable of finding the solutions to the problems. This leads to solutions being thrust upon the juniors, which they resent and hence do not feel committed to implementing them.

Employees Suggestion Plan: While these plans are in place in several countries, they have become the moving spirit for job satisfaction. All suggestions are given due credit and as the suggestions are made after thorough investigations and experimentation, they are implemented. Employees feel highly motivated to see their ideas implemented. Quality circles help generate the suggestions and on an regular basis the Japanese worker keeps sending the suggestions with an yearly average of minimum 50 to maximum 1000 suggestions, where the average for the American worker comes to about 3.

Problems in Japan are considered beneficial because they provide the firm with impetus to overcome them and improve the firm's efficiency even further.

Japanese business culture believes that for furthering the cause of the firm they need people with good education. The firms believe in collective decision-making with upward flow of decisions. The main points of their business culture are given below.

- Authority with seniority
- Respect for age
- Life long employment
- Loyalty to the firm
- Participation in the quality circles
- Group information and decisions in quality circles
- Emphasis on productivity
- Debt financing is facilitated by the banks
- Slow decision process but fast implementation

Tasks for the students: Compare and contrast the Japanese and Indian cultural stream. How can the Indian business learn from their Japanese counterparts?

CASE STUDY 10

McDonald Worldwide

If one name stands out in fast food quality eatery it is the Mac. After enjoying great success in the US, they diversified into overseas operations, using the franchisee route. In the US, they have the following competitors:

- Burger King Corporation: They have enjoyed the number two position in the restaurant business. In 1991, they sold worth $5.4 billion worth of goods from nearly 5400 outlets. They tried nutritional foods with low calorie content.
- Wendy's International Inc.: In 1991, they sold goods worth $1.1 billion with 3776 outlets. They started with salad bars for the health conscious customers.
- PepsiCo. Inc. included Kentucky Fried Chicken, Pizza Hut and Taco Bar. Each of these has their own business philosophy; Taco is for smaller menu low prices, while KFC (the new name to get rid of the fried tag) was the first to tap international market, and Pizza Hut came out with innovative pizzas.

MacDonald went for a three-pronged strategy for business as given below.

1. Maximize sales and profits at their existing outlets
2. Adding restaurants
3. Improving international profitability

As a result they changed their focus of business along the following lines:

1. Lowest prices of their products
2. Easiest availability with top service and convenient locations
3. Trendiest products and messages with latest gimmickry
4. Widest variety of foods

Their slogan became: "We are the easiest eating place that satisfies customers best and gives them best value."

Their new mission became, "Value and customer satisfaction is the new message. The object of our message would be long-term brand building, and evoking nostalgia for the magic moments for the customers when they had visited us and felt happy and satisfied."

Recruitment policy included, "bring a friend", which would earn the employee a fifty-dollar gift for helping the firm.

The firm's earnings per share increased from $1.95 to $2.35 from 1989 to 1991, while profit margin stayed at 17.9% during this period.

Franchisee Operations

Mac Donald usually has the franchisee arrangement on the following basis:

- The franchisee has to pay an initial fee
- Continued payment on the basis of gross sales at the rate of 12 per cent of the sales.
- Minimal rental payment
- The lease is generally for a period of 20 years
- Franchisee has to pay property tax, insurance, maintenance charges and a refundable non-interest bearing security deposit.

The corporate revenue from the franchisee operations is given below.

	1991-million $	1990- million $	1989-million $
Rent from franchisees	798.2	690.7	597.6
Percentage fees	970.4	914.0	854.8
Initial fees	17.9	16.0	12.3
Total revenue	1786.5	1620.7	1464.7

Corporate Controls

Corporate officers frequently visited the restaurants to exchange notes with the franchisees. Besides there was a three-day examination twice a year to look at everything from the roof to the ketchup dispensers and the restaurants were graded on quality, service, and cleanliness. They were not graded on value, because as independent business people they were free to set the prices. In addition, suggestions were made to improve the place.

Tasks for the students: Please discuss the firm's mission statement and how is it going about fulfilling it through its overseas operations.

CASE STUDY 11

Nations Strategies

With the advent of 21st century, the time has come to look at the great divide between the rich and the poor nations. Some nations have remained poor in spite of having great mineral resources, brilliant people, while others with much less have forged ahead in the race of economic achievements. The deciding factor becomes, whether the nation wants to divide the wealth amongst the populace or increase it through free market enterprise.

In countries like India free market enterprise has been considered a bad word from the time the country became independent in 1947. Socialistic pattern of society, mixed economy with greater emphasis on government controlled and owned public sector were the norms, while the private sector was considered a necessary evil. Taking the cue from the then USSR, India wanted better distribution of wealth (or whatever of it was available at the time in the country) among the people of the country. Without making a value judgment of the decision, only on the hindsight, it can be assessed as a total disaster, as despite all efforts, the wealth remained with the wealthy, who in fact became more wealthy and poor remained poor.

Countries like India and Africa, with huge reservoir of natural resources, minerals, and forests and diversity in climatic conditions, remained poor. Countries, which became rich, were the Japan with no natural resource worth the name, earthquake disaster prone countryside, totally devastated after the world war came up economically, rose like the proverbial sphinx. In case of Japan, the national spirit of its population coupled with the market economy which governed the country's growth were responsible for the unprecedented success.

China, which had remained submerged in the communist philosophy, could emerge as a progressive nation only after it opened its economy to the western world shedding its former economic policies. It was caused by the liberal economic thought from the US and from the practical example of their erstwhile neighbouring developed island nation Hong Kong, which has become part of China now.

Market economy has come up as a panacea for most economic ills of the world and yet several nations consider it as taboo. The market economy, open world markets are looked down upon as some people and some countries consider it as anti-poor people. The imbalance, the rich-poor divide, is the direct result of such thinking; which limits the progress to redistribution of wealth rather than creation of wealth. The underdeveloped nations suffer from low education levels, increase in population, which aggravates the economic distribution further. The success of market economy can be seen in nations like Holland, where the country has hardly any natural wealth, sea has submerged part of the country and yet the population enjoys the fruits of market economy, they are free to earn their living any way they want to, spend the earnings as they like. The product price is not controlled by the government but by the market forces like competition, brand image.

In controlled economies the rich poor divide continues unabated; it results in the youth of the country, who have watched the progress made by other nations and not finding similar opportunities either leave the country or take to guns to make a fast buck. The theory of redistribution of wealth from the rich to poor has never been the option as the bureaucracy involved in the process takes the major part for its own benefit, leaving very little for the poor.

Today, even nations like China have learnt that when the cake is small nobody gets a big piece. It is better to bake a few more cakes than to give small portions to the people, and only creating more wealth rather than dividing it can do this.

The level of prosperity of nations can be measured by assessing the purchasing power of its citizens. Going by the Maslow's hierarchy of needs, are the citizens able to afford the daily needs of life in the following manner:

1. Physiological needs: Can the citizens afford to get meals of their choice for their families, can they get the clothing, medication, education and house for their families?
2. Safety needs: Can the citizens look after their family's security requirements?
3. Social needs: Can they afford to welcome and look after guests and their sociological needs?
4. Need for personal esteem: Can they get prestigious work with job opportunities in the country?
5. Need for self-actualization: Can they become self-actualized by attaining higher levels of physical, mental and spiritual satisfaction?

No one can for a moment deny the severe problems of poverty-stricken nations. But the answer starts with taking the money from the affluent and giving it to the poor? If the money comes first, the poor would not even know what to do with it, unless the country can produce or otherwise provide the citizens with the things they can use to satisfy the needs as per the hierarchy of needs given above. For this purpose, the country needs to push its economic structure along with that of more affluent countries and align their markets together.

The rich nations have to realize that as their own markets become saturated, they will have to cultivate the virgin markets of the poor nations for their products. For this purpose, it is a sound business sense for them to bring up the economies of their future markets by making investments in production, marketing and outsourcing from these poor nations. On the part of the poor nations it becomes incumbent on them to open their markets for not only foreign products but also for foreign direct investments. Once the realization comes that it is going to serve the purpose of both the rich and poor nations their economic divide would slowly but surely start diminishing.

In India, poor can be seen either taking out scraps of food from the bins or using guns to snatch from the rich. The mafia gangs of Bihar are only symptoms of the deep-rooted malaise from which the entire country is suffering albeit in different degrees of ailment. From Kerala a large number of persons migrate to the oil rich Middle East to work as labour, and they bring the petro-dollars back for the families.

Theoretically if India was to visualize its condition if it had opted for market economy right in the year 1950 and not as late as 1991, India would have achieved the kind of growth equal to or even surpassing some other nations of the far east, including Korea, Hong Kong, Taiwan, Singapore. However, instead of lamenting on the time lost, India must move forward with the reforms, which were started in 1991.

Most rich nations have no idea of the sufferings of poor nations on account of poverty. Till twenty years the west considered India a nation of snake charmers and of cattle on the road of beggars. Even now while there are several 5 star hotels, beauty pageants, there are also starvation deaths, malnutrition among children. Lot needs to be done.

While India propounded the theory of "Vasudhaiv Kutumbkam", meaning that the world is a family; the country has kept itself aloof and isolated in real commercial terms. With numerous entry barriers for foreigners to come to India for business, protection of Indian firms, India also acquired, perhaps justifiable, the reputation of a rigid and corrupt bureaucracy, which further became a major deterrent for foreign investors for the country. Or, Indians can continue to lament their fate as the most fatalist people, keep cursing the rich for their wealth and in all humility trust the Almighty to bring succour to them, without moving a finger of their own. Let the Lord Krishna's benevolent voice become our guiding factor. He had told Arjun on the battlefield that it is the duty of all human beings to do their Karma and yet leave the benefits from the Karma on to the God Himself. Let the Indians feel happy that there are rich nations in the world and instead of cursing them, take their help in business so that while the rich progress, India too does just the same. The alternative, even while it is not possible is that even the rich become poor with no benefit for the poor as the redistribution of wealth, if it ever was to happen would not get the poor the products they want; they would not know what to do with all that moneys and the rich would not get the markets they are looking for.

It is in this context the role of the UN and its agencies like the WTO becomes extremely important. WTO should be involved in solving the existing entry barriers between nations rather than going into the product specifications from the less developed countries matching the needs of the rich nations. In this case also WTO should let the market decide what it wants and what it does not want, the price and other terms of business. This singular service should be real focus and it can be hoped that in this twenty-first century, the political unrest can be quelled with economically open markets across the world. The apparent paradox that both the rich and poor nations can jointly make the rich richer and the poor not so poor is the new reality of business world of the century.

CASE STUDY

12

LG Group

India has made remarkable achievements in the recent time, especially after their earlier failure in strategic tie-ups as Goldstar, which led them to carry out their operations in India all alone as subsidiary of the Korean giant.

Ever since its inception in India 'LG India' has made an impressive beginning and has shown commendable progress on all parameters of keeping in touch with the market. This report aims to establish the factors included in the strategic marketing plan of LG in India (in the colour television market) that has contributed to its rise to glory. This report begins by giving the origin and background of the company which includes the strategic intents of the organization, and then the company and its environment have been studied. This includes the discussion of the General Business Environment Factors affecting the company and Industry Analysis (Porter's Five Forces), which provide the outline of the competitors, and their analysis, which is followed by a SWOT Analysis to highlight the company's strengths, weakness, opportunities and threats faced. The 7's strategy of McKenzie has also been analyzed for LG. The next part involves the critical success factors, which have been the major factors to help the organization to achieve the success in the industry, and competitive advantages followed by a discussion of the company's strategies. The last part then includes alternative strategic recommendations that provides a base on which the company can work up on and achieve their objective of gaining the largest market share in the CTV segment and finally the conclusion made of the research carried.

The world of consumer durable is becoming more and more complicated, compared to what it was about 5 years back. Consumer electronic goods are now going digital. Companies are coming out with technologically advanced products researched in-house and being launched in India more or less simultaneously with the rest of the world. Some of the really high tech consumer durables to be seen in the market are so advanced that they seem to be from the future world. For example, the Internet televisions have pre-installed Internet software and there is no need of a personal computer.

With multinationals zeroing in onto the Indian consumer durable market, emotions are ranging from excitement to despair. Excitement is coming from the world-class products being launched by the technologically advanced multinationals and despair for the Indian manufactories faced by constricting market conditions.

Inherent advantages that the MNCs had were their superior products, worldwide experience, greater spending and sustaining powers. On the other hand, the Indian companies had easily recognized brands, wide distribution networks and first hand knowledge of the Indian mindset and market conditions.

It is to be seen who will emerge as the winner and survive the price wars brand wars and the huge marketing expenses.

Gone are the days when word of mouth publicity sufficed and household goods were bought off the shelf. People no longer buy cash down as they are confronted with various choices. Customers are confronted with multiple choices and a huge price range, suitable for all pockets. All the companies are desperately trying to capture market share. It is no longer within the persuasive powers of the salesman to complete a deal. The customer is being wooed and so are the deals, for it is in his hand to promote the sale of a company's goods at the last minute, the point of purchase.

Year 1997-98 can be characterized by the stiff competition for the mind space of the Indian consumer. During this period the industry grew by 10.2% compared to 1997(4.3% growth rate). Reason being that the MNCs were improving their market and the Indian companies were not found very far behind on this front. Deals were structured keeping in mind the changing buyer profile. Industry's perception of the Indian consumer durable market in terms of volume and product attributes has refined over a period of time.

It is not necessary that the products that have been a great success outside the country will continue to perform well on the Indian soil. Indian consumer looks for value for money in these products apart from some peculiar product attribute. Decline in the economic growth of the country had a negative impact on almost all the industries; consumer durables were not an exemption. Majority of the wholly owned MNCs that have come to Indian market in the last few years are still in red. The Indian companies continue making profits albeit at reduced margins.

Background and Assumptions

Origin

The Lucky Group (now known as LG) has its origins dating late back to January 5, 1957 when founder Chairman Hwoi Koo had invested all his personal assets in its formation with great success is in many rounds of reinvestment by the late 1950s, Mr. Koo announced his intention to get into electronics after much painstaking research and planning the Goldstar Company (now known as LG Electronics) was founded on 1.10.1958.

LG Electronics India Limited

After being appointed one of the official sponsors of CTV kits for the Asian Games in New Delhi 1982, LG disappeared for the next 12 years. Then in 1995 it came together with a technical collaboration with Delhi based Bestavision Group and in 1996 tried to set up a joint venture with the CK Birla Group. However, both these attempts to take off failed. Finally getting affirmation by the foreign investment promotion board to set up a 100% subsidiary in India, LG Electronics Limited was incorporated on January 1997 as a fully owned subsidiary of LG Electronics (South Korea). The first employee joined on April 1, 1997 and within 5 months it opened 18 fully operational branch offices across the country. Since then there has been no looking back and they have been constantly studying customer needs, setting up the infrastructure, recruiting people and reaching out to dealers.

Vision and Mission Statements

Vision

"The best global company"

Mission

"To bring the smiling face to every home across the globe".

The mission and vision statements of LG are simple, short, and precise; however, they fail to answer the five questions of Peter Drucker, i.e.

- What is our business?
- Who is the customer?
- What is the value to the customer?
- What will our business be?
- What should our business be?

Inferences from the mission statement help us to answer the above questions:

Q. What is our business?
LG's product range varies from colour televisions (CTV's) to fridges, microwave ovens, air-conditioners, washing machines, monitors and others.

Q. What are our customers?
LG's customers include both households and firms.

Q. What is our value to the customer?
LG's focus on 'value' rather than price. It has built upon the 'health' platform.

Q. What will our business be?"
Short-term goals – Constant innovations and development of newer better products.

Q. What should our business be?
Long-term goals – To be the market leader in the CTV segment by constant customer satisfaction.

LG' corporate logo incorporates five concepts and sentiments.
→ World
→ Future
→ Youth
→ Humanity
→ Technology
(A&M 2000, May, Issue)

The corporate logo has been designed very intelligently and carefully so as to encompasses the entire global market and caters to all needs.

General Business Environmental Factors Affecting LG Electronics

Political and legal factors

The budget in the year 2000 has had a negative impact on the consumer electronics industry, leading to an increase in the already high product prices. The main reason for the fall in TV sales is the high taxes that the consumer electronics industry has to bear. As compared to any similar country, where the TV industry has to pay 17-18 per cent as Value Added Tax (VAT), the Indian companies have to pay different taxes at each level for manufacturing and sales as well as separate municipal tax and customs duties, all adding up to almost 70-80 per cent of the end price paid by the consumer. The industry suffered a hit of nearly six per cent. Some companies passed on this additional tax burden to the consumer, resulting in increased prices. Other companies that did not pass on this burden to the consumers took steps like reducing advertising expenditure and other overhead costs.

Political changes with respect to change in the government may affect the policies and the rules established for business development such as import and export policies. Also change in the level of taxation, direct and indirect will leads to price sensitivity.

With relaxation in customs duty by the Indian Government, the company can import upgraded, innovative products from the parent company in Korea.

Economic factors

Level of inflation as well as savings is likely to increase in the Indian economy as a result of rise in the disposable income levels of the middle class.

The company carrying out export and imports has to face certain changes in custom duties and exchange rate which have been in fluctuating mode in the recent past, which has forced the company to change the policies accordingly.

Social-cultural factors

Consumers' lifestyles are improving and the liking for higher value products is on the increase. This helps LG to innovate and differentiate the products based up on the living standards of people.

Consumers are accepting higher value products at reasonably higher prices, which is a positive sign for the company to cater to the premium segments and also follow the pricing and quality combination for masses.

The segment of multiple ownerships is growing at a fast rate bringing users to pick more than one set, which may help the company to concentrate now on volumes with different models to satisfy a complete family.

Technological factors

High levels of technological developments are being witnessed by the industry. The industry being ruled by major multinationals have a competitive environment, thus by keeping a constant watch on technological advancements and quickly responding to the changes in technological world will help the organization to survive in the cut-throat competition.

The company imports most of its technology from the parent company. The technology so imported has to be suited according to the tastes and the needs of the Indian consumers.

Global factors

Liberalization means that more and more companies will be exploring the business environment in India. Hence, there would be more and more competition in an already saturated marketplace.

Advanced nations might dump their bulk goods in the Indian market at cheaper prices, thus giving a serious competition for well-established brands like LG.

Demographic

As India possesses largest middle class group, which has untapped market which can be a potential for LG to capture. Also the middle class now being quality and health conscious serves as another potential market segment for their health supportive products.

Industrial Competitive Analysis

Using Michael Porter's Five Forces Model

Bargaining power of buyers

Although in the CTV industry buyer's power is high as there is abundance of supply. The buyer has the option to choose from a wide variety of choice but LG CTV operates in the premium segment where the number of players is few and buyers are left with little option. Also the customer in the Indian premium segment does not tend to bargain.

Bargaining power of suppliers

In the CTV segment there are wide ranges of suppliers. Furthermore, there have been more and more diversification and companies are entering and expanding into the Indian market. The bargaining power of the suppliers is low as the number of competitors in the premium segment are few, namely, Samsung, Sony, and LG.

Threat from Substitute Products

With technological advancement, computers have incorporated some of the features of CTVs, as a result of which they act as a substitute for CTVs.

Apart from the above, the traditional substitutes like radio and cinema theatres have always been there.

Threat of new entrants

New players should not be easily dismissed because although they are new to the market they come with a vast pool of experience and expertise behind them. Therefore, the LG CTV has to be prepared for head on challenges. Further, with globalization the consumers are becoming more and more demanding. Hence, the CTV market has to be well aware of emerging trends and charges and accordingly formulate strategies. The year 2003 will be remembered as being a landmark one, with several multinational brands trying to re-enter an already overcrowded Indian market. Chinese mega brands Haier and TCL have returned despite biting the dust the first time round; Korean brand Daewoo has forged an equity tie-up with Anchor Electronics for its second trial in the Indian market. Japanese major Aiwa has also been relaunched in the country by Sony, which acquired it globally.

Rivalry Amongst Existing Players

The major existing players in the CTV segments in India against LG are Samsung, Sony, Sansui, Onida, and BPL, etc. Samsung having a major market share in the flat television (FTV's) market, which is followed by the Japanese multinational Sony. Since both the companies have been in India for a long time, comparatively they have an edge over LG. But when compared to the overall colour television market, LG has an upper hand on all the other companies since it holds the highest market share with 18%. To grab the major market share for the flat televisions also, LG must come out with marketing plans and separately handle the flat television market to differentiate it with the other LG products.

Graphical Analysis for Existing Players for CTV's in India

The flat television market in India is headed by the three multinational companies as they have better marketing and operational strategies to out do the Indian counterparts besides quality parameter. The effect has been clearly depicted in the chart where BPL has least market share among branded product suppliers.

Although being in the third place for FTV's competition, this year LG has emerged as the leader in the overall segment of colour televisions with a percentage of 18, when compared to the Samsung fighting on the second position, to be followed by Onida with 11%. The others including the local made TV's constituted to total of 47%.

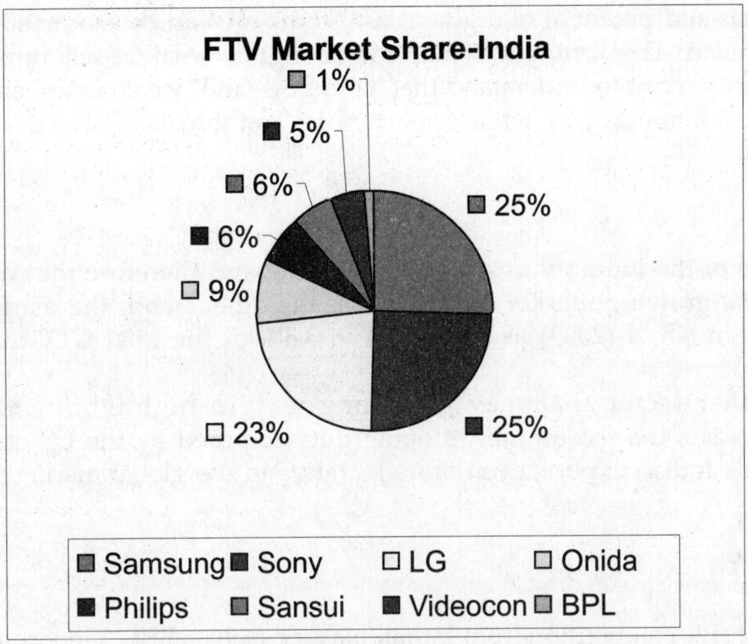

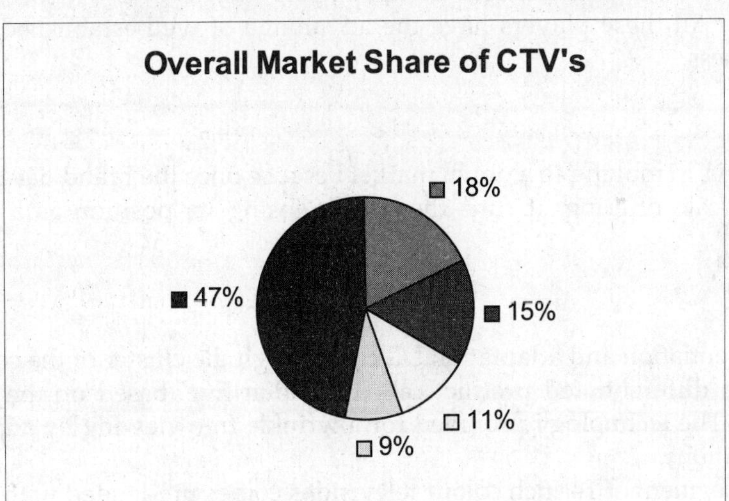

SWOT Analysis

A common technique utilized in management and business is the SWOT Analysis. This technique does not only provide answers to operating issue but also helps to identify relevant problems, from which more informed decisions can be made. OTSW (opportunities, threats, strengths, and weakness) analysis provides four key titles with which analysis and potential of a given case/company can be examined. The acronym can be examined. The acronym stands for strengths, weaknesses, opportunities and threats. It is important to understand that 'strengths' and 'weaknesses' emerge from the firm's internal circumstances, while opportunities and threats exist in the firm's external environment.

Opportunities

Growth rates of the industry as a whole are rising and therefore the company stands to gain on the growing market of CTV's. On the other hand, the market growth for FTV's has been 8.8 % (2003) as compared to 3.8% of the total CTV market in April 2002.

Yet another factor that may go a long way in highlighting the industry's competitiveness is the recent anti-dumping duty imposed by the US on Chinese TVs. This has made Indian exports even more lucrative in the global market than before.

Threats

Competition

LG faces intensive competition from Indian players such as BPL, Videocon, Onida, Aiwa and Samsung. All these players have the advantage of well-established networks and brand awareness.

Positioning

LG has a danger in moving to a down market because once the brand has been associated with a downscale offering; it runs the risk of losing its position as a higher quality brand name.

Strengths

Product differentiation and adaptation LG cut through the cluster of the colour television market with a differentiated product called 'Golden Eye' based on the health USP of the company. The technology provided for a wrinkle free viewing by adjusting itself to lighting conditions.

Its youth segment of 14-inch colour televisions comes pre-loaded with a cricket game and an extra remote control. The idea was developed just before the World Cup and in a cricket crazy country like India it caused sales to rise.

(Economic Times, July 2000)

Innovation

Product innovation is a continuous process at LG. The reason for survival in this competitive marketplace is the ability to launch new models with innovative features. Innovation at LG involves many functions like:

It also launched the 'Sampoorna' range of CTVs. These involved multilingual on screen displays in 5 Indian languages.

The R&D department of LG works for two major objectives:

- To develop and modify the products suiting to the Indian conditions.
- To keep a customized focus on the changing environmental and cultural conditions.

Well-Developed Promotion Plans

LG has one of the best promotional plans in the whole industry. Its whole plan is systematically developed using various promotional tools.

It also promotes itself with the help of well-decorated mobile showrooms, which move all over India to create curiosity and awareness among the people.

Distribution strategy: Since its inception LG has laid stress on proper channel merchandising and management. Due to a very calculated network expansion plan, LG has the fastest dealer network and also the highest dealer productivity. Dealer loyalty and retention have been a high priority from the beginning.

The distribution graphic for LG TV is given below.

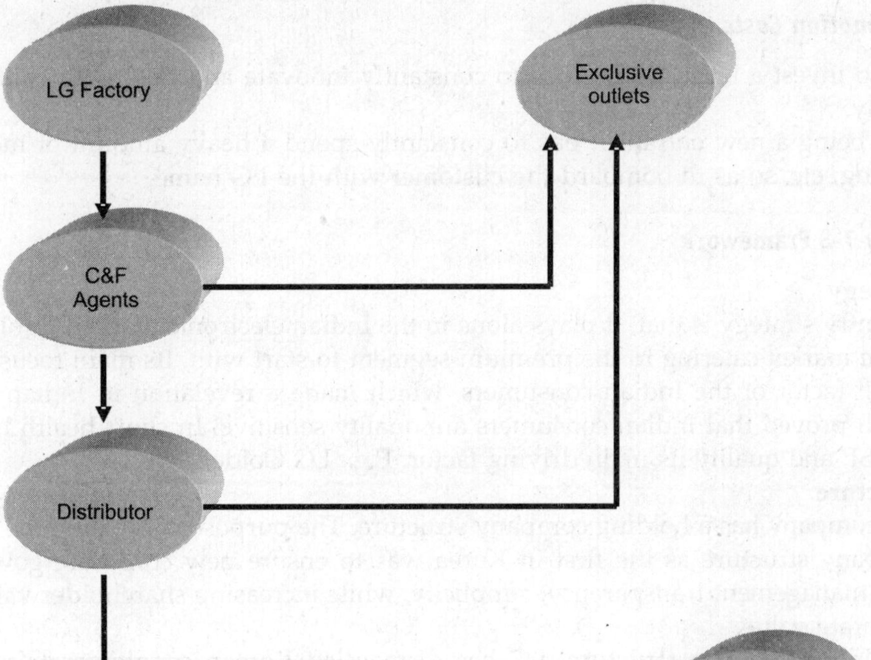

Brand image

LG has a popular brand image in the global market. LG has extended its popularity in the Indian market as well by providing high quality products mainly concentrating on the health parameter.

Company's objectives and policies

While all CTV players were playing on price. LG was the first to play on value and features. Hence, this differentiation policy acted as a main strength for the company.

Weaknesses

Dealer margins/schemes

Although LG went to the best dealers it gave them few schemes or extra discounts comparatively as its competitors, which cost them losing some dealers to their competitors like Samsung, which provide better options for dealers.

High Promotion Costs

LG has to invest a lot in R&D so as to constantly innovate and deal with competition effectively.

Also being a new entrant it has to constantly spend a heavy amount of money on advertising, etc. so as to bombard the customer with the LG name.

McKinsey 7-S Framework

1. **Strategy**
   LG entry strategy is that, it plays alone in the Indian electronic market. It followed a Niche market catering to the premium segment to start with. Its main focus was on health factor of the Indian consumers, which made a revelation in Indian market, which proved that Indian consumers are quality sensitive. In short health has been its USP and quality its main driving factor. E.g.: LG Golden Eye.
2. **Structure**
   The company has a holding company structure. The purpose of creating the holding company structure as the first in Korea was to ensure new corporate governance with management transparency, simplicity, while increasing shareholder value, and corporate value.

   Under this new structure, LG has dismantled Korean conglomerate's chronic problem of cross-payment guarantees between the affiliates. Now, the holding companies are responsible for all the investment portfolios of its subsidiaries and each business unit is responsible only for their business operations. It provides the subsidiary companies independence and freedom to strengthen their core business competitiveness without having to worry about equity investments nor their affiliates.

3. **Style (Pioneering spirit)**

LG Electronics takes the initiative in leading the development of Korea's electronics industry through a pioneering spirit of transforming vision into reality. In 1959, the company manufactured the radio, the first undertaking of its kind in Korea. Furthermore, the company achieved other firsts in the country by developing telephones, refrigerators, and black & white television sets. LG Electronics is one of the country's pioneers, spearheading Korea's electronics industry since its inception 40 years ago. This success was made possible because of LG Electronics' boldness in product innovations and its fearlessness in accepting many challenges. LG Electronics espouses and believes in the dictum No Success without Challenge as it proudly exercises its global leadership in the field of digital TV and other state-of-the-art products.

4. **Shared values**

(i) Labour Management Relations

LG Electronics chooses to promote harmony and build constructively on a labour-management relationship rather than an employee-employer relationship. This illustrates that management and workers are not in a vertical relationship, but in a horizontal one, with each party on equal footing and working together based on mutual trust and respect. By shifting the paradigm from an employee-employer relationship to that of labour-management, LG Electronics and its members discard the old vertical relationships of pursuing and keeping their respective shares. Instead, a horizontal relationship type is embraced wherein workers and management assume their functions and roles in pursuit of a common goal: boosting competitiveness and enhancing the quality of life while promoting mutual trust and respect. Because of this harmonious relationship, the company's labour and management work together to establish and cultivate a world-class corporate culture.

This culture is necessary for LG Electronics as it strives to become one of the world's top companies. Such a relationship is transformed into a value-creation relationship whereby both parties endeavour to address mutual problems and create new values together.

(ii) Management by Principle

LG Electronics management seeks to employ fair and transparent methods in all its transactions to compete fairly and to elicit customer acceptance and loyalty. LG Electronics aims to become a superior and highly competitive company based on customer-oriented services. A fair and transparent management is one of LG Electronics' corporate ethical criteria. LG Electronics strongly believes that this is the way towards achieving the status of a superior, world-class corporation. The company will continue to pursue its goals together with its partners in an environment of mutual trust and cooperation.

5. **Skills**

Embracing the slogan of No. 1 LG, LG Electronics is continuously steering various reform initiatives to secure global competitiveness. The company has been undertaking 'Super A' pioneering activities since 1993, seeking to strengthen its competitiveness and create profitability. The company is also practising TL 2005, a technological management strategy aimed at building and sustaining prominence in the global market. In addition, LG Electronics is carrying out the Six Sigma Campaign to achieve an ideal management base. LG Electronics is exerting its best efforts to respond positively to the fast-changing business environment and to shore up its global competitiveness in its core businesses. Embracing the slogan of No. 1 LG, LG Electronics is continuously steering various reform initiatives to secure global competitiveness. The company has been undertaking 'Super A' pioneering activities since 1993, seeking to strengthen its competitiveness and create profitability. The company is also practicing TL 2005, a technological management strategy aimed at building and sustaining prominence in the global market. In addition, LG Electronics is carrying out the Six Sigma Campaign to achieve an ideal management base. LG Electronics is exerting its best efforts to respond positively to the fast-changing business environment and to shore up its global competitiveness in its core businesses.

6. **Staff**

   The employees of LG have been taken care of very well, so as to motivate them to produce the best. The company achieved the Six-sigma certification, which was the result of the best of training and motivation techniques used by the personnel department. The employees are sent to Korea for extensive training programme to lever the employee's abilities at full.

Strategies Adopted by LG

In a short span of just 26 months, since its inception in May 1997, the brand has attained a brand awareness level of about 90% in the consumer durable Indian market.

Considering the fact that LG electronics is a Korean multinational, entering the Indian market meant establishing itself in a different market altogether with varied cultures and consumer tastes and preferences. Also that so many multinationals are entering into the country, it is evident that each and every company has a cutting edge over another. These global corporations are deviating from their international methodologies and improvising their strategies for local markets.

LG's localization of strategy covers the following areas:

Entry Strategy: The strategy that LG has adopted is presenting an Indianised face to its products but keeping the technology at global standards.

Operations: LG opted for starting its own manufacturing facility at Greater Noida. The 20-month schedule to commission its manufacturing plant was compressed to 10 months. It is always better to establish as fully owned subsidiaries. It is considered better if the company has a local partner but, since LG's earlier two attempts had already failed, it decided to do it all alone this time rather than acquisitions or mergers.

Products: LG decided to go in for Product Adaptation Strategy. Globally LG does not operate in the direct cool refrigerator, semi-automatic washing machine and 21 inch CTV's. But the company had to develop these products for the Indian market because these areas constitute a major bulk of buys for the Indian consumer. Also LG launched, Sampoorna, India's first TV with a devanagiri script on screen display on the 50th anniversary of Indian independence. LG's strategy of localizing its products to suit Indian tastes added to its strength.

Segmentation: The company decided to enter the high-end middle-class onward segment in the initial stages, since most of the Indian brands were targeting the low and middle end customers. In the past 3 years due to LG's distinct strategy it has carved a niche for itself in a crowded segment of 20 manufacturers.

Brand: The company launched its products in the country with "LG, the global leader". It did not opt for any established brands in the country to be associated with it.

Leadership: At LG electronics, keeping the localized strategy in mind, the strategic areas such as sales and marketing are headed by an Indian. Generally, it happens that the senior management is deprived of Indians in a transnational but LG did not want to follow this path, it wanted that an Indian should head the marketing division because he would be versed of the Indian market and cultures. Ultimately it is this that determined whether the company wants to make profits or obtain a market share. LG definitely wants to be the leader in the consumer electronics industry. Seeing the progress that the company has made in the past 3 years, it has revised its plans for becoming the number one consumer electronics company to the year 2003 from 2005. In the year 2000, its turnover in India was comprised nearly 2 per cent of its global turnover. This is significant for a multinational that has been in the market for just two years.

LG's Globalization strategy for India

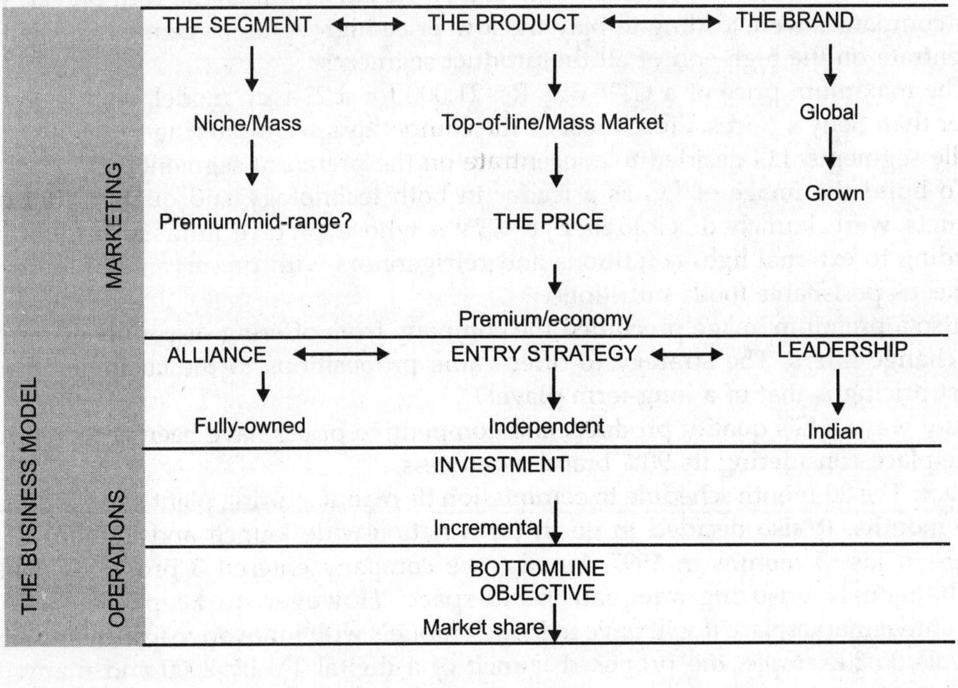

Channels of distribution at LG.

LG's Marketing Success

Before launching itself in the market in 1997, it carried out an extensive research study to understand consumer motivations to create magnetic products, price them strategically, position them sharply and keep making the magnetism more potent. Having understood the finer differences in consumer motivations, it opted for differentiation over the other players.

In a broad perspective, LG's sales and marketing success can be attributed to its 7 Ps of marketing. In addition to the products, price, place and promotion, the key factors that have contributed to LG's success are the following 3 additional Ps:

(i) Pace
(ii) People
(iii) Passion

The most important winning factor of the sales and marketing has been its '*Passion*'. It is this attribute within all the workers that drives the other 6 Ps.

However, LG's marketing strategy is based on 3 Ps, apart from the conventional 4 Ps of marketing:

- Premium pricing to maintain margins
- Breathtaking pace to create riches
- Deep penetration to increase volumes.

Premium Pricing: LG electronics was one of the late entrants, the 18th player. While other companies were jostling to play the low price high volumes game, LG decided to concentrate on the high end of all the product segments.

The maximum price of a CTV was Rs. 21,000 for a 21-inch model, was 10 per cent higher than Sony's prices. Since most of the competitors were catering to the lower and middle segments, LG decided to concentrate on the premium segments.

To build the image of LG as a leader in both technology and quality, innovative products were launched: Golden Eye CTV's whose picture adjusts automatically according to external light conditions and refrigerators with preserve nutrition system that keeps perishable foods nutritious.

Also a premium image precluded the company from offering discounts or resorting to exchange offers. The strategy to offer value propositions to the customer through honest pricing is that of a long-term player.

Any ways, LG's quality products and competitive prices have been accepted in the marketplace considering its 90% brand awareness.

Pace: The 20-month schedule to commission its manufacturing plant was compressed to 10 months. It also decided to go in for a nation-wide launch and appointed 1000 dealers in just 5 months in 1997. Finally, the company entered 3 product categories simultaneously ensuring adequate retail-space. However, to keep pace with the competitive marketplace it will have to launch models with innovative features at regular intervals. For example, the proposed launch of a digital TV by 2000 and many other digital products is a step towards this direction.

Penetration: Pace was followed by aggressive penetration. Having established 18 branch offices and C&F agents in Goa and Pondicherry to take advantage of the sales tax benefits in these areas and towns like Ranchi, Raipur and Nagpur the company has expanded its dealer network to 2,500. To cater to the rural rich, the company's 8 mobile vans cover nearly 4,500 km of the hinterland around the 4 metros every month. The estimated annual ad expense and market support expenses were to the tune of Rs. 28 crore in 1999.

LG believes in "Value Marketing". It is exactly opposite of what Akai Stands for. Akai is pushing volumes by sacrificing value. On the other hand, LG is sacrificing volume for value. The refusal to interpret Indian price sensitivity as value-insensitivity seems to have pushed LG into delving deep into consumer behaviour for insights missed by excessively self-centric companies. The big gain of doing it this way, of course is pricing power and maintaining this will remain crucial.

Product positioning: The Unique Selling Proposition (USP) is based on health.

The company wanted a USP for its products that no other company in the industry had. Hence, it piggybacked on health. This is a niche which none of the other company's had thought of. Each of its product lines were positioned based on health:

1. Golden Eye television–Ensuring wrinkle free viewing
2. Refrigerators–PN system (preserve nutrition system)
3. Air-conditioners–Health Air AC's
4. Washing Machines–Chaos Punch +3-Fabricare system
5. Microwave Over–Health wave cooking system

Product Life Cycle, Strategies and Objectives

According to the stages of the product life cycle, LG is in the growth stage considering the company's success over the past 3 years. Marketing objectives and strategies for the introductory and the growth stage are summarized.

	Introduction	Growth
Marketing objectives	To offer technological superior products in the market	Preparing for "Digitally yours" image for the new millennium
Strategies:		
Product	Offering about in total 23 products to the premium end of the market	Launching digitally superior products for all its product ranges
Price	Initially prices high to cater the premium end	Catering to the mass market via its diverse prices
Distribution	Selective	Intensive
Promotion	Heavy advertising to create awareness about its products	More into corporate advertising, i.e. promotion the brand

Critical Success Factors and Core Competencies

LG's CSF's:

Dealership network

The network only has dealers who believe in the magnetic charm of LG's products. Market-addressed processes in terms of product development and better communication that are in harmony with the market generate this. A unique understanding of special needs of the Indian consumer drives these processes.

Developing quality products

LG is a popular global company with name recognition and a strong reputation. At the nucleus of it has a keen focus on quality, matched by intense consumer orientation. LG has differentiated itself by taking the 'health' plank in most product areas. For example, LG's Golden Eye CTV sales depend not only on CTV demand in general, but are also concerned with consumer's sensitivity to eye care. The core competence with respect to developing quality products is stringent quality controls in the assembly processes.

Product innovation

Product innovation at LG is a continuous process. It is a part of its entire policy. From 12 models at the time of its launch in 1997, LG has come a long way in strengthening its CTV product line. At present it has 25 models. The average time between new products launch being just mere 6 months. Its product line includes high-end projection Flatron TV at one end and Sampoorna sets for down scale markets on the other hand.

The main core competencies considering product innovation is with respect to its R&D and technology. Innovation at LG involves many functions such as six sigma, TDR, Fi-10, and TPI-50, etc.

Entire marketing plan

LG's marketing plan is based on 3Ps - Premium 'Pricing' to maintain margins, breathtaking 'Pace' to create niches and deep penetration to increase volumes. Its marketing strategy revolves around aggression with differentiation. LG's strength was to understand customer motivations, to create magnetic products, price them strategically and position them sharply making magnetism more potent.

LG's marketing plan focuses deeply on value marketing and it refused to interpret the Indian consumer's price sensitivity to value insensitivity.

Competitive Advantage

Competitive advantage can be defined as something that is unique, sustainable and profitable.

1. Differentiation strategy
2. Distribution

Distribution

LG's main competitive advantage is with respect to its effective distribution. LG sells through 18 branches across India in more than 1800 towns and cities. The company has 162 distributors and more than 3000 dealers. LG has been constantly placing emphasis on proper channel management. It has an extensive, calculated network expansion plan with the fastest dealer network and also the highest dealer productivity as compared to other companies. Dealer loyalty and retention is given high priority.

Physical distribution

While dealing with logistics, i.e., transportation, inventory management, warehousing and order processing, LG has been continuously implementing strict cost control measures. It attempts to keep inventory levels at minimum possible levels, the plant keeping no more than 7 days stock of material from vendors and 15-20 days of imported part. Strict guidelines for branch offices have been laid emphasizing low inventory. They are advised at the end of the month to keep not more than 40% of the requirement of the next month, to be replenished by the 15th.

By stopping credit to dealers LG forces them to make demand projections which also force them to move the products off the shelf faster to keep their own cash from getting blocked. Hence, LG's distribution acts as its main competitive advantage.

Differentiation strategy

LG began as a 'value-deliver' in a market where intensity of competition derived to such an extent that survival would be doubtful. The marketing plan of LG involves the creation of magnetic products to justify customer acceptance. LG has gone for a product differentiation strategy coupled with high levels of adaptation keeping in mind customer motivation and a strategy of localizing its products to suit Indian tastes while keeping the technology global. Its product features and product variety have successfully penetrated the Indian market.

Recommendations Planned by the Inner Group

LG's performance on the marketing platform has been outstanding and the company is essentially a go-getter, yet it might need to revise certain aspects of its strategy to perform all the more better in the future. An attempt has been made to list down all such possible recommendations that might be worthy of consideration.

LG has managed to gain an excellent repute of a premium product. As it ventures into new territories it is recommended to look into the following:

Evaluating options

The danger of moving to a downmarket is that the brand runs the risk of losing its position as a high quality brand. To avoid such negative repercussions the following moves could be considered.

Launch a new brand

One way to avoid the negative aspects of accessing a downscale market is to launch a new brand, since a connection with the LG brand might confuse the customers and cannibalize the core-brands image. The new brand should be promoted with the mother company LG as the promoter or co-driving force.

An example of such a case is AIWA, which is created by Sony. However, new brands are not easy to introduce and it takes time to build awareness, establish perception of quality and developing a customer base.

Promotions

Being the costs of promotion very high to create brand equity in India, which lead LG provide few discounts and low margins for the dealers. Now as the company is penetrating into local market to cater the masses, to the lower-middle and lower income group, it must provide better margins , schemes and discounts so that to promote their products through dealers and channel members along with few advertisements and promotions addressing those segments.

Technological breakthrough

As the computers are posing a major threat to not only LG but to the overall television industry, a technological breakthrough or a innovation such as a television incorporated with the computer abilities like surfing through the TV and storage abilities must be developed so that the company can counter the threat posed by the computers and DVD's.

Following these recommendations, the company can gain total market share which has been its objective and stand ready to face the competition ahead where the companies are trying back to play in Indian CTV market.

CONCLUSION

Lucky Group (the then Gold Star) which tried its hand in Indian electronics market with corporate strategic tie-ups leading to no way, which resulted in packing bags and fly back. In 1997, when it came back as the LG (Lucky Group) it had some different plans all over. Firstly, it didn't try for any strategic tie-ups rather it went alone as a subsidiary to take on the Indian CTV's market. Secondly, it had done its homework this time, such as knowing the Indian consumer, innovating and working on their Indian USP of health which helped not only to create a niche in the market they made the market head in the year 2003 by leading the overall CTV's market share.

Following are the financial information about LG since its establishment in India.

Turnover for 1997 Rs. 125 crore

Turnover for 1998 Rs. 485 crore that is 288% increase since previous year

Turnover for 1999 Rs. 1056 crore that is 117.77% increase since previous year.

Turnover for 2000 Rs. 1903 crore that is 80.20% increase since previous year

Turnover for 2001 Rs. 2216 crore is 59% increase since previous year.

Turnover for 2002 crossed Rs. 3000 crore that is 37% increase since previous year.

LG had its own market of niche as it catered its products to the premium segment, with the USP of health. The company changed the traditionally followed principle of price sensitive Indian market to health sensitive Indian market. Now as the objective of LG is achieving the highest market share, the company must take on the ever growing middle class and a secondary market, i.e., lower-middle income group to achieve its objective following its basic way of promoting and quality products with innovation as major strength.

Tasks for the Students: Find out the flaws in the LG strategies and recommend what you consider as the right strategies for them.

CASE STUDY 13

Microsoft Inc. USA

Microsoft genesis begins with a 14-year old Bill Gates getting a computer as present from his mother. He along with his three friends started a club for development computer software as computer hackers. In 1973, Gates went to Howard to look for business opportunities. A little later Microsoft was found as a partnership firm. In 1980, IBM came to Microsoft with an opportunity unparalleled in the short history of Microsoft. Later on when UNIX System came and Microsoft software was not so popular, its relations with IBM became strained. In 1991, it also got into problems with the US Government's Federal Trade Commission, which felt that Microsoft is going to monopolize the PC Software, through Windows.

Start any computer around the world and more than ninety per cent you will find it running on Microsoft windows operating system. The firm is as controversial as it is successful and influential. It touches the lives of billions of people and it has changed the way people manage and work in offices, homes, factories and how they correspond with others.

It is a firm, which evokes intense feelings of love or hatred it is Microsoft! Its founder Bill Gates is already a cult figure, worshipped and idolized by millions of young and old in the world. From a middle-class family, he inherited his acumen from his mother and shrewdness from his father. In just twenty years he is the richest man on the planet.

Where do they go from here?

Microsoft strives to produce innovative products to meet the evolving needs of the knowledgeable customers.

Mission: Microsoft started in 1975, with a mission to create software for the personal computer that empowers and enriches people at home and at their workplace, at schools and in the laboratories.

Vision: Its early vision was to see a computer on every desk, every home and it is now coupled with a strong commitment to Internet technologies expanding the reach and power of PC users.

Values: Microsoft's values are enshrined in the following tenets:

- Customers: Helping them achieve their goals by listening to them and quickly delivering new innovative products; building relationships based on trust, respect and understanding and service support.
- Innovation: Moving with the speed of light for bringing new products in the market to remain competitive with reduced costs as well.
- Partners: Helping them grow in their business
- Integrity: Acting with utmost integrity Microsoft's team is guided by what is right for their customers.
- People: The team must have an exciting challenging career with growth opportunity and well balanced home and work life.
- Entrepreneurial culture: The team must remain passionate about the work, contributing to evolution of technology to remain competitive.
- Diversity: The team is encouraged for diverse activities, with equal chance of promotion and increments for the members.
- Community: Microsoft feels responsible to the community in which they operate and wants to make a meaningful difference in its life.

Finance as on June 1999
Net revenue $19.75 billion
Net income $7.79 billion
Microsoft headcount and revenue growth is given below.

Year	Headcount	Revenue $B	%Growth	Income $ M	%Growth
1990	5635	1.18	47	279	63
1991	8226	1.85	56	463	66
1992	11542	2.78	50	708	53
1993	14430	3.79	36	953	35
1994	15017	4.71	25	1150	20
1995	17801	6.08	29	1450	27
1996	20561	9.05	49	2200	51
1997	22232	11.94	32	3450	57
1998	27055	15.26	28	4490	30
1999	31575	19.75	29	7790	79

The headcount is in the vicinity of 40,000.

Microsoft has been living in the shadow of its illustrious founder. While Bill Gates has many friends, his opponents believe he is shrewd and manipulative and wants to dominate the world. Microsoft needs to improve its image to come out of the predicament it faces today.

In 1995 the firm almost lost the battle of Internet to Netscape and Sun Microsystems and Microsoft was caught napping. Microsoft needs feedback from marketing to their

R&D to get the latest customers needs. Microsoft must make more friends than foes. It should not consider that it is a **Know All** firm. It could consider splitting in to several small firms with independent decision-making under one over all umbrella.

IBM is reeling under competitive pressure and does not know what hit them. Microsoft must not fall in the same trap. If they do not learn from history than history is likely to repeat itself.

Task for the students: Discuss the strengths and weaknesses of Microsoft and recommend a marketing strategy which would help them in retaining their leadership position.

CASE STUDY 14

Whirlpool a Case Study

Pride, Passion and Performance

Whirlpool of India is a late entrant in the white goods industry in India. However, its name and its brand image was already established in the country. Yet the firm resorted to heavy advertising and promotion to catch up with the existing players. Today, it has become a household name in the urban India, mainly due to its product quality and the quality of service provided by its personnel.

Whirlpool's vision is to have a presence in every home of the country – with Pride, Passion and Performance. They believe they create the world's best home appliances to make people's life easier and more enjoyable for people around the world.

- Pride in the work and in the employees. It is measured by vigorous process of determining the commitment, capabilities, and contribution of the employees.
- Passion for creating unmatched customer loyalty for their brands, which is measured by growth in revenues, market share and market position and brand loyalty.
- Performance results should excite and reward the global investors with superior results and other stakeholders. The results are measured by calculating the economic value additions and not just the return on investment.

Whirlpool is committed to achieving global leadership by creating value for its three major stakeholders as follows:

- Customers: The firm has customer focus in all their markets, products and services and it continuously measures the customer satisfaction to ensure that they prefer Whirlpool brand. Through their Worldwide Excellence System they achieve improvement in their results and attain breakthroughs in lowest defect levels, low supply cycle time. It enables them to exceed customer expectations and outperform competition
- Employees: The firm creates culture for high performance that encourages the employees to contribute to the tasks fully as individuals and as teams. In dynamic

environment diversity and pursuit of world-class performance is obtained from the employees.
- Shareholders: With the aim of global leadership the firm delivers great shareholder value to stay in the top twenty-five per cent firms in the field.

Worldwide Excellence System (WES) is the blueprint for Whirlpool quality management. It constitutes the operating system for achieving its objectives as follows:
- Leadership and people—at all levels people must act to reach the excellence
- Strategic planning, fact based management and quality of process and products are the major internal processes for achieving excellence
- Measurement and results set out for meaningful quantifiable measurements, which can be tracked down for improving quality
- Customer satisfaction constitutes of commitment of the firm, customers expectations, service standards, relationships and satisfactory resolution of complaints

WES also provides a feedback loop where the response of customers to the products and services is fed back into the system, driving further process improvement and refining the direction of effort.

Whirlpool Corporation of the USA is a leading manufacturer and marketer of major home appliances. The firm manufactures in 13 countries and markets in 170 countries under brand names of Whirlpool, Kitchen Aid, and Roper.

Whirlpool India is a subsidiary of Whirlpool Inc. it has acquired majority stake in Kelvinator of India in 1996. It started with the following four products under Whirlpool brand:
- Refrigerators
- Washing Machines
- Air-conditioners
- Microwave Ovens

Keeping core businesses of white goods they have discontinued unrelated and not core lines. As a result it has divested from compressors and automotive division.

Management strategy

The firm is following expansionist strategy to avail the opportunities in the Indian market. The strategy has the following thrust areas:
- To register growth in the market through brand leadership to make Whirlpool a dominant brand.
- To make external focus of satisfying customer needs.
- To achieve business growth through high volumes, high quality and low costs.
- To focus on core competencies and to have the best capabilities in the industry.
- To have high profit and most efficient cost structure in the industry.

Strategy industry analysis

Consumer durable industry is characterized by the following:

- Formidable entry barriers, of terms of brand equity, distribution and service network.
- Manufacturers of most durables is neither capital- nor technology-intensive, the need for constant product innovation, makes R&D a key factor.
- Rationalization of duties and opening up of the economy has attracted a host of global players.
- Increase competitive pressures and over zealous capacity creation have resulted in lower margins, which are expected to aggravate.
- The market for most consumer durables are in the nascent stage and penetration levels are low.
- The sector is price sensitive and each durable is a lifetime purchase
- Refrigerators and washing machines sales are seasonal. Peak periods for refrigerators are the summer months, and for washing machines monsoon season

Consumer durables market in India is estimated at Rs. 100 bn. The rural market, which has fifty per cent of the target group, has lower levels of penetration. Favourable personal tax, politics and increase in credit financing are expected to increase spending capability on durables. Realizing the potential of annual growth rate of 24% is predicted over next three years and helped by the liberal foreign investment politics most MNCs have either established base in India through tie-ups.

The refrigerator market has two segments, the direct cool type and the frost-free type. Its penetration levels are given below:

- Urban 32%
- Rural 10%

Growth rate of Consumer Durables

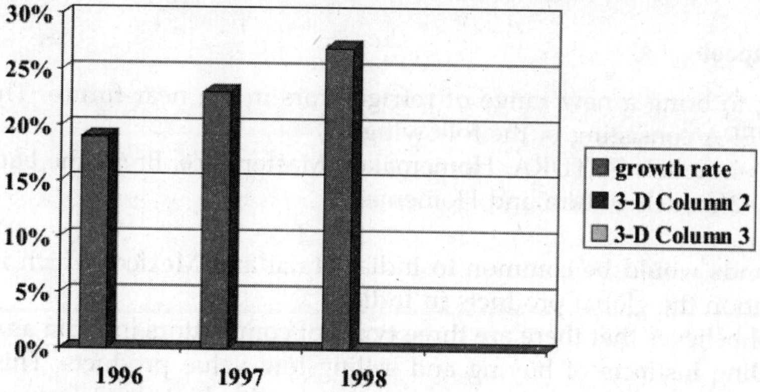

Installed capacity in the country is 3.2 million units per annum while the demand is 2.8 million units only.

Whirlpool is selling refrigerators both as direct cool, and frost-free types in different sizes, and have introduced the first CFC Free no frost refrigerator. Its campaign, "ICE ICE BABY" has helped the firm in achieving great success.

Market share in percentage of refrigerators in India is as follows:

Whirlpool	Godrej GE	Electrolux	Videocon	BPL	Others
21	31	24	10	5	9

Refrigerators installed capacity in million units in India is given below.

Whirlpool	Godrej GE	BPL	Voltas	Electrolux	LG	Samsung	Daewoo	Others
1.4	1.3	0.3	0.55	0.3	0.4	0.2	0.2	0.5

Washing Machine Competition

In washing machines Whirlpool competes with the following firms:

Firms	Market share in %
Whirlpool	18
Videocon	35
Godrej GE	12
BPL	22
Others	13

Whirlpool marketing strategy can be summarized as follows:

1. To place whirlpool washing machine with every customer in every price segment
2. Marketing only top loading machines
3. Started with top of the line front loading machine
4. Whirlpool creative campaign 1-2,1-2 has been a big success.

Plans of Whirlpool

It is planning to bring a new range of refrigerators in the near future. This would be known as OPERA consisting of the following:

- 180 litres –4 models FUTURA, Homemaker, Masterpiece, Break the barrier
- 210 litres –2 models Futura and Homemaker

These brands would be common to India, Brazil and Mexico, which is part of the policy to position the global products in India.

Whirlpool believes that there are three types of competitors in India as given below.

1. Basic trading instincts of buying and selling low value products. This is going to continue for a while. Some large competitors with high brand awareness in the country, which is not built on a strong platform of differentiation.
2. There are the South-East Asian types, not just the Koreans. A number of technology driven firms, pack their gizmos with features and some are good with futuristic plans.

3. The best products and technology do not build big business or brands, which depends on consumer perception. There is competition from the developed countries of the west. They have a different approach involving clear differentiated product for the firm and its brand. Who is going to succeed will depend on the policies and plans the firms have for India. Whirlpool wants to place its strategy on the third category.

Whirlpool's growth will depend on the following aspects:

- The industry's phase is of consolidation and the number of players will reduce in a few years, which would have a positive impact on sales
- Possible decline in commodity prices in international market for steel, copper could lead top procurement savings for lower manufacturing costs
- Phasing out of CFC products is to benefit Whirlpool as it has launched an array of CFC Free products conforming to Montreal protocol
- Four percent levy on import duty and rupee depreciation is likely to affect firm's cost structure, as a large proportion of raw material are imported. The firm is on an indigenization drive for sourcing components to overcome dependence on imports
- Whirlpool keeps more than one supplier for its components
- Most global majors are competing in India, due to its vast potential market. Indian firms also compete.

Task for the students: Organize SWOT Analysis of Whirlpool and give your own marketing plan for the firm.

CASE STUDY 15

Price Waterhouse

Price Waterhouse represents what the will, determination and grit of just two people can do to transform an entire, hitherto neglected sector of world economy: accounting and consultancy.

Traditionally an accountancy firm, it was started by Samuel Price and Edwin Waterhouse in 1849 in London UK. In 1930, the partners fanned out across the world, establishing semi-autonomous practice for accountancy investigations, liquidation and other financial services.

It was only from 1980 PW started Management consultancy in a big way as several firms started accepting consultancy as a useful profession. PW has added technical research to their portfolio, an advance technology centre in Artificial Intelligence in the US with a $410 million Development Center in London for IT Skills.

PW's USP comes from combining the roles of a consultant and an implementer.

PW's Vision reads as follows:

The firm is committed to turning strategic insight into tactical action (Strategic Implementation), for our clients. In doing so we provide them with high quality, leading edge, industry focused services and solutions, wherever they do business.

Their mission statement reads as follows to be the global consultants to TOP -LAYER firms by solving their complex business problems.

The international growth phase of PW began the two world wars, where partnerships were set up in different parts of the world. These were mainly offices to serve audit clients in the first instance. Tax consultancy services were added in the large offices. Today, PW has 434 offices in 119 countries.

The highly regarded Emerson Research firm rates PW as simply one of the best in its 1998 clients satisfaction survey of high technology firms PW ranked first, in eleven of thirteen client satisfaction categories among 293 audit clients of the big six firms. PW earned five star status in four categories and it bagged more number one rankings than any other big six firms.

Category	PWs ranking
Overall client satisfaction	1*
Responsiveness of the partners	1* five star
Understanding clients' needs /expectations	1
Audit and accounting services	1 five star
Information technology services	1*
Corporate finance	1*five star
Tax services	1*
Contribution to success of the client's business	1*
Staff responsiveness	1*five star
Proactive contribution	1* five star
Consultancy services	1

Clients have singled out PW among the big six in serving high technology firms as can be seen from below:

"They have a high degree of responsiveness and professionalism"

"Overall they are exceptional"

"I think they do mergers and acquisitions very well. It is a speciality of PW"

Auditing is a competitive area and therefore the firm has diversified its management consultancy to cover such industries as entertainment, media and high tech. To keep abreast of industry trends PW has formed a new consulting group on of electronics and on-line financial services.

PW is restructuring itself along product lines, as opposed to territorial divisions to serve the full range of its multinational clients. The purpose of the renewal efforts is helping firms in implementing strategies to improve business performance and Shareholder values. Affecting organizational and strategic change using IT for competitive advantage and meeting audit and tax requirements with greater speeds with improved software packages.

Price Waterhouse

PW was established in India in 1980 as a part of the worldwide network of Price Waterhouse. PW has access to worldwide resources in terms of experience and expertise. It has the largest professional resource based in India enabling it to have a greater subject and sector specialization with 41 partners, around 1500 professional staff and supported by a panel external technical or professional experts.

Various disciplines include the following:

- Audit and business advisory services ABS
- Tax
- Management consultancy services MCS
- Corporate finance recovery and disputes CFRD

Clientele includes large and prestigious organizations in the following areas:

- MNCs

- Indian private sector
- Public sector or government
- Bilateral donor agencies/foreign embassies
- Multilateral funding/development agencies.

PW is registered with World bank, ADB, UNDP, UNESCO, IDBI, and FIEO. Besides, it has regular working and consultative relationship with various Indian ministries.

PW has over the years acquired specialization in the following industrial sectors:

- Agro-based industry, including food processing
- Banking, finance and insurance services
- Engineering and electronics
- Finance and insurance
- Hotel and leisure
- Informatics including software
- International funding/ development agencies
- Mining
- Manufacturing and allied industries
- Retail trade-consumer goods
- Transportation
- Telecom
- Petroleum utilities including power and water

PW has other divisions operating in India as follows:

- Price Waterhouse Associates
- Price Waterhouse & Co
- Choksey & Co
- IPAN

Price Waterhouse India is a separate Profit Center for the parent firm; it is their SBU (Strategic Business Unit). Partners of Indian operations who have stock options in the parent firm. The parent firm does regular internal audit in order to ensure that the SBU conforms to their strict guidelines.

In order to scan the competitive environment Porter's Five Force Model is used as given below:

Bargaining power of the customers: It is moderate as the customers have choice to select from the consultants, but it is not high as most of them are providing certain specific and specialized services.

Bargaining power of the suppliers: They include the business schools and the Institute of Chartered Accountants of India. Their bargaining power is moderate as consultancy is a refined form of business dealings - an aspect highly appealing to intelligent experts. The managerial talent of business schools prefers to join the consultants.

Threat of new entrants–the threat of new firms entering the area is high as it is growing and in a profitable business.

Threat of substitute products would come from internal experts of the clients. The threat from them is low as the internal experts may not have the vat resources, which are with the consultants. Firms generally prefer to go the consultants.

Competition among rival firms is high. The major players include the following:

- Anderson worldwide
- Vooz Allen
- PA Consulting group
- PE consultants
- Mackenzie
- Boston Consulting Group
- KPMG

Critical Success Factors for the consultancy firms like PW are as follows:

- Consultants form the backbone of the firm/two basic characteristics of consultants are high intelligence and expertise in different areas as needed. John Foden CEO of PA Consulting group identifies three characteristics of an ideal consultant, which are: (a) ability to listen, (b) capacity for analyzing the situation and capacity to come up with creative knowledge base solutions.
- HR Planning: (a) recruitment they employ meticulous care in recruiting management trainees from the best of the schools.
- Career development opportunities: The promotions are performance related
- Pay package
- Continuous training and skill upgradation
- Establishment of relationship with clients
- Uniqueness of ideas
- Development of new ideas
- Experience
- Latest management ideas
- Efficient management information systems

The dictum is that the firm is as good as its clients.

CASE STUDY 16

Infosys–Worldwide

Narayan Murthy is one of the few Indians, who understood the software market worldwide and got on to the business early to come to the forefront. Today he is a respected name in the world software industry. As a promoter of ITL he has made it the leading firm in its product range.

ITL is a leading Indian firm in software services and packages for exports and the domestic market. Its clients include several fortune 500 companies. Indian software industry is fragmented with several players in the field. India's USP in the global market is that there is a large English speaking trained workforce, which is still relatively available at low cost.

ITL has grown in strength with special products developments like, in 2000 for Y2K solutions, IntERPryz for ERP, and InEuro for Euro banking services. It is the first Indian firm to be listed on the US Stock Exchange NASDAQ after its successful issue of ADR in 1999.

Management of ITL is totally inspired by its CMD, Narayan Murthy and it is characterized by the following qualities:

- Technically qualified professional management
- Having rich experience of large export orders
- Stakeholder friendly approach
- Positioning in high growth areas
- HR policies for merit recognition
- Focus on core areas

India's Position

Till 2000 Indian industry had a boom time in software. Only the events of 11th September 2001 have brought the industry down at least temporarily. India's competitive advantage lies in the following areas:

- Cost-effective software
- World-class quality
- High reliability
- Rapid delivery

India's position can be seen from the following matrix:

High		India
Quality and sophistication	Philippines	
	China	CIS
Low	Mexico	
	Low	High

Technical expertise

Software industry in India is given in the following table.

Year	1997	1998	1999	2000
Exports US M $	1755	2700	3900	5700
Domestic M Rs.	63100	100400	158600	245000

In 1999, the growth of the industry was 46% and it was expected to grow at 50%, but the USA catastrophe of 11 September 2001derailed the momentum of growth.

Top ten firms of India had the following turnover in million rupees in 1998:

1	TCS	10836
2	WIPRO	4816
3	HCL	3455
4	NIIT	3254
5	PENTAFOUR	2845
6	INFOSYS	2576
7	IBM GLOBAL	2428
8	TATA INFOTECH	2117
9	SATYAM	1784
10	PATNI GROUP	1375

Infosys has focused on providing software services with branded products and has moved on to software products.

- Services: revenue is 74% of total revenue of Infosys
- Branded Services: their share is 22%
- Products: account for just 3% of the revenue

Infosys's vision is to become a globally respected firm, which provides best of the software solutions by the best in class people.

Its mission is to grow with protected margins by focusing on horizontal applications and vertical industries.

Infosys goals are to have development centres for software in different parts of the world to provide quality speedy solutions at affordable prices.

Its objective is to restrict revenue generation of any division to less than 25%.

Infosys's competitive position is given below.

Market share	Market growth: High	Market growth: Low
High	Infosys Wipro	TCS
Low	Satyam NIIT	Rolta Pentafour

Infosys is in the Star position of the BCG Matrix.

Infosys track record is envious, with its shares surpassing the industry norms, including the ADR, which is also performing well in the market. Infosys could be planning on the following lines to keep its growth rate.

- Geographic expansion—Infosys gets the major share of business from the North American market as can be seen from the table given below.

Revenue area	1999 in lakh Rs.	%	1998 in lakh Rs.	%
North America	41739.11	82	21224.46	81
Europe	4753.03	9	2317.20	9
Rest of the world	3533.27	7	1552.10	6
India	1248.43	2	942.81	4
Total	51273.83	100	26036..57	

Europe and Japan are almost not there, which came in focus after 11th September 2001. Infosys would do well to open its markets in untapped areas so far.

- As a cash rich firm Infosys could be planning joint ventures in India and overseas to utilize its cash profits and zero debt status.
- Infosys could extend the services offered. Its present portfolio includes the following services.
  (i) Apparels
  (ii) Commodity trading
  (iii) Customer management
  (iv) e-business

(v) Financial services
(vi) Insurance
(vii) Logistics
(viii) Manufacturing
(ix) Retailing

Infosys could plan entry in the following fast pace areas as well.

(a) Aviation
(b) Healthcare
(c) Tourism
(d) Transport
(e) Security industry
(f) Telecom
(g) Training in software development
(h) Retailing in the country

Tasks for the student: Please do the SWOT Analysis of the firm and plan out the best marketing strategy for Infosys.

CASE STUDY 17

Hindustan Graphite Electrodes

In B to B market, HEG stands out as a firm not well known beyond its customer group and yet it has shown to the world what the correct strategies can do in highly competitive international and Indian markets.

The Indian graphite industry is a 700 crore industry, which has garnered around 10 per cent of the world trade of the product. It is also an industry that has continued to grow even when the entire industry and business both worldwide and in India, has been shrinking for the last decade. The graphite electrode industry has its fortunes linked to that of secondary steel production through the electric arc furnace EAF, technology and other factors like the structure of domestic industry, electrode production technology and costs, exports, accessibility to raw materials and customers. India beats the developed countries of the world in terms of cost of production because of its lower fixed costs, labour and overheads.

The Indian graphite electrode industry is having only three major domestic players. HEG Ltd. is a leading graphite electrode maker and also operates the single largest graphite electrode plant in South Asia. Supporting a global perceptive the firm has decided not to restrict itself to the domestic market and it aims at achieving a respectable market share worldwide.

HEG's strength include possession of sophisticated electrode manufacturing technology, ISO 9002 certification, competent workforce and management. Reduced risks of business cycle because of horizontal diversifications deep financial resources and related backward diversifications.

HEG's weaknesses include dependence on imported raw materials, high levels of inventory, poor cash flow, stiff and bureaucratic organization structure and a weak RD.

Intense competition, exchange rate fluctuations, changing technology, high bargaining powers of customers and suppliers are some of the threats facing HEG.

Growing demand for graphite electrodes in fast developing countries HEGs global experiences and image, installed production base are some of the plus points.

The Indian Graphite Electrode (GE), industry is concentrated as there are three major players in India. Between them they share Rs. 700 crore market, the Jhunjhunwalas and the Bangurs share the battleground.

The Jhunjhunwala's own the country's largest GE factory HEG. The Bangur group through its own firms Carbon Everflow Ltd. (CEL), and GIL are the biggest in the GE industry in India. The total installed capacity of the industry HEG, GIL AND CEL is 54000 tons, with HEG having 40% share and the other two of Bangur group having the balance.

The biggest threat today is the imports, which are eating into the market of the domestic players, as imported GEs are available at much lower cost. This has happened after the rationalization of duty structure, which went against the domestic industry.

Imports and exports of GE is given below.

Year	Imports in tons	Exports in tons
1993	475	11148
1994	500	15003
1995	3080	17001
1996	5500	18291
1997	4000	21000

The dramatic increase in imports since 1994 was primarily because Chinese producers were dumping their products in India at low prices $1100 per ton, while the average price in the international market was $2600 per ton. In 1997, dumping duty was imposed on China and there was a drop in the total GE imports in the country in 1997.

At present the scenario can be described as being between the devil and the deep sea. At a time when domestic players were fighting to create a strong base, infiltration started. These foes are none other than the mighty international players, while Indians are fighting for survival. The present sentiment is down as players are crying hoarse about the international players are resorting to dumping practices and the industry is feeling ignored by the government. Duties on imported electrodes have been reduced.

The fact that the user industry, the steel making is doing reasonably well, does not ensure good days for the GE industry. The size of GE is the main cause for its sufferings. For a government with an agenda the state of steel industry and the GE industry, the formers gets the concessions and not the GE industry.

HEG Ltd. is the leading GE maker as it also operates the single largest GE plant in South Asia. HEG Ltd. an ISO 9002, firm has its GE plant at Bhopal. HEG has facilities for GE production and specialities, set up in technical collaboration with Societe Des Electrodes ET Refractaries Savoie (SERS), a subsidiary of Pechiney of France. HEG is India's largest exporter with 55% of its produce being exported to more than 40 countries of the world.

HEGs vision statement is powerful as given below.

Vision–to have a global perspective

Mission–never restrict to the domestic market and aim at achieving respectable world market share.

Goals–investments to be made for new facilities for growth in market share. Product mix to be expanded with quality improvement.

Objectives–the major thrust is on producing GE at low cost and focus on higher segment of the users ready to pay the price or better quality product.

HEGs market segments are as given below.

- High efficiency product segment of Essar Steels Tisco in India and Sigri of Germany and Ucar Carbon of the USA.
- The middle segment wants value for money product.
- The lower end segment is the one competing with the Chinese players.

HEG has defined its marketing policy in the following words:

- Ensure full customer satisfaction with prompt service, courteous behaviour and motivate the employees for such efficient service
- Locate customer complaints and nip them in the bud only
- Build relationship with the customers
- Work at the relationship all the time
- Keep generating enthusiasm in the customers with special attention, gifts.
- Approach new customers and provide them with prompt courteous service.

HEG is focussed on providing value to the customers and not just satisfaction. customers are retained through superior service and products. New customers come through HEG's efforts and the word of mouth publicity provided by its customers.

HEG has selected the following foreign markets where they have got a good market share:

- North America
- South America
- Europe
- South-East Asia
- Middle East

The countries where HEG does business are 40, some of them are the following: USA, Canada, Italy, France, Australia, Taiwan, Singapore, South Korea,

SWOT Analysis of HEG:

- Strengths: Leading GE maker in India with 45% market share, exports 55% produce exported to 40 countries in the world. Has ISO 9002 certification, well up in finance and management areas
- Weaknesses: Dependence on imported raw materials, heavy inventory of finished goods due to recession, poor R&D
- Opportunities: Growing demand of the product in developing nations, it has global marketing experience
- Threats: Severe international competition, including the one from China. GEs demand is a derived demand and it depends on the demand of steel, which fluctuates with the country's GNP.

Michael Porter's 5 Force Model Analysis:

- Threat of new entrants is less as the industry requires huge capital; existing players have achieved Economies of Scale
- Supplier's bargaining power: They have great bargaining power as they are well organized and a few in number
- Customer's bargaining power is high as the product is undifferentiated, has large production base and imports are available at competitive prices
- Threat of substitute products is not there, but the steel making technology is undergoing changes, which threatens to do away with GEs
- Existing firms rivalry is intense as the product made is same, in large quantities by all the players

Improvement Opportunities/Problems of the industry:

- Middle segment has Chinese products where HEG had a stronghold earlier.
- Changes in steel making technology
- Challenges of possible price wars
- Political instabilities in the world
- Success or failure of quality programme of HEG.

Marketing Solutions

1. To fight the price competition from China HEG should start building relationships with the customers, to enlighten them on the hidden extra expenses they have to undergo when they use inferior Chinese products.
2. HEG should plan down sizing its operations to become cost-effective
3. Eliminate non-value adding tasks
4. Arrange order based production and inventories
5. Organize cross-functional teams for greater coordination
6. Along with international sales agents, HEG should start their own marketing operations in the countries they have a strong footing

Task for the students: Define the goals, which HEG should set for itself and the methods it should use for achieving the same

Global Business Discussion Questions

Guidelines for attempting the questions

1. Time management in answering questions; pick up difficult questions for spending more time on them
2. Write legibly
3. Read the questions twice or thrice to understand them fully
4. Make an outline of your answers before starting to write the answers
5. Keep a flow in style, make a lucid essay
6. The answers should reflect your full knowledge on the subject

7. State your conclusions and recommendations in an unambiguous manner; try to make them hard hitting but to the point.

Questions

1. Define the following:
   Global business
   (a) Merchandise export and import
   (b) Service export and import
   (c) Licensing agreements
   (d) Franchising
   (e) FDI
   (f) Joint ventures
   (g) Portfolio investments
   (h) MNCs
   (i) Economies of scale
2. What are the major objectives of IB?
3. The role of technology in IB
4. Lowering of entry barriers in most countries, reasons thereof
5. Effect of competition on IB
6. Difference of IB for small and large businesses
7. The role of social sciences like economics, culture, politics in IB
8. Differences in the competitive environment in IB and domestic business
9. Evolution of IB in companies
10. Reasons why more companies are starting with global focus in India

Second Set of Discussion Questions

1. How operations differ in the global context from national?
2. Do countries compete with each other? If yes how?
3. Do ethical and social responsibilities of host country pose problems for a company? How these complicate the company's operations?

Third set of questions:

1. Define and discuss the importance of the following in IB:
   (a) Culture and cultural imperialism
   (b) Group membership
   (c) Hierarchy of needs
   (d) Culture shock
   (e) Polycentrism
   (f) Ethnocentrism
   g. Geo-centrism
2. Is it useful for companies to look at group memberships in the global business?
3. What are the major problems in communications globally?
4. What is a political system and what are its major functions?

5. What are the major differences in a democratic government and totalitarianism as the base of a government?
6. How managers can face host government's interventions?
7. Countries have different laws for protecting the consumers. How can managers cope with them?
8. What are the legal issues faced by companies in IB? What is WTOs role in IB?
9. What are the characteristics of a market economy.
10. Discus the factors and demand conditions as a part of country's global competitiveness.
11. Define balance of payment, theory of absolute advantage, product life cycle and interdependence

Fourth set of questions

1. What are the main features of democratic parliamentary form of government?
2. Discuss the differences in multiparty and single party democratic system
3. Discuss the use of lobbyists in planning political strategy
4. How theocratic legal system affects business?
5. What is mixed economy?
6. Define GDP and GNP.
7. Per capita income and purchasing power parity can be used to define a country's wealth. Discuss.
8. What is inflation and how does it affect business performance?
9. What are the major benefits of privatization and how it can be made successful?
10. What is meant by the following:
    (a) Import substitution
    (b) Favourable balance of payment
    (c) PLC
    (d) Absolute advantage
    (e) Acquired advantage
    (f) Country size advantage

Fifth set of questions

Explain the following:

1. WTO
2. MFN
3. Dumping
4. Tariff
5. Ad valorem duty
6. Quota system
7. Foreign exchange control
8. Import restrictions and local employment
9. Protection of new industries
10. Non-economic objectives of governmental interference in global trade

Sixth set of questions

1. Describe regional integration for trade
2. Geographic proximity as a factor of economic integration
3. Political dimensions of economic integration
4. Economies of scale
5. Describe the following a economic entities:
   (a) EU
   (b) NAFTA
   (c) ASEAN
   (d) FDI
6. Why companies resort to FDIs?
7. Exports versus direct investment?
8. Transportation costs in foreign trade.

Seventh set of questions

Discuss the following:

1. Global vertical integration
2. Political motivations of FDIs
3. Gains of FDIs
4. Exchange rates
5. Spot rate, forward rate, and settlement, inter-bank market and transactions
6. Arbitrage
7. IMF
8. Special Drawing Rights
9. Free Fluctuating Rates
10. Market implications of exchange rate changes

Eighth set of questions

1. Impact of MNCs on local business.
2. MNCs decisions in one country, how they impact the business in other countries?
3. Difficulties encountered by MNCs because of differences in home and host country conditions.
4. FDIs and balance of payment and their impact on home and host country's business.
5. Are countries affected by foreign control of key industries?
6. MNCs capital induction can become a bargaining power with the host country's government. Discuss.
7. What are the differences and similarities in domestic and global negotiations?
8. Discuss the bilateral agreements on FDIs.
9. How can MNCs improve their brand equity?
10. Differences in approach to Intellectual Property Rights among nations.
11. Growth of global business modes over a period of time, discuss the methods employed.

12. How to rank countries for taking marketing decisions? How to prioritize them?
13. Discuss the different types of political risks in global business.
14. What factors affect the cost of manufacturing overseas?
15. What are the strategic alliances?
16. Reasons for making divestment decisions.
17. What are licensing franchising and joint ventures?

Set of ninth questions

1. Define the global and multi-domestic planning process.
2. When should companies adopt global or multi-domestic decision process?
3. Corporate culture needed for a global player.
4. How the demand of product be assessed in global market?
5. What are the differences between domestic and global marketing?
6. What are the possible trade channels available and what are their strengths?
7. What are the important factors used in fixing export prices?
8. What are the types of exporters in India?
9. What are the letters of credit and how many types of LCs are available.
10. What are the accepted accounting principles?
11. How do the exchange crates appear in the budgeting process?

Set of tenth questions

1. How does HRM differs in global business from domestic business?
2. Relationship required between home and host country management.
3. What is the difference between expatriates, locals, home country persons and third country persons?

Index